Sociology For The Seventies □
A Contemporary Perspective

Sociology For The Seventies
A Contemporary Perspective

Edited by

MORRIS L. MEDLEY *Department of Sociology*
Indiana State University, Terre Haute, Indiana

JAMES E. CONYERS *Department of Sociology*
Indiana State University, Terre Haute, Indiana

JOHN WILEY & SONS, INC.
NEW YORK □ LONDON □ SYDNEY □ TORONTO

COPYRIGHT © 1972, BY JOHN WILEY & SONS, INC.

ALL RIGHTS RESERVED. PUBLISHED SIMULTANEOUSLY IN CANADA.

NO PART OF THIS BOOK MAY BE REPRODUCED BY ANY MEANS, NOR TRANSMITTED, NOR TRANSLATED INTO A MACHINE LANGUAGE WITHOUT THE WRITTEN PERMISSION OF THE PUBLISHER.

LIBRARY OF CONGRESS CATALOGUE CARD NUMBER: 70-168640

ISBN 0-471-59015-0

PRINTED IN THE UNITED STATES OF AMERICA.

10 9 8 7 6 5 4 3 2 1

The Contributors

RAZIEL ABELSON *Professor of philosophy at New York University. He is a frequent contributor to philosophical journals and author of the book* Ethics and Meta-Ethics.

MICHAEL R. ALDRICH *A student leader of the Society for Legalization of Marijuana.*

CAROL ANDREAS *Professor of sociology at Oakland University. She is a prominent proponent of women's liberation and is currently focusing her research and writing on this subject. Her book,* Humankind, *is currently in press.*

HOWARD S. BECKER *Past president of the Society for the Study of Social Problems. He is presently a professor of sociology at Northwestern University. His numerous publications, such as* Outsiders *and* The Other Side, *reflect an "activist" perspective.*

MARK CHESLER *A member of the sociology department at the University of Michigan. He has been associated with the Center for Research on Utilization of Scientific Knowledge.*

SHIRLEY CHISHOLM *The Honorable Shirley Chisholm is the first black congresswoman in the United States. She represents the 12th Congressional District, the Bedford-Stuyvesant area, of New York City. Representative Chisholm has been active in the projects of broadening the powers of the Department of Housing and Urban Development and sponsoring a "Full Opportunity Act" and a bill to abolish the House Un-American Activities Commission.*

RUSSELL DYNES *Professor of sociology at Ohio State University; he has recently published a monograph on organized behavior in disasters. As codirector of the Disaster Research Center, he is doing research on community functioning in acute and diffused types of crises.*

v

HOWARD J. EHRLICH *One of the founders of the National University Conference, and at present a member of the sociology department of the University of Iowa. His research has focused primarily on public opinion and social movements.*

EDGAR Z. FRIEDENBERG *Professor of social foundations and sociology at the State University of New York at Buffalo. He is the author of* The Vanishing Adolescent, Coming of Age in America, The Dignity of Youth and Other Atavisms, *and numerous articles that have appeared in a variety of journals.*

JOHN GAGNON *Associate professor of sociology and Director of the Laboratory for Social Relations at the State University of New York at Stony Brook. He is the coauthor of the volume* Sex Offenders *(1965) and coeditor of the book* Sexual Deviance *(1967) and has in press works on the end of adolescence, the anomie of affluence, and two books of collected papers.*

DAVID J. GRAY *Chairman of the Division of the Social Sciences at Kirkland College. He is a contributor to the professional journals and has five articles in the* Encyclopedia International.

ALLEN GINSBERG *World-renowned poet and essayist. The* New Yorker *has described him as not merely a poet but a guru of the world-wide "amalgamated hippie-pacifist-activist-visionary-orgiastic-anarchist-orientalist-psychedelic underground."*

CHARLES V. HAMILTON *Professor of political science at Columbia University. He is a coauthor with Stokely Carmichael of* Black Power: The Politics of Liberation in America.

JOSEPH S. HIMES *Professor of sociology at the University of North Carolina in Greensboro. He has published in a variety of journals and is highly respected for his work on intergroup relations. Dr. Himes is a past president of the Southern Sociological Society.*

RICHARD HOFSTADTER *[the late] DeWitt Clinton professor of American history at Columbia University. He is the author of* Anti-Intellectualism in American Life *and numerous other books and articles dealing with political behavior in American society.*

JOHN HOWARD *Member of the sociology department at Rutgers University. His research interests include the relationship between community structure and the participation of the poor in the war on poverty, and institutional resistance to innovation in the public schools. He is coeditor of the anthology,* Where It's At.

TERRY ANN KNOPF *Research associate at the Lemberg Center for the Study of Violence, Brandeis University, in charge of the Center's Civil Disorder Clearinghouse, a research and service division. She is the author of a recent work on security patrols entitled* Youth Patrols: An Experiment in Community Participation.

PAUL KURTZ *Editor of* The Humanist.

JAMES H. LAUE *Lecturer on sociology in the Laboratory of Community Psychiatry, Department of Psychiatry at Harvard Medical School. His major research at present is an attempt to synthesize a body of theory and practice of community crisis intervention for professionals as well as indigenous community residents.*

RALPH LINTON *Ralph Linton, now deceased, was, perhaps, the most respected anthropologist of his time. His thoughts were recorded in a direct and penetrating manner. Among his many publications, the following works would seem clearly to deserve the label "classic":* The Study of Man *(1936) and* The Cultural Background of Personality *(1945).*

JOHN LOFLAND *Associate professor of sociology at the University of California, Davis. His writings include* Deviance and Identity, Doomsday Cult, *and* Field Research in Sociology. *He has taught at the University of Michigan and Sonoma State College.*

JAMES MCEVOY III *Assistant professor of sociology at the University of California, Davis. He is the author of* Radicals or Conservatives: The Contemporary American Right *and editor of* Black Power and Student Rebellion.

C. WRIGHT MILLS *C. Wright Mills died in 1962 at the age of 46; although his career was brief, he left a tremendous impact on contemporary sociology. Among his more well-known books are* White Collar: The American Middle Class *(1951);* The Power Elite *(1956);* The Causes of World War III *(1958); and* The Sociological Imagination *(1959).*

E. L. QUARANTELLI *Professor of Sociology at Ohio State University and codirector of the Disaster Research Center. His current research focuses on the emergence of new groups in emergency situations and the violation of legal norms during disasters.*

JEANE LOFLIN ROTHSEIDEN *Formerly Miami Area Representative for the Social Research Center, University of Michigan; she is now a consultant for Policy Management Systems, Washington, D.C.*

BRUCE M. RUSSETT *Professor of political science and Director of the World Data Analysis Program at Yale University. He is the author of numerous books and articles, most of which deal with a macroanalysis of political behavior.*

NORA SAYRE *New York correspondent for* The New Statesman; *she has contributed to many publications here and abroad. She recently devoted several months of research to the Black Panthers and interviewed many of their leaders and critics.*

RICHARD SCHMUCK *Member of the department of sociology at the University of Oregon. He was formerly associated with the University of Michigan Center for Research on Utilization of Scientific Knowledge.*

JOHN FINLEY SCOTT *Professor of sociology at the University of California, Davis. His research focuses on kinship in complex societies and the role of norms in sociological theory.*

WILLIAM SIMON *Program director in sociology and anthropology at the Institute for Juvenile Research in Chicago. His interests are the sociology of urban youth, particularly their problems with sex and drugs.*

JOHN P. SISK *Professor of English at Gonzaga University, and a former chairman of the English department. His works have appeared in* Commonweal, The New York Times, Ramparts, Commentary, *and other publications. A book,* Person and Institution, *is forthcoming.*

ATHELSTAN SPILHAUS *Noted urbanist who formerly served as President of the Franklin Institute, Philadelphia; Dean of the Institute of Technology, University of Minnesota; Director of Research, New York University; and president of Aqua International Corporation.*

JOHN RAPHAEL STAUDE *Professor of sociology at Sonoma State College. He is the author of* Max Scheler: An Intellectual Portrait *and editor of* Culture and Society, *an interdisciplinary reader in sociology of knowledge.*

RICHARD STERNE *Director of Social Research, Council of Social Agencies, Rochester, New York and adjunct associate professor of sociology, State University College, Brockport, New York.*

ROBERT S. WEISS *Lecturer in sociology in the department of psychiatry of the Harvard Medical School, working in its Laboratory of Community Psychiatry.*

ROGER R. WOOCK *Associate professor of education at the University of Calgary. He is coeditor of* Man Against Poverty: World War III *and coauthor of* Social Foundations of Urban Education.

JAMES W. VANDER ZANDEN *Associate professor of sociology at Ohio State University. He is also consulting editor for* Sociological Inquiry. *Dr. Vander Zanden has written numerous articles on race relations and is the author of the text,* American Minority Relations.

MICHAEL WYSCHOGROD *Teaches in the philosophy department of City College of the City University of New York. He is the author of* Kierkegaard and Heidegger: The Ontology of Existence.

To our students, for providing us with many insights in understanding the purposes and goals of education, we offer this volume as a partial repayment.

Preface

A PRIMARY GOAL OF AN UNDERGRADUATE COURSE IN SOCIOLOGY SHOULD BE to sensitize the student to the discipline. This task can be fully accomplished only by offering the student an introduction to the excitement and stimulation of an intellectual experience with a wide range of perceptive authors.

This book is a selective overview of the discipline rather than a comprehensive coverage of the entire field. Space limitations prevent a complete overview; however, the articles included are wide in scope. We have chosen the activist perspective as the nexus for a probing examination of several issues currently confronting sociology and American society in general. But we do not envision this book as a "radical reader."

In selecting articles, four general criteria were followed.
1. Does the article demonstrate sociological substance?
2. Does the selection raise important questions about issues in contemporary America?
3. Will the article be of interest to the undergraduate student?
4. Is the selection written in a clear and concise manner?

No attempt was made to shelter the student from necessary nomenclature. But care has been taken to avoid the inclusion of needless jargon. We paid constant attention to the anticipated interests of our potential audience, and deliberately avoided articles that play upon statistical enumeration of the trite or the obvious. Instead, we focused our attention on ideas and questions of the activist perspective in contemporary sociology—that is, the sociology of involvement, of change, of dissent, and of seeking new directions.

We tried to organize the materials in the most readable and usable way for an undergraduate sociology course. Each Part is preceded by an introduction that helps the student to understand the various interrelated articles. There is also an introduction to each selection, which summarizes the major ideas and findings presented in the article and gives the student a frame of reference. Reflective questions follow each article. They should be scanned before reading the selection and should be studied afterward.

A teacher has an obligation (regardless of his media) to reveal an intellectual point of view, and we have done this here. We have taken a professional position regarding the responsibility of sociologists to become actively involved with the social world in which they live. We hope that the student will accept our position as an expressed point of view and not as an attempt to offer a definitive and unchallengeable truism. We believe that the mind develops most creatively when it is confronted by challenge, criticism, and diversity. We therefore hope that this book will help the student to acquire an intellectual cynicism and curiosity that will encourage him to seek and develop his own position regarding the nature and role of sociology in American society.

It is our wish that this volume will awaken students to the vitality, excitement, and relevance of sociology for themselves and for society. Our selections provide a critical elaboration of ideas and principles taught in many undergraduate sociology courses. Consequently, we envision this book as a supplement to the instructor and to his primary text—not as a replacement for either.

MORRIS MEDLEY
JAMES CONYERS

Acknowledgments

We are indebted to many invaluable people. We give our profound thanks to the contributors, since their work will offer students an enjoyable intellectual experience. We also thank many unknown reviewers for their careful and constructive criticisms. We are especially grateful to our student assistants, Jeanne Hohl, Jane Hosapple, and Pat Murphy for their secretarial competence. Finally, we thank Ronald St. John and Scott Alderton of Wiley for their skillful editorial assistance and friendly encouragement.

M. M.
J. C.

CONTENTS

PART ONE □ A CONTEMPORARY SOCIOLOGICAL PERSPECTIVE

1 □ THE SOCIOLOGICAL IMAGINATION: THE PROMISE
C. Wright Mills   7

2 □ VALUE-FREE SOCIOLOGY: A DOCTRINE OF HYPOCRISY AND IRRESPONSIBILITY
David J. Gray   14

3 □ WHOSE SIDE ARE WE ON?
Howard S. Becker   26

4 □ THE IMPOSSIBLE POSSIBLE PHILOSOPHERS' MAN: A DISCUSSION OF THE SOCIOLOGIST AS ACTIVIST
Howard J. Ehrlich   39

PART TWO □ CULTURE AND THE DEVELOPMENT OF SELF

5 □ ONE HUNDRED PER CENT AMERICAN
Ralph Linton   49

6 □ PSYCHOSEXUAL DEVELOPMENT
William Simon and John Gagnon   53

7 □ THE FUND OF SOCIABILITY
Robert S. Weiss   68

8 □ THE USES OF FAILURE
John H. Gagnon   79

9 □ ALIENATED YOUTH AND THE CULT OF THE OCCULT
John Raphael Staude   86

10 □ THE MAKING OF A BLACK MUSLIM
John R. Howard   96

PART THREE □ PIVOTAL INSTITUTIONS AND INTERACTING PEOPLE

11 □ THE PARANOID STYLE IN AMERICAN POLITICS
Richard Hofstadter   113

12 □ STUDENT ACTIVISTS AND HIGHER EDUCATION
Roger R. Woock   123

13 □ SORORITIES AND THE HUSBAND GAME
John Finley Scott   131

14 □ MAKING IT IN AMERICA
John P. Sisk   142

15 □ PSYCHEDELICS AND RELIGION: A SYMPOSIUM
Raziel Abelson, Allen Ginsberg and Michael Wyschogrod   155

16 □ THE PRICE OF WAR
Bruce M. Russett   171

PART FOUR □ INDIVIDUALS AND SOCIETY IN CRISIS

17 □ CHANGING PERSPECTIVES AND THE TOPICS OF DEVIANCE
John Lefland   189

18 □ FEMININITY IN THE LESBIAN COMMUNITY
William Simon and John H. Gagnon   198

19 □ THE PENTHEUS APPROACH
Michael R. Aldrich   209

20 □ THE FUNCTIONS OF RACIAL CONFLICT
Joseph S. Himes   218

21 □ BLACK PANTHERS
Nora Sayre   234

22 □ RACISM AND ANTI-FEMINISM
Shirley Chisholm   243

23 □ Master-Slave Clashes as Forerunners of Patterns in Modern American Urban Eruptions
Richard S. Sterne and Jeane Loftin Rothseiden   252

24 □ What Looting in Civil Disturbances Really Means
Russell Dynes and E. L. Quarantelli   265

25 □ Sniping—A New Pattern of Violence?
Terry Ann Knopf   276

Part Five □ Reactions to a Society in Turmoil

26 □ Social Change, Dissent, and Violence
James H. Laue   297

27 □ The Black Revolution: A Primer for White Liberals
Charles V. Hamilton   314

28 □ The Klan Revival
James W. Vander Zanden   321

29 □ An Interview with Abbie Hoffman and Jerry Rubin
Paul Kurtz   332

30 □ Content Analysis of a Super Patriot Protest
James McEvoy, Mark Chesler and Richard Schmuck   352

31 □ The Revolt Against Democracy
Edgar Z. Friedenberg   366

32 □ Notes on the Liberation of Women
Carol Andreas   379

33 □ "So That Man Might Live Better"
Athelstan Spilhaus   390

PART ONE
A Contemporary Sociological Perspective

> Where it is a duty to worship the sun, it is pretty sure to be a crime to examine the laws of heat.
>
> VISCOUNT MORLEY

BOB FITCH / BLACK STAR

To BETTER UNDERSTAND CONTEMPORARY AMERICAN SOCIOLOGY, ONE needs to examine the sources and development of the discipline. Although sociology may trace its intellectual beginnings to the ancient philosophers, perhaps the greatest debt to the past is owed to the nineteenth-century European scholars. The Frenchman Auguste Comte (1798-1857) is credited with coining the term "sociology," with the appearance of the fourth volume of his *Cours de Philosophie Positive,* in 1839.[1] Comte envisioned a science of society based on systematic observation and classification, rather than on speculation and intuition. Although Comte is considered by many to be the "father of sociology," perhaps his greatest contribution has been the synthesizing and integration of the works and ideas of Saint Simon (1760-1825).[2] Simon was, undoubtedly, one of the most brilliant scholars of the eighteenth and nineteenth centuries.

The nineteenth-century Europeans had a great concern with social change, as was reflected in Herbert Spencer's (1820-1903) application of the grand theory of social evolution, which was introduced in his monumental work *Principles of Sociology,* first published in 1876. Although the original form of Spencer's theory has little support among contemporary sociologists, it aided in stimulating others to seek explanations for social phenomena through sociology. From Germany, the impact of theories developed by Karl Marx (1818-1883), Max Weber (1864-1920), and Ferdinand Tonnies (1855-1936) continue to influence sociology. In France, Le Play (1806-1882), and Emile Durkheim (1858-1917) were influencial in affecting the intellectual direction of sociology in America. The noted Italian economist Pareto (1848-1923), whose writings on the social system provided a wealth of intellectual discussion in America, particularly during the 1930's, represents the principal contribution of southern Europe to modern sociology. A great intellectual debt is owed to all of these men and to their counterparts of the nineteenth-century academic circles.

Sociology in America emerged, in part, as a reaction to political and social issues of the nineteenth century. America in the late 1800's was a nation shaped by the civil war, industrialization, urbanization, and the influx of massive immigration. Sociologists in America, as in Europe, were divided on the issue of social change and man's ability to direct the social process. The problems created by the rapid and often unplanned change of the 1800's brought about an involvement of sociology with social reforms and social problems of American life. Many of the early sociologists were either former ministers or sons of ministers, and nearly all came from rural backgrounds; thus their reaction and response to the quagmire of problems and confusion was perhaps understandable.

---

[1] G. Duncan Mitchell, *A Hundred Years of Sociology* (Chicago: Aldine Publishing Company, 1968), p. 3.
[2] Harry Elmer Barnes, *An Introduction to the History of Sociology* (Chicago: The University of Chicago Press, 1966), pp. 73-74.

4 □ A CONTEMPORARY SOCIOLOGICAL PERSPECTIVE

These men often viewed sociology as a device for social engineering and envisioned social change as being synonymous with social progress.[3]

Sociology has been taught at the university level in the United States since the early 1880's. The first courses were introduced at Boston College, William and Mary College, Indiana University, Yale, Columbia and the University of Chicago.

Teaching many of these early courses were the "founders" of American sociology. These men frequently developed grand systems to explain the social phenomena of men acting in groups. Among the leading scholars of this early period in American sociology were such men as Lester Ward (1841–1913), Albion Small (1854–1926), Edward Ross (1866–1958), William Graham Sumner (1840–1910), Charles Cooley (1864–1929) and Franklin Giddings (1855–1931). The insight and theoretical formulations of these scholars helped to form an intellectual base for contemporary American sociology.

Under the direction of Albion Small, the American Sociological Society was formed, with Lester Ward becoming the Society's first president in 1905. Following the formation of the Society, widespread acceptance of sociology as a distinct discipline gained popularity, and courses were soon being offered in many liberal arts colleges and numerous land-grant institutions.[4]

Between World War I and the Great Depression, sociology entered a second distinctive phase, which might be labeled "the age of scientism." The major emphasis of this period was on scientific study for the sake of science, not necessarily for the benefit of man. World War I was extremely disillusioning to many students of human behavior who had formerly viewed man as an essentially rational creature. The intellectual and social conditions following the war provided an impetus among scholars to apply the scientific method in attempting to explain human behavior. By the mid-1930's, sociology had developed a perspective and method somewhat different from the other behavioral sciences, and had empirically delved into numerous areas of human behavior. Many of these early studies produced results that have been critically labeled as empirical generalizations. Nevertheless, many of the early empirical studies provided later sociologists with a wealth of data from which explicit propositions and studies of verification have been developed.

The worldwide depression of the 1930's, along with World War II, had a considerable impact on American sociology. A reconsideration of the philosophy of the "age of scientism" resulted in a renewed interest in applying the knowledge and method of sociology to the benefit of society. This position was given eloquent support in 1939 when Robert Lynd's book *Knowledge For What?*

---

[3] Roscoe C. Hinkle, Jr. and Gisela J. Hinkle, *The Development of Modern Sociology* (Garden City, N.Y.: Doubleday and Company, Inc., 1954), pp. 1–4.
[4] The division of time used in this introduction to discuss the phases through which sociology has passed is indebted to the work of Hinkle and Hinkle.

became widely read among both laymen and academicians; however, not all sociologists of this period were in accord with the "return to the utilitarian" justification of sociology. Lead by George Lundberg (1895–1966), a neopositivist whose thoughts were disseminated to a vast audience through his book *Can Science Save Us?*, a plea arose for sociologists to remain value-free and to maintain a rigid separation between their role as sociologists and that as citizens.

Since 1950, sociology appears to be firmly enmeshed in an era of synthesis. A kind of academic maturity appears to be prevailing; thus, the petty differences and scholarly defensiveness that have often been identified with sociology appear to be relegated to a subservient position. Robert Merton's conceptual development of the theories of the middle range has had an immeasurable impact on the discipline in the past two decades. Merton has developed an orientation to the study of social phenomena that is sensitive to the reciprocity and complementariness of both the *verstehen* and the empirical orientation positions.[5]

The admonishment of C. Wright Mills (1916–1962), as stated in *The Sociological Imagination,* challenging sociology to become relevant, has apparently struck a sensitive chord in the mind of many sociologists. The academic orientation of contemporary sociology appears to rest on the premise that the most substantial gains will come through the development of significant propositions founded on sound theory and tested by verifiable studies. This approach, which seems to be gaining support, appears to represent a genuine synthesis between the grand theoretical approach and the attempt to secure empirical generalizations.

As sociology moves into the 1970's, the image of the sociologist appears to be undergoing a revolutionary revision. An activist-oriented sociology appears, in this time of general academic discontent, to be gathering support among both sociologists and students. The current movement is commonly labeled "new sociology."[6]

The "new sociology" probably owes its birth to C. Wright Mills, whose penetrating style lead many of his contemporaries into a reevaluation of their intellectual positions. The "cause," so eloquently stated by Mills, has been continued and expanded under the leadership of many contemporary sociologists, such as Irving Horowitz, Sidney Peck, Alvin Gouldner, Nathan Hare, David Gottlieb, and Oliver C. Cox. In addition to the above individuals, the revival of Marxism, plus the power of the civil rights and peace movements, have also contributed immeasurably to modifying the substance and direction of current sociological pursuits.

The goal of the current movement, as stated by its spokesmen, is an attempt

[5] Robert K. Merton, *Social Theory and Social Structure* (Glencoe, Ill.: The Free Press, 1949).
[6] Irving Louis Horowitz (Ed.), *The New Sociology* (New York: Oxford University Press, 1965).

to radicalize sociology. The new sociologist is challenging the functionality of traditional institutions, questioning the validity of "sacred" concepts, and seeking to develop explanatory propositions that will provide the impetus for social change. He is no longer satisfied with the antiseptic sociology called for by the "value-free sociologist." In direct contrast to the ethically detached value-free sociology of some of his predecessors, he views the world as his laboratory and values the opportunity to be innovative and to initiate humane change. The new sociologist is often described as a radical, an activist, and one who is oriented toward a humanistic philosophy of man—in short, he is involved in the workings and substance of the society that confronts him.

There are those within the discipline who undoubtedly view the new sociology as being devastating to the scientific study of human behavior; however, we believe that the current challenge issued by the new sociologist constitutes the real health of our field. Sociology will, we feel, become a more viable and more honest discipline as a result of the new sociology.

1 □ THE SOCIOLOGICAL IMAGINATION: THE PROMISE

C. Wright Mills

C. Wright Mills, one of the most respected and controversial sociologists of this century, is sometimes called the "sociologist in anger." He earned this title by producing some of the most scathing and intellectually penetrating criticisms of the society and the world, which he so desperately sought to awaken to the sociological imagination. In this article, Mills calls for the use of an intellectual imagination that would dispel the academic minutiae of the rigid empiricist and the vast meanderings of the grand theorist. Mills disparagingly contends that much of the work presently labeled sociology is unimaginative and makes no significant contribution either to the discipline or to the betterment of society. The sociological imagination is, to Mills, a matter of personal involvement coupled with a sense of responsibility. □

PERHAPS THE MOST FRUITFUL DISTINCTION WITH WHICH THE SOCIOLOGICAL imagination works is between "the personal troubles of milieu" and "the public issues of social structure." This distinction is an essential tool of the sociological imagination and a feature of all classic work in social science.

Troubles occur within the character of the individual and within the range of his immediate relations with others; they have to do with his self and with those limited areas of social life of which he is directly and personally aware. Accordingly, the statement and the resolution of troubles properly lie within the individual as a biographical entity and within the scope of his immediate milieu—the social setting that is directly open to his personal experience and to some

From *The Sociological Imagination* by C. Wright Mills. Copyright © 1959 by Oxford University Press, Inc. Reprinted by permission.

extent his willful activity. A trouble is a private matter: values cherished by an individual are felt by him to be threatened.

Issues have to do with matters that transcend these local environments of the individual and the range of his inner life. They have to do with the organization of many such milieux into the institutions of an historical society as a whole, with the ways in which various milieux overlap and interpenetrate to form the larger structure of social and historical life. An issue is a public matter: some value cherished by publics is felt to be threatened. Often there is a debate about what that value really is and about what it is that really threatens it. This debate is often without focus if only because it is the very nature of an issue, unlike even widespread trouble that it cannot very well be defined in terms of the immediate and everyday environments of ordinary men. An issue, in fact, often involves a crisis in institutional arrangements, and often too it involves what Marxists call "contradictions" or "antagonisms."

In these terms, consider unemployment. When, in a city of 100,000 only one man is unemployed, that is his personal trouble, and for its relief we properly look to the character of the man, his skills, and his immediate opportunities. But when in a nation of 50 million employees, 15 million men are unemployed, that is an issue, and we may not hope to find its solution within the range of opportunities open to any one individual. The very structure of opportunities has collapsed. Both the correct statement of the problem and the range of possible solutions require us to consider the economic and political institutions of the society, and not merely the personal situation and character of a scatter of individuals.

Consider war. The personal problem of war, when it occurs, may be how to survive it or how to die in it with honor; how to make money out of it; how to climb into the higher safety of the military apparatus; or how to contribute to the war's termination. In short, according to one's values, to find a set of milieux and within it to survive the war or make one's death in it meaningful. But the structural issues of war have to do with its causes; with what types of men it throws up into command; with its effects upon economic and political, family and religious institutions with the unorganized irresponsibility of a world of nation-states.

Consider marriage. Inside a marriage a man and a woman may experience personal troubles, but when the divorce rate during the first four years of marriage is 250 out of every 1,000 attempts, this is an indication of a structural issue having to do with the institutions of marriage and the family and other institutions that bear upon them.

Or consider the metropolis—the horrible, beautiful, ugly, magnificent sprawl of the great city. For many upper-class people, the personal solution to "the problem of the city" is to have an apartment with private garage under it in the heart of the city, and forty miles out, a house by Henry Hill, garden by Garrett Eckbo, and a hundred acres of private land. In these two controlled environments—with a small staff at each end and a private helicopter connection—most people could solve many of the problems of personal milieux caused by the facts of the city. But all this, however splendid, does not solve the public issues that the structural fact of the city poses. What should be done with this wonderful monstrosity? Break it all up into scattered units, combining residence and work? Refurbish it as it stands? Or, after evacuation, dynamite it and build new cities according to new plans in new places? What should those plans be? And who is to decide and to accomplish whatever choice is made? These are structural issues; to confront them and to solve them requires us to consider political and economic issues that affect innumerable milieux.

In so far as an economy is so arranged that slumps occur, the problem of unemployment becomes incapable of personal solution. In so far as war is inherent in the nation-state system and in the uneven industrialization of the world, the ordinary individual in his restricted milieu will be powerless—with or without psychiatric aid—to solve the troubles this system or lack of system imposes upon him. In so far as the family as an institution turns women into darling little slaves and men into their chief providers and unweaned dependents, the problem of a satisfactory marriage remains incapable of purely private solution. In so far as the overdeveloped megalopolis and the overdeveloped automobile are built-in features of the overdeveloped society, the issues of urban living will not be solved by personal ingenuity and private wealth.

What we experience in various and specific milieux, I have noted, is often caused by structural changes. Accordingly, to understand the changes of many personal milieux we are required to look beyond them. And the number and variety of such structural changes increase as the institutions within which we live become more embracing and more intricately connected with one another. To be aware of the idea of social structure and to use it with sensibility is to be capable of tracing such linkages among a great variety of milieux. To be able to do that is to possess the sociological imagination.

What are the major issues for publics and the key troubles of private individuals in our time? To formulate issues and troubles, we must ask what values are cherished yet threatened, and what values are cherished and supported, by the characterizing trends of our period. In the case both of threat and of support we must ask what salient contradictions of structure may be involved.

When people cherish some set of values and do not feel any threat to them, they experience *well-being*. When they cherish values but *do* feel them to be threatened, they experience a crisis either as a personal trouble or as a public issue. And if all their values seem involved, they feel the total threat of panic.

But suppose people are neither aware of any cherished values nor experience any threat? That is the experience of *indifference,* which if it seems to involve all their values, becomes apathy. Suppose, finally, they are unaware of any cherished values, but still are very much aware of a threat? That is the experience of *uneasiness,* of anxiety, which, if it is total enough, becomes a deadly unspecified malaise.

Ours is a time of uneasiness and indifference—not yet formulated in such ways as to permit the work of reason and the play of sensibility. Instead of troubles—defined in terms of values and threats—there is often the misery of vague uneasiness; instead of explicit issues there is often merely the beat feeling that all is somehow not right. Neither the values threatened nor whatever threatens them has been stated; in short, they have not been carried to the point of decision. Much less have they been formulated as problems of social science.

In the 'thirties there was little doubt except among certain deluded business circles that there was an economic issue which was also a pack of personal troubles. In these arguments about "the crisis of capitalism," the formulations of his work probably set the leasing terms of the issue, and some men came to understand their personal troubles in these terms. The values threatened were plain to see and cherished by all; the structural contradictions that threatened them also seemed plain. Both were widely and deeply experienced. It was a political age.

But the values threatened in the era after World War Two are often neither widely acknowledged as values nor widely felt to be threatened. Much private uneasiness goes unformulated; much public malaise and many decisions of enormous structural relevance never become public issues. For those who accept such inherited values as reason and freedom, it is the uneasiness itself that is the trouble; it is the indifference itself that is the issue. And it is this condition, of uneasiness and indifference, that is the signal feature of our period.

All this is so striking that it is often interpreted by observers as a shift in the very kinds of problems that need now to be formulated. We are frequently told that the problems of our decade, or even the crises of our period, have shifted from the external realm of economics and now have to do with the quality of individual life—in fact with the question of whether there is soon going to be anything that can properly be called individual life. Not child labor but comic books, not poverty but mass leisure, are at the center of concern. Many great public issues as well as many private troubles are described in terms of "the psychiatric"—often, it seems, in a pathetic attempt to avoid the large issues and problems of modern society. Often this statement seems to rest upon a provincial narrowing of interest to the Western societies, or even to the United States—this ignoring two-thirds of mankind; often, too, it arbitrarily divorces the individual life from the larger institutions within which that life is enacted and which on occasion bear upon it more grievously than do the intimate environments of childhood.

Problems of leisure, for example, cannot even be stated without considering problems of work. Family troubles over comic books cannot be formulated as problems without considering the plight of the contemporary family in its new relations with the newer institutions of the social structure. Neither leisure nor its debilitating uses can be understood as problems without recognition of the extent to which malaise and indifference now form the social and personal climate of contemporary American society. In this climate, no problems of "the private life" can be stated and solved without recognition of the crisis of ambition that is part of the very career of men at work in the incorporated economy.

It is true, as psychoanalysts continually point out, that people do often have "the increasing sense of being moved by obscure forces within themselves which they are unable to define." But it is *not* true, as Ernest Jones asserted that "man's chief enemy and danger is his own unruly nature and the dark forces pent up within him." On the contrary: "Man's chief danger" today lies in the unruly forces of contemporary society itself, with its alienating methods of production, its enveloping techniques of political domination, its international anarchy—in a word, its pervasive transformations of the very "nature of man and the conditions and aims of his life."

It is now the social scientist's foremost political and intellectual task—for here the two coincide—to make clear the elements of contemporary uneasiness and indifference. It is the central demand made upon him by other cultural workmen—by physical scientists and artists, by the intellectual community in general. It is because of this task and these demands, I believe, that the social sciences are becoming the common denominator of our cultural period, and the sociological imagination our most needed quality of mind.

In every intellectual age some one style of reflection tends to become a common denominator of cultural life. Nowadays, it is true, many intellectual fads are widely taken up before they are dropped for new ones in the course of a year or two. Such enthusiasms may add spice to cultural play, but leave little or no intellectual trace. That is not true of such ways of thinking as "Newtonian physics" or "Darwinian biology." Each of these intellectual universes became an influence that reached far beyond any special sphere of idea and imagery. In terms of them, or in terms derived from them, unknown scholars as well as fashionable commentators came to re-focus their observations and re-formulate their concerns.

During the modern era, physical and biological science has been the major common denominator of serious reflection and popular metaphysics in Western societies. "The technique of the laboratory" has been the accepted mode of procedure and the source of intellectual security. That is one meaning of the idea of an intellectual common denominator: men can state their strongest convictions in its terms; other terms and other styles of reflection seem mere vehicles of escape and obscurity.

That a common denominator prevails does not of course mean that no other styles of thought or modes of sensibility exist. But it does mean that more general intellectual interests tend to slide into this area, to be formulated there most sharply, and when so formulated, to be thought somehow to have reached if not a solution, at least a profitable way of being carried along.

The sociological imagination is becoming, I believe, the major common denominator of our cultural life and its signal feature. This quality of mind is found in the social and psychological sciences, but it goes far beyond these studies as we now know them. Its acquisition by individuals and by the cultural community at large is slow and often fumbling; many social scientists are themselves quite unaware of it. They do seem to know that the use of this imagination is central to the best work that they might do, that by failing to develop and to use it they are failing to meet the cultural expectations that are coming to be demanded of them and that the classic traditions of their disciplines make available to them.

Yet in factual and moral concerns, in literary work and in political analysis the qualities of this imagination are regularly demanded. In a great variety of expressions, they have become central features of intellectual endeavor and cultural sensibility. Leading critics exemplify these qualities as do serious journalists—in fact the work of both is often judged in these terms. Popular categories of criticism—high, middle, and low-brow, for example—are now at least as much sociological as aesthetic. Novelists—whose serious work embodies the most widespread definitions of human reality—frequently possess this imagination, and do much to meet the demand for it. By means of it, orientation to the present as history is sought. As images of "human nature" become more problematic, an increasing need is felt to pay closer yet more imaginative attention to the social routines and catastrophes which reveal (and which shape) man's nature in this time of civil unrest and ideological conflict. Although fashion is often revealed by attempts to use it, the sociological imagination is not merely a fashion. It is a quality of mind that seems most dramatically to promise an understanding of the intimate realities of ourselves in connection with larger social realities. It is not merely one quality of mind among the contemporary range of cultural sensibilities—it is *the* quality whose wider and more adroit use offers the promise that all such sensibilities—and in fact, human reason itself—will come to play a greater role in human affairs.

Reflective Questions

1. What distinction does Mills see as an essential tool of the sociological imagination? Why?

2. Why does Mills claim that to understand the changes of many personal milieux we are required to look beyond them?

3. How does Mills suggest that we determine the major issues for publics and the key troubles of private individuals in our time?

4. Why does Mills believe that the social sciences are becoming the common denominator of our cultural period, and the sociological imagination our most needed quality of mind?

5. What, according to Mills, is the sociological imagination?

2 □ VALUE-FREE SOCIOLOGY: A DOCTRINE OF HYPOCRISY AND IRRESPONSIBILITY

David J. Gray

During the past decade a noticeable schism has become visible within the sociological establishment. This division focuses on intellectually weighing the value-free sociology of the 1950's against the activist orientation of the 1960's. This paper presents a caustic commentary that serves as a rebuttal of the position taken by the ethically neutral sociologist. The primary thesis of the paper is revealed in the first sentence: the value-free position will not serve the best interest of sociology. Professor Gray develops his argument around the need for the sociologist to be aware of his values and to accept them in the hope that the result will produce contributions to expanding existing knowledge in areas of value to humanity. Gray presents a very defensible case for the sociologist to become involved with the realities of the world, and lucidly issues a plea for sociologists to be relevant. The student of sociology quickly realizes that no one is amoral or value-free, and on accepting this premise, he is in a more realistic position from which to observe human behavior. □

*Ethically neutral, value free—
tweedle dum, tweedle dee.
Nazi S.S., Schweitzer humane—
value free, all the same.*[1]

From *The Sociological Quarterly*, April, 1968, pp. 176–185. Reprinted by permission of The Midwest Sociological Society and the author.
[1] David J. Gray, "Ode to Behavioral Science," *William and Mary Review*, 4:70.

THE CENTRAL THESIS OF THIS PAPER IS THAT THE VALUE-FREE DOCTRINE FOR so long dominant in the sociological discipline will not serve. While in many quarters this thesis may be viewed as an act of sociological heresy, absolute originality in its formulation cannot be claimed. For several decades a minority voice, critical of the ethically-neutral pose of the discipline, has attempted to make itself heard—Znaniecki, Lynd, Redfield, Bierstedt, Sorokin, Gouldner, Nisbet, Mills, Stein, Vidich, Horowitz—to mention but some of the more outstanding. But the desire within the discipline to appear scientific—narrowly defined to mean quantitatively precise—has been sufficiently strong to overpower whatever question has been raised.

It is not that the relevant arguments articulated by this minority have been answered. Rather, they generally have been ignored. As Gouldner has stated: "Today, all the powers of sociology, from Parsons to Lundberg, have entered into a tacit alliance to bind us to the dogma 'thou shalt not commit a value judgment.' "[2] Moreover, the admonition "thou shalt not" has been transformed in the minds of many sociologists to mean that, in fact, they "do not." In short, the claim of objectivity, typically proclaimed to convince others of sociology's truly scientific worth, has more generally succeeded in convincing sociologists themselves that the claim, repeated often enough, is somehow evidence of the fact.

But the fact, of course, is quite otherwise. Values have not been absent from the discipline; and, more than that, sociological contributions which sociologists themselves have long regarded as among the most significant have not lacked judgments of human value. Far more to the point, the power of these works rests in part on the fact that such judgments were made.

Verification of this assertion is easily provided. And, since it was Max Weber who originated the discipline's distinction between statements of fact and statements of value,[3] Weber's classic work, *The Protestant Ethic and the Spirit of Capitalism,* serves as a most appropriate starting point. Concerning the "iron cage" of materialism which Weber felt had been fostered by the rise of bureaucratically-organized capitalism, his final evaluation was delivered in words which scarcely can be regarded as value-free.

> . . . mechanized petrification, embellished with a sort of convulsive self-importance. For of the last stage of this cultural development, it might well be truly said: "Specialists without spirit, sensualists without

[2] Alvin W. Gouldner, "Anti-Minotaur: The Myth of a Value-Free Sociology," *Social Problems,* 9:199 (Winter, 1962).
[3] Though, as Gouldner has noted, it was Weber's purpose to "depoliticize" the German university of his time to prevent divergent political loyalties from interfering with academic work his effort, unfortunately, more generally succeeded in "amoralizing" his chosen discipline. *Ibid.,* p. 203.

heart; this nullity imagines that it has attained a level of civilization never before achieved."[4]

Weber was not unaware that he had entered an arena forbidden to the sociological endeavor. For in his very next line he stated: "But this brings us to the world of judgments of value and of faith, with which this purely historical discussion need not be burdened."[5] But the fact remains that the judgment was made. And who would have it otherwise? How else should a study of the Protestant ethic and the spirit of capitalism conclude if not with a judgment by the scholar most intimately acquainted with the subject? Indeed, without the final judgment, the power of Weber's classic work would be curtailed.

And what of Durkheim? First of all, the felt necessity to grasp the continuity of past, present, and future is clearly evident in his published work. The chief characteristic of our whole historical development, he wrote,

is to have swept cleanly away all the older social forms of organization. One after another, they have disappeared either through the slow usury of time or through great disturbances, but without being replaced.[6]

The statement is one of great scope. And while modern sociology would discourage this broad endeavor because of the difficulty of securing verification, Durkheim's *Suicide* stands as a classic rather unchallenged by any more modern work on the subject. Moreover, Durkheim, as Weber, did not ultimately shy away from the value question. In concluding his study of suicide, he asked, in rather nonobjective language: "Is the evil (suicide) then incurable?"[7] And beyond that: "By what means shall we try to overcome it?"[8] These concerns are hardly those of the disinterested observer. Rather, they are those of the competent scholar who, upon completion of a careful and reasonably objective study, understands the necessity of being pertinent, i.e., concerned with the plight of mankind. Moreover, he was not ashamed to wish mankind well.

Hence, aside from their great intellectual capacity, it is quite clear that these two sociologists whom the field still regards as among its masters possessed at least two main qualities: (1) they focused their attention on those social forces responsible for the essential drift of social life; and (2) while in the conduct of their studies they attempted to view the data as objectively as possible, ultimately, they did not refrain from offering their most reasoned judgments.

[4] Max Weber, *The Protestant Ethic and the Spirit of Capitalism* (New York: Charles Scribners' Sons, 1958), p. 182.
[5] *Ibid.*
[6] Emile Durkheim, *Suicide*, tr. John A. Spaulding and George Simpson (Glencoe, Ill.: The Free Press, 1951), p. 388.
[7] *Ibid.*, p. 378.
[8] *Ibid.*, p. 370.

For those who may feel that verification requires more than two examples, the following queries are offered for consideration: Did not August Comte, the acknowledged father of the sociological discipline, recommend sociocracy? Did not Toennies write a little more warmly concerning *Gemeinschaft* as opposed to *Gesellschaft*? Did not Cooley describe primary relationships as warm, intimate, personal; and secondary relationships[9] as cold, superficial, impersonal? Did not Veblen, firmly grounded on utilitarianism as a value, equate conspicuous leisure and consumption with waste? Does not Freud's *Civilization and Its Discontents* offer a judgment in its very title? And, finally, is it not true that sociologists generally have felt that all of the foregoing have been particularly significant? And why? Certainly not because these works were value-free. Quite the contrary. In each case (and the list could be multiplied), in addition to a rather sound analysis of the nature of social life, a value position is either explicitly stated or implicitly contained.

And who would have it otherwise? Who would really prefer that the works of Weber, Durkheim, Toennies, Cooley, Veblen, etc. be altered to conform to the dictates of a truly value-free sociology? To raise the question is to know the answer. As one well realizes as he contemplates the prospect, while the judgments offered have rarely been flawless, without the judgment the power of the work is impaired. To insist upon value neutrality concerning the contributions of the foregoing would require not alteration but emasculation.

Thus, if value commitment is so evident in significant sociological works, how can the modern commitment to a value-free sociology be explained? The attraction of Weber's logic in the original formulation of the value-free doctrine is, of course, fundamental. But, as Gouldner has observed, logic aside, we may be sure that the attraction of the value-free doctrine rests in part on the fact that "it is somehow useful to those who believe it."[10] And it is especially useful "to those young, and not so young, men who live off sociology rather than for it, and who think of sociology as a way of getting ahead in the world by providing them with neutral techniques that may be sold on the open market to any buyer."[11] Similarly, Horowitz, who has noted that the less marketable specialties such as sociological theory, the history of social thought, and the sociology of religion have been outflanked by the far more lucrative specialties of medical and industrial sociology, writes: " 'Who pays how much for what' . . . best explains the dominant motif in American sociology."[12]

---

[9] Cooley himself did not actually use this term. Rather than being explicitly stated, it was implicit in his chapter on "Primary Groups." See C. H. Cooley, *Social Organization* (Glencoe, Ill.: Free Press, 1956).
[10] Gouldner, *op. cit.*, p. 200.
[11] *Ibid.*, p. 206.
[12] Irving L. Horowitz in the Introduction of *The New Sociology*, ed. Irving L. Horowitz (New York: Oxford University Press, 1965), p. 8.

On this score, the words of the major American proponent of a value-free sociology, George Lundberg, are worth recalling. For, though perhaps he did not intend it, the advice of Lundberg has served his value-free followers well. "Physical scientists," Lundberg noted, are far "less likely to be disturbed than social scientists when a political upheaval comes along, because the work of the former is recognized as of equal consequence under any regime."[13] Should the full impact of Lundberg's observation not be sufficiently appreciated, he stated more precisely the virtue of his position for one concerned with survival or success in his individual career: "The services of *real* [i.e., value-free] social scientists would be as indispensable to Fascists or to Communists and Democrats, just as are the services of physicists and physicians."[14]

Lundberg surely has a point. But one should note that German physicians who systematically froze human beings in tubs of ice and, in the conduct of sterilization experiments, sent electrical charges through female ovaries were quite useful to the Nazi regime. While to some these examples may seem extreme, one must recognize nonetheless that the behavior of these German scientists falls quite within the limits of the value-free model offered. And, should one demur from sociological studies designed to increase the effectiveness of political terror under a Nazi regime, at this point he becomes, in Lundberg's terms, a less-than-perfect or even unreal social scientist.

Can Science Save Us? asked Lundberg in the title of his famous work. For society as a whole (which is what he had in mind), the answer remains unclear. For the value-free social scientist, however, it is difficult to conceive of a doctrine better calculated to insure the survival of the individual social scientist.

Thus, the value-free doctrine of contemporary sociology appears deficient on two main counts: (1) it is hypocritical—since, while widely proclaimed, it has consistently fallen short of delivery, and especially in the discipline's most significant works; (2) it is inappropriate—for if the discipline which claims to know most about the nature of social life does not offer its most reasoned judgments, to whom does the obligation fall? It would seem to those less competent to make them—which would also seem absurd.

It is not that sociologists should "make policy," an accusation often made by those wedded to the value-free doctrine when it is suggested that informed judgments on matters of moment are appropriate. On this matter, sociologists flatter themselves unnecessarily. Policy will be made, as it always has been, by those in positions of ultimate authority—despite either the fears or the wishes of Ph.D.'s in sociology. The point is, however, that policy, especially in a society characterized by a rapid pace of social change, is continually being formulated

[13] George A. Lundberg, *Can Science Save Us?* (New York: Longmans, Green and Co., 1961), p. 56.
[14] *Ibid.*, p. 57.

and modified. Hence, those in positions of authority might well benefit from the judgments of a competent and responsible sociology. Certainly, well-founded, informed sociological judgment can do little harm and, on occasion, might do considerable good.

The point here need not be misinterpreted. By no means is one recommending a license to offer value judgments at random, resulting in a "this I believe"-type sociology. Rather, it is to proceed as significant minds always have—that is, after a careful, fair-minded, and reasonably objective consideration of the facts —to offer whatever meaningful judgment seems appropriate. Moreover, in offering such a judgment, one's scientific or scholarly role need not be compromised. If, for example, an oceanographer knows, on the basis of the data before him, that a tidal wave appears imminent in approximately twenty-seven minutes, is he any less a scientist if he indicates, out of concern for ocean-side residents, that it might be a good idea for them to evacuate? Likewise, if the social scientist sees in his data an impending racial crisis, is he (or his data? or sociology? or science?) in any way compromised should he attempt to convince the city authorities to take certain measures for the good of all urban residents concerned? Obviously not. To be responsible has always been a virtue. Yet, a value-free, amoral sociological doctrine has attempted to convince us otherwise. As Lynd, quoting a line from Auden's poetry, asked his value-free sociological colleagues almost thirty years ago, are we really to be encouraged to continue "lecturing on navigation while the ship is going down"?[15]

But, under the influence of value-free dogma, this is precisely what we have been doing. As opposed to Durkheim, who stated in concluding *Suicide:* "Thus a monograph on suicide has a bearing beyond the special class of facts which it particularly embraces. The questions it raises are closely connected with the most serious practical problems of the present time."[16] Furthermore, as noted above, Durkheim went on to make certain recommendations for the solution of these problems. Indeed, the final chapter of *Suicide,* thirty-two pages in length, bears the title "Practical Consequences." The contrast between Durkheim and contemporary sociology, however, is sharp. Consider the following—no straw man but, indeed, a contribution centrally in the mainstream of modern sociology. Published by the *American Sociological Review* and entitled "The Socio-Economic Status of Cities and Suburbs," the article encourages the reader to believe that he will be confronted by a source which in some way will further his understanding of the modern urban age. When the final summation is delivered, however, his expectations are left rather unfulfilled:

In conclusion, we must emphasize that our own efforts to reconstruct

---

[15] Robert S. Lynd, *Knowledge For What?* (New York: Grove Press, Inc., 1964), p. 3.
[16] Durkheim, *op. cit.,* p. 391.

the past development of urban residential structure are speculative. They are based on a thin line of evidence derived from cross-sectional observations of broad status groups in cities of different age. One hesitates to assert on the basis of these materials, that a determinate "evolutionary sequence" occurs with the maturation of urban areas. Longitudinal inferences cannot be readily derived from cross-sectional observations. Nothing presented here denies the existence of an historical series of outward shifts of higher status groups from the center to the periphery, but proof of such a sequence is not established in this study.[17]

Given the tortured verbal style, combined with the tentative and hesitant conclusion, an intelligent citizenry (including a fair number of sociologists) concerned with life in the Twentieth Century may be forgiven if it turns to *Harper's* or the *Atlantic Monthly* for intellectual guidance. For the fact is that, as opposed to the writings of Weber and Durkheim, modern value-free sociology has very little to say. As Gerth and Landau have observed:

It was not until 1940, after the hot war was underway, that the *American Journal of Sociology* decided to publish an article on the Nazi Party. In all, from 1933 to 1947, only two articles on National Socialism appeared in the *Journal*. A fifty-year index of the *Journal* shows exactly three listings under Marx or Marxism, and under Lenin (or Leninism) there are no citations. By and large, the sociologists of today have shut the world crisis out of their vision, focusing their intellectual energy on the crisis of the family, while the Chinese revolution, involving 600,000,000 people—perhaps the greatest mass movement of mankind—is totally neglected.[18]

But "so what?" ask those firmly convinced of the value of being value-free. Who is to say that a knowledge of Nazism in 1937 is any more or less important than that concerning the status of a randomly selected sample of 117 retail druggists in Madison, Wisconsin? Clearly a judgment is called for and clearly a judgment must be made. Lynd's judgment offered in *Knowledge for What?* is worth recalling:

No economist collects the dates on the coins passed over the counter of a soda fountain, . . . and no sociologist interested in urban problems

---

[17] Leo F. Schnore, "The Socio-Economic Status of Cities and Suburbs," *The American Sociological Review* (Feb., 1963), p. 85.
[18] Hans Gerth and Saul Landau, "The Relevance of History to the Sociological Ethos," *Studies on the Left*, 1:1 (Fall, 1959). Reprinted in *Sociology on Trial*, eds. Maurice Stein and Arthur Vidich (Englewood Cliffs, N.J.: Prentice-Hall, Inc., 1963), p. 31.

counts and compares the number of bricks in the buildings on a slum block and on a Park Avenue block. Why do we train scientists? To give them refined techniques of observation, analysis, and control, to be sure. But, even more important, the outstanding characteristic of a well-trained scientist is his ability to distinguish "significant" from "insignificant" problems and data. Good scientific training sensitizes one to important problems. . . . Research without an actively selective point of view becomes the ditty bag of an idiot, filled with bits of pebbles, straws, feathers, and other random hoardings.[19]

Thus, in answer to the question: "Who is to judge?"—as if we are all so equally incompetent and blind—let me suggest that matters such as the threat of nuclear annihilation, racial strife in urban areas, the social consequences of automation, and the viability of the Great Society are certainly among those which virtually all intelligent and informed citizens view as matters of consequence. As Barrington Moore has said of Marx, Durkheim, Weber, and Mosca:

There was a strong historical current in the thinking of all these men. Through different lenses and from widely differing political standpoints all of them saw as their scientific problems those which the course of human history had put on the agenda as the significant ones of their epoch.[20]

It is worth asking why the case at the present time should be so different.

Again, misinterpretation here is unnecessary. The recommendation is not that sociology should be solely social problem or social issue-oriented. Rather, it is that sociology should be relevant—as Marx, Weber, Durkheim, and Mosca were. Contemporary research concerning small groups, marriage and the family, etc. should certainly continue. But what we surely should not do is avoid issues of consequence simply because they require human judgment or because they are not very susceptible to the methodological tools we happen to have at hand. Unquestionably, scientific methodology is very helpful, indeed, even indispensable, for the investigation of certain kinds of subject matter. But, to allow methodological technique to dictate our human concerns would seem the height of intellectual folly. For, aside from the appropriateness of the investigative technique employed, clearly, it is the issue which remains primary. "To proceed in the reverse fashion—i.e., to permit technique to determine our interests—puts us, as it already has, on a methodologically reliable highway which leads, how-

[19] Lynd, op. cit., p. 183.
[20] Barrington Moore, "Strategy in Social Science," Political Power and Social Theory: Six Studies (Cambridge, Mass.: Harvard Univ. Press, 1958). Chap. IV reprinted in Sociology on Trial, op. cit., p. 67.

22 □ A Contemporary Sociological Perspective

ever, into rather barren intellectual territory."[21] Indeed, as Ross and Van Den Hagg have attempted to remind their sociological colleagues, "to discuss only what is scientifically testable" is "to ignore much that is vital and to lay undue stress on the trivial." In fact, "the greater part of human experience" is thereby "excluded from articulate reflection."[22] Testability, verifiability, reliability to be sure: but what great difference can it make if that which is reliable is also trivial?

That scientific methodology is important no one can deny. Yet, when one reflects on the fact that methodology finally is only a means, its current worship within the discipline reminds one of Robert Merton's "ritualist" who has become so involved in the means that he loses sight of, or even renounces, the end. As Merton said of "ritualism," it represents that adjustment committed to the proposition "that high ambitions invite frustration and danger whereas lower aspirations produce satisfaction and security."[23] Ritualism, thus, is that mode of adaptation in which one seeks an "escape from the dangers and frustrations which seem . . . inherent in the competition for major cultural goals by abandoning these goals and clinging all the more closely to the safe routines and the institutional norms."[24] While, for Merton, the frightened individual employee and the rigid bureaucrat are the examples on centerstage, the applicability of his analysis to a discipline plagued by "methodological inhibition"[25] is by no means inappropriate. For, while the current emphasis on formal verification via quantification is so strong as to indicate that one can hardly know anything by any other means, it is perfectly clear that the works of Weber, Toennies, Simmel, Cooley, Mead, Sumner, Veblen (i.e., contributions which scarcely contain a number) do not measure up to this modern "scientific" requirement. And one suspects that if all of the foregoing "arm-chair theorists" had been advised in their formative years by convinced advocates of modern scientism, perhaps certain rather imaginative concepts such as that of the looking-glass self, the generalized other, conspicuous leisure, and conspicuous consumption might never have seen the light of day. As Nisbet has commented on the deficiency of contemporary sociology's method-worship:

Only that is scientific—so runs the folklore of scientism—that proceeds from an unambiguous and precisely delimited problem, drawn from statistically aseptic data, to a carefully tailored hypothesis. All else is, by

---

[21] David J. Gray, "Sociology as a Science: A Dysfunctional Element," *American Journal of Economics and Sociology,* 21:346 (Oct., 1962).
[22] Ralph Ross and Ernest Van Den Haag, *The Fabric of Society* (New York: Harcourt, Brace and Co., 1957), p. 5.
[23] Robert K. Merton, *Social Theory and Social Structure* (Glencoe, Ill.: The Free Press, 1959), p. 150.
[24] *Ibid.,* p. 151.
[25] C. Wright Mills, *The Sociological Imagination* (New York: Oxford University Press, 1959), Chap. III.

definition, art or philosophy. It is hard to think of a better way to apotheosize the routine and insignificant.[26]

And, in a truly value-free context, how could it be otherwise? Since no one can legitimately distinguish the trivial from the consequential, in an age of scientism, the trivial inevitably triumphs. For if verification—the keynote of modern scientism—is required, verification of the minuscule is far more easily achieved.

The ultimate consequence is that the critical (i.e., evaluative) quality of an intellectual discipline is lost. And while sociologists may congratulate themselves on their newly attained "scientific" status, the fact is that as opposed to being truly value-free, rather, they have become but professional handmaidens of the going value system.[27] In effect, by refusing to make value judgments themselves, they have tacitly accepted the values of others. No longer truly intellectual, they have assumed a new role as employees, consultants, or technicians serving the present establishment which, on the matter of values, is by no means so shy. As a result, sociologists may be more prosperous, to be sure, but, in a confirmation of Weber's prophesy concerning "specialists without spirit," as ethically-neutral practitioners in a modern bureaucratic world, they now are "useful only because they can be used."[28]

The final question thus becomes: "how should a relevant sociology proceed?" And the fundamental answer is that the erroneous and self-congratulatory sociological allegiance to the value-free doctrine must be foregone. Specifically, we should understand that human judgment, which, in part, must involve human values, is indispensable in the selection of a subject to be investigated. We have often admitted this, but have continued to tell ourselves and anyone else who would listen that, nevertheless, we were still value-free. Secondly, admitting that values are involved, we should then proceed to select subjects and issues worthy of investigation. The specific question we must ask ourselves here is: "Of what relevance is this particular matter for mankind?" And the investigation of the sexual attitudes of 127 sophomore co-eds even though calculated to the third decimal point, if unrelated to anything else in society or the world at large, does not recommend itself as a matter of great relevance. Thirdly, having selected an important subject, we should proceed to investigate it—quantitatively, and with as much methodological sophistication as is available, if possible, but analytically, with as scholarly and objective a regard for the facts as is humanly possible, if not. Finally, having completed our investigation of a significant matter, we should take it as the duty of that discipline which studies social life most carefully to provide, where or when appropriate, our most reasoned

---

[26] Robert A. Nisbet, "Sociology as an Art Form," *Pacific Sociological Review*, 5:70 (Fall, 1962).
[27] Horowitz, *op. cit.*, p. 10.
[28] Gouldner, *op. cit.*, p. 213.

judgments concerning whatever issue may be at stake. No one need always listen; nor, need it be assumed that the judgment offered is beyond question. Rather, it is to be taken precisely in the vein in which it is offered—a judgment by that scholar intimately acquainted with the subject under consideration, offered for the possible enlightenment and betterment of mankind.

Hence, what is recommended in the present paper is the legitimacy and, indeed, indispensability of value judgment for the sociological discipline. While to some this may seem an act of sacrilege, by no means can anything so revolutionary be claimed. For the fact is that what is presented here comes to no more than a recommendation to proceed as Weber and Durkheim and other significant scholars did, and still do. That there are very few Webers and Durkheims (a point often underlined in the conventional sociological wisdom), while true, is superfluous. The point is that there may be some—and, for any significant discipline, their encouragement or discouragement and the model which they provide is a matter of critical importance. For even if contemporary talents are limited—as they surely always are—the issues of the twentieth century remain. And if that discipline which claims to know the most about social life refuses to investigate significant issues and to deliver its best judgments concerning them, to repeat, to whom does this important obligation fall? Under the guise of science, the value-free doctrine has encouraged us to say: "Who cares?" The question which a significant intellectual discipline must ask itself, however, is whether or not this posture of irrelevance and irresponsibility is appropriate. To date, the value-free doctrine has led us to conclude that it is. Only when this conclusion is reversed can the sociological discipline hope to rejuvenate, on any substantial basis, the intellectual vitality it earlier possessed and which only a violation of the value-free doctrine in modern sociology has managed to keep alive. And only then will a worthy and important discipline replace a large amount of well-verified irrelevance with a body of relevant knowledge truly worth communicating to a receptive and appreciative audience.

Reflective Questions

1. What is the basis for Gray's argument that the value-free doctrine will not serve the best interest of sociology?

2. On what counts does Gray claim the value-free doctrine to be deficient?

3. What is the meaning of the quote, "... are we really to be encouraged to continue lecturing on navigation while the ship is going down?"?

4. How does Gray respond to the question, "how should a relevant sociology proceed?"?

3 □ WHOSE SIDE ARE WE ON?

Howard S. Becker

Becker first delivered this paper as the presidential address to the annual meeting of the Society for the Study of Social Problems in August 1966. He discusses and analyzes the charge that the sociologist who demonstrates a value stand is biased and therefore his research is invalid. According to Becker, by refusing to accept the hierarchy of credibility, the activist sociologist is considered to have disrespect for the entire established order and consequently provokes charges of bias. To the accusations of bias, Becker responds: ". . . there is no position from which sociological research can be done that is not biased in one or another way." The "real" problem facing the sociologist is to take care that his research meets the high standards of quality scientific work and to be certain that his biases are not reflected in such a manner as to invalidate the results of his research. A possible solution suggested by Becker to the charges of bias is to apply rigorous standards to the design and methodology of a research project and to state carefully the limitations and boundaries of the findings. From this article, one can understand the impossibility of maintaining neutrality when confronted with issues. Even to remain mute is to take a position. □

TO HAVE VALUES OR NOT TO HAVE VALUES: THE QUESTION IS ALWAYS WITH US. When sociologists undertake to study problems that have relevance to the world we live in, they find themselves caught in a crossfire. Some urge them not to take sides, to be neutral and do research that is technically correct and value free. Others tell them their work is shallow and useless if it does not express a deep commitment to a value position.

From *The Journal of Social Problems*, Vol. 14, No. 3, Winter 1967, pp. 239–247. Reprinted by permission of The Society for the Study of Social Problems and the author.

This dilemma, which seems so painful to so many, actually does not exist, for one of its horns is imaginary. For it to exist, one would have to assume, as some apparently do, that it is indeed possible to do research that is uncontaminated by personal and political sympathies. I propose to argue that it is not possible and, therefore, that the question is not whether we should take sides, since we inevitably will, but rather whose side we are on.

I will being by considering the problem of taking sides as it arises in the study of deviance. An inspection of this case will soon reveal to us features that appear in sociological research of all kinds. In the greatest variety of subject matter areas and in work done by all the different methods at our disposal, we cannot avoid taking sides, for reasons firmly based in social structure.

We may sometimes feel that studies of deviance exhibit too great a sympathy with the people studied, a sympathy reflected in the research carried out. This feeling, I suspect, is entertained off and on both by those of us who do such research and by those of us who, our work lying in other areas, only read the results. Will the research, we wonder, be distorted by that sympathy? Will it be of use in the construction of scientific theory or in the application of scientific knowledge to the practical problems of society? Or will the bias introduced by taking sides spoil it for those uses?

We seldom make the feeling explicit. Instead, it appears as a lingering worry for sociological readers, who would like to be sure they can trust what they read, and a troublesome area of self-doubt for those who do the research, who would like to be sure that whatever sympathies they feel are not professionally unseemly and will not, in any case, seriously flaw their work. That the worry affects both readers and researchers indicates that it lies deeper than the superficial differences that divide sociological schools of thought, and that its roots must be sought in characteristics of society that affect us all, whatever our methodological or theoretical persuasion.

If the feeling were made explicit, it would take the form of an accusation that the sympathies of the researcher have biased his work and distorted his findings. Before exploring its structural roots, let us consider what the manifest meaning of the charge might be.

It might mean that we have acquired some sympathy with the group we study sufficient to deter us from publishing those of our results which might prove damaging to them. One can imagine a liberal sociologist who set out to disprove some of the common stereotypes held about a minority group. To his dismay, his investigation reveals that some of the stereotypes are unfortunately true. In the interests of justice and liberalism, he might well be tempted, and might even succumb to the temptation, to suppress those findings, publishing with scientific candor the other results which confirmed his beliefs.

But this seems not really to be the heart of the charge, because sociologists who study deviance do not typically hide things about the people they study.

They are mostly willing to grant that there is something going on that put the deviants in the position they are in, even if they are not willing to grant that it is what the people they studied were originally accused of.

A more likely meaning of the charge, I think, is this. In the course of our work and for who knows what private reasons, we fall into deep sympathy with the people we are studying, so that while the rest of the society views them as unfit in one or another respect for the deference ordinarily accorded a fellow citizen, we believe that they are at least as good as anyone else, more sinned against than sinning. Because of this, we do not give a balanced picture. We focus too much on questions whose answers show that the supposed deviant is morally in the right and the ordinary citizen morally in the wrong. We neglect to ask those questions whose answers would show that the deviant, after all, has done something pretty rotten and, indeed, pretty much deserves what he gets. In consequence, our overall assessment of the problem being studied is one-sided. What we produce is a whitewash of the deviant and a condemnation, if only by implication, of those respectable citizens who, we think, have made the deviant what he is.

It is to this version that I devote the rest of my remarks. I will look first, however, not at the truth or falsity of the charge, but rather at the circumstances in which it is typically made and felt. The sociology of knowledge cautions us to distinguish between the truth of a statement and an assessment of the circumstances under which that statement is made; though we trace an argument to its source in the interests of the person who made it, we have still not proved it false. Recognizing the point and promising to address it eventually, I shall turn to the typical situations in which the accusation of bias arises.

When do we accuse ourselves and our fellow sociologists of bias? I think an inspection of representative instances would show that the accusation arises, in one important class of cases, when the research gives credence, in any serious way, to the perspective of the subordinate group in some hierarchical relationship. In the case of deviance, the hierarchical relationship is a moral one. The superordinate parties in the relationship are those who represent the forces of approved and official morality; the subordinate parties are those who, it is alleged, have violated that morality.

Though deviance is a typical case, it is by no means the only one. Similar situations, and similar feelings that our work is biased, occur in the study of schools, hospitals, asylums and prisons, in the study of physical as well as mental illness, in the study of both "normal" and delinquent youth. In these situations, the superordinate parties are usually the official and professional authorities in charge of some important institution, while the subordinates are those who make use of the services of that institution. Thus, the police are the superordinates, drug addicts are the subordinates; professors and administrators, principals and teachers, are the superordinates, while students and pupils are the subordinates; physicians are the superordinates, their patients the subordinates.

All of these cases represent one of the typical situations in which researchers accuse themselves and are accused of bias. It is a situation in which, while conflict and tension exist in the hierarchy, the conflict has not become openly political. The conflicting segments or ranks are not organized for conflict; no one attempts to alter the shape of the hierarchy. While subordinates may complain about the treatment they receive from those above them, they do not propose to move to a position of equality with them, or to reverse positions in the hierarchy. Thus, no one proposes that addicts should make and enforce laws for policemen, that patients should prescribe for doctors, or that adolescents should give orders to adults. We can call this the *apolitical* case.

In the second case, the accusation of bias is made in a situation that is frankly political. The parties to the hierarchical relationship engage in organized conflict, attempting either to maintain or change existing relations of power and authority. Whereas in the first case subordinates are typically unorganized and thus have, as we shall see, little to fear from a researcher, subordinate parties in a political situation may have much to lose. When the situation is political, the researcher may accuse himself or be accused of bias by someone else when he gives credence to the perspective of either party to the political conflict. I leave the political for later and turn now to the problem of bias in apolitical situations.[1]

We provoke the suspicion that we are biased in favor of the subordinate parties in an apolitical arrangement when we tell the story from their point of view. We may, for instance, investigate their complaints, even though they are subordinates, about the way things are run just as though one ought to give their complaints as much credence as the statements of responsible officials. We provoke the charge when we assume, for the purposes of our research, that subordinates have as much right to be heard as superordinates, that they are as likely to be telling the truth as they see it as superordinates, that what they say about the institution has a right to be investigated and have its truth or falsity established, even though responsible officials assure us that it is unnecessary because the charges are false.

We can use the notion of a *hierarchy of credibility* to understand this phenomenon. In any system of ranked groups, participants take it as given that members of the highest group have the right to define the way things really are. In any organization, no matter what the rest of the organization

[1] No situation is necessarily political or apolitical. An apolitical situation can be transformed into a political one by the open rebellion of subordinate ranks, and a political situation can subside into one in which an accommodation has been reached and a new hierarchy been accepted by the participants. The categories, while analytically useful, do not represent a fixed division existing in real life.

chart shows, the arrows indicating the flow of information point up, thus demonstrating (at least formally) that those at the top have access to a more complete picture of what is going on than anyone else. Members of lower groups will have incomplete information, and their view of reality will be partial and distorted in consequence. Therefore, from the point of view of a well socialized participant in the system, any tale told by those at the top intrinsically deserves to be regarded as the most credible account obtainable of the organizations' workings. And since, as Sumner pointed out, matters of rank and status are contained in the mores,[2] this belief has a moral quality. We are, if we are proper members of the group, morally bound to accept the definition imposed on reality by a superordinate group in preference to the definitions espoused by subordinates. (By analogy, the same argument holds for the social classes of a community.) Thus, credibility and the right to be heard are differentially distributed through the ranks of the system.

As sociologists, we provoke the charge of bias, in ourselves and others, by refusing to give credence and deference to an established status order, in which knowledge of truth and the right to be heard are not equally distributed. "Everyone knows" that responsible professionals know more about things than laymen, that police are more respectable and their words ought to be taken more seriously than those of the deviants and criminals with whom they deal. By refusing to accept the hierarchy of credibility, we express disrespect for the entire established order.

We compound our sin and further provoke charges of bias by not giving immediate attention and "equal time" to the apologies and explanations of official authority. If, for instance, we are concerned with studying the way of life inmates in a mental hospital build up for themselves, we will naturally be concerned with the constraints and conditions created by the actions of the administrators and physicians who run the hospital. But, unless we also make the administrators and physicians the object of our study (a possibility I will consider later), we will not inquire into why those conditions and constraints are present. We will not give responsible officials a chance to explain themselves and give their reasons for acting as they do, a chance to show why the complaints of inmates are not justified.

It is odd that, when we perceive bias, we usually see it in these circumstances. It is odd because it is easily ascertained that a great many more studies are biased in the direction of the interests of responsible officials than the other way around. We may accuse an occasional student of medical sociology of having given too much emphasis to the complaints of patients. But it is not obvious that most medical sociologists look at things from the point of view of the doctors?

[2] William Graham Sumner, "Status in the Folkways," *Folkways,* New York: New American Library, 1960, pp. 72–73.

A few sociologists may be sufficiently biased in favor of youth to grant credibility to their account of how the adult world treats them. But why do we not accuse other sociologists who study youth of being biased in favor of adults? Most research on youth, after all, is clearly designed to find out why youth are so troublesome for adults, rather than asking the equally interesting sociological question: "Why do adults make so much trouble for youth?" Similarly, we accuse those who take the complaints of mental patients seriously of bias; what about those sociologists who only take seriously the complaints of physicians, families and others about mental patients?

Why this disproportion in the direction of accusations of bias? Why do we more often accuse those who are on the side of subordinates than those who are on the side of superordinates? Because, when we make the former accusation, we have, like the well socialized members of our society most of us are, accepted the hierarchy of credibility and taken over the accusation made by responsible officials.

The reason responsible officials make the accusation so frequently is precisely because they are responsible. They have been entrusted with the care and operation of one or another of our important institutions: schools, hospitals, law enforcement, or whatever. They are the ones who, by virtue of their official position and the authority that goes with it, are in a position to "do something" when things are not what they should be and, similarly, are the ones who will be held to account if they fail to "do something" or if what they do is, for whatever reason, inadequate.

Because they are responsible in this way, officials usually have to lie. That is a gross way of putting it, but not inaccurate. Officials must lie because things are seldom as they ought to be. For a great variety of reasons, well-known to sociologists, institutions are refractory. They do not perform as society would like them to. Hospitals do not cure people; prisons do not rehabilitate prisoners; schools do not educate students. Since they are supposed to, officials develop ways both of denying the failure of the institution to perform as it should and explaining those failures which cannot be hidden. An account of an institution's operation from the point of view of subordinates therefore casts doubt on the official line and may possibly expose it as a lie.[3]

For reasons that are a mirror image of those of officials, subordinates in an apolitical hierarchical relationship have no reason to complain of the bias of sociological research oriented toward the interests of superordinates. Subordinates typically are not organized in such a fashion as to be responsible for the overall operation of an institution. What happens in a school is credited or debited to the faculty and administrators; they can be identified and held to account. Even

[3] I have stated a portion of this argument more briefly in "Problems of Publication of Field Studies," in Arthur Vidich, Joseph Bensman, and Maurice Stein (Eds.), *Reflections on Community Studies,* New York, John Wiley and Sons, 1964, pp. 267–281.

though the failure of a school may be the fault of the pupils, they are not so organized that any one of them is responsible for any failure but his own. If he does well, while others all around him flounder, cheat and steal, that is none of his affair, despite the attempt of honor codes to make it so. As long as the sociological report on his school says that every student there but one is a liar and a cheat, all the students will feel complacent, knowing they are the one exception. More likely, they will never hear of the report at all or, if they do, will reason that they will be gone before long, so what difference does it make? The lack of organization among subordinate members of an institutionalized relationship means that, having no responsibility for the group's welfare, they likewise have no complaints if someone maligns it. The sociologist who favors officialdom will be spared the accusation of bias.

And thus we see why we accuse ourselves of bias only when we take the side of the subordinate. It is because, in a situation that is not openly political, with the major issues defined as arguable, we join responsible officials and the man in the street in an unthinking acceptance of the hierarchy of credibility. We assume with them that the man at the top knows best. We do not realize that there are sides to be taken and that we are taking one of them.

The same reasoning allows us to understand why the researcher has the same worry about the effect of his sympathies on his work as his uninvolved colleague. The hierarchy of credibility is a feature of society whose existence we cannot deny, even if we disagree with its injunction to believe the man at the top. When we acquire sufficient sympathy with subordinates to see things from their perspective, we know that we are flying in the face of what "everyone knows." The knowledge gives us pause and causes us to share, however briefly, the doubt of our colleagues.

When a situation has been defined politically, the second type of case I want to discuss, matters are quite different. Subordinates have some degree of organization and, with that, spokesmen, their equivalent of responsible officials. Spokesmen, while they cannot actually be held responsible for what members of their group do, make assertions on their behalf and are held responsible for the truth of those assertions. The group engages in political activity designed to change existing hierarchical relationships and the credibility of its spokesmen directly affects its political fortunes. Credibility is not the only influence, but the group can ill-afford having the definition of reality proposed by its spokesmen discredited, for the immediate consequence will be some loss of political power.

Superordinate groups have their spokesmen too, and they are confronted with the same problem: to make statements about reality that are politically effective without being easily discredited. The political fortunes of the superordinate group—its ability to hold the status changes demanded by lower groups to a minimum—do not depend as much on credibility, for the group has other kinds of power available as well.

When we do research in a political situation we are in double jeopardy, for the spokesmen of both involved groups will be sensitive to the implications of our work. Since they propose openly conflicting definitions of reality, our statement of our problem is in itself likely to call into question and make problematic, at least for the purposes of our research, one or the other definition. And our results will do the same.

The hierarchy of credibility operates in a different way in the political situation than it does in the apolitical one. In the political situation, it is precisely one of the things at issue. Since the political struggle calls into question the legitimacy of the existing rank system, it necessarily calls into question at the same time the legitimacy of the associated judgments of credibility. Judgments of who has a right to define the nature of reality that are taken for granted in an apolitical situation become matters of argument.

Oddly enough, we are, I think, less likely to accuse ourselves and one another of bias in a political than in an apolitical situation, for at least two reasons. First, because the hierarchy of credibility has been openly called into question, we are aware that there are at least two sides to the story and so do not think it unseemly to investigate the situation from one or another of the contending points of view. We know, for instance, that we must grasp the perspectives of both the resident of Watts and of the Los Angeles policeman if we are to understand what went on in that outbreak.

Second, it is no secret that most sociologists are politically liberal to one degree or another. Our political preferences dictate the side we will be on and, since those preferences are shared by most of our colleagues, few are ready to throw the first stone or are even aware that stone-throwing is a possibility. We usually take the side of the underdog; we are for Negroes and against Fascists. We do not think anyone biased who does research designed to prove that the former are not as bad as people think or that the latter are worse. In fact, in these circumstances we are quite willing to regard the question of bias as a matter to be dealt with by the use of technical safeguards.

We are thus apt to take sides with equal innocence and lack of thought, though for different reasons, in both apolitical and political situations. In the first, we adopt the commonsense view which awards unquestioned credibility to the responsible official. (This is not to deny that a few of us, because something in our experience has altered them to the possibility, may question the conventional hierarchy of credibility in the special area of our expertise.) In the second case, we take our politics so for granted that it supplants convention in dictating whose side we will be on. (I do not deny, either, that some few sociologists may deviate politically from their liberal colleagues, either to the right or the left, and thus be more liable to question than convention.)

In any event, even if our colleagues do not accuse us of bias in research in a political situation, the interested parties will. Whether they are foreign politicians who object to studies of how the stability of their government may be maintained in the interest of the United States (as in the *Camelot* affair)[4] or domestic civil rights leaders who object to an analysis of race problems that centers on the alleged deficiencies of the Negro family (as in the reception given to the Moynihan Report),[5] interested parties are quick to make accusations of bias and distortion. They base the accusation not on failures of technique or method, but on conceptual defects. They accuse the sociologist not of getting false data but of not getting all the data relevant to the problem. They accuse him, in other words, of seeing things from the perspective of only one party to the conflict. But the accusation is likely to be made by interested parties and not by sociologists themselves.

What I have said so far is all sociology of knowledge, suggesting by whom, in what situations and for what reasons sociologists will be accused of bias and distortion. I have not yet addressed the question of the truth of the accusations, of whether our findings are distorted by our sympathy for those we study. I have implied a partial answer, namely, that there is no position from which sociological research can be done that is not biased in one or another way.

We must always look at the matter from someone's point of view. The scientist who proposes to understand society must, as Mead long ago pointed out, get into the situation enough to have a perspective on it. And it is likely that his perspective will be greatly affected by whatever positions are taken by any or all of the other participants in that varied situation. Even if his participation is limited to reading in the field, he will necessarily read the arguments of partisans of one or another side to a relationship and will thus be affected, at least, by having suggested to him what the relevant arguments and issues are. A student of medical sociology may decide that he will take neither the perspective of the patient nor the perspective of the physician, but he will necessarily take a perspective that impinges on the many questions that arise between physicians and patients; no matter what perspective he takes, his work either will take into account the attitude of subordinates, or it will not. If he fails to consider the questions they raise, he will be working on the side of the officials. If he does raise those questions seriously and does find, as he may, that there is some merit in them, he will then expose himself to the outrage of the officials and of all those sociologists who award them the top spot in the hierarchy of credibility. Almost all the topics that sociologists study, at least those that have some relation to the real world around us, are seen by society as morality plays and we shall find ourselves, willy-nilly, taking part in those plays on one side or the other.

[4] See Irving Louis Horowitz, "The Life and Death of Project Camelot," *Transaction*, 3 (Nov./Dec., 1965), pp. 3–7, 44–47.
[5] See Lee Rainwater and William L. Yancey, "Black Families and the White House," *ibid.*, 3 (July/August, 1966, pp. 6–11, 48–53).

There is another possibility. We may, in some cases, take the point of view of some third party not directly implicated in the hierarchy we are investigating. Thus, a Marxist might feel that it is not worth distinguishing between Democrats and Republicans, or between big business and big labor, in each case both groups being equally inimical to the interests of the workers. This would indeed make us neutral with respect to the two groups at hand, but would only mean that we had enlarged the scope of the political conflict to include a party not ordinarily brought in whose view the sociologist was taking.

We can never avoid taking sides. So we are left with the question of whether taking sides means that some distortion is introduced into our work so great as to make it useless. Or, less drastically, whether some distortion is introduced that must be taken into account before the results of our work can be used. I do not refer here to feeling that the picture given by the research is not "balanced," the indignation aroused by having a conventionally discredited definition of reality given priority or equality with what "everyone knows," for it is clear that we cannot avoid that. That is the problem of officials, spokesmen and interested parties, not ours. Our problem is to make sure that, whatever point of view we take, our research meets the standards of good scientific work, that our unavoidable sympathies do not render our results invalid.

We might distort our findings, because of our sympathy with one of the parties in the relationship we are studying, by misusing the tools and techniques of our discipline. We might introduce loaded questions into a questionnaire, or act in some way in a field situation such that people would be constrained to tell us only the kind of thing we are already in sympathy with. All of our research techniques are hedged about with precautionary measures designed to guard against these errors. Similarly, though more abstractly, every one of our theories presumably contains a set of directives which exhaustively covers the field we are to study, specifying all the things we are to look at and take into account in our research. By using our theories and techniques impartially, we ought to be able to study all the things that need to be studied in such a way as to get all the facts we require, even though some of the questions that will be raised and some of the facts that will be produced run counter to our biases.

But the question may be precisely this. Given all our techniques of theoretical and technical control, how can we be sure that we will apply them impartially and across the board as they need to be applied? Our textbooks in methodology are no help here. They tell us how to guard against error, but they do not tell us how to make sure that we will use all the safeguards available to us. We can, for a start, try to avoid sentimentality. We are sentimental when we refuse, for whatever reason, to investigate some matter that should properly be regarded as problematic. We are sentimental, especially, when our reason is that we would prefer not to know what is going on, if to know would be to violate some sympathy whose existence we may not even be aware of. Whatever side we are on, we must use our techniques impartially enough that a belief to which we are especially sympathetic could be proved untrue. We must always inspect our work carefully enough to know whether our techniques and theories are open enough to allow that possibility.

Let us consider, finally, what might seem a simple solution to the problems posed. If the difficulty is that we gain sympathy with underdogs by studying them, is it not also true that the superordinates in a hierarchical relationship usually have their own superordinates with whom they must contend? Is it not true that we might study those superordinates or subordinates, presenting their point of view on their relations with their superiors and thus gaining a deeper sympathy with them and avoiding the bias of one-sided identification with those below them? This is appealing, but deceptively so. For it only means that we will get into the same trouble with a new set of officials.

It is true, for instance, that the administrators of a prison are not free to do as they wish, not free to be responsive of the desires of inmates, for instance. If one talks to such an official, he will commonly tell us, in private, that of course the subordinates in the relationship have some right on their side, but that they fail to understand that his desire to do better is frustrated by his superiors or by the regulations they have established. Thus, if a prison administrator is angered because we take the complaints of his inmates seriously, we may feel that we can get around that and get a more balanced picture by interviewing him and his associates. If we do, we may then write a report which *his* superiors will respond to with cries of "bias." They, in their turn, will say that we have not presented a balanced picture, because we have not looked at *their* side of it. And we may worry that what they say is true.

The point is obvious. By pursuing this seemingly simple solution, we arrive at a problem of infinite regress. For everyone has someone standing above him who prevents him from doing things just as he likes. If we question the superiors of the prison administrator, a state department of corrections or prisons, they will complain of the governor and the legislature. And if we go to the governor and the legislature, they will complain of lobbyists, party machines, the public and the newspapers. There is no end to it and we can never have a "balanced picture" until we have studied all of society simultaneously. I do not propose to hold my breath until that happy day.

We can, I think, satisfy the demands of our science by always making clear the limits of what we have studied, marking the boundaries beyond which our findings cannot be safely applied. Not just the conventional disclaimer, in which we warn that we have only studied a prison in New York or California and the findings may not hold in the other forty-nine states—which is not a useful procedure anyway, since the findings may very well hold if the conditions are the same elsewhere. I refer to a more sociological disclaimer in which we say, for instance, that we have studied the prison through the eyes of the inmates and not through the eyes of the guards or other involved parties. We warn people, thus, that our study tells us only how things look from that vantage point—what kinds of objects guards are in the prisoners' world—and does not attempt to explain why guards do what they do or to absolve the guards of what may seem, from the prisoners' side, morally unacceptable behavior. This will not protect us from accusations of bias, however, for the guards will still be outraged by the unbalanced picture. If we implicitly accept the conventional hierarchy of credibility, we will feel the sting in that accusation.

It is something of a solution to say that over the years each "one-sided" study will provoke further studies that gradually enlarge our grasp of all the relevant facets of an institution's operation. But that is a long-term solution, and not much help to the individual researcher who has to contend with the anger of officials who feel he has done them wrong, the criticism of those of his colleagues who think he is presenting a one-sided view, and his own worries.

What do we do in the meantime? I suppose the answers are more or less obvious. We take sides as our personal and political commitments dictate, use our theoretical and technical resources to avoid the distortions that might introduce into our work, limit our conclusions carefully, recognize the hierarchy of credibility for what it is, and field as best we can the accusations and doubts that will surely be our fate.

Reflective Questions

1. When are sociologists most likely to be accused of bias?

2. Why are sociologists who are on the side of the subordinates more apt to be accused of bias than those who are on the side of superordinates?

3. How does the hierarchy of credibility operate differently in the political situation than it does in the apolitical one?

4. What does Becker mean by the "problem of infinite regress"?

4 □ THE IMPOSSIBLE POSSIBLE PHILOSOPHERS' MAN: A DISCUSSION OF THE SOCIOLOGIST AS ACTIVIST

Howard J. Ehrlich

This paper first appeared in the *Sociological Focus* as an invited discussion of the presidential address presented by Dr. William V. D'Antonio at the 1969 joint meeting of the Ohio Valley and Midwest Sociological Societies. Ehrlich argues that, in reality, the sociologist has supported the ideological positions of the established institutions. The fact that a number of contemporary activist sociologists are challenging the established social and political interests is the primary reason for much of the current attention being focused on them. Whether a sociologist should be an activist is viewed by Ehrlich as a moot question. The present marginality of the radical sociologist may provide, according to Ehrlich, an atmosphere most conducive to professional creativity and productivity. An analogy may be drawn between the black artists who have long dominated the field of rhythm and blues and the contemporary radical sociologist. Perhaps we will find, as a result of the current conflict and "suffering," the development of a sociology with "soul" coming to influence the thinking and research of future sociologists. □

THE SOCIOLOGIST HAS ALWAYS BEEN AN ACTIVIST, AND THE UNIVERSITY HAS never been neutral. As long as the activism of the sociologist was consonant with the partisanship of the university, there were no serious professional or

From *Sociological Focus*, Vol. 2, No. 4, Summer, 1969, pp. 31–35. Reprinted, in slightly revised form, by permission of The Ohio Valley Sociological Society and the author.

institutional problems. Activism, in this context, has always been rewarded. When the activism of scholars violated the norms of professional behavior, those intent on preserving these norms invoked the idea of role segregation. As long as the scholar's political behaviors did not offend the university's sponsors, and/or were ineffective or not highly visible, there have been no serious professional or institutional problems. Although the idea of a "citizen's role" and a "scholar's role" is a sociological soporific, it was too essential a weapon in the ideological arsenal of the liberal academician to be challenged successfully. The members of the academy took the idea of role segregation as a premise on which to build an irrelevant curriculum—a curriculum built upon the wishes of scholars and established societal and political interests.

The 1960's generated an ethos of campus activism in a context of war, racial, and urban crises. The concatenation of events represents a decade of unique historical force.

For sociologists, activist or not, it should be clear that most Americans are unaware of the extent of social injustice that pervades this society. When injustice does become apparent, most people are unprepared to interpret the causes of such injustice as social. Prevailing interpretations of social phenomena tend strongly to be psychological. Individual persons may be mean, bigoted, aberrant, or violent, but social institutions are benign. Some policemen may be pigs, but the social organization of police is seldom questioned by the public.

When social interpretations are made, most Americans cast them in a national-revolutionary framework. This is, if the cause of injustice is not to be found in the existing social order, and if the psychological deficit of those who proclaim such injustice is undetermined, then clearly civil disorder must be the consequence of an external conspiracy. Thus in the Harris survey of September 9, 1968, 82 per cent of this national sample report "communists" as a (major or minor) cause of "the breakdown of law and order in this country."

Out of ignorance of social facts and social theory, and perhaps also out of a growing sense of personal alienation and fear, Americans stand strongly opposed to direct action and civilly disobedient protests in race relations, in opposition to the war, and in the agitation for a meaningful education on the campus. Most people are well aware that these tactics represent a direct challenge to the existing order, but since they do not view the causes of such problems as social they must conclude that such tactics "will hurt more than help" the cause of justice. After all, radical action can not be rationalized unless social injustice prevails.

In the context of the events of the 1960's, and in view of our collective failure to communicate the societal causes and social significance of these events, many sociologists have shifted to a new perspective. They have come to learn that social analysis without advocacy, that criticism without action, is an empty bag. It may be inflated by words, but any pressure will reveal its essential emptiness.

Still another void confronts the sociologist who eschews an active involvement and commitment to his subject matter. He may soon be confined to the laboratory, the paid volunteer, vital statistics, and computer simulation. The sociologist as sociologist may soon no longer be able to claim a mandate to study some groups and some phenomena. Already our fund of good will has been dissipated in some communities and in some ethnic and political groupings. I suspect that the days of suspicious toleration or altruistic cooperation are waning. The new keyword in field research will be *trust*; and it will be a trust based on the mutual collaboration of the sociologist and his host population. I think that a radical activist perspective will increase the relevance of social research for the host and for society. It will probably not affect its competence.

I do not believe that radical activism is necessarily divisive for sociology (although it will upset a few departments), nor will it diminish the scientific quality of research. Those who think so fail to comprehend the nature of the scientific enterprise. As long as we can agree upon methods of procedure and a logic of justification, we minimize the incursions of bias whatever their source. It is in the areas of ethics and morality that the lines of battle are being drawn. The substantive issues all focus upon our view of the good society, and the decade of the 1960's has made clear that there is no fundamental American consensus on this issue. And there certainly is no consensus among sociologists.

Surely it ought to be the fundamental objective of the social sciences to formulate a view of utopia. It becomes our challenge, as it has always been the challenge to radical social theorists, to ground our vision in a theory of society and personality that is consistent with the available evidence. While I do not reject the idea current in some radical strategies that all scholarship and research be judged by its relevance to this utopian vision, I cannot always make this judgment even with regard to my own work. And I do not believe that we can easily make such judgments today except in a negative sense. That is, I think we can sometimes tell rather clearly when social research serves established anti-utopian objectives. The involvement of social scientists in counter-insurgency research is (unfortunately) a good example.

There is one sense in which a utopian or radical position may serve the cause of social science even beyond that normally attributed to the value of diversity. I want to suggest, as a serious hypothesis that derives from Simmel's discussion of the stranger and Stonequist's commentary on the marginal man, that marginality is one necessary condition for creativity. It may be that a fuller comprehension of the society in which we live may require that we be somewhat marginal to it. A cross-cultural perspective, which most of us agree today is so necessary, may in fact draw its strength from its effects in inducing a marginal perspective.

The rise of organized factions of radical scholars in the American academy and the extraordinary impact of radical activism in the 1960's has brought with it the attempts of political and academic elites to control and suppress these activities. In 1960, D'Antonio and I collaborated on a statement on the nature of democratic political organization. I think that while we both still accept that statement, I have become less sanguine about its adequacy in characterizing political organization in the United States.

Certainly the basic elements of the democratic process include the ideas of effective opposition, of equality of access to political resources, of the vote, and of free and open competition for ideas and leadership. Democracy, of course, has always been construed as an institution of political order, and not as a means of governing complex organizations. Yet the essential failure of democracy in America may well derive from our national failure to accept this mode of decision making as fundamental to all social institutions.

I believe that as sociologists presumably committed to the idea of democracy, we must now give thought to maximizing the effective opposition of our colleagues through establishing caucuses of minority and political activists within our professional associations. Much as pseudo-liberal chairmen are now scouring the country for that rare Black sociologist, so they ought to be out searching for voices of minority opposition and utopian vision.

I would like to end my discussion with some comments directed at my radical colleagues, and conclude with a word to those not so committed. Our public commitment as radicals serves us as a collective symbol for our identity and for our solidarity. We identify ourselves as radicals because we seek fundamental changes in society. And we identify ourselves as radicals because we are willing to use nonconventional means of civil disobedience and direct action to achieve the changes we seek. As radicals we stand in consensus that this society is not what we seek, and we live—particularly in the university—in a paradoxically hostile environment. The university's major function is often defined as the transmission of traditional knowledge. But the new university must, and can, function as the critic of existing knowledge. The task of criticism logically implies a knowledge of history and tradition, and it takes sociological precedence as the goal of the university in modern society. It is in our commitment to radical action that we find ourselves in a campus and a societal context of opposition and conflict.

The nature and by-products of this conflict bring about two dilemmas that we should consider. Extensive or protracted conflict always produces careerists: persons whose entire social existence takes meaning from the conflict. Just the same, most of us are careerists, not in the sense of making conflict an end, but in the sense that there is no foreseeable end to our conflict. One cost of living in a hostile environment is that we tend to demand too much of ourselves. Our political commitments, while always a part of us, must always be balanced against our other commitments as scholars, scientists, artists, workers, and as human beings. If that cry of the streets, "Fuck for peace," were only true, then some of our problems might be easily solved.

One difference between the new left and the old is the great concern for personal autonomy. This concern has its political manifestation in the demand for participatory democracy. It has its individual expression in the search for a different life-style. The expression of this search is often to be found in the rejection of ostensively middle-class patterns of behavior and in actions which are sometimes calculated for their sensationalism. Style is important, but styles on the left are as transient as those devised by the centrists of Madison Avenue, and the pressures to conform are often no different.

Doing one's own thing—or, in the rhetoric of my student days, being authentic—is a necessary guide to individual action. But social organization always entails constraints on behavior: some things can not be done. The radical's dilemma remains that of determining when the individual good takes precedence over the social good, and vice-versa. The incredible burden of this choice is that such decisions have been traditionally mandated to institutions and not to individuals. Furthermore, there are no stock judicial precedents by which society can cope with civil disobedience, nor is there a well-developed social theory by which individuals can clearly claim their mandate.

I close now by addressing myself to those who have been puzzled by my remarks. I shall provide a poet's solution. The title I gave to this discussion is taken from Wallace Stevens' poem, *Asides on the Oboe*. Stevens begins his work, his reflections on man and war and violence:

> The prologues are over. It is a question, now,
> Of final belief. So, say that final belief
> Must be in a fiction. It is time to choose.

Reflective Questions

1. What is the basis for the author's argument that sociologists and universities have never been neutral?

2. When injustice becomes apparent, why are most people unprepared to interpret the causes of such injustice as social?

3. What, according to Ehrlich, are the goals of the radical sociologist?

4. How does the poem that concludes this article relate to the thesis of the author's argument?

PART TWO □ CULTURE AND THE DEVELOPMENT OF SELF

Because we do not use quarter tones in music, many of us do not hear them in Oriental music. How many people, seeing a painting, automatically dislike it because it is not familiar? And, most important of all, how many ideas do we reject without a hearing simply because our experience pattern can bring up no recognition parallel?

JOHN STEINBECK

PHOTO NEWS SERVICE / PIX

THE ARTICLES CONTAINED IN THIS PART EXAMINE ONE OF THE MOST significant of all sociological concepts—culture. It is so important to the understanding of human behavior that many sociologists would argue that culture is the most basic and useful concept that has been developed by the disciplines of sociology and anthropology. Although definitions of culture are often stated rather simply, the concept is somewhat difficult to grasp because man and his culture are inseparable.

One of the most comprehensive definitions of culture comes from the classic work of anthropologist Edward B. Tyler. According to Tyler, culture is " . . . that complex whole which includes knowledge, belief, art, morals, law, custom, and any other capabilities and habits acquired by man as a member of society."[1] Thus, culture includes the totality of man's social heritage. "Culture, then, is man's contribution to his environment."[2]

Sociologists frequently speak of culture as having two forms: (1) the material culture and (2) the nonmaterial culture. The material culture consists of the tangible objects of the culture coupled with the manner in which they are used. The buildings that constitute the physical portion of your university are a part of the material culture. In addition, man uses and creates an intangible social environment or nonmaterial culture. The nonmaterial culture consists of beliefs, customs, ideas, and ideologies that contribute to the patterns of human behavior—for example, folkways, mores, laws, and taboos.

It appears obvious to even a casual observer that not all members of any given society participate on the same cultural level. Anthropologist Ralph Linton has identified three types of cultural participation.[3] Every society has certain cultural universals that are required for all members of the society. These are behavior patterns that are considered necessary for the continued existence of the society. A second level of participation revolves around cultural alternatives. These are patterns of behavior that permit a diversified approach to a situation; each of several approaches are acceptable by the society, such as saying "hello" or "good day" when greeting a friend. Either of the above remarks are accepted in our society. The third type of cultural participation discussed by Linton is concerned with cultural specialties. These have a uniqueness that is shared by only a few members of the society. All societies, simple or complex, include specialists or persons considered to be members of categories, often on the basis of the division of labor; however, we must realize that there are subcultures derived from culture specialties that are not predicated upon the work role, such as teenage groups, college groups, peace groups, and gangs.

[1] Edward Burnett Tyler, *Primitive Culture* (London: J. Murray, 1871).
[2] Henry Pratt Fairchild (Ed.), *Dictionary of Sociology* (Paterson, N.J.: Littlefield, Adams and Co., 1961), p. 8.
[3] Ralph Linton, *The Study of Man* (New York: Appleton-Century-Crofts, Inc., 1936), pp. 272–274.

Closely related to Linton's discussion of levels of cultural participation are the concepts of subculture and contracultures. Within nearly all societies there are people with behavior patterns considerably different from the generally held patterns. A subculture is a collection of people who, in addition to sharing the norms of the larger culture, possess particular norms that differentiate it from the larger culture as well as other subcultures—for instance, jazz musicians, nurses, doctors, and "hippies." The behavior patterns of members of a contraculture are not only different, but also exhibit a way of life that may be seen as being in direct contrast to the general societal norms—for example, yippies and American Maoists.

Whatever a man may be, he is, in some sense, a reflection of his society, particularly of that portion whose members are significant to him. How a person becomes a functioning member of the society in which he lives has been a point of disagreement and discussion among students of human behavior for many years. The process whereby the human organism becomes a human being is labeled by the sociologist the "socialization process." It is through this process that the individual comes to acquire his concept of self. The ability to perceive selfhood is probably the primary distinction between man and the lower anthropoids.

The self may be viewed as "a personality's conception of its own personality."[4] Essentially self is the awareness an individual possesses that permits him to realize differences between himself and others. At birth an individual is asocial; however, he possesses the potential to become a social creature. This transformation from a human organism to a human being is a result of social interaction, which begins at birth. The pattern of transformation is achieved through the socialization process. Lindesmith and Strauss suggest that "The child becomes socialized when he has acquired the ability to communicate with others and to influence and be influenced by them through use of speech."[5] As an individual's intellectual and emotional awareness is expanded, his social world is likewise enlarged.

Frederick Elkin defines socialization as "The process by which someone learns the ways of a given society or social group so that he can function within it."[6] The socialization process may be considered a dynamic, continuous process that provides the individual with the knowledge to function in the social environment in which he exists. The impact of the socialization process is ongoing and ceases only in death.

---

[4] Fairchild, *op. cit.*, p. 269.
[5] Alfred R. Lindesmith and Anselm L. Strauss, *Social Psychology* (New York: Holt, Rinehart and Winston, Inc., 1968), p. 234.
[6] Frederick Elkin, *The Child and Society* (New York: Random House, 1960), p. 121.

5 □ ONE HUNDRED PER CENT AMERICAN

Ralph Linton

The following satirical essay was written to develop a very significant point: that the ignorance of the derivation of our culture is an important variable in understanding ethnocentrism. In a most humorous manner, Linton tells us that if we truly understood the sources of our culture we would probably be far less likely to see ourselves as superior to other peoples. The essay very poignantly reveals how the most basic culture traits and complexes of the "American Way of Life" are really not American at all, but rather have been diffused from various other cultures. Linton's article has become a classic description of the impact of diffusion on the development and change of cultures. □

THERE CAN BE NO QUESTION ABOUT THE AVERAGE AMERICAN'S AMERICANISM or his desire to preserve this precious heritage at all costs. Nevertheless, some insidious foreign ideas have already wormed their way into his civilization without his realizing what was going on. Thus dawn finds the unsuspecting patriot garbed in pajamas, a garment of East Indian origin; and lying in a bed built on a pattern which originated in either Persia or Asia Minor. He is muffled to the ears in un-American materials; cotton, first domesticated in India; linen, domesticated in the Near East; wool from an animal native to Asia Minor; or silk whose uses were first discovered by the Chinese. All these substances have been transformed into cloth by a method invented in Southwestern Asia. If the weather is cold enough he may even be sleeping under an eiderdown quilt invented in Scandinavia.

On awakening he glances at the clock, a medieval European invention, uses

From *The American Mercury*, 40 (April, 1937), pp. 427–429.

one potent Latin word in abbreviated form, rises in haste, and goes to the bathroom. Here, if he stops to think about it, he must feel himself in the presence of a great American institution; he will have heard stories of both the quality and frequency of foreign plumbing and will know that in no other country does the average man perform his ablutions in the midst of such splendor. But the invidious foreign influence pursues him even here. Glass was invented by the ancient Egyptians, the use of glazed tiles for floors and walls in the Near East, porcelain in China, and the art of enameling on metal by Mediterranean artisans of the Bronze Age. Even his bathtub and toilet are but slightly modified copies of Roman originals. The only purely American contribution to the ensemble is the steam radiator.

In this bathroom the American washes with soap invented by the ancient Gauls. Next he cleans his teeth, a subversive European practice which did not invade America until the latter part of the eighteenth century. He then shaves, a masochistic rite first developed by the heathen priests of ancient Egypt and Sumer. The process is made less of a penance by the fact that his razor is of steel, an iron-carbon alloy discovered in either India or Turkestan. Lastly, he dries himself on a Turkish towel.

Returning to the bedroom, the unconscious victim of un-American practices removes his clothes from a chair, invented in the Near East, and proceeds to dress. He puts on close-fitting tailored garments whose form derives from the skin clothing of the ancient nomads of the Asiatic steppes and fastens them with buttons whose prototypes appeared in Europe at the close of the Stone Age. This costume is appropriate enough for outdoor exercise in a cold climate, but is quite unsuited to American summers, steam-heated houses, and Pullmans. Nevertheless, foreign ideas and habits hold the unfortunate man in thrall even when common sense tells him that the authentically American costume of gee string and moccasins would be far more comfortable. He puts on his feet stiff coverings made from hide prepared by a process invented in ancient Egypt and cut to a pattern which can be traced back to ancient Greece, and makes sure they are properly polished, also a Greek idea. Lastly, he ties about his neck a strip of bright-colored cloth which is a vestigial survival of the shoulder shawls worn by seventeenth-century Croats. He gives himself a final appraisal in the mirror, an old Mediterranean invention, and goes downstairs to breakfast.

Here a whole new series of foreign things confronts him. His food and drink are placed before him in pottery vessels, the popular name of which—china—is sufficient evidence of their origin. His fork is a medieval Italian invention and his spoon a copy of a Roman original. He will usually begin the meal with coffee, an Abyssinian plant first discovered by the Arabs. The American is quite likely to need it to dispel the morning-after effects of over-indulgence in fermented drinks, invented in the Near East; or distilled ones, invented by the alchemists of medieval Europe. Whereas the Arabs took their coffee straight, he will probably sweeten it with sugar, discovered in India; and dilute it with cream, both the domestication of cattle and the technique of milking having originated in Asia Minor.

If our patriot is old-fashioned enough to adhere to the so-called American breakfast, his coffee will be accompanied by an orange, domesticated in the Mediterranean region, a cantaloupe domesticated in Persia, or grapes, domesticated in Asia Minor. He will follow this with a bowl of cereal made from grain domesticated in the Near East and prepared by methods also invented there. From this he will go on to waffles, a Scandinavian invention, with plenty of butter, originally a Near-Eastern cosmetic. As a side dish he may have the egg of a bird domesticated in Southeastern Asia or strips of the flesh of an animal domesticated in the same region, which have been salted and smoked by a process invented in Northern Europe.

Breakfast over, he places upon his head a molded piece of felt, invented by the nomads of Eastern Asia, and, if it looks like rain, puts on outer shoes of rubber, discovered by the ancient Mexicans, and takes an umbrella, invented in India. He then sprints for his train—the train, not the sprinting, being an English invention. At the station he pauses for a moment to buy a newspaper, paying for it with coins invented in ancient Lydia. Once on board he settles back to inhale the fumes of a cigarette invented in Mexico, or a cigar invented in Brazil. Meanwhile, he reads the news of the day, imprinted in characters invented by the ancient Semites by a process invented in Germany upon a material invented in China. As he scans the latest editorial pointing out the dire results to our institutions of accepting foreign ideas, he will not fail to thank a Hebrew God in an Indo-European language that he is a one hundred per cent (decimal system invented by the Greeks) American (from Americus Vespucci, Italian geographer).

Reflective Questions

1. Why might a person with a limited knowledge of the sources of his culture be more likely to exhibit an ethnocentric attitude than one who understands his culture's debts?

2. Is ethnocentrism ever purposefully taught? Give examples.

3. Is ethnocentrism necessarily undesirable or can it serve positive functions?

4. How might you respond to an individual who claimed to be "one hundred per cent American"?

5. Can you think of any cultural traits or complexes other than those discussed by Linton that have been diffused into the American culture?

6. Are there any culture traits or complexes that are truly American contributions to our culture?

6 □ PSYCHOSEXUAL DEVELOPMENT

William Simon □ John Gagnon

The main impact of this article is the rejection of the Freudian view that sexual development is a continuous contest between biological drives and cultural restraint. As an alternative to this widely held view, Simon and Gagnon state that in the sexual realm, sociocultural factors dominate biological influences in human life. The authors reject the views that impute sexual significance to some childhood behavior—that hold that psychosexual drives are fixed biological attributes—and posit the notions that sexual behaviors often express and serve nonsexual purposes and that sexual behavior is *scripted* behavior. Sexual behavior, therefore, is not a mechanistic expression of a primordial drive. There is no play without a *script*, the authors contend. Nothing sexual occurs unless actors organize elements into an appropriate script. Foreplay suggests this, according to Simon and Gagnon. Although there are some biological differences due to hormonal functions, the impact of this article is that social scripts predominate. Cross-cultural information, social differences within each sex, and differences among social and economic groups are cited to lend credence to social cultural primacy in sexual development.

The remainder of the essay is devoted to an elaboration of variations in sexual development by social scripts—for instance, infantile and early childhood, adolescence, male-female, and adult sexual activity—concluding by affirming the view that sexual development can be best viewed as a variable social invention. □

ERIK ERIKSON HAS OBSERVED THAT, PRIOR TO SIGMUND FREUD, "SEXOLOGISTS" tended to believe that sexual capacities appeared suddenly with the onset of adolescence. Sexuality followed those external evidences of physiological change

Copyright © March 1969, by TRANS-action, Inc., New Brunswick, New Jersey.

53

that occurred concurrent with or just after puberty. Psychoanalysis changed all that. In Freud's view, libido—the generation of psychosexual energies—should be viewed as a fundamental element of human experience at least beginning with birth, and possibly before that. Libido, therefore, is essential, a biological constant to be coped with at all levels of individual, social, and cultural development. The truth of this received wisdom, that is, that sexual development is a continuous contest between biological drive and cultural restraint should be seriously questioned. Obviously sexuality has roots in biological processes, but so do many other capacities including many that involve physical and mental competence and vigor. There is, however, abundant evidence that the final states which these capacities attain escape the rigid impress of biology. This independence of biological constraint is rarely claimed for the area of sexuality, but we would like to argue that the sexual is precisely that realm where the sociocultural forms most completely dominate biological influences.

It is difficult to get data that might shed much light on the earliest aspects of these questions: Adults are hardly equipped with total recall and the pre-verbal or primitively verbal child does not have ability to report accurately on his own internal state. But it seems obvious—and it is a basic assumption of this paper—that with the beginnings of adolescence many new factors come into play, and to emphasize a straight-line developmental continuity with infant and childhood experiences may be seriously misleading. In particular, it is dangerous to assume that because some childhood behavior appears sexual to adults, it must be sexual. An infant or a child engaged in genital play (even if orgasm is observed) can in no sense be seen as experiencing the complex set of feelings that accompanies adult or even adolescent masturbation.

Therefore, the authors reject the unproven assumption that "powerful" psychosexual drives are fixed biological attributes. More importantly, we reject the even more dubious assumption that sexual capacities or experiences tend to translate immediately into a kind of universal "knowing" or innate wisdom—that sexuality has a magical ability, possessed by no other capacity, that allows biological drives to be expressed directly in psychosocial and social behaviors.

The prevailing image of sexuality—particularly that of the Freudian tradition—is that of an intense, high-pressure drive that forces a person to seek physical sexual gratification, a drive that expresses itself indirectly if it cannot be expressed directly. The available data suggest to us a different picture—one that shows either lower levels of intensity, or, at least, greater variability. We find that there are many social situations or life-roles in which reduced sex activity or even deliberate celibacy is undertaken with little evidence that the libido has shifted in compensation to some other sphere.

A part of the legacy of Freud is that we have all become remarkably adept at discovering "sexual" elements in nonsexual behavior and symbolism. What we suggest instead (following Kenneth Burke's three-decade-old insight) is the reverse—that sexual behavior can often express and serve nonsexual motives.

No Play Without A Script

We see sexual behavior therefore as *scripted* behavior, not the masked expression of a primordial drive. The individual can learn sexual behavior as he or she learns other behavior—through scripts that in this case give the self, other persons, and situations erotic abilities or content. Desire, privacy, opportunity, and propinquity with an attractive member of the opposite sex are not, in themselves, enough; in ordinary circumstances, nothing sexual will occur unless one or both actors organize these elements into an appropriate script. The very concern with foreplay in sex suggests this. From one point of view, foreplay may be defined as merely progressive physical excitement generated by touching naturally erogenous zones. The authors have referred to this conception elsewhere as the "rubbing of two sticks together to make a fire" model. It would seem to be more valuable to see this activity as symbolically invested behavior through which the body is eroticized and through which mute, inarticulate motions and gestures are translated into a sociosexual drama.

A belief in the sociocultural dominance of sexual behavior finds support in cross-cultural research as well as in data restricted to the United States. Psychosexual development is universal—but it takes many forms and tempos. People in different cultures construct their scripts differently; and in our own society, different segments of the population act out different psychosexual dramas—something much less likely to occur if they were all reacting more or less blindly to the same superordinate urge. The most marked differences occur, of course, between male and female patterns of sexual behavior. Obviously, some of this is due to biological differences, including differences in hormonal functions at different ages. But the significance of social scripts predominate; the recent work of Masters and Johnson, for example, clearly points to far greater orgasmic capacities on the part of females than our culture would lead us to suspect. And within each sex—especially among men—different social and economic groups have different patterns.

Let us examine some of these variations, and see if we can decipher the scripts.

Childhood

Whether one agrees with Freud or not, it is obvious that we do not become sexual all at once. There is continuity with the past. Even infant experiences can strongly influence later sexual development.

But continuity is not causality. Childhood experiences (even those that appear sexual) will in all likelihood be influential not because they are intrinsically sexual, but because they can affect a number of developmental trends, *including* the sexual. What situations in infancy—or even early childhood—can be called psychosexual in any sense other than that of creating potentials?

The key term, therefore, must remain potentiation. In infancy, we can locate some of the experiences (or sensations) that will bring about a sense of the body and its capacities for pleasure and discomfort and those that will influence the child's ability to relate to others. It is possible, of course, that through these primitive experiences, ranges are being established—but they are very broad and overlapping. Moreover, if these are profound experiences to the child—and they may well be that—they are not expressions of biological necessity, but of the earliest forms of social learning.

In childhood, after infancy there is what appears to be some real sex play. About half of all adults report that they did engage in some form of sex play as children; and the total who actually did may be half again as many. But, however the adult interprets it later, what did it mean to the child at the time? One suspects that, as in much of childhood role-playing, their sense of the adult meanings attributed to the behavior is fragmentary and ill-formed. Many of the adults recall that, at the time, they were concerned with being found out. But here, too, were they concerned because of the real content of sex play, or because of the mystery and the lure of the forbidden that so often enchant the child? The child may be assimilating outside information about sex for which, at the time, he has no real internal correlate or understanding.

A small number of persons do have sociosexual activity during preadolescence—most of it initiated by adults. But for the majority of these, little apparently follows from it. Without appropriate sexual scripts, the experience remains unassimilated—at least in adult terms. For some, it is clear, a severe reaction may follow from falling "victim" to the sexuality of an adult—but, again, does this reaction come from the sexual act itself or from the social response, the strong reactions of others? (There is some evidence that early sexual activity of this sort is associated with deviant adjustments in later life. But this, too, may not be the result of sexual experiences in themselves so much as the consequence of having fallen out of the social main stream and, therefore, of running greater risks of isolation and alienation.)

In short, relatively few become truly active sexually before adolescence. And when they do (for girls more often than boys), it is seldom immediately related to sexual feelings or gratifications but is a use of sex for nonsexual goals and purposes. The "seductive" Lolita is rare; but she is significant: She illustrates a more general pattern of psychosexual development—a commitment to the social relationships linked to sex before one can really grasp the social meaning of the physical relationships.

Of great importance are the values (or feelings, or images) that children pick up as being related to sex. Although we talk a lot about sexuality, as though trying to exorcise the demon of shame, learning about sex in our society is in large part learning about guilt; and learning how to manage sexuality commonly involves learning how to manage guilt. An important source of guilt in children comes from the imputation to them by adults of sexual appetites or abilities that they may not have, but that they learn, however imperfectly, to pretend they have. The gestural concomitants of sexual modesty are learned early. For instance, when do girls learn to sit or pick up objects with their knees together? When do they learn that the bust must be covered? However, since this behavior is learned unlinked to later adult sexual performances, what children must make of all this is very mysterious.

The learning of sex roles, or sex identities, involves many things that are remote from actual sexual experience, or that become involved with sexuality only after puberty. Masculinity or femininity, their meaning and postures, are rehearsed before adolescence in many nonsexual ways.

A number of scholars have pointed, for instance, to the importance of aggressive, deference, dependency, and dominance behavior in childhood. Jerome Kagan and Howard Moss have found that aggressive behavior in males and dependency in females are relatively stable aspects of development. But what is social role, and what is biology? They found that when aggressive behavior occurred among girls, it tended to appear most often among those from well-educated families that were more tolerant of deviation. Curiously, they also reported that "it was impossible to predict the character of adult sexuality in women from their preadolescent and early adolescent behavior," and that "erotic activity is more anxiety-arousing for females than for males," because "the traditional ego ideal for women dictates inhibition of sexual impulses."

The belief in the importance of early sex-role learning for boys can be viewed in two ways. First, it may directly indicate an early sexual capacity in male children. Or, second, early masculine identification may merely be an appropriate framework within which the sexual impulse (salient with puberty) and the socially available sexual scripts (or accepted patterns of sexual behavior) can most conveniently find expression. Our bias, of course, is toward the second.

But, as Kagan and Moss also noted, the sex role learned by the child does not reliably predict how he will act sexually as an adult. This finding also can be interpreted in the same two alternative ways. Where sexuality is viewed as a biological constant which struggles to express itself, the female sex role learning can be interpreted as the successful repression of sexual impulses. The other interpretation suggests that the difference lies not in learning how to handle a pre-existent sexuality, but in learning how to *be* sexual. Differences between men and women, therefore, will have consequences both for *what* is done sexually, as well as *when*.

Once again, we prefer the latter interpretation, and some recent work that we have done with lesbians supports it. We observed that many of the major elements of their sex lives—the start of actual genital sexual behavior, the onset and frequency of masturbation, the time of entry in sociosexual patterns, the number of partners, and the reports of feelings of sexual deprivation—were for these homosexual women almost identical with those of ordinary women. Since sexuality would seem to be more important for lesbians—after all, they sacrifice much in order to follow their own sexual pathways—this is surprising. We concluded that the primary factor was something both categories of women share—the sex-role learning that occurs before sexuality itself becomes significant.

Social class also appears significant, more for boys than girls. Sex-role learning may vary by class; lower-class boys are supposed to be more aggressive and put much greater emphasis on early heterosexuality. The middle and upper classes tend to tolerate more deviance from traditional attitudes regarding appropriate male sex-role performances.

Given all these circumstances, it seems rather naive to think of sexuality as a constant pressure, with a peculiar necessity all its own. For us, the crucial period of childhood has significance not because of sexual occurrences, but because of nonsexual developments that will provide the names and judgments for later encounters with sexuality.

Adolescence

The actual beginnings and endings of adolescence are vague. Generally, the beginning marks the first time society, as such, acknowledges that the individual has sexual capacity. Training in the postures and rhetoric of the sexual experience is now accelerated. Most important, the adolescent begins to regard those about him (particularly his peers, but also adults) as sexual actors and finds confirmation from others for this view.

For some, as noted, adolescent sexual experience begins before they are considered adolescents. Kinsey reports that a tenth of his female sample and a fifth of his male sample had experienced orgasm through masturbation by age 12. But still, for the vast majority, despite some casual play and exploration that post-Freudians might view as masked sexuality, sexual experience begins with adolescence. Even those who have had prior experience find that it acquires new meanings with adolescence. They now relate such meanings to both larger spheres of social life and greater senses of self. For example, it is not uncommon during the transition between childhood and adolescence for boys and, more rarely, girls to report arousal and orgasm while doing things not manifestly sexual—climbing trees, sliding down bannisters, or other activities that involve genital contact—without defining them as sexual. Often they do not even take it seriously enough to try to explore or repeat what was, in all likelihood, a pleasurable experience.

Adolescent sexual development, therefore, really represents the beginning of adult sexuality. It marks a definite break with what went on before. Not only will future experiences occur in new and more complex contexts, but they will be conceived of as explicitly sexual and thereby begin to complicate social relationships. The need to manage sexuality will rise not only from physical needs and desires, but also from the new implications of personal relationships. Playing, or associating, with members of the opposite sex now acquires different meanings.

At adolescence, changes in the developments of boys and girls diverge and must be considered separately. The one thing both share at this point is a reinforcement of their new status by a dramatic biological event—for girls, menstruation, and for boys, the discovery of the ability to ejaculate. But here they part. For boys, the beginning of a commitment to sexuality is primarily genital; within two years of puberty all but a relatively few have had the experience of orgasm, almost universally brought about by masturbation. The corresponding organizing event for girls is not genitally sexual but social: they have arrived at an age where they will learn role performances linked with proximity to marriage. In contrast to boys, only two-thirds of girls will report ever having masturbated (and, characteristically, the frequency is much less). For women, it is not until the late twenties that the incidence of orgasm from any source reaches that of boys at age 16. In fact, significantly, about half of the females who masturbate do so only after having experienced orgasm in some situation involving others. This contrast points to a basic distinction between the developmental processes for males and females: males move from privatized personal sexuality to sociosexuality; females do the reverse and at a later stage in the life cycle.

The Turned-On Boys

We have worked hard to demonstrate the dominance of social, psychological, and cultural influences over the biological; now, dealing with adolescent boys, we must briefly reverse course. There is much evidence that the early male sexual impulses—again, initially through masturbation—are linked to physiological changes, to high hormonal inputs during puberty. This produces an organism that, to put it simply, is more easily turned on. Male adolescents report frequent erections, often without apparent stimulation of any kind. Even so, though there is greater biological sensitization and hence masturbation is more likely, the meaning, organization, and continuance of this activity still tends to be subordinate to social and psychological factors.

Masturbation provokes guilt and anxiety among most adolescent boys. This is not likely to change in spite of more "enlightened" rhetoric and discourse on the subject (generally, we have shifted from stark warnings of mental, moral, and physical damage to vague counsels against nonsocial or "inappropriate" behavior). However, it may be that this very guilt and anxiety gives the sexual experience an intensity of feeling that is often attributed to sex itself.

Such guilt and anxiety do not follow simply from social disapproval. Rather, they seem to come from several sources, including the difficulty the boy has in presenting himself as a sexual being to his immediate family, particularly his parents. Another source is the fantasies or plans associated with masturbation —fantasies about doing sexual "things" to others or having others do sexual "things" to oneself; or having to learn and rehearse available but proscribed sexual scripts or patterns of behavior. And, of course, some guilt and anxiety center around the general disapproval of masturbation. After the early period of adolescence, in fact, most youths will not admit to their peers that they did or do it.

Nevertheless, masturbation is for most adolescent boys the major sexual activity, and they engage in it fairly frequently. It is an extremely positive and gratifying experience to them. Such an introduction to sexuality can lead to a capacity for detached sex activity—activity whose only sustaining motive is sexual. This may be the hallmark of male sexuality in our society.

Of the three sources of guilt and anxiety mentioned, the first—how to manage both sexuality and an attachment to family members—probably cuts across class lines. But the others should show remarkable class differences. The second one, how to manage a fairly elaborate and exotic fantasy life during masturbation, should be confined most typically to the higher classes, who are more experienced and adept at dealing with symbols. (It is possible, in fact, that this behavior, which girls rarely engage in, plays a role in the processes by which middle-class boys catch up with girls in measures of achievement and creativity and, by the end of adolescence, move out in front. However, this is only a hypothesis.)

The ability to fantasize during masturbation implies certain broad consequences. One is a tendency to see large parts of the environment in an erotic light, as well as the ability to respond, sexually and perhaps poetically, to many visual and auditory stimuli. We might also expect both a capacity and need for fairly elaborate forms of sexual activity. Further, since masturbatory fantasies generally deal with relationships and acts leading to coitus, they should also reinforce a developing capacity for heterosociality.

The third source of guilt and anxiety—the alleged "unmanliness" of masturbation—should more directly concern the lower-class male adolescent. ("Manliness" has always been an important value for lower-class males.) In these groups, social life is more often segregated by sex, and there are, generally, fewer rewarding social experiences from other sources. The adolescent therefore moves into heterosexual—if not heterosocial—relationships sooner than his middle-class counterparts. Sexual segregation makes it easier for him than for the middle-class boy to learn that he does not have to love everything he desires, and therefore to come more naturally to casual, if not exploitative, relationships. The second condition—fewer social rewards that his fellows would respect—should lead to an exaggerated concern for proving masculinity by direct displays of physical prowess, aggression, and visible sexual success. And these three, of course, may be mutually reinforcing.

In a sense, the lower-class male is the first to reach "sexual maturity" as defined by the Freudians. That is, he is generally the first to become aggressively heterosexual and exclusively genital. This characteristic, in fact, is a distinguishing difference between lower-class males and those above them socially.

But one consequence is that although their sex lives are almost exclusively heterosexual, they remain homosocial. They have intercourse with females, but the standards and the audience they refer to are those of their male fellows. Middle-class boys shift predominantly to coitus at a significantly later time. They, too, need and tend to have homosocial elements in their sexual lives. But their fantasies, their ability to symbolize, and their social training in a world in which distinctions between masculinity and femininity are less sharply drawn, allow them to withdraw more easily from an all-male world. This difference between social classes obviously has important consequences for stable adult relationships.

One thing common in male experience during adolescence is that while it provides much opportunity for sexual commitment, in one form or another, there is little training in how to handle emotional relations with girls. The imagery and rhetoric of romantic love is all around us; we are immersed in it. But whereas much is undoubtedly absorbed by the adolescent, he is not likely to tie it closely to his sexuality. In fact, such a connection might be inhibiting, as indicated by the survival of the "bad-girl-who-does" and "good-girl-who-doesn't" distinction. This is important to keep in mind as we turn to the female side of the story.

WITH THE GIRLS

In contrast to males, female sexual development during adolescence is so similar in all classes that it is easy to suspect that it is solely determined by biology. But, while girls do not have the same level of hormonal sensitization to sexuality at puberty as adolescent boys, there is little evidence of a biological or social inhibitor either. The "equipment" for sexual pleasure is clearly present by puberty, but tends not to be used by many females of any class. Masturbation rates are fairly low, and among those who do masturbate, fairly infrequent. Arousal from "sexual" materials or situations happens seldom, and exceedingly few girls report feeling sexually deprived during adolescence.

Basically, girls in our society are not encouraged to be sexual—and may be strongly discouraged from being so. Most of us accept the fact that while "bad boy" can mean many things, "bad girl" almost exclusively implies sexual delinquency. It is both difficult and dangerous for an adolescent girl to become too active sexually. As Joseph Rheingold puts it, where men need only fear sexual failure, women must fear both success and failure.

Does this long period of relative sexual inactivity among girls come from repression of an elemental drive, or merely from a failure to learn how to be sexual? The answers have important implications for their later sexual development. If it is repression, the path to a fuller sexuality must pass through processes of loss of inhibitions, during which the girl unlearns, in varying degrees, attitudes and values that block the expression of natural internal feelings. It also implies that the quest for ways to express directly sexual behavior and feelings that had been expressed nonsexually is secondary and of considerably less significance.

On the other hand, the "learning" answer suggests that women create or invent a capacity for sexual behavior, learning how and when to be aroused and how and when to respond. This approach implies greater flexibility; unlike the repression view, it makes sexuality both more and less than a basic force that may break loose at any time in strange or costly ways. The learning approach also lessens the power of sexuality altogether; all at once, particular kinds of sex activities need no longer be defined as either "healthy" or "sick." Lastly, subjectively, this approach appeals to the authors because it describes female sexuality in terms that seem less like a mere projection of male sexuality.

If sexual activity by adolescent girls assumes less specific forms than with boys, that does not mean that sexual learning and training do not occur. Curiously, though girls are, as a group, far less active sexually than boys, they receive far more training in self-consciously viewing themselves—and in viewing boys—as desirable mates. This is particularly true in recent years. Females begin early in adolescence to define attractiveness, at least partially, in sexual terms. We suspect that the use of sexual attractiveness for nonsexual purposes that marked our preadolescent "seductress" now begins to characterize many girls. Talcott Parsons' description of how the wife "uses" sex to bind the husband to the family, although harsh, may be quite accurate. More generally, in keeping with the childbearing and child-raising function of women, the development of a sexual role seems to involve a need to include in that role more than pleasure.

To round out the picture of the difference between the sexes, girls appear to be well-trained precisely in that area in which boys are poorly trained—that is, a belief in and a capacity for intense, emotionally-charged relationships and the language of romantic love. When girls during this period describe having been aroused sexually, they more often report it as a response to romantic, rather than erotic, words and actions.

In later adolescence, as dates, parties, and other sociosexual activities increase, boys—committed to sexuality and relatively untrained in the language and actions of romantic love—interact with girls, committed to romantic love and relatively untrained in sexuality. Dating and courtship may well be considered processes in which each sex trains the other in what each wants and expects. What data is available suggests that this exchange system does not always work very smoothly. Thus, ironically, it is not uncommon to find that the boy becomes emotionally involved with his partner and therefore lets up on trying to seduce her, at the same time that the girl comes to feel that the boy's affection is genuine and therefore that sexual intimacy is more permissible.

In our recent study of college students, we found that boys typically had intercourse with their first coital partners one to three times, while with girls it was ten or more. Clearly, for the majority of females first intercourse becomes possible only in stable relationships or in those with strong bonds.

"Woman, What Does She Want?"

The male experience does conform to the general Freudian expectation that there is a developmental movement from a predominantly genital sexual commitment to a loving relationship with another person. But this movement is, in effect, reversed for females, with love or affection often a necessary precondition for intercourse. No wonder, therefore, that Freud had great difficulty understanding female sexuality—recall the concluding line in his great essay on women: "Woman, what does she want?" This "error"—the assumption that female sexuality is similar to or a mirror image of that of the male—may come from the fact that so many of those who constructed the theory were men. With Freud, in addition, we must remember the very concept of sexuality essential to most of nineteenth century Europe—it was an elemental beast that had to be curbed.

It has been noted that there are very few class differences in sexuality among females, far fewer than among males. One difference, however, is very relevant to this discussion—the age of first intercourse. This varies inversely with social class—that is, the higher the class, the later the age of first intercourse—a relationship that is also true of first marriage. The correlation between these two ages suggest the necessary social and emotional linkage between courtship and the entrance into sexual activity on the part of women. A second difference, perhaps only indirectly related to social class, has to do with educational achievement: here, a sharp border line seems to separate from all other women those who have or have had graduate or professional work. If sexual success may be measured by the percentage of sex acts that culminate in orgasm, graduate and professional women are the most sexually successful women in the nation.

Why? One possible interpretation derives from the work of Abraham Maslow: Women who get so far in higher education are more likely to be more aggressive, perhaps to have strong needs to dominate; both these characteristics are associated with heightened sexuality. Another, more general interpretation would be that in a society in which girls are expected primarily to become wives and mothers, going on to graduate school represents a kind of deviancy—a failure of, or alienation from, normal female social adjustment. In effect, then, it would be this flawed socialization—not biology—that produced both commitment toward advanced training and toward heightened sexuality.

For both males and females, increasingly greater involvement in the social aspects of sexuality—"socializing" with the opposite sex—may be one factor that marks the end of adolescence. We know little about this transition, especially among noncollege boys and girls; but our present feeling is that sexuality plays an important role in it. First, sociosexuality is important in family formation and also in learning the roles and obligations involved in being an adult. Second, and more fundamental, late adolescence is when a youth is seeking, and experimenting toward finding, his identity—who and what he is and will be; and sociosexual activity is the one aspect of this exploration that we associate particularly with late adolescence.

Young people are particularly vulnerable at this time. This may be partly due to the fact that society has difficulty protecting the adolescent from the consequences of sexual behavior that it pretends he is not engaged in. But, more importantly, it may be because, at all ages, we all have great problems in discussing our sexual feelings and experiences in personal terms. These, in turn, make it extremely difficult to get support from others for an adolescent's experiments toward trying to invent his sexual self. We suspect that success or failure in the discovery or management of sexual identity may have consequences in personal development far beyond merely the sexual sphere—perhaps in confidence and feelings of self-worth, belonging, competence, guilt, force of personality, and so on.

Adulthood

In our society, all but a few ultimately marry. Handling sexual commitments inside marriage makes up the larger part of adult experience. Again, we have too little data for firm findings. The data we do have come largely from studies of broken and troubled marriages, and we do not know to what extent sexual problems in such marriages exceed those of intact marriages. It is possible that, because we have assumed that sex is important in most people's lives, we have exaggerated its importance in holding marriages together. Also, it is quite possible that, once people are married, sexuality declines relatively, becoming less important than other gratifications (such as domesticity or parenthood); or it may be that these other gratifications can minimize the effect of sexual dissatisfaction. Further, it may be possible that individuals learn to get sexual gratification, or an equivalent, from activities that are nonsexual, or only partially sexual.

The sexual desires and commitments of males are the main determinants of the rate of sexual activity in our society. Men are most interested in intercourse in the early years of marriage—woman's interest peaks much later; nonetheless, coital rates decline steadily throughout marriage. This decline derives from many things, only one of which is decline in biological capacity. With many men, it is more difficult to relate sexually to a wife who is pregnant or a mother. Lower-class adult men receive less support and plaudits from their male friends for married sexual performance than they did as single adolescents; and we might also add the lower-class disadvantage of less training in the use of auxiliary or symbolic sexually stimulating materials. For middle-class men, the decline is not as steep, owing perhaps to their greater ability to find stimulation from auxiliary sources, such as literature, movies, music, and romantic or erotic conversation. It should be further noted that for about 30 percent of college-educated men, masturbation continues regularly during marriage, even when the wife is available. An additional (if unknown) proportion do not physically masturbate, but derive additional excitement from the fantasies that accompany intercourse.

But even middle-class sexual activity declines more rapidly than bodily changes can account for. Perhaps the ways males learn to be sexual in our society make it very difficult to keep it up at a high level with the same woman for a long time. However, this may not be vital in maintaining the family, or even in the man's personal sense of well-being, because, as previously suggested, sexual dissatisfaction may become less important as other satisfactions increase. Therefore, it need seldom result in crisis.

About half of all married men and a quarter of all married women will have intercourse outside of marriage at one time or another. For women, infidelity seems to have been on the increase since the turn of the century—at the same time that their rates of orgasm have been increasing. It is possible that the very nature of female sexuality is changing. Work being done now may give us new light on this. For men, there are strong social-class differences—the lower class accounts for most extramarital activity, especially during the early years of marriage. We have observed that it is difficult for a lower-class man to acquire the appreciation of his fellows for married intercourse; extramarital sex, of course, is another matter.

In general, we feel that far from sexual needs affecting other adult concerns, the reverse may be true: adult sexual activity may become that aspect of a person's life most often used to act out other needs. There are some data that suggest this. Men who have trouble handling authority relationships at work more often have dreams about homosexuality; some others, under heavy stress on the job, have been shown to have more frequent episodic homosexual experiences. Such phenomena as the rise of sadomasochistic practices and experiments in group sex may also be tied to nonsexual tensions, the use of sex for nonsexual purposes.

It is only fairly recently in the history of man that he has been able to begin to understand that his own time and place do not embody some eternal principle or necessity, but are only dots on a continuum. It is difficult for many to believe that man can change, and is changing, in important ways. This conservative view is evident even in contemporary behavioral science; and a conception of man as having relatively constant sexual needs has become part of it. In an ever-changing world, it is perhaps comforting to think that man's sexuality does not change very much, and therefore is relatively easily explained. We cannot accept this. Instead, we have attempted to offer a description of sexual development as a variable social invention—an invention that in itself explains little, and requires much continuing explanation.

Reflective Questions

1. Do you feel that too much sexual significance is imputed to the play activities of children in American culture?

2. What effect will the women's liberation movement have on the social definitions of male and female sex roles in America?

3. What are some of the nonsexual motives or social purposes served and expressed by sexual behavior?

4. What differences and similarities exist between the sexual development of humans and other animals? What effects do the differences have on the emergence of human society?

7 □ THE FUND OF SOCIABILITY

Robert S. Weiss

Social relationships, whether viewed from sociological or psychological frames of reference, are important to all of us. Robert Weiss offers some answers to the following two questions: Why do people require relationships with one another? What needs are being expressed? Two approaches are commonly taken in coming to grips with these types of questions. One comes from sociology, and sees relationships as important; they are ways by which society organizes the thinking and behavior of its members. The other comes from psychology, and rests on the theory that individuals have needs satisfied through relationships, with serious consequences if the needs are not fulfilled through appropriate relationships.

Weiss studies parents without partners as well as a limited number of married couples. After finding that relationships of parents without partners did not appreciably alter the course of loneliness and that intact married couples needed other relationships than those provided by marriage, the author establishes five "functional" categories of *relationships:* (1) intimacy—effective emotional integration; (2) social integration—sharing or striving for similar objectives; (3) opportunity for nurturant behavior—responsibility for the well-being of a child; (4) reassurance of worth—attesting to one's competence in some role; and (5) assistance—making available a resource or guidance. Within limits, Weiss believes, "we cannot limit our relations with others without incurring a serious loss." □

WHY DO PEOPLE REQUIRE RELATIONSHIPS WITH ONE ANOTHER? WHAT NEEDS are being expressed? We recognize constantly, sometimes with surprise, how important relationships are to us. Newly divorced individuals are distressed by

© Copyright July/August, 1969, by TRANS-action, Inc., New Brunswick, New Jersey. Reprinted by permission of TRANS-Action and the author.

loneliness, even as they congratulate themselves on having ended a conflict-laden marriage. Individuals who work alone, such as writers, complain of isolation, even as they prize their autonomy. Travelers on shipboard, separated from their network of friends, may find themselves greeting with enthusiasm an acquaintance from their home town who, in other circumstances, they might have barely acknowledged. In all these ways social needs express themselves. What can be their nature?

In trying to find answers to this question, people have generally taken two lines of argument. One, associated with some schools of sociology, has been to assert that relationships which are close, so close they may be called primary, provide the individual with his understandings of reality, his moral values, his goals, even his sense of self. Relationships are important because through them the society organizes the individual's thinking and acting. Essentially, the society teaches its members what they want.

The second view, associated more with psychology than with sociology, has been that people have a number of needs or requirements which only relationships can satisfy, and that without appropriate relationships the individual will suffer. These needs are intrinsic to the individual, and are not formed by the society in which he lives. They may include needs for recognition, for affection, for power, for prestige, for belonging, and many more.

How can we move from these fairly general theoretical positions to a testable formulation of why people require relationships? Perhaps the simplest hypothesis we can phrase, one which would seem to be an implication of the first view but not of the second, is that of the "fund of sociability." According to this idea individuals require a certain amount of interaction with others, which they may find in various ways. They may with equal satisfaction have a few intense relationships or have a large number of relationships of lesser intensity. They would experience stress only if the total amount of relating to others was too little or too great.

The "fund of sociability" idea seemed to us to be a useful starting point in our effort to learn more regarding the assumptions, content, and functions of social ties. The research strategy that seemed to us a promising way to test this hypothesis was to seek out a group of individuals, all of whom had lost an important relationship but who also had the opportunity for unlimited sociability. It might then be seen whether increased sociability in some way compensated for the loss of the relationship.

For about a year, a colleague and I attended meetings of the Boston chapter of Parents Without Partners, a national organization of people who have children but who are living alone because of separation, divorce, or the death of their spouse. By listening to discussions of their past and current problems, and also from interviews with a good many members and former members, we hoped to be able to specify the nature of the losses sustained by these men and women with the end of their marriages, and the way in which membership in Parents Without Partners was useful to them.

We found that most members had joined simply because they were lonely, although there may well have been other reasons, including concern for their children or the desire to help others. The loneliness resulted directly from the absence of the marital relationship, rather than from such secondary factors as change in social role.

According to the "fund of sociability" hypothesis, we should expect to find members reporting that they had been lonely and restless after the dissolution of the marriage, but that interaction with others in Parents Without Partners had made up some part of that loss. We found, however, that although Parents Without Partners offered its members help with a host of difficulties, the sociability of belonging did not particularly diminish the sense of loneliness. Dating helped a good deal, but friendship did not. Although many members, particularly among the women, specifically mentioned friendship as the main contribution they received from Parents Without Partners, and these friendships sometimes became very close and very important to the participants, they did not compensate for the loss of the marriage. Friends and activities (discussion groups were perhaps the best) made the loneliness easier to manage, but they did not end it or even appreciably diminish it. One woman said, "Sometimes I have the girls over, and we talk about how hard it is. Misery loves company, you know."

Simple Sociability Not Satisfactory

Clearly the social needs satisfied in marriage, and, apparently, in dating, were not satisfied by simple sociability, no matter how much of it there was. But this raised the question of whether friendship was simply inadequate to supply the kind of interaction required, or whether friendship supplied something quite different, something that might not be found in marriage.

It seemed to us that friendship did offer something distinct from what marriage provides. But how to test this? We needed to find people who were married, but without friends. If friendships met social needs distinct from those met by marriage, then people without friends should be in distress, even though married. However, if friendship provided only a kind of time-filling sociability, then married people without friends should get along almost as well as married people with friends.

We began with a pilot study of six couples who had moved to the Boston suburbs from at least two states away. Our respondents were all middle-class and they had moved to Boston because of the husband's job.

Soon after the move, all but two of the wives were seriously unhappy; they were feeling a sense of social isolation similar in intensity (albeit shorter in duration) to the sense of emotional isolation that seemed to follow the dissolution of a marriage in others. The problem appeared to be that the housebound wife had no one with whom she could share the concerns of her daily life. Husbands could not really discuss with interest the dilemmas of child care nor the burdens of housework, and though they sometimes tried, they simply could not function properly as a friend. They might even compound the difficulty by saying they couldn't understand what was happening to their wives, and sometimes be downright unsympathetic because of what they felt were their own more serious problems of proving themselves on the new job. They were not troubled by the lack of people with whom they could share common interests, because at work they found men to talk to about the things that concerned them; the job, politics, sports, the local driving patterns, and the like. Two of the men with whom we worked listed for us the people they talked with during the day, and the number was impressive.

Meanwhile, the newcomer wives were likely to become painfully bored. In the absence of anyone with whom they could share their interests, they found housework and child care increasingly unrewarding. One wife who had been socially active and had considered herself reasonably happy in her former home began to drink heavily. Another wanted her husband to give up the promotion that had brought him to the Boston area, and to return to her parents' home town.

Of the two wives who did not seem to suffer from newcomer blues, the first was a woman who had no children and who immediately solved the problem of social isolation by going to work. The other was married to a man who in a previous move had bought a house in an old and settled neighborhood where friendships were well-established. To escape social isolation, she began taking night-school classes, and as her husband said when he talked with us, he hardly saw her except when they passed each other in the driveway. This time the husband moved into a new development where other homes were also owned by newcomers to the region, and spent his first weekend making friends with the new neighbors.

It now appeared clear to us that just as friendships do not provide the functions ordinarily provided by marriage, neither does marriage provide the functions ordinarily provided by friendship. Our current work on the nature of marriage suggests that marriages may vary in this, but nevertheless we believe that even in the most companionate of marriages, some important interests will not be shared within the marriage, and for women in the social group of the newcomer sample and even to a greater degree among poorer women the concerns of managing a family are not shared with the husband.

At this point, the hypothesis of a "fund of sociability" could be confidently rejected. It was clear that there were different kinds of relationships, providing different functions. The question then arose, how many relationships seemed to be necessary, and what functions did they seem to provide?

On the basis of further work with Parents Without Partners, we have been led to develop a theory that might be characterized as "the functional specificity of relationships." We believe that individuals have needs which can only be met within relationships, that relationships tend to become relatively specialized in the needs for which they provide, and as a result individuals require a number of different relationships for well-being.

Although there are many variations in the way people organize their lives, one can in general say that relations with kin seem to be reliable as sources of help, but not as sources of companionship; friends offer companionship, but not intimacy; and marriage or a near-marital relationship offers intimacy, but rarely friendship. We are not sure why this specialization develops. Undoubtedly, much has to do with underlying cultural definitions of the relationship. If wholehearted commitment between friends is difficult—and this seems the case in adult American life—then it will be possible for friends to share interests, but extremely difficult for them to develop the level of trust which would permit emotional intimacy.

The marriage relationship may be an exception to the generalization that relationships are specialized in function. In marriage each spouse provides for the other a degree of emotional integration, and also provides collaboration in managing the mechanics of life. But even here there may be conflicts between the way of relating to one another that is associated with the one function, and that associated with the other. In terms of the collaborative relationship, for example, it may be reasonable for a wife to criticize her husband's capacity to earn, but since she is also a source of emotional integration, her criticism can be devastating.

The specialization of relationship is probably always incomplete. Undoubtedly every friendship involves some emotional exchange and has the potential for more. Yet going beyond the understood assumptions of the relationship can endanger it. When it happens, for example, that one partner in a friendship seeks to move the relationship to one in which there is an assumption of unbounded trust, the more usual assumptions of the friendship may be temporarily flooded out. The consequence is likely to be uneasiness when the friends later find it necessary to return to the old basis. Generally there is so much resistance to changes of definition of a relationship that if a person loses the relationship that provided a particular function—as through the death of a spouse—he will be able only temporarily to alter his remaining relationships to fill the gap. Among members of Parents Without Partners, for example, we found a good deal of bitterness that stemmed from the failure of their friends to respond to their new relational needs.

Five Categories of Relationships

On the basis of our material we believe we can identify five categories of relational functions, each for the most part provided by a different relationship. All these functions seem to us to be necessary for well-being.

1. *Intimacy,* for want of a better term, is used to characterize the provision of an effective emotional integration in which individuals can express their feelings freely and without self-consciousness. It seems to us that this function of relationships prevents the individual from experiencing the sense of emotional isolation that is expressed in the term "loneliness." For a relationship to provide intimacy, there must be trust, effective understanding, and ready access. Marriage provides such a relationship and so, often, does dating, at least for a time. Occasionally a woman may establish a relationship of this kind with a close friend, her mother, or a sister. And under some circumstances a man may establish a relationship of this sort with a friend.

It may be noted, parenthetically, that the relationship between sexual involvement and emotional intimacy, when the individuals concerned are potentially appropriate sexual partners, is quite complex and may well vary by social group and by circumstance. Certainly sex and intimacy are not necessarily associated. Still, rather fragmentary evidence suggests that in the groups we have worked with, individuals who are potentially appropriate partners may find it difficult to maintain a non-sexual emotionally intimate relationship. Where individuals are not appropriate sexual partners there is no apparent difficulty in maintaining such a relationship.

2. *Social integration* is provided by relationships in which participants share concerns, either because of similar situations ("we are in the same boat") or because they are striving for similar objectives (as in relationships among colleagues). Such relationships allow a good deal of sharing of experience, information, and ideas. They provide the basis for exchange of favors, and sometimes for more substantial help (though not for help continued over time). Among women this function is usually provided by friendships; among men, by relations with colleagues, as well as by friendships. The absence of this relationship may be experienced as a sense of social isolation and will, we suspect, be accompanied by feelings of boredom.

3. *Opportunity for nurturant behavior* is provided by relationships in which the adult takes responsibility for the well-being of a child. Our impression, based on experience with Parents Without Partners, is that men seem able to act as foster fathers to children not their own, but that it is much more difficult for women to act as foster mothers. The conditions for the expression of nurturance—and the nature of nurturance—may be different in men and

women. We suspect that absence of this function may be signaled by a sense that one's life is unfulfilled, meaningless, and empty of purpose.

4. *Reassurance of worth* is provided by relationships that attest to an individual's competence in some role. Colleague relationships, and the social support and mutual respect they imply, can do this for some men, particularly those whose work is difficult or highly valued. Successful family life may function in this way for other men, competence or worth here depending not on particular skills, but on the ability to support and defend a family. Women who work may also find their employment a source of reassurance of worth. Women who do not work must look to relationships with husbands, children, and acquaintances for recognition of their competence in making and managing a home. The loss of any system from which recognition of work, value, or competence may be gained will, we believe, result in decreased self-esteem.

5. *Assistance* through the provision of services or the making available of resources, although a primary theme in kin relationships, may be provided by a number of other relationships as well, including friendships and relationships with neighbors. However it seems to be only among close kin that one may expect assistance that is not limited in time and extent. It is the importance of this function for the poor that leads to the development of relational patterns in which kin ties are of primary importance. We suspect that the absence of any relationship providing the assurance of assistance if needed would be reflected in a sense of anxiety and vulnerability.

In addition, there seems to be a sixth function which can be provided by relationships that some people find important. This function might be characterized as *guidance,* and may be provided by mental-health professionals such as social workers or psychiatrists, or by ministers and priests, among others.

Undoubtedly there are individual differences in capacity to withstand the absence of one or another of the functions without giving way to restlessness and to the development of such symptoms as loneliness and boredom. On the basis of accounts of individuals who have successfully weathered long periods of isolation, one might suspect that individuals who have more rigid character structures might be better able to forego the absence of some relational functions. One device that seems to have helped these men and women was to establish a detailed daily routine from which they did not deviate.

It is difficult at this point to say that any one of the relational functions is more important than another. The absence of intimacy can clearly be disorganizing for many individuals, and for most it would be accompanied by painful loneliness, but we are not able at this time to say that it is a more serious deficit than the absence of opportunity for nurturance. I have known childless couples to be as downcast by difficulties in adopting a baby as a lonely person might be by difficulties in finding love. It seems as though the absence of any relational function will create some form of dissatisfaction, accompanied by restlessness and occasional spells of acute distress.

This theory, like any theory of human nature, has implications for the way in which we might deal with individuals in difficult situations. We might consider two possible areas of application of these ideas: to the problem of relational loss, and to the problem of aging.

There are many forms of relational loss. There is the loss of friends that comes with moving from one area to another, the loss of colleagues that accompanies retirement, the loss of newly adult children from home, the loss of a spouse through death or divorce. Each of these losses would seem to have two aspects: first, the trauma that accompanies the damage to the individual's life organization; and, second, the deficit in the individual's life that is a result of the continuing absence of the functions once provided by the now-lost relationship. When individuals move from one area to another, the trauma aspect may be nothing more than sadness at leaving old friends and old associations, and not especially serious. The primary problem of relocation is that of deficit in the wife's relationships, the absence of new friends in the new situation. In conjugal bereavement, the loss by death of a spouse, the pain of loss is ordinarily very great and, for a good while, the trauma of the loss will be the primary source of distress. Yet even when this has been resolved, the life of the widow or widower is apt to continue to be unsatisfactory because of problems of relational deficit. It can be helpful to a widow or widower to recognize these two consequences of loss and to acknowledge that loneliness may be an unavoidable response to an unsatisfying situation rather than an inability to resolve the disruption of loss. Being able to identify what is wrong makes it easier to find remedies.

To turn to aging, the theory alerts us to the disturbances of social relationships that come with time. These include departure of children, retirement, possibly the loss of spouse, and, as a result of all the preceding, painful and sometimes bewildering reorientation of central life concerns.

When their children leave, the older couple may find a freedom they have not known for decades, but they also lose their opportunity for nurturance. They may continue to help their now-grown children, and they may be able periodically to indulge their grandchildren, but they probably will never again have the sense of being essential to someone else, which is at least one of the functions small children seem to provide for their parents.

Retirement Removes Important Basis for Self-Esteem

Retirement varies in its implications, but for many men, as Eugene A. Friedmann and Robert J. Havighurst have shown, it removes from their lives an important basis for self-esteem. The parallel, for a woman, would be the loss of a home to keep up. This too can occur in time, but usually at a considerably later point in a woman's life than retirement occurs in a man's. It must be said, though, that the loss of children from the home may constitute a partial retirement for women.

With bereavement, the aged person may have no access to intimacy, and despite remaining relationships with grown children, other relatives, and friends, may begin to experience chronic loneliness. The absence of an intimate tie, we suspect, makes it difficult for an individual to maintain an even emotional balance. Since his emotional responses are not communicated and responded to, they go unchecked, uncorrected by another's perceptions. The result may be distortions either in the direction of pathological distrust or in the direction of depression which are difficult to interrupt.

The aged will lose friends through death, including old friends with whom so much is shared that the relationships are irreplaceable. But they also may give up friends because the interests and concerns that were central to the friendship no longer have meaning for them. Losing her husband may change a woman's life so much that she may no longer have anything in common with her married friends. Retirement may make irrelevant a man's relationships with former colleagues. And at the same time these bases for former friendships are lost, the afflictions of age—sickness, limited income, dependence—may produce new central life concerns which can be shared by few others. The aged who become seriously ill, or crippled, or have a chronic condition that requires frequent medical care, cannot share with anyone their feelings about these physical problems, even though they may well find them the central concerns of their lives. Small wonder, then, if an aged person who is ill seeks out a doctor just to talk about his condition, even at the risk of being thought a hypochondriac.

The aged, therefore, are vulnerable to relational losses that bring in their wake feelings of loneliness, boredom, and worthlessness, and a sense that they are no longer of critical importance to anyone else. These feelings, taken together, have sometimes been characterized as a psychological syndrome that accompanies age. A simpler explanation is that these feelings are normal reactions to relational deficits, reactions that would be found in any group similarly afflicted.

This appraisal suggests that the social and emotional distresses that accompany age can be remedied, but only by relationships that supply the required functions. It gives us a guide to the sort of relationships that may help and the sort that probably will not. For the retired, activities that clearly benefit others, or display competence in an important or valued way, may substitute for employment; but a make-work task, a hobby, or just keeping busy will not.

The appraisal also suggests that relational losses can be repaired. Should loss take place, and this is almost inevitable with age, then the view taken here suggests that it would be better to advise such people that they attempt to establish new relationships that will provide the same functions, rather than "gracefully" accept constriction.

But this recommendation could be made universally. Beyond a certain point we cannot limit our relations with others without incurring serious loss. Just as it is bad advice to tell a widow to live for the children, or to tell someone who is aged to accept the inevitable losses, it is bad advice to tell a young person to forego intimacy for a time while he concentrates on his studies.

Reflective Questions

1. What effect does prolonged social isolation have on people?

2. How best might loneliness be minimized in our lives? Are positive consequences associated with loneliness?

3. What suggestions would you give for increasing the quality of social relationships in America? In the world?

4. To what extent is the problem of aging in America one of a loss of relational ties?

8 □ THE USES OF FAILURE

John H. Gagnon

The orientation of our culture is not toward failure. This proposition can be inferred from the small amount of time given to the phenomenon of failure, an event that occurs many times in the lives of individuals and groups. Gagnon tells us that there are "no college courses teaching us how to fail, or how to substitute one set of goals for another when attainment of the first becomes impossible." Although the essay by Gagnon is rooted, by example, in educational experiences, it is clear that it could well apply to other institutional sectors of life in which failure, or "an accommodation to diminished expectations," is common. The implications are clear. Either we will have to devote more attention to the social psychological management of failure, or appreciably modify an "overly optimistic and excessively competitive" society. The stigma attached to failure might be more acute than the burdens of success. □

SETTLING FOR SECOND BEST (OR EVEN THIRD OR FOURTH) IS SOMETHING FEW of us are prepared for in any public way. There are no school or college courses in how to fail, or how to substitute one set of goals for another when attainment of the first becomes impossible. Although we are told that it is "not whether one wins or loses, but how one plays the game," we are still exhorted "to try and try again." Yet the crisis of failure, or an accommodation to diminished expectations, is a common experience. Few of us achieve all that we want and, ultimately, through the trick of biology, there is inevitably too little time to do all the things one might have desired, or of which one might have thought himself capable. The social-psychological mechanisms of the management of

From *Change Magazine,* May/June 1969, pp. 27–31. Reprinted by permission of *Change Magazine* and the author.

failure remain an unexplored area, and one could find a dozen reasons in the character of American society to account for this particular failure of nerve. But the central question is not why psychology and sociology have failed to attend to this task, but, rather, the positive use of individual failure in the operation of society as a whole, and especially in the university.

In *Equality of Educational Opportunity,* by James Coleman and others, there is substantial evidence to support the structuring of education, at least at the elementary and high school levels, around a school and classroom mix of children of varying academic talents. Coleman's evidence argues against the existence of the track system and other forms of ability discrimination in the schools on the ground that in mixed situations the less academically talented do better and the more academically talented do no worse. Why, in social-psychological terms, those students who are conventionally labelled as less talented perform better in these situations is unclear; but the evidence is that many *do* perform better and that they come to be more like those who appeared originally to be more talented.

From this evidence at the elementary and high school levels, some might wish to suggest that as a society we should reduce ability discrimination in colleges and graduate schools as well. That is, we should begin in college admissions to reduce the differences in ability selection *between* colleges to produce a greater spread of ability among *all* colleges, rather than having some colleges filled with high-ability students, other colleges where the ability of students is lower, and others where the distribution of ability is lower still. However, such ability mixing in colleges and graduate schools—unlike at the elementary and high school levels—might well prove to be counter-productive in terms of the distribution of individuals of varying abilities among occupational careers. In short, while ability mixing evidently pays off when relatively general skills are being learned, ability segregation may be necessary in this society for the sake of effective occupational selection and training. In this sense, academic failure at the college level, no matter how personally crushing, functions to the advantage of society-at-large.

From the research of James A. Davis ("The Campus as a Frog Pond," *American Journal of Sociology,* July 1966), for example, it is clear that institutional quality and grade point averages are independent attributes. In other words, regardless of the quality of a college as measured by the ability of its students, the college grades on a curve. Thus at colleges having a large number of bright students there is the same tendency on the part of the faculty to give B's and C's as in colleges where the students are generally less bright. At the higher quality schools there is a consistent tendency for the faculty to require more work for the same grades. As ability segregation increases—that is, as admission standards go up—grade distribution does not tend to change, rather the amount of required work increases. The end result is that a very bright young man who goes to Harvard will find himself in competition with many other very bright young people for a limited number of high grades. Given the intensity of competition for a scarce resource, the odds are that—unlike in high school where the academic pond was larger—he will not end up in the top of the class or get the best grades. Ironically, the very same young man would find himself at the top of the heap had he gone to a less prestigious college where the standards for entry were not so high.

Davis implies some criticism of this situation when he correctly notes that the worst student, in terms of grades, at a high quality school is nonetheless probably at or near the top of the national ability distribution. And Davis rightly observes that a "feeling of success" is important in career choice, and that the student who goes to college in pursuit of a career requiring academic excellence (again in terms of grades) and who suddenly finds himself at the bottom of the grading heap may have difficulty adjusting to a required change in career choice. But for such a student, the adjustment is both unavoidable and rapid; failure leaves little alternative. In high school, where there exists a relatively wide range of abilities among students, the very bright, the bright and the near bright—if they are not disadvantaged by race or poverty—have relatively easy times getting good grades, running up high scores on the Scholastic Aptitude Test and ranking relatively high in their classes. Even in the best private schools, where there is significant academic competition, the bright students have few doubts of their ultimate abilities. They realize they may not *all* get into the most prestigious or the most intellectual colleges, but they know all will get into *some* high-quality institution. Often, moreover, they will get in with little intellectual effort—there are, after all, their colleagues in the lower fifty to sixty percent of the ability spectrum who will not go to college at all—and they will enroll with high career aspirations. In Davis' data, about forty percent of the students who entered what he calls high-quality colleges were initially committed to "high performance academic career fields"—the physical and biological sciences, the humanities and fine arts, law and medicine. Even in moderate- and low-quality institutions, Davis' data shows approximate high-expectation proportions of twenty-five and twenty percent.

But at the college level, the academic game operates differently, especially at the high-quality institutions. Many students, no longer propped up by a convenient cushion of academic non-achievers, find themselves in classes full of high achievers, many of whom work very hard. Readjustment of expectations and, ultimately, career choices quickly occurs. When incoming freshmen at one high-quality college in the Midwest were asked recently if they expected to make the dean's list, about ninety percent said yes; within a few months the proportion that expected to make it dropped to the accurate proportion of about fifteen percent.

What many students find out, even at low-quality institutions, is that college is a place of at least partial failure. For those too inarticulate to ask for help, college is a place of total failure, a place from which one returns without a degree. For many others, it is a place at which to shift to lower expectations. As problematic to individuals as this process undoubtedly is, having, in Davis' words, "frog ponds" of varying ability dimensions may well be a useful device for the allocation of talent to various occupations and career lines. For if the large proportions of young people who overselect the high-status occupations and career lines on entering college were maintained, there would be a direct line between the ability distribution of students on entry into college and the ability distribution of graduates in the preferred graduate school fields and the prestigious professions. The high-status careers thus would get most of the bright college graduates, while fields of lesser status would get the less able, at least as predicted by SAT scores and other college measures.

Fortunately for American society, this does not happen. Instead, many bright young people find themselves in colleges where, because there are entire classrooms filled with equally bright people, they fail—at least relatively—and thus must make other choices. It is here that the problem of academic failure presents itself most dramatically, causing widespread shifts in career interests from the hard sciences to the soft, from mathematics and pure physics to engineering, from engineering to sociology, and from still other areas to journalism, education and business. Not only is there movement from "academic high performance" fields to areas of lesser performance, there is movement within the high performance fields. For example, at one high-quality state institution in the East which emphasizes science, there is traditionally a substantial movement away from career choices in the physical and biological sciences over the four undergraduate years. As freshmen, some three hundred students typically will opt for a biology major, but by their senior year only eighty will be left; losses of the same dimensions are common in physics, mathematics and chemistry. For women students, the movement is nearly totally to the field of education; for men, the move most commonly is to engineering, the social sciences and the humanities.

Given the highly structured prestige ranking of career choices, it seems that bright students must be pushed, rather than drawn, into career fields of lower prestige, which require talented people as much as the high-status fields. The societal solution is to make the individual bear the burden of change through academic selection. When the high-prestige occupation was medicine, the high selectivity of the medical schools (whether on academic or non-academic grounds) forced talented applicants into physiology, anatomy and the rest of the biological sciences where their work (and *not* the work of the practicing physicians they would have preferred to have been) laid the groundwork for a revolution in medical technology. This stratification mechanism also works in reverse. Students who originally do not choose high-performance academic fields as freshmen often do so later, after winning high grades. This happens in colleges of all quality levels. For these students, the mechanism flips over and rewards hard work and application.

In graduate and professional schools, the ability range narrows still further, screening out the bottom of the ability range that did not enter graduate or professional school. Aside from those who go on to graduate school primarily to increase salary levels in educational occupations, the same process of accommodation to failure occurs. In the very best graduate schools there is again a prestige ranking of career options. Nuclear physics, for instance, is a more prestigious and attractive choice than solid state physics, yet even in departments composed of the most able graduate students, not all can work at the side of the local Nobel Laureate. Thus, once again, competition presses students into becoming experimentalists or working in lower prestige fields, and again society benefits. Those who make specialty changes from physics, for example, to lower prestige areas in the best graduate schools often later become the most productive and able researchers in their fields. The medical school is another example of this process. Outside of certain metropolitan-wide medical centers, the most prestigious of medical specialties is surgery. Yet by the end of medical school, many young doctors have settled for less prestigious specialties, even at the medical schools with the highest standards of entry. And out of this process, society often gets its best psychiatrists, pathologists and proctologists.

The actual process of failing—or selecting-down to fields of less prestige—is an important source of development for lower-status fields, both within and outside the high-performance domain. It seems clear that if students succeed in getting good grades in their field, they are unlikely to change fields. If talent is to be distributed among all fields, the experience of failure is often required. If we increased the ability distributions among colleges, then far more original career choices would be carried through to the end. The very bright and the bright would continue to have the near-bright as a cushion at each institution, and the pattern of actual career choice would follow more closely the pattern of original career selection. Only by shortening the ability dimension at individual institutions—by building into the American university the process of academic failure—does society deflect some of the very bright and the bright from high-prestige career choices to those fields that are less prestigious, but which are perhaps in greater need of a larger share of the nation's best talent.

One cannot fail to see that from an individual point of view this is often an uncomfortable manner of distributing talent. The emotional cost to some individuals surely is high, and there is considerable angst and pain in trying to survive in a high-quality school. By failing to attain one's favored occupational choice, there is potential for a powerful attack on one's sense of personal competence. The test for the individual is to maintain a sense of continuing personal worth and competence ("there are other things that I can do well") in the face of evidence that others are more talented in one's first-chosen career.

In the lower-quality colleges and among what appear to be the less-talented students, the mechanisms of altering career choice are more obscure. The less-talented often go to college with lower aspirations to start, and they are more likely to aim for non-academic fields. In such cases, those who are bright, but not bright enough to get into the high-quality schools, may nevertheless find their way to academic fields; they may, in fact, by not having gone to a high-quality school, be better able to make a high-prestige career choice, given the relative caliber of their classroom competition. If, however, they are in fact less talented, they may well be relegated to the lower ranks of the high-status fields.

This necessary accommodation to failure may, indeed, be an unnoticed contributor to the current levels of student discontent, especially on the high-quality campuses. For the narrowness of the ability spectrum in these schools insures that many young people of real ability will find themselves for the first time facing the harsh fact of personal and intellectual failure. This is not to overindividualize the origins of campus conflicts or to denigrate the reality of the political and social demands of activist students. But the level of discontent conceivably reflects the excessive increase in standards without a concomitant expansion of mechanisms for managing transitions in career choice, once failure has been tasted. The mechanism itself, clearly an unintended consequence of mass education, may simply be inadequate to the needs of both the individual and society.

Failure is a hard taskmaster which visits nearly everyone. It becomes, however, a major problem in a society which is both overly optimistic and excessively competitive. For the result is a process which first instills in the brightest of our youth the highest hopes and then places our young people in competitive races which only a few can win.

Reflective Questions

1. Is failure simply a matter of individual motivation or psychology?

2. Is human interaction largely a matter of winning and losing? If yes, do you see any way to modify the situation?

3. Could you develop typologies of failure and the varied consequences of each for individuals and the social system?

9 □ ALIENATED YOUTH AND THE CULT OF THE OCCULT

John Raphael Staude

Professor Staude offers an exploration into the current interest in, and acceptance of, occult philosophy among middle-class American youth. A plausible argument is presented to explain why alienated youth are turning to the mystic philosophy of the East in their quest for truth and reality. Staude views the followers of the occult as hedonists; but perhaps we are all hedonistic—some are simply more long-range hedonistic than are the youthful adherents to the occult movement. The author considers the cult of the occult to be more than a mere fad or fashion; the source of strength that nurtures the movement is the experience of alienation and disillusionment of the young with the values and goals of the society in which they are expected to function. "Mysticism," according to Staude, "offers a sense of identity with the original and all-inclusive Source and Goal of the universe, the one eternal principle, God." Of course, only time will reveal whether the occult philosophy proves to satisfy the quest of the young; however, there appears to be evidence that an increasing number of alienated youth see the cult of the occult as a feasible alternative to existing institutional solutions. □

I

LET ME PREFACE MY DISCUSSION BY SAYING THAT THESE ARE SIMPLY SOME *tentative* reflections and observations about alienated youth and the cultural revolution we are currently living through. I will take as my starting point Louis Wirth's admonition that the sociology of knowledge should concern itself not merely with the ideas and modes of thinking that happen to flourish but with

Paper presented at the Midwest Sociological Society Meeting, May 1970. Reprinted by permission of the author.

the social and cultural setting in which these occur. Wirth advised us to "take account of the factors that are responsible for the *acceptance* or the *rejection* of certain ideas by certain groups in society, and of the motives and interests that prompt certain groups consciously to promote these ideas and to disseminate them among wider sections."[1] Specifically I am asking: how can we account for the growing acceptance of mystical and occult ideas and the rejection of scientific rationalism among an increasing number of American high school and college students?

Evidence that there is in fact a growing interest in and acceptance of occult and mystical ideas in the youth culture is not hard to find. I could play you some popular recordings such as Buffy Saint Marie's rendition of Leonard Cohen's prose poem, "God is alive. Magic is afoot." Or we might listen to Donovan, the Scottish romantic bard turned guru, recount his tale of the origins of the gods and mythology in the lost continent of Atlantis, a tale which he advises us the Elders of our world cannot understand despite all their learning and so-called science. We could listen to Johnny Rivers record, "Realization," to Blind Faith, to Ravi Shankar's Sitar or to the Beatles. But then we'd all be dancing and contact high and you probably wouldn't want to listen to my paper any more than I would feel like standing up here and presenting it. So instead I'm going to trust that you are all familiar with the album, "Hair" and that though you may not have seen the show, you have heard that we are living in the "Age of Aquarius," a time of "golden living dreams of visions," of "mystic crystal revelation and a mind of true liberation." I could easily cite other media such as psychedelic poster art, the new cinema, the living theatre, the reports of the occult scene in *Esquire, McCall's,* and other slick magazines, and the TV talk shows where astrologers, gurus, and Holy Men are appearing frequently.

To relate these happenings to the college and university world, let me reproduce for you an interview conducted by a *New York Times*[2] correspondent in the Harvard Coop. (The interviewer is a little square and heavy handed, but I think the student's responses are typical enough.)

INTERVIEWER: "You believe—really believe—that astrology's true?"
STUDENT: "Why not?"
INTERVIEWER: "What about the *I-Ching?* Did you read that, too?"
STUDENT: "Yes, sir."
INTERVIEWER: "And mystic Tarot cards and books on the Tarot—Do you take those seriously?"
STUDENT: "Un-huh."
INTERVIEWER: "What the hell are you studying anyhow?"

[1] Louis Wirth. Preface to Karl Mannheim. *Ideology and Utopia,* New York, Harcourt, Brace & World, 1936, p. xxviii.
[2] The New York Times Book Review, February 15, 1970.

STUDENT: "Physics."
INTERVIEWER: "You're kidding."
STUDENT: "I'm not kidding. I'm studying physics, and there's a lot in elemental particles that's weirder than astrology."
INTERVIEWER: "But don't you reserve judgment in both cases—you know, scientific skepticism?"
STUDENT: "That's just rationalism (the last word said with muted contempt). There's other ways to see the world."

Here is an excerpt from another interview, this time with a girl who the interviewer caught browsing in Carlos Castaneda's *The Teachings of Don Juan*, a current campus best-seller about the mescaline trips of an Indian medicine man. In discussing the book the girl's one complaint was at the anthropologist-author's attempt at an anthropological analysis of Don Juan, the medicine man, but for the "stoned" mental prowess of the old Indian, and his ease at slipping into boundary states of consciousness she expressed unreserved praise.

STUDENT: "What do you mean by 'objective'?"
INTERVIEWER: "You know, objective—not seeing things colored by one's own personal feelings."
STUDENT: "Why would you want to do that? Wow, that's deadly!"

The Interviewer then asked the same girl her opinion about another best-seller among college students, R. D. Laing's *The Politics of Experience*. Laing, as you probably know defines "true sanity" as being in one way or another the dissolution of the normal ego, which he calls our "false self, competently adjusted to our alienated social reality." This false self is replaced by the "inner archetypal mediators of divine power." Through this death a rebirth occurs, the ego now being "the servant of the divine, no longer its betrayer."

INTERVIEWER: "What's so important about Laing?"
STUDENT: "Well, he's one of the only ones in psychiatry that makes fantasy legitimate. He's not always knocking you over the head with reality."

I could cite similar responses from my own experience with students in various parts of the country, but I think that the point can be summed up in one youngster's response: "We're on a God-trip, man. God-consciousness is where it's at. We got high and now we want to learn how to stay high forever."

Today we see among the young a growing interest in a large variety of exotic metaphysical and magical cults which come under the general category of "Ways of Liberation" from the "illusion" of Ego. These techniques offer the adept a sense of unity and community with the Godhead. Of course, there are also satanic cults, witchcraft and black magic, things which have been brought to public attention as a result of the Sharon Tate affair, but the cult of the demonic I see as simply a part of the more general search for identity and self-realization now going on. I believe that Black and White magic, and witchcraft in general is spreading among the youth, but I see it as a subcategory within the much wider movement of spiritual renewal which I want to discuss today.

What is it that the I Ching, the Tarot, astrology, and other forms of fortune telling such as palmistry, graphology, numerology, scientology, etc. all have in common? They all reject the relevance of rational planning, and they all presuppose that there are supernatural forces or fate that shape the destiny of the individual regardless of his actions or wishes. In short they are deterministic. There is a pattern and meaning in human life that is beyond human will. (Reality is not as it appears.) Furthermore, they postulate the interrelatedness of all parts of reality, and man is often viewed as a microcosm linked to the macrocosmic source of all being. Individuality is viewed as an illusion, and our destiny is pre-ordained.

A very important principle of occult philosophies is that they are generally contained in "secret teachings" revealed only to illuminati or initiates. The latter have succeeded in transcending the illusions of the "status game" thereby freeing themselves to develop the latent potentialities in human nature which lie dormant in other men. It is assumed that man is evolving "spiritually" as well as physically, and that yogis, fakirs, and saints have at various times manifested these superior psychic powers. The Secret Teachings generally offer a practical technique for realizing these latent possibilities of human evolution. Self-knowledge is viewed as the goal of all study; education to be worthy of the name must be an "education of consciousness."

The Guide or Guru has become a familiar figure on American college campuses for a generation of "Seekers". He teaches Wisdom (*Heils-und Erlosungswissen*) in contrast to the practical and theoretical knowledge of control and achievement (*Leistungswissen*) offered by most academics.[3] The Beat Prophet, Allen Ginsberg[4] recently commented that Academe meant a grove of trees where there should be taught not just knowledge but wisdom and suggested that Tibetan teachers should be installed on university campuses. By wisdom he meant non-verbal, non-conceptual sensory training in expansion of consciousness teaching students to attain higher states of awareness without the aid of language. He spoke of the need to avoid brainwashing, and the need for psychic transformation. Tim Leary and other Gurus have been developing and teaching techniques of consciousness expansion for several years now.

Last October, in San Francisco[5] there was a "Holy Man Jam" at the

---

[3] See my discussion of these terms in *Max Scheler,* New York: Free Press, 1967, p. 189.
[4] See the profile of Allen Ginsberg as "Paterfamilias" to the youth culture in *The New Yorker* (August 17 and 24, 1968).
[5] See the *San Francisco Oracle,* Vol. 1, No. 7 (October 1969).

Family Dog, a popular rock entertainment hall. Six thousand people came, not to hear The Band, or Crosby, Stills and Nash, but to see the "Holy Men": Timothy Leary, Dr. Warwick, the Tantric Buddhist mountain yogi, Master Choy, the Tai Chi master, Steve Gaskin, a well known occultist teacher in the Bay Area, Allen, the world messiah, Askoe Fakir with his Hindu Folk Band, and others. It seems hard to believe that these fakirs could outsell the top rock groups. Yet it is true. Alan Watts, Tim Leary, Baba Ram Das (formerly Richard Alpert, Ph.D.), and of course, *the* prophet Allen Ginsberg, are known and respected by youth as much as the leading rock musicians and probably a good deal more.

The new religion is a religion of joy and delight, of "mystic crystal revelation . . . and a mind of true liberation." It is an outrageously rollicking, exuberant, often militant hedonism—spontaneity, authenticity, sexual and sensual pleasure and delight. (In a way Wilhelm Reich is as much a prophet of the new religion as is Timothy Leary, his latter-day disciple and apostle of hedonism.) In all registers and on all levels (to use structuralist terminology) one can see a similar spirit burgeoning forth.

There have been similar periods in Western cultural history; the most obvious analogies that come to mind are the spurt of re-birth and renewal that blazed across the Western horizon in the Renaissance. Then, too, men talked of the impending millenium, and went out to convert all men to the joyful Word of Revelation. Then, too, men saw visions, and believed that they must live in the present, joyfully and alive, before the world came to an end. Then, too, they kicked off the traces of an atrophied scholasticism (the reigning science of the age) and created the counter-culture of humanism and hermeticism. In this same period large numbers of men and women, puzzled by the political and social troubles of the time, turned to magic and to witchcraft, to astrology and various forms of divination. A study of the growth of witchcraft in the later Middle Ages reveals that practitioners of the black arts purchased from the Devil: joy, riches, pleasure and earthly paradise in exchange for their souls' eternal salvation (delayed gratification). Members of the Church of Satan then as now preached philosophy of indulgence instead of abstinence.

In short, I suggest that we are in the throes of a spiritual, religious, cultural renaissance, similar to the prototypical Renaissance of the 12th–16th centuries. To judge the import of this religious and cultural renewal movement in purely political terms, to focus solely on the student activists who have gained so much attention of late, is to miss some of the deeper, and I believe, more lasting aspects of the current youth culture.

II

What social, psychological, or cultural forces can help us to understand this shift in the foci of interest among American youth? Some say that the current interest in religion and mysticism can be dismissed as a passing fad: it is simply the "in-thing" and the young will soon go on to another craze. However, I see it as symptomatic of a deepening spiritual crisis, a disillusionment with science, planning and rationality similar to the disenchantment with Enlightenment that spurred the cultural revolution of romanticism. Here is something that we cannot dismiss as a passing fad. It has deep roots, and it is going to grow.

The simplest explanation, I think, is in terms of "alienation" and "disillusionment." Today many a student is alienated from his own social, cultural and religious background when he comes to college, if not before. Professors attack and ridicule the values of his parents. But what do they offer instead, in place of the old time religion to give meaning to life? They are the high priests of the esoteric religion of science. The young are told that if they work very hard, they may eventually get the degree and then also become high priests. Many are finding that self-denial, postponement of gratification, rational planning does not seem to pay off. Formerly, in the 1920's and 1930's the student knew what his career plans were. College was simply a stage along the way, but he could get by with a gentlemanly "C." College was not to be taken too seriously. Today we are beginning to see students again not taking college very seriously. The metaphysical "C" is coming into vogue, or rather no grades at all, as they are said to be irrelevant as are all status distinctions.

The young are rebelling. They want to know the meaning of life and they don't want to wait. They want Paradise now. So they turn to Eastern mysticism and philosophy and to a lesser extent to Western Romanticism and Existentialism for answers in their quest for meaning. All of these philosophies preach the absurdity of meritocratic status distinctions. They offer the student an escape from the pressure to succeed, to achieve, which weighs heavily upon him almost from kindergarten. (I am reminded of the stories of the competition among parents to get their children in the best nursery schools to prepare them for college.) The young are finally throwing over the traces and saying "Fuck you."

Certainly these students are alienated from the academy, from the moral climate of the time, from their parents and from themselves, but not as random individuals. They are participants in a counter culture which is fundamentally challenging the Western objective scientific rationalist cultural tradition. However, to understand alienation we must see not only the alienated as objects of therapy, but also the alienator, the agency or system which may well be in deeper need of and the proper object for therapy. Current psychotherapeutic usage needs to be enriched by Marx's dialectical perspective.

What makes the alienation of youth a cultural phenomenon is the fact that it strikes beyond ideology to the level of consciousness, seeking to transform our deepest sense of the self, the other, and the environment. In his recent book, *The Making of a Counter Culture: Reflections on the Technocratic Society and Its Youthful Opposition,* **Theodore Rozak** sums it up this way:

A heroic generalization about this still embryonic culture is to say that what the young are up to is nothing less than a reorganization of the prevailing state of personal and social consciousness. From a culture that has a long-standing, entrenched commitment to an egocentric and intellective mode of consciousness, the young are moving toward a sense of identity that is *communal* and *nonintellective*. I think the disjuncture is just that great—as great in its implications (though obviously not as yet in historical influence) as the disjuncture between Greco-Roman rationality and Christian mystery. Against the traditional Cartesian *cogito,* with its blunt, initial assertion of individuality and logicality, the counter culture opposes the community and visionary aspiration. This really amounts to an assault on the reality of the ego as an isolable and purely cerebral unit of identity.

The politics of the student activist is basically to reorganize personal and social consciousness rather than to extend New Deal liberalism. The effort of the hippie to accomplish this same reorganization of consciousness is far more serious and engaged, albeit in cultural rather than in political terms, than those of us whose assumptions of personal and social identity are those of the Enlightenment and the Protestant Ethic can see. This is not to obscure the very real strategic differences between New Left politicos and hippies but rather to prevent these distinctions from obscuring the fundamental shape of the counter culture which they share in creating.[6]

The youth of the counter culture, having broken with the Western rationalistic individualists, skeptical tradition of the last 300 years in favor of a communal, personalist, "committed" life style, now are searching for sacral foundations to sustain and celebrate their new identity. This quest for the sacred in an odd amalgam of Eastern and Western terms is itself another sign of how deeply alienated from the immediate Western intellectual and cultural tradition the counter culture actually is.

The traditional intellectual style of higher education in the United States has been analytical and morally detached. This tradition assumes that truth is enormously complex but ultimately inert and that, therefore, an increasingly microscopic and fragmentary rationality is needed to unravel it. Only a strict posture of moral detachment will avoid compromising its essential inertness. The style of Objective Analysis assumes that the primary responsibility of the

---

[6] Karl Garrison has tried to test sociologically the religious character of the New Left, basing his analysis on Howard Becker's sacred/secular typology and on Becker's theory that when secular—ordinary, neutral, relative—values become dominant in a given culture, then a quest for the sacred often becomes manifest in its youth. His conclusion, after six months' research among a group of student activists, is that they are indeed engaged in that sacral quest. See Myron B. Bloy, Jr., "Alienated Youth and the Chaplain" in *The Religious Situation,* 1969 (Boston: Beacon Press, 1969), p. 656.

individual scientist, scholar or artist is to his subject and craft. For the research and teacher this implies that one should attempt to examine one's material as objectively, as impersonally as possible in order to minimize the danger that one's own point of view might distort the interpretation of the material.[7]

The counter culture is evolving an alternative and morally committed style. Its members assume that truth is finally unitive (albeit mysterious) and alive, and that, therefore, successively larger more inclusive perceptions of reality must be discovered and that only moral engagement is responsive to its essential sentience. This Engaged Style invites an existential absorption of experience rather than the channeling of investigation toward particular ends, and it resists the effort of analytic teachers to discipline the expression of feeling for the purpose of communication persuasion, and achievement.[8] It is individualist, vigorous in its opposition to the prevailing educational system, articulating a critique of existing curricula and teaching that lack "relevance" to contemporary life and issues.

III

We have seen that young Americans apparently have some grounds for wishing to reject scientific rationalism and the meritocratic social order. To what, on the other hand, can we attribute their acceptance of the occultist ideology described earlier in this paper? The most common explanation is drugs. The drug experience is surely a fundamental part of student life today, and as such has opened the way to exploration of mystical states of consciousness, but I believe that drug use is as much symptomatic as causal in relation to the spiritual renewal I am describing. As Seekers, the young try drugs along with meditation, the Tarot, I Ching, astrology, etc. For our explanation I believe we must look to the metaphysical anxiety the young experience in face of their alienation, disillusionment and identity-confusion.

The question is what frame of reference can we turn to to make sense out of the world we're living in? The young have turned to the "Wise Men" of the Establishment, the scientists and sociologists, the whole lot, and found them wanting. Then some of the young, like the Beatles, decided to find out what wise men in other parts of the world had to say and they discovered an alternative frame of reference and an alternative symbolic reference group; the Holy Men, the Sages, Mystics, Wise men of the East. For example Hermann Hesse's *Siddhartha,* the Sage of the East sees all dualisms contained within human experience; he sees the order and coherence behind the appearance of chaos. The sky is one aspect of human experience; the jungle another. The sage, whose life is ordered and at peace, and whose life includes all forms of relationships

[7] James S. Ackerman. "Two Styles: A Challenge to Higher Education," *Daedalus* (Summer 1969), p. 855.
[8] *Ibid.,* 861.

possible to man is a "lesser whole" who has reached a kind of integration sustained and measured by the organic order of the "greater whole." He is at peace with himself because the peace of the "greater whole," the peace that surpasses all understanding, is within him. He is at peace with other men because his relationships to them are in his consciousness, expressions of, and contained in his relationship to the greater whole. They fit into a universal picture. Each piece of the jigsaw puzzle is where it belongs. The image of the whole is clear.

My thesis is very simple: young people are turning to mysticism and the occult as an attempt to find meaning in a world in which they feel alienated and disillusioned with the liberal progressivist ideology of their parents and with totalistic ideologies like socialism and Communism. Objectively the social structural factors such as poverty, racism, the draft, crime, violence, rape of the environment, and especially lack of understanding between the generations, produces an alienated "unhappy consciousness" among young people. Given the fact of the apparent failure of the student movement to attain peace and social reforms, many students are becoming anti-political. They are seeking meaning in extra-political contexts such as mysticism and metaphysics.

Mysticism offers a sense of identity with the original and all-inclusive Source and Goal of the universe, the one eternal principle, God. A further payoff for the alienated young person suffering from identity confusion is a sense of belonging and a feeling of being accepted as a "brother" regardless of his success or failure in the meritocratic competitive rat race. Martyrdom and persecution promote a sense of group identity. The current Hippies and long-haired youth may be compared to the early Christians preaching universal love and identification with the poor and downtrodden. This faith, hope and love carried the early Christians through many hard periods. A similar faith inspires the youth. Our country may be failing miserably politically but this is viewed as one more sign of the futility of the rationalistic meritocratic order.

IV

How are we to react to this "cult of the occult"? Probably many of us will view these explorations into the occult as a pathetic regression to primitivism, to forms of consciousness that we consider a result of human weakness, the human—all too human—need for certitudes and absolutes in a time of rapid social change. Personally, I view the "cult of the occult" more optimistically. Certainly the dangers of irrationalism are there. The cult of the unconscious as a source of liberating wisdom can easily lead to the *Blut und Boden* ideology of Nazi Germany and there is clearly a strongly anti-rationalist strain in the Youth movement today. But there is also the potential that Youth, exploring new and old "ways of liberation" may develop an understanding of other peoples, of the Humanity Comte idealized, and ultimately of themselves.

Reflective Questions

1. Why are the followers of occult philosophies more likely to come from the middle class than from the lower or upper classes?

2. In what sense could the cult of the occult be considered a "cop out" and an avoidance of facing reality?

3. What social, psychological, and/or cultural forces contribute to the interest of the occult among American youth?

4. What are the possible consequences to the individual and to society of short-range hedonism versus long-range hedonism?

5. What contribution might the mystic ideology of the occult make to the development of a sense of identity?

10 □ THE MAKING OF A BLACK MUSLIM

John R. Howard

The black community in America is composed of many groups competing for adherence to its approach to solving racial problems in America. One such group is the closely knit Nation of Islam, popularly known as Black Muslims. John Howard interviewed 19 West Coast recruits to the Nation of Islam and followed them through their process of commitment. Howard found that the two major sources of attraction for recruits were (1) an emphasis on black nationalism and (2) an emphasis on self-help. Socialization into this religious group consists of a host of activities designed to decrease non-Muslim contact and assimilate Muslim ideology and the truths of Elijah Muhammad, the messenger of Allah, whose mission is that of being sent to awaken the black man. Defections from the movement occur, according to Howard, because it has no effective mechanism for handling individual grievances or expressions of dissatisfaction. □

You were black enough to get in here. You had the courage to stay. Now be man enough to follow the honorable Elijah Muhammad. You have tried the devil's way. Now try the way of the Messenger.
        MINISTER WILLIAM X, *in a West Coast Black Muslim mosque*

THE LOST-FOUND NATION OF ISLAM IN THE WILDERNESS OF NORTH AMERICA, commonly known as the Black Muslim movement, claims a small but fanatically devoted membership among the Negroes of our major cities. The way of the "Messenger" is rigorous for those who follow it. The man or woman who

Copyright © December 1966, by TRANS-action, Inc., New Brunswick, New Jersey. Reprinted by permission.

becomes a Muslim accepts not only an ideology but an all-encompassing code that amounts to a way of life.

A good Muslim does a full day's work on an empty stomach. When he finally has his one meal of the day in the evening, it can include no pork, nor can he have drink before or a cigarette after; strict dietary rules are standard procedure, and liquor and smoking are forbidden under any circumstances. His recreation is likely to consist of reading the Koran or participating in a demanding round of temple-centered activities, running public meetings or aggressively proselytizing on the streets by selling the Muslim newspaper, *Muhammad Speaks*.

Despite allegations of Muslim violence (adverse publicity from the slaying of Malcolm X supports the erroneous notion that Muslims preach violence), the member's life is basically ascetic. Why then in a non-ascetic, hedonistically-oriented society do people become Muslims? What is the life of a Muslim like? These are questions I asked in research among West Coast members. Specifically, I wanted to know:

- What perspective on life makes membership in such an organization attractive?
- Under what conditions does the potential recruit develop those perspectives?
- How does he happen to come to the door of the temple for his first meeting?
- The Black Muslims are a deviant organization even within the Negro community; the parents or friends of many members strongly objected to their joining. So how does the recruit handle pressures that might erode his allegiance to the organization and its beliefs?

Presenting my questions as an effort to "learn the truth" about the organization, I was able to conduct depth interviews with 19 West Coast recruits, following them through the process of their commitment to the Nation of Islam.

Two main points of appeal emerged—black nationalism and an emphasis on self-help. Some recruits were attracted primarily by the first, and some by the second. The 14 interviewees who joined the organization for its aggressive black nationalism will be called "Muslim militants." The remaining five, who were attracted more by its emphasis on hard work and rigid personal morality, may be aptly termed "Protestant Ethic Muslims."

Muslim Militants: Beating the Devil

Of the 14 Muslim militants, some came from the South, some from border states, and some from the North. All lived in California at the time of the interviews; some migrated to the state as adults, others were brought out by their families as children. They varied in age from 24 to 46, and in education from a few years of grade school to four years of college. Regardless of these substantial differences in background, there were certain broad similarities among them.

At some point, each one had experiences that led away from the institutionally-bound ties and commitments that lend stability to most people's lives. Nine had been engaged in semi-legal or criminal activities. Two had been in the military, not as a career but as a way of postponing the decision of what to do for a living. None had a stable marital history. All of them were acutely aware of being outsiders by the standards of the larger society—and all had come to focus on race bias as the factor which denied them more conventional alternatives.

Leroy X came to California in his late teens, just before World War II:

I grew up in Kansas City, Missouri, and Missouri was a segregated state. Negroes in Kansas City were always restricted to the menial jobs. I came out here in 1940 and tried to get a job as a waiter. I was a trained waiter, but they weren't hiring any Negroes as waiters in any of the downtown hotels or restaurants. The best I could do was busboy, and they fired me from that when they found out I wasn't Filipino.

Leroy X was drafted, and after a short but stormy career was given a discharge as being psychologically unfit.

I tried to get a job, but I couldn't so I started stealing. There was nothing else to do—I couldn't live on air. The peckerwoods didn't seem to give a damn whether I lived or died. They wouldn't hire me and didn't seem to worry how I was going to stay alive. I started stealing.

I could get you anything you wanted—a car, drugs, women, jewelry. Crime is a business like any other. I started off stealing myself. I wound up filling orders and getting rid of stuff. I did that for fifteen years. In between I did a little time. I did time for things I never thought of doing and went free for things I really did.

In my business you had no friends, only associates, and not very close ones at that. . . . I had plenty of money. I could get anything I wanted without working for it. It wasn't enough, though.

Bernard X grew up in New York City:

As a kid . . . you always have dreams—fantasies—of yourself doing something later—being a big name singer or something that makes you outstanding. But you never draw the connection between where you are and how you're going to get there. I had to—I can't say exactly when,

13, 14, 15, 16. I saw I was nowhere and had no way of getting anywhere.
    Race feeling is always with you. You always know about The Man but I don't think it is real, really real, until you have to deal with it in terms of what you are going to do with your own life. That's when you feel it. If you just disliked him before—you begin to hate him when you see him blocking you in your life. I think then a sense of inevitability hits you and you see you're not going to make it out—up—away—anywhere—and you see The Man's part in the whole thing, that's when you begin to think thoughts about him.

Frederick 2X became involved fairly early in a criminal subculture. His father obtained a "poor man's divorce" by deserting the family. His mother had children by other men. Only a tenuous sense of belonging to a family existed. He was picked up by the police for various offenses several times before reaching his teens. The police patrolling his neighborhood eventually restricted him to a two-block area. There was, of course, no legal basis for this, but he was manhandled if seen outside that area by any policeman who knew him. He graduated in his late teens from "pot" to "shooting shit" and eventually spent time in Lexington.

William 2X, formerly a shoeshine boy, related the development of his perspective this way:

You know how they always talk about us running after white women. There have always been a lot of [white] servicemen in this town—half of them would get around to asking me to get a woman for them. Some of them right out, some of them backing into it, laughing and joking and letting me know how much they were my friend, building up to asking me where they could find some woman. After a while I began to get them for them. I ran women—both black and white. . . . What I hated was they wanted me to do something for them [find women] and hated me for doing it. They figure "any nigger must know where to find it. . . ."

Things Begin to Add Up

Amos X grew up in an all-Negro town in Oklahoma and attended a Negro college. Because of this, he had almost no contact with whites during his formative years.

One of my aunts lived in Tulsa. I went to see her once when I was in college. I walked up to the front door of the house where she worked. She really got excited and told me if I came to see her anymore to come around to the back. But that didn't mean much to me at the time. It is only in looking back on it that all these things begin to add up.

After graduating from college, Amos joined the Marines. There he began to "see how they [the whites] really felt" about him; by the end of his tour, he had concluded that "the white man is the greatest liar, the greatest cheat, the greatest hypocrite on earth." Alienated and disillusioned, he turned to professional gambling. Then, in an attempt at a more conventional way of life, he married and took a job teaching school.

I taught English. Now I'm no expert in the slave masters' language, but I knew the way those kids talked after being in school eight and nine years was ridiculous. They said things like "mens" for "men." I drilled them and pretty soon some of them at least in class began to sound like they had been inside a school. Now the principal taught a senior class in English and his kids talked as bad as mine. When I began to straighten out his kids also he felt I was criticizing him. . . . That little black man was afraid of the [white] superintendent and all those teachers were afraid. They had a little more than other so-called Negroes and didn't give a damn about those black children they were teaching. Those were the wages of honesty. It's one thing to want to do an honest job and another thing to be able to. . . .

With the collapse of his career as a public school teacher and the break-up of his marriage, Amos went to California, where he was introduced to the Muslim movement.

I first heard about them [the Muslims] in 1961. There was a debate here between a Muslim and a Christian minister. The Muslims said all the things about Christianity which I had been thinking but which I had never heard anyone say before. He tore the minister up.

Finding an organization that aggressively rejected the white man and the white man's religion, Amos found his own point of view crystallized. He joined without hesitation.

Norman Maghid first heard of the Muslims while he was in prison.

I ran into one of the Brothers selling the paper about two weeks after I got out and asked him about the meetings. Whether a guy could just go and walk in. He told me about the meetings so I made it around on a Wednesday evening. I wasn't even bugged when they searched me. When they asked me about taking out my letter [joining the organization] I took one out. They seemed to know what they were talking about. I never believed in non-violence and love my enemies, especially when my enemies don't love me.

Muhammad Soule Kabah, born into a family of debt-ridden Texas sharecroppers, was recruited into the Nation of Islam after moving to California.

I read a series of articles in the Los Angeles *Herald Dispatch,* an exchange between Minister Henry and a Christian minister. It confirmed what my grandfather had told me about my African heritage, that I had nothing to be ashamed of, that there were six thousand books on mathematics in the Library of the University of Timbucktoo while Europeans were still wearing skins. Also my father had taught me never to kow-tow to whites. My own father had fallen away. My parents didn't want me to join the Nation. They said they taught hate. That's funny isn't it? The white man can blow up a church and kill four children and the black man worries that an organization which tells you not to just take it is teaching hate.

Protestant Ethic Muslims: Up by Black Bootstraps

The Protestant Ethic Muslims all came from backgrounds with a strong tradition of Negro self-help. In two cases, the recruit's parents had been followers of Marcus Garvey; another recruit explicitly endorsed the beliefs of Booker T. Washington; and the remaining two, coming from upwardly mobile families, were firm in the belief that Negroes could achieve higher status if they were willing to work for it.

When asked what had appealed to him about the Muslims, Norman X replied:

They thought that black people should do something for themselves. I was running this small place [a photography shop] and trying to get by. I've stuck with this place even when it was paying me barely enough to eat. Things always improve and I don't have to go to the white man for anything.

Ernestine X stressed similar reasons for joining the Muslims.

You learned to stand up straight and do something for yourself. You learn to be a lady at all times—to keep your house clean—to teach your children good manners. There is not a girl in the M·G·T who does not know how to cook and sew. The children are very respectful; they speak only when they are spoken to. There is no such thing as letting your children talk back to you the way some people believe. The one thing they feel is the Negroes' downfall is men and sex for the women, and women and sex for the men, and they frown on sex completely unless you are married.

Despite their middle-class attitudes in many areas, Protestant Ethic Muslims denounced moderate, traditional civil rights organizations such as the NAACP, just as vigorously as the militant Muslims did. Norman X said that he had once belonged to the NAACP but had dropped out.

They spent most of their time planning the annual brotherhood dinner. Besides it was mostly whites—whites and the colored doctors and lawyers who wanted to be white. As far as most Negroes were concerned they might as well not have existed.

Lindsey X, who had owned and run his own upholstery shop for more than 30 years, viewed the conventional black bourgeoisie with equal resentment.

I never belonged to the NAACP. What they wanted never seemed real to me. I think Negroes should create jobs for themselves rather than going begging for them. That's why I never supported CORE.

In this respect Norman and Lindsey were in full accord with the more militant Amos X, who asserted:

They [the NAACP and CORE] help just one class of people. . . . Let something happen to a doctor and they are right there; but if something happens to Old Mose on the corner, you can't find them.

The interviews made it clear that most of the Protestant Ethic Muslims had joined the Nation because, at some point, they began to feel the need of organizational support for their personal systems of value. For Norman and Lindsey, it was an attempt to stop what they considered their own backsliding after coming to California. Both mentioned drinking to excess and indulging in what they regarded as a profligate way of life. Guilt feelings apparently led them to seek Muslim support in returning to more enterprising habits.

COMMITMENT TO DEVIANCE

The Nation of Islam is a deviant organization. As such it is subject to public scorn and ridicule. Thus it faces the problem of consolidating the recruit's allegiance in an environment where substantial pressures operate to erode this allegiance. How does it deal with this problem?

The structural characteristics of the Nation tend to insulate the member from the hostility of the larger society and thus contribute to the organization's survival. To begin with, the ritual of joining the organization itself stresses commitment without questions.

At the end of the general address at a temple meeting, the minister asks those nonmembers present who are "interested in learning more about Islam" to step to the back of the temple. There they are given three blank sheets of ordinary stationery and a form letter addressed to Elijah Muhammad in Chicago:

> Dear Savior Allah, Our Deliverer:
> I have attended the Teachings of Islam, two or three times, as taught by one of your ministers. I believe in it. I bear witness that there is no God but Thee. And, that Muhammad is Thy Servant and Apostle. I desire to reclaim my Own. Please give me my Original name. My slave name is as follows:

The applicant is instructed to copy this letter verbatim on each of the three sheets of paper, giving his own name and address unabbreviated at the bottom. If he fails to copy the letter perfectly, he must repeat the whole task. No explanation is given for any of these requirements.

Formal acceptance of his letter makes the new member a Muslim, but in name only. Real commitment to the Nation of Islam comes gradually—for example, the personal commitment expressed when a chain smoker gives up cigarettes in accordance with the Muslim rules even though he knows that he could smoke unobserved. "It's not that easy to do these things," Stanley X said of the various forms of abstinence practiced by Muslims. "It takes will and discipline and time, . . . but you're a much better person after you do." Calvin X told of periodic backsliding in the beginning, but added, "Once I got into the thing deep, then I stuck with it."

This commitment and the new regimen that goes with it have been credited with effecting dramatic personality changes in many members, freeing alcoholics from the bottle and drug addicts from the needle. It can be argued, however, that the organization does not change the member's fundamental orientation. To put it somewhat differently, given needs and impulses can be expressed in a variety of ways; thus, a man may give vent to his sadism by beating up strangers in an alley or by joining the police force and beating them up in the back room of the station.

"Getting into the thing deep" for a Muslim usually comes in three stages:

• Participation in organizational activities—selling the Muslim newspaper, dining at the Muslim restaurant, attending and helping run Muslim meetings.

- Isolation from non-Muslim social contacts—drifting away from former friends and associates because of divergent attitudes or simply because of the time consumed in Muslim activities.
- Assimilation of the ideology—marking full commitment, when a Muslim has so absorbed the organization's doctrines that he automatically uses them to guide his own behavior and to interpret what happens in the world around him.

The fact that the organization can provide a full social life furthers isolation from non-Muslims. Participation is not wholly a matter of drudgery, of tramping the streets to sell the paper and studying the ideology. The organization presents programs of entertainment for its members and the public. For example, in two West Coast cities a Negro theatrical troupe called the Touring Artists put on two plays, "Jubilee Day" and "Don't You Want to Be Free." Although there was a high element of humor in both plays, the basic themes—white brutality and hypocrisy and the necessity of developing Negro self-respect and courage—were consonant with the organization's perspective. Thus the organization makes it possible for a member to satisfy his need for diversion without going outside to do so. At the same time, it continually reaches him with its message through the didactic element in such entertainment.

Carl X's experiences were typical of the recruit's growing commitment to the Nation. When asked what his friends had thought when he first joined, he replied: "They thought I was crazy. They said, 'Man, how can you believe all that stuff?'" He then commented that he no longer saw much of them, and added:

When you start going to the temple four or five times a week and selling the newspaper you do not have time for people who are not doing these things. We drifted—the friends I had—we drifted apart. . . . All the friends I have now are in the Nation. Another Brother and I get together regularly and read the Koran and other books, then ask each other questions on them like, "What is Allah's greatest weapon? The truth. What is the devil's greatest weapon? The truth. The devil keeps it hidden from men. Allah reveals it to man." We read and talk about the things we read and try to sharpen our thinking. I couldn't do that with my old friends.

Spelled out, the "stuff" that Carl X had come to believe, the official Muslim ideology, is this:

- The so-called Negro, the American black man, is lost in ignorance. He is unaware of his own past history and the future role which history has destined him to play.

- Elijah Muhammad has come as the Messenger of Allah to awaken the American black man.
- The American black man finds himself now in a lowly state, but that was not always his condition.
- The Original Man, the first men to populate the earth, were non-white. They enjoyed a high level of culture and reached high peaks of achievement.
- A little over 6,000 years ago a black scientist named Yakub, after considerable work, produced a mutant, a new race, the white race.
- This new race was inferior mentally, physically, and morally to the black race. Their very whiteness, the very mark of their difference from the black race, was an indication of their physical degeneracy and moral depravity.
- Allah, in anger at Yakub's work, ordained that the white race should rule for a fixed amount of time and that the black man should suffer and by his suffering gain a greater appreciation of his own spiritual worth by comparing himself to the whites.
- The time of white dominance is drawing near its end. It is foreordained that this race shall perish, and with its destruction the havoc, terror, and brutality which it has spread throughout the world shall disappear.
- The major task facing the Nation of Islam is to awaken the American black man to his destiny, to acquaint him with the course of history.
- The Nation of Islam in pursuing this task must battle against false prophets, in particular those who call for integration. Integration is a plot of the white race to forestall its own doom. The black bourgeoisie, bought off by a few paltry favors and attempting to ingratiate themselves with the whites, seek to spread this pernicious doctrine among so-called Negroes.
- The Nation of Islam must encourage the American black man to begin now to assume his proper role by wresting economic control from the whites. The American black man must gain control over his own economic fortunes by going into business for himself and becoming economically strong.
- The Nation of Islam must encourage the so-called Negro to give up those habits which have been spread among them by the whites as part of the effort to keep them weak, diseased, and demoralized. The so-called Negro must give up such white-fostered dissolute habits as drinking, smoking, and eating improper foods. The so-called Negro must prepare himself in mind and body for the task of wresting control from the whites.
- The Nation of Islam must encourage the so-called Negro to seek now his own land within the continental United States. This is due him and frees him from the pernicious influence of the whites.

The Problem of Defection

Commitment to the Nation can diminish as well as grow. Four of the members I interviewed later defected. Why?

These four cases can be explained in terms of a weak point in the structure of the Nation. The organization has no effective mechanisms for handling grievances among the rank and file. Its logic accounts for this. Muslim doctrine assumes that there is a single, ultimate system of truth. Elijah Muhammad and, by delegation, his ministers are in possession of this truth. Thus only Elijah Muhammad himself can say whether a minister is doing an adequate job. The result is the implicit view that there is nothing to be adjudicated between the hierarchy and its rank and file.

Grievances arise, however. The four defectors were, for various reasons, all dissatisfied with Minister Gerard X. Since there were no formal mechanisms within the organization for expressing their dissatisfaction, the only solution was to withdraw.

For most members, however, the pattern is one of steadily growing involvement. And once the ideology is fully absorbed, there is virtually no such thing as dispute or counter-evidence. If a civil rights bill is not passed, this proves the viciousness of whites in refusing to recognize Negro rights. If the same bill *is* passed, it merely proves the duplicity of whites in trying to hide their viciousness.

The ideology also provides a coherent theory of causation, provided one is willing to accept its basic assumptions. Norman X interpreted his victory over his wife in a court case as a sign of Allah's favor. Morris X used it to account for the day-to-day fortunes of his associates.

Minister X had some trouble. He was sick for a long time. He almost
died. I think Allah was punishing him. He didn't run the temple
right. Now the Brothers make mistakes. Everyone does—but Minister X
used to abuse them at the meetings. It was more a personal thing.
He had a little power and it went to his head. Allah struck him
down and I think he learned a little humility.

When a man reasons in this fashion, he has become a fully committed member of the Nation of Islam. His life revolves around temple-centered activities, his friends are all fellow Muslims, and he sees his own world—usually the world of an urban slum dweller—through the framework of a very powerful myth. He is still doing penance for the sins of Yakub, but the millennium is at hand. He has only to prepare.

The Nation of Islam does not in any real sense convert members. Rather it attracts Negroes who have already, through their own experiences in white America, developed a perspective congruent with that of the Muslim movement. The recruit comes to the door of the temple with the essence of his ideas already formed. The Black Muslims only give this disaffection a voice.

Reflective Questions

1. What prior movements in the black community have espoused black nationalism?

2. Is the separation of whites and blacks necessary in the "ultimate" solution of the race problem?

3. Why isn't the Nation of Islam more widely followed in the black community?

4. How many black nationalist groups do you know about? What differences and similarities exist between them?

Part Three
Pivotal Institutions and Interacting People

I have examined man's wonderful inventions. And I tell you that in the arts of life man invents nothing, but in the arts of death he outdoes Nature herself, and produces by chemistry and machinery all the slaughter of plague, pestilence, and famine. The peasant . . . eats and drinks what was eaten and drunk by peasants 10,000 years ago; and the house he lives in has not altered as much in a thousand centuries as the fashion of a lady's bonnet in a score of weeks. But when he goes out to slay, he carries a marvel of mechanism that lets loose at the touch of a finger all the hidden molecular energies, and leaves the javelin, the arrow, the blow-pipe of his fathers far behind.

G. B. SHAW

TED COWELL / BLACK STAR

THE CONCEPT OF INSTITUTION, LIKE ITS COUNTERPART, CULTURE, IS A frequently used concept; however, it is often used in a nonsociological frame of reference. The social institution, like culture, is rather difficult to define in the sociological nomenclature. Perhaps the most widely accepted definition is that offered by Harry Estill Moore, who defines a social institution as "an enduring, complex, integrated, organized behavior pattern through which social control is exerted and by means of which the fundamental social desires or needs are met."[1]

Moore posits the argument that institutions constitute collective solutions to human needs; therefore, the more basic the need, the more fundamental the institution. Although sociologists do not universally accept the above contention, and certainly not all will agree to the needs basic to human life, we suggest that at least five needs may be viewed as fundamental to the social being. The needs that we consider basic to the contemporary American, followed by the institution primarily responsible for satisfying those needs, are presented in Table 1.

TABLE 1

Basic Need	Fundamental Institution
Procreation	Family
Order	Polity
Resources	Economy
Socialization	Education
Meaning	Religion

The institutions in the table are frequently described as the pivotal institutions of society.

Obviously, the orientation in Table 1 does not constitute an all-inclusive theory of human behavior; however, the approach appears to focus on a plausible argument for examining collective social interaction. Perhaps the most valid criticisms of the needs approach is its inability to explain the origin of the needs and the type of structures needed to fulfill them.

In view of Moore's definition, it is clear that the term institution is a concept for perceiving systems of organized social relationships. The institution, therefore, infers a set of prescribed behavior patterns that satisfy the needs of the individuals who constitute society. Do institutions always function to meet the fundamental social desires or needs? The answer to the above question would,

---

[1] Harry Estill Moore in Henry Pratt Fairchild (Ed.), *The Dictionary of Sociology and Related Sciences* (Paterson, N.J.: Littlefield, Adams and Co., 1961), p. 157.

of course, be negative. The result of the institution's failure to meet the basic needs is a malfunctioning society. An institution or institutions that lead to malfunction in society are said to be sociopathic. Read Bain suggests that an institution may be regarded as sociopathic when:[2]

1. It fails to satisfy needs effectively.
2. It interferes with the satisfaction of human needs by other institutions.
3. Its ideology contains internal inconsistencies.
4. It fails to adjust to technological and ideological changes in its own and related institutions.
5. It wastes human and other resources.

Everyone will not agree when and if the above conditions are present in our institutions; however, we believe that many of our basic institutions are currently demonstrating manifest symptoms of a sociopathic nature, that they are not designed to deliver to all the people, are not flexible in the alternatives they provide, and are essentially upper middle class in orientation. These themes are apparent in the following articles as features of pivotal institutions are examined.

[2] Read Bain, "The Concept of Sociopathy", *Sociology and Social Research,* 38 (September/October, 1953), pp. 3–6.

11 □ THE PARANOID STYLE IN AMERICAN POLITICS

Richard Hofstadter

In this article, the author examines the literature of paranoid political groups in America and presents the basic components of the paranoid style. Some of the common features of the paranoid style are the beliefs that (1) history is a conspiracy; (2) an all-out crusade is needed to defeat the powerful conspiracy before time runs out; (3) only "they" are capable of perceiving the full implications of the conspiracy; and (4) the enemy possesses some unusual source of power. In addition, the paranoid is seen to be a militant leader who sees the conflict as one between absolute good and absolute evil. The absolute evil enemy must be totally eliminated. Hofstadter summarizes by saying that paranoid literature starts out with strong moral commitment, accumulates "evidence," and then reaches fantastic conclusions. Current dilemmas in the political life of contemporary America demonstrate the timeliness of Hofstadter's characterization of American politics. □

LET US NOW ABSTRACT THE BASIC ELEMENTS IN THE PARANOID STYLE. THE central image is that of a vast and sinister conspiracy, a gigantic and yet subtle machinery of influence set in motion to undermine and destroy a way of life. One may object that there *are* conspiratorial acts in history, and there is nothing paranoid about taking note of them. This is true. All political behavior requires strategy, many strategic acts depend for their effect upon a period of secrecy, and anything that is secret may be described, often with but little exaggeration, as conspiratorial. The distinguishing thing about the paranoid style is not that

© Copyright 1964 by Richard Hofstadter. Reprinted from *The Paranoid Style in American Politics and Other Essays* by Richard Hofstadter, by permission of Alfred A. Knopf, Inc. and the author. Footnotes have been renumbered.

its exponents see conspiracies or plots here and there in history, but that they regard a "vast" or "gigantic" conspiracy as *the motive force* in historical events. History *is* a conspiracy, set in motion by demonic forces of almost transcendent power, and what is felt to be needed to defeat it is not the usual methods of political give-and-take, but an all-out crusade. The paranoid spokesman sees the fate of this conspiracy in apocalyptic terms—he traffics in the birth and death of whole worlds, whole political orders, whole systems of human values. He is always manning the barricades of civilization. He constantly lives at a turning point: it is now or never in organizing resistance to conspiracy. Time is forever just running out. Like religious millenarians, he expresses the anxiety of those who are living through the last days and he is sometimes disposed to set a date for the apocalypse. "Time is running out," said Welch in 1951. "Evidence is piling up on many sides and from many sources that October 1952 is the fatal month when Stalin will attack."[1] The apocalypticism of the paranoid style runs dangerously near to hopeless pessimism, but usually stops short of it. Apocalyptic warnings arouse passion and militancy, and strike at susceptibility

---

[1] *May God Forgive Us* (Chicago, 1952), p. 73. Dr. Fred C. Schwarz of the Christian Anti-Communism Crusade is more circumspect. In his lectures he sets the year 1973 as the date for the Communists to achieve control of the world, if they are not stopped. Most contemporary paranoid spokesmen speak of a "Communist timetable," of whose focal dates they often seem to have intimate knowledge.

Probably the most spectacular American instance of such adventism is the case of William Miller, who flourished in New York in the 1830's. The offspring of a line of Baptist preachers, Miller became preoccupied with millenarian prophecies, and made calculations which indicated that Christ would come at first in 1843, and then on October 22, 1844, and became the leader of an adventist sect with a considerable following. On the appointed day, Millerites gathered to pray, many abandoned their worldly occupations, and some disposed of their property. The Miller movement waned after the fatal day, but other adventists, more cautious about their use of dates, carried on.

A notable quality in Miller's work was the rigorously logical and systematic character of his demonstrations, as was his militant opposition to Masonry, Catholicism, and other seductions. His lieutenants and followers, A. Whitney Cross has remarked, "found the world beyond rescue, legislatures corrupt, and infidelity, idolatry, Romanism, sectarianism, seduction, fraud, murder, and duels all waxing stronger." Cross argues that the Millerite movement was not so far from the mainstream of American Protestantism as some might think: "The Millerites cannot be dismissed as ignorant farmers, libertarian frontiersmen, impoverished victims of economic change, or hypnotized followers of a maniac thrown into prominence by freak coincidences, when the whole of American Protestantism came so very close to the same beliefs. Their doctrine was the logical absolute of fundamentalist orthodoxy, as perfectionism was the extreme of revivalism. . . . All Protestants expected some grand event about 1843, and no critic from the orthodox side took any serious issue on basic principles with Miller's calculations." *The Burned-Over District* (Ithaca, N.Y., 1950), pp. 320–1; see Ch. 17 for a good account of the Millerite movement.

For the story of an interesting contemporary prophetic cult and some sober reflections on the powerful resistance of true believers to overwhelming disconfirmation, see L. Festinger, H. W. Riecken, and S. Schachter: *When Prophecy Fails* (Minneapolis, 1956).

to similar themes in Christianity. Properly expressed, such warnings serve somewhat the same function as a description of the horrible consequences of sin in a revivalist sermon: they portray that which impends but which may still be avoided. They are a secular and demonic version of adventism.

As a member of the avant-garde who is capable of perceiving the conspiracy before it is fully obvious to an as yet unaroused public, the paranoid is a militant leader. He does not see social conflict as something to be mediated and compromised, in the manner of the working politician. Since what is at stake is always a conflict between absolute good and absolute evil, the quality needed is not a willingness to compromise but the will to fight things out to a finish. Nothing but complete victory will do. Since the enemy is thought of as being totally evil and totally unappeasable, he must be totally eliminated— if not from the world, at least from the theater of operations to which the paranoid directs his attention.[2] This demand for unqualified victories leads to the formulation of hopelessly demanding and unrealistic goals, and since these goals are not even remotely attainable, failure constantly heightens the paranoid's frustration. Even partial success leaves him with the same sense of powerlessness with which he began, and this in turn only strengthens his awareness of the vast and terrifying quality of the enemy he opposes.

This enemy is clearly delineated: he is a perfect model of malice, a kind of amoral superman: sinister, ubiquitous, powerful, cruel, sensual, luxury-loving. Unlike the rest of us, the enemy is not caught in the toils of the vast mechanism of history, himself a victim of his past, his desires, his limitations. He is a free, active, demonic agent. He wills, indeed he manufactures, the mechanism of history himself, or deflects the normal course of history in an evil way. He makes crises, starts runs on banks, causes depressions, manufactures disasters, and then enjoys and profits from the misery he has produced. The paranoid's interpretation of history is in this sense distinctly personal: decisive events are not taken as part of the stream of history, but as the consequences of someone's will. Very often the enemy is held to possess some especially effective source of power: he controls the press; he directs the public mind through "managed news"; he has unlimited funds; he has a new secret for influencing the mind (brainwashing); he has a special technique for seduction (the Catholic confessional); he is gaining a stranglehold on the educational system.

This enemy seems to be on many counts a projection of the self: both the ideal and the unacceptable aspects of the self are attributed to him. A fundamental paradox of the paranoid style is the imitation of the enemy. The enemy, for example, may be the cosmopolitan intellectual, but the paranoid will outdo him

---

[2] "The systems are diametrically opposed: one must and will exterminate the other." Edward Beecher: *The Papal Conspiracy Exposed and Protestantism Defended* (Boston, 1855), p. 29.

in the apparatus of scholarship, even of pedantry. Senator McCarthy, with his heavily documented tracts and his show of information, Mr. Welch with his accumulations of irresistible evidence, John Robison with his laborious study of documents in a language he but poorly used, the anti-Masons with their endlessly painstaking discussions of Masonic ritual—all these offer a kind of implicit compliment to their opponents. Secret organizations set up to combat secret organizations give the same flattery. The Ku Klux Klan imitated Catholicism to the point of donning priestly vestments, developing an elaborate ritual and an equally elaborate hierarchy. The John Birch Society emulates Communist cells and quasi-secret operation through "front" groups, and preaches a ruthless prosecution of the ideological war along lines very similar to those it finds in the Communist enemy. Spokesmen of the various Christian anti-Communist "crusades" openly express their admiration for the dedication, discipline, and strategic ingenuity the Communist cause calls forth.[3]

David Brion Davis, in a remarkable essay on pre-Civil War "countersubversive" movements, has commented on the manner in which the nineteenth-century nativist unwittingly fashioned himself after his enemy:

As the nativist searched for participation in a noble cause, for unity in a group sanctioned by tradition and authority, he professed a belief in democracy and equal rights. Yet in his very zeal for freedom he curiously assumed many of the characteristics of the imagined enemy. By condemning the subversive's fanatical allegiance to an ideology, he affirmed a similarly uncritical acceptance of a different ideology; by attacking the subversive's intolerance of dissent, he worked to eliminate dissent and diversity of opinion; by censuring the subversive for alleged licentiousness, he engaged in sensual fantasies; by criticizing the subversive's loyalty to an organization, he sought to prove his unconditional loyalty to the established order. The nativist moved even farther in the direction of his enemies when he formed tightly-knit societies and parties which were often secret and which subordinated the individual to the single purpose of the group. Though the nativists generally agreed that the worst evil of subversives

---

[3] This has now become a fashionable trend in more respectable quarters. Stephen Shadegg, known for his success in Senator Goldwater's senatorial campaigns, writes: "Mao Tse-tung . . . has written a valuable book on the tactics of infiltration. In it he says: 'Give me just two or three men in a village and I will take the village.' In the Goldwater campaigns of 1952 and 1958 and in all other campaigns where I have served as a consultant I have followed the advice of Mao Tse-tung." *How to Win an Election* (New York, 1964), p. 106. Writing about cold-war strategy, Goldwater himself declares: "I would suggest that we analyze and copy the strategy of the enemy; theirs has worked and ours has not." *Why Not Victory?* (New York, 1962), p. 24.

was their subordination of means to ends, they themselves recommended the most radical means to purge the nation of troublesome groups and to enforce unquestioned loyalty to the state.[4]

Much of the function of the enemy lies not in what can be imitated but in what can be wholly condemned. The sexual freedom often attributed to him, his lack of moral inhibition, his possession of especially effective techniques for fulfilling his desires, give exponents of the paranoid style an opportunity to project and freely express unacceptable aspects of their own minds. Priests and Mormon patriarchs were commonly thought to have especial attraction for women, and hence licentious privilege. Thus Catholics and Mormons—later Negroes and Jews—lent themselves to a preoccupation with illicit sex. Very often the fantasies of true believers serve as strong sado-masochistic outlets, vividly expressed, for example, in the concern of anti-Masons with the alleged cruelty of Masonic punishments. Concerning this phenomenon, Davis remarks:

Masons disemboweled or slit the throats of their victims; Catholics cut unborn infants from their mothers' wombs and threw them to the dogs before their parents' eyes; Mormons raped and lashed recalcitrant women, or seared their mouths with red-hot irons. This obsession with details of sadism, which reached pathological proportions in much of the literature, showed a furious determination to purge the enemy of every admirable quality.[5]

Another recurring aspect of the paranoid style is the special significance that attaches to the figure of the renegade from the enemy cause. The anti-Masonic movement seemed at times to be the creation of ex-Masons; it certainly attached the highest significance and gave the most unqualified credulity to their revelations. Similarly anti-Catholicism used the runaway nun and the apostate priest, anti-Mormonism the ex-wife from the harem of polygamy; the avant-garde anti Communist movements of our time use the ex-Communist. In some part the special authority accorded the renegade derives from the obsession with secrecy so characteristic of such movements: the renegade is the man or woman who has been in the secret world of the enemy, and brings forth with him or her the final verification of suspicions which might otherwise have been doubted by a skeptical world. But I think there is a deeper eschatological significance attached to the person of the renegade: in the spiritual wrestling match between good and evil which is the paranoid's archetypal model of the world struggle,

---

[4] David Brion Davis: "Some Themes of Counter-Subversion: An Analysis of Anti-Masonic, Anti-Catholic, and Anti-Mormon Literature," *Mississippi Valley Historical Review,* XLVII (September 1960), 223.
[5] Ibid., p. 221.

the renegade is living proof that all the conversions are not made by the wrong side. He brings with him the promise of redemption and victory.

In contemporary right-wing movements a particularly important part has been played by ex-Communists who have moved rapidly, though not without anguish, from the paranoid left to the paranoid right, clinging all the while to the fundamentally Manichean psychology that underlies both. Such authorities on communism remind one of those ancient converts from paganism to Christianity of whom it is told that upon their conversion they did not entirely cease to believe in their old gods but converted them into demons.

A final aspect of the paranoid style is related to that quality of pedantry to which I have already referred. One of the impressive things about paranoid literature is precisely the elaborate concern with demonstration it almost invariably shows. One should not be misled by the fantastic conclusions that are so characteristic of this political style into imagining that it is not, so to speak, argued out along factual lines. The very fantastic character of its conclusions leads to heroic strivings for "evidence" to prove that the unbelievable is the only thing that can be believed. Of course, there are highbrow, lowbrow, and middlebrow paranoids, as there are likely to be in any political tendency, and paranoid movements from the Middle Ages onward have had a magnetic attraction for demi-intellectuals. But respectable paranoid literature not only starts from certain moral commitments that can be justified to many non-paranoids but also carefully and all but obsessively accumulates "evidence." Paranoid writing begins with certain defensible judgments. There *was* something to be said for the anti-Masons. After all, a secret society composed of influential men bound by special obligations could conceivably pose some kind of threat to the civil order in which they were suspended. There was also something to be said for the Protestant principles of individuality and freedom, as well as for the nativist desire to develop in North America a homogeneous civilization. Again, in our time innumerable decisions of the Second World War and the cold war can be faulted, and it is easy for the suspicious to believe that such decisions are not simply the mistakes of well-meaning men but the plans of traitors.

The typical procedure of the higher paranoid scholarship is to start with such defensible assumptions and with a careful accumulation of facts, or at least of what appear to be facts, and to marshal these facts toward an overwhelming "proof" of the particular conspiracy that is to be established. It is nothing if not coherent—in fact, the paranoid mentality is far more coherent than the real world, since it leaves no room for mistakes, failures, or ambiguities. It is, if not wholly rational, at least intensely rationalistic; it believes that it is up against an enemy who is as infallibly rational as he is totally evil, and it seeks to match his imputed total competence with its own, leaving nothing unexplained and comprehending all of reality in one overreaching, consistent theory. It is nothing if not "scholarly" in technique. McCarthy's 96-page pamphlet *Mc-*

Carthyism contains no less than 313 footnote references, and Mr. Welch's fantastic assault on Eisenhower, *The Politician,* is weighed down by a hundred pages of bibliography and notes. The entire right-wing movement of our time is a parade of experts, study groups, monographs, footnotes, and bibliographies. Sometimes the right-wing striving for scholarly depth and an inclusive world view has startling consequences: Mr. Welch, for example, has charged that the popularity of Arnold Toynbee's historical work is the consequence of a plot on the part of Fabians, "Labour Party bosses in England," and various members of the Anglo-American "liberal establishment" to overshadow the much more truthful and illuminating work of Oswald Spengler.[6]

What distinguishes the paranoid style is not, then, the absence of verifiable facts (though it is occasionally true that in his extravagant passion for facts the paranoid occasionally manufactures them), but rather the curious leap in imagination that is always made at some critical point in the recital of events. John Robison's tract on the Illuminati followed a pattern that has been repeated for over a century and a half. For page after page he patiently records the details he has been able to accumulate about the history of the Illuminati. Then, suddenly, the French Revolution has taken place, and the Illuminati have brought it about. What is missing is not veracious information about the organization, but sensible judgment about what can cause a revolution. The plausibility the paranoid style has for those who find it plausible lies, in good measure, in this appearance of the most careful, conscientious, and seemingly coherent application to detail, the laborious accumulation of what can be taken as convincing evidence for the most fantastic conclusions, the careful preparation for the big leap from the undeniable to the unbelievable. The singular thing about all this laborious work is that the passion for factual evidence does not, as in most intellectual exchanges, have the effect of putting the paranoid spokesman into effective two-way communication with the world outside his group—least of all with those who doubt his views. He has little real hope that his evidence will convince a hostile world. His effort to amass it has rather the quality of a defensive act which shuts off his receptive apparatus and protects him from having to attend to disturbing considerations that do not fortify his ideas. He has all the evidence he needs; he is not a receiver, he is a transmitter.

Since I have drawn so heavily on American examples, I would like to emphasize again that the paranoid style is an international phenomenon. Nor is it confined to modern times. Studying the millennial sects of Europe from the eleventh to the sixteenth century, Norman Cohn finds, in his brilliant book *The Pursuit of the Millennium,* a persistent psychological complex that closely resembles what I have been considering—a style made up of certain marked preoccupations and fantasies: "the megalomanic view of oneself as the Elect,

---

[6] *The Blue Book of the John Birch Society* (n.p., 1961), pp. 42–3.

wholly good, abominably persecuted yet assured of ultimate triumph; the attribution of gigantic and demonic powers to the adversary; the refusal to accept the ineluctable limitations and imperfections of human existence, such as transience, dissention, conflict, fallibility whether intellectual or moral; the obsession with inerrable prophecies . . . systematized misinterpretations, always gross and often grotesque . . . ruthlessness directed towards an end which by its very nature cannot be realised—towards a total and final solution such as cannot be attained at any actual time or in any concrete situation, but only in the timeless and autistic realm of phantasy."[7]

The recurrence of the paranoid style over a long span of time and in different places suggests that a mentality disposed to see the world in the paranoid's way may always be present in some considerable minority of the population. But the fact that movements employing the paranoid style are not constant but come in successive episodic waves suggests that the paranoid disposition is mobilized into action chiefly by social conflicts that involve ultimate schemes of values and that bring fundamental fears and hatreds, rather than negotiable interests, into political action. Catastrophe or the fear of catastrophe is most likely to elicit the syndrome of paranoid rhetoric.

In American experience, ethnic and religious conflicts, with their threat of the submergence of whole systems of values, have plainly been the major focus for militant and suspicious minds of this sort, but elsewhere class conflicts have also mobilized such energies. The paranoid tendency is aroused by a confrontation of opposed interests which are (or are felt to be) totally irreconcilable, and thus by nature not susceptible to the normal political processes of bargain and compromise. The situation becomes worse when the representatives of a particular political interest—perhaps because of the very unrealistic and unrealizable nature of their demands—cannot make themselves felt in the political process. Feeling that they have no access to political bargaining or the making of decisions, they find their original conception of the world of power as omnipotent, sinister, and malicious fully confirmed. They see only the consequences of power—and this through distorting lenses—and have little chance to observe its actual machinery. L. B. Namier once said that "the crowning attainment of historical study" is to achieve "an intuitive sense of how things do not happen."[8] It is precisely this

---

[7] *The Pursuit of the Millennium* (London, 1957), pp. 309–10; see also pp. 58–74. In the Middle Ages millenarianism flourished among the poor, the oppressed, and the hopeless. In Anglo-American experience, as Samuel Shepperson has observed, such movements have never been confined to these classes, but have had a more solid middle-class foundation. "The Comparative Study of Millenarian Movements," in Sylvia Thrupp (ed.): *Millennial Dreams in Action* (The Hague, 1962), pp. 49–52.

[8] L. B. Namier: "History," in Fritz Stern (ed.): *The Varieties of History* (New York, 1956), p. 375.

kind of awareness that the paranoid fails to develop. He has a special resistance of his own, of course, to such awareness, but circumstances often deprive him of exposure to events that might enlighten him. We are all sufferers from history, but the paranoid is a double sufferer, since he is afflicted not only by the real world, with the rest of us, but by his fantasies as well.

Reflective Questions

1. How do you account for the emergence of paranoia in American politics?

2. Is paranoia a common feature of social movements?

3. How is it that leaders who exemplify the paranoid style that Hofstadter describes are able to secure a following?

4. What suggestions do you have for eliminating or minimizing distrust, suspicion, insecurity, and paranoia from the character of American politics?

12 □ STUDENT ACTIVISTS AND HIGHER EDUCATION

Roger R. Woock

Professor Woock develops a paper designed to provide the basis for a more insightful understanding of the current unrest among student activists. He very perceptively cuts through the superfluous rhetoric and misleading images that often dominate the current polarization of generations, to reveal the gut issues that have led to confrontation. The author identifies the participants, their strengths, weaknesses, tactics, and issues. He concludes by offering five recommendations for reducing student criticism and revolts. In general, the recommendations suggest that administrators examine and act to eliminate the very realistic dysfunctional elements that students have so discernibly revealed within the system. □

"OUR EARTH IS DEGENERATE . . . CHILDREN NO LONGER OBEY THEIR PARENTS." From that 6,000-year-old lament carved in stone by an Egyptian priest down to the present day, social commentators have perennially decried the disobedience of the young of their times.

In an historical sense, there is nothing particularly new about the recent disturbances, uprisings or revolutions that have been taking place on American campuses. Nor are they unique geographically since students in societies as different as Mexico, France, Poland, the Soviet Union and Czechoslovakia have been complaining, struggling, rebelling and rioting against both their societies and their universities.

One seemingly new phenomenon that has disturbed the casual observer of the American student revolt is its apparent unity and organization. Similar

From *Bell Telephone Magazine*, January–February, 1969, pp. 20–25. Reprinted by permission of *Bell Telephone Magazine* and the author.

demands and tactics are used to confront university administration and local government officials across the country. Yet this supposed unity is more fiction than fact and is most probably a result of the coverage provided by the mass media. The tendency to see just one student movement and just one set of demands is unfortunate because it prevents a real understanding of the situation.

Who are the students involved?

"The present generation of young people in our universities is the best informed, the most intelligent, the most idealistic this country has ever known. This is the experience of teachers everywhere. It is also the most sensitive to public issues and the most sophisticated in political tactics. Perhaps because they enjoy the affluence to support their ideals today's undergraduate and graduate students exhibit as a group a higher level of social conscience than preceding generations."

This quotation from the Cox Commission Report, an analysis of the crisis at Columbia University, may well be true. But the first thing that needs to be said about students in American universities is that most of them are politically and socially uncommitted. In none of the recent student confrontations at Columbia, Wisconsin, Berkeley or at smaller colleges and universities throughout the country has student activity and participation involved anywhere near the majority. In a few cases the majority provided quiet and passive support and in many cases not even this.

The fact that demands have been made by a minority of university students does not, of course, reflect on their merit; nor does it reduce the seriousness of the situation since there is evidence that the student activists are of a higher intellectual and academic caliber than nonactivists.

University Reform Sought

Among those students who do participate in demonstrations and sit-ins, the largest number might fairly be labeled "liberal." These are students who are opposed to the Vietnam war, who believe that more nonwhites should be admitted to American colleges and universities, who would like to see stronger civil rights legislation, including open housing ordinances. Even the moderate National Student Association, a nationwide organization of college student governments, is concerned with these issues.

In addition to supporting these social goals, the liberal student is also interested in moderate university reform. He supports more student participation on university committees and increased contact between faculty members and students. The liberal student's view is that none of the social or university problems represent a fundamental failure of the system but rather mistakes or aberrations that can be removed by making the government aware of the citizen's desire and by consultation with university officials.

A smaller group of students may be reasonably called "radicals." These students support the same social and university goals as the liberal students but differ significantly in their judgment about the methods needed to achieve them. A radical student viewing the war in Vietnam, for example, is likely to judge it to be part of a larger pattern of American foreign policy rather than an isolated error. He views the "systematic exploitation" of nonwhite Americans not merely as casual cruelty but as an important part of the social structure of American society.

In the area of university life, the radical student views the deans and administrators as members of the power structure in society and, as such, very unlikely to willingly give up their power and authority. Radical students maintain that more disruptive tactics are likely to be successful; they believe sit-ins and lock-ins or lock-outs are necessary in order to achieve their objectives.

They argue, for example, that their tactics at Columbia University were in large measure successful. Of the three stated objectives, all have been in large measure achieved. The students were clearly responsible for stopping construction of the new gymnasium on the adjacent public park site used by Harlem residents; for Columbia severing its relationship with the Institute for Defense Analysis; and for the early resignation of Columbia's president, Grayson Kirk. In addition, during the fall semester Columbia made every effort to involve students in a great variety of university committees on which they were unrepresented before the Spring agitation.

Besides the inactive, liberal and radical students, there is another small group that may frankly be described as "revolutionary." These are students who are devoted to effecting radical change in the university and wish to use the university as a base for creating a revolutionary situation in the larger society. Although few in number and not very influential among other students, the revolutionaries, because of their extreme statements and occasional violent actions, have been focused on by the mass media.

When a Tom Hayden or a Mark Rudd calls for more Columbias or more Chicagos (i.e., the violent confrontation surrounding the Democratic convention last August), mass media present such statements as being representative of all active students in American universities. This is simply not true. The gap between revolutionary rhetoric and the real possibility of wide-scale violence or revolution à la France or Germany is a vast one.

The one issue which clearly unites the widest political spectrum of students is opposition to the war in Vietnam. This unpopularity is particularly widespread among young men of fighting age, since a personal stake in draft resistance must be added to the political, social and ideological reasons for opposing the war. It seems to be only on the Vietnam issue that the liberals, radicals or revolutionaries can persuade some of their inactive and uncommitted fellow students to join them. Even here the number of students who have been seriously active has been small. Participants in anti-Vietnam events at Columbia since May 1965 ranged from 18 engaged in a sit-in up to 800 who demonstrated against permitting the U.S. Marine Corps to set up recruiting tables on campus. Even the 800, however, represents a figure of less than five per cent of the total student body of Columbia University and Barnard College.

NONWHITES OFFER RALLYING POINT

The treatment of nonwhite Americans is the other social issue on which liberal, radical and revolutionary students can on occasion combine their efforts. Besides the general feeling of outrage and indignation at the role of minority group members in American society, students are particularly sympathetic to the special problems of nonwhite students in colleges and universities. At large urban universities that are situated adjacent to poor black communities, students view the effects of racial discrimination and poverty firsthand. These on-the-spot observations result in a considerably more militant posture. Add to this the fact that some large universities are, in effect, slum landlords, and the students' reactions are not especially difficult to understand.

Separate from but overlapping with the Vietnam war, race relations and poverty in the United States is the role of the university in relation to the larger society and its centers of power. Student activists want the university to become more independent from the power center in American society. This demand points to an extremely complicated problem, that is, the nature of the relationship between government-industry and the university.

SOME PROFESSORS SUPPORT ACTIVISTS

In recent years the special skills and knowledge of university faculty members have become increasingly important to both government and industry. John Kenneth Galbraith in *The New Industrial State* has gone so far as to suggest that knowledge itself is replacing capital as the most important input in the development of American industry. Another factor is the rising cost of education. Research grants are a vital source of income for most top-level universities in the United States.

Student activists' demands for a more independent stance are supported by a fairly sizeable number of faculty members. At the very least, many professors feel that American universities are maneuvering themselves into a position from which they will be unable to fulfill one of their historic and extremely important functions, that of criticizing society objectively. How much unbiased analysis may be expected from a political science department that has just received a $2 million Federal grant to devise more effective methods of political and para-military warfare? Other faculty members argue that it would be suicidal for the university to cut itself off from contact with and possible influence on the centers of power.

The major academic issues to which student activists have been addressing themselves are the nature and quality of the curriculum and the lack of contact between students and faculty in the university community. Criticisms of curriculum are related to the closeness of the particular discipline to problems in contemporary society. Most frequently and vociferously attacked have been sociology, political science, anthropology, psychology, economics, and to some extent, history. To a lesser degree philosophy, English literature and the humanities have been criticized, while practically no concern has been directed toward the natural sciences or mathematics. Student criticisms of the social sciences are twofold: (1) That by and large they avoid discussion and analysis of controversial problems in American society; and (2) When these problems are dealt with, it is from an "establishment" point of view.

Student demands for more freedom and individual responsibility in their personal lives should also be mentioned. Here again is an issue that unites a broad spectrum of students since almost all judge the traditional "in loco parentis" as old-fashioned.

Perhaps because of student unanimity, universities have been moving rapidly to provide the freedom demanded. Indeed, some universities have removed themselves from the role of parental guardian even before student demands could be organized and articulated. It is probably safe to say that within the next five to 10 years practically all nonreligiously affiliated institutions of higher learning will have relaxed social regulations to the point where students will have complete control of their social life.

STUDENTS NOT TAKEN SERIOUSLY

One of the more interesting aspects of the student revolt is the amount of attention it has captured in both the mass media and academic journals. More and more professors are rushing into print with their insights on either particular university conflicts or the general situation. Much of the academic writing is defensive in nature and treats student demands and behavior as without merit. Indeed, an entire recent issue of the quarterly, *The Public Interest,* was devoted to "The Universities" without once considering that something might be basically wrong with the structure of American higher education. One could better understand this inability to take students seriously or to consider them reasonable and rational if it did not come from academics who teach and presumably interact with students.

One might hazard a generalization that it is the failure of the academic community, both administrators and faculty, to take students seriously that forces them to become more radical both in goals and means. Students at Columbia had petitioned for a year to persuade the university to stop construction plans for the gymnasium. They got nowhere. In most cases their efforts were not even acknowledged. But in a week of forceful occupation of university buildings, the students succeeded in what they had been unable to achieve by more moderate means. The lessons of Columbia will not be lost on other students who have had little success in capturing the attention of their faculties and administrations.

Suggestions for solving problems presented by the student revolt are generally addressed solely to university administrators. In fact, they most often consist of sophisticated ways of conning students and/or splitting the activists into conflicting groups. It is quite clear that student demands cannot be dealt with solely by university administrators. Other groups must be involved.

The general public must stop viewing activists as either "kooks"—that is, irrational, emotional children—or, conversely, as dedicated agents of a vast conspiracy with connections in other parts of the world, particularly behind the Iron Curtain. Both of these views are widespread and are sometimes held by the same people.

The mass media can assist by devoting less attention to the sensational aspects of student activities, playing down the incidents of violence or force and the occasional extreme dress style, long hair, beards, beads, etc. The mass media should concentrate more on a reasonable in-depth analysis of what the students are saying and what changes they are seeking.

Alumni—particularly of those universities that have been the scenes of confrontations between students and administration and/or police—have a crucial role to play. So far alumni response has been confined to shrill demands for a university crackdown on dissidents. More helpful would be a position of openness and support for administrators. It is particularly difficult for an administrator to deal responsibly and effectively with student demands when he knows that alumni groups, along with boards of trustees or regents, are not likely to support agreements he makes with students.

Five Steps Recommended

Finally, there are a number of steps that the faculties and administrations of American universities must take:

1. Increase student participation in many areas of college life. This includes giving students the right to regulate their personal and social lives and adding students to almost all faculty and administrative committees. Tokenism—the appointment of one student or a "student adviser" to various committees—will clearly not be satisfactory to the activists.

2. Universities must meet demands for increased interaction between students and faculty. This must include a reduction in class size and an increase in seminars, tutorials and independent study under individual faculty direction. The problem here is financial. Indeed, many deans and college presidents argue

that they would like nothing better than to provide such increased contact. But they are unable to do so. Alumni and the general public must develop additional financial resources that would enable colleges and universities to provide a rich and meaningful intellectual experience.

3. Changes in the curriculum suggested by students must be carefully considered, especially in the social sciences. Courses that look objectively and critically at the whole structure of American society must be provided.

4. Serious attention must be given to the present relationship between the university and government and industry. At the very least this means a completely open and frank description of the relationship that exists. The university should be accountable to the public and its students for the research it does and the financial support it receives. Beyond that attempts should be made to consider carefully changes that would support the university as an independent and critical institution.

5. For universities located in urban areas, special attempts must be made to improve relationships between the university and the surrounding community. It may mean that universities must change their real estate practices to meet the needs and demands of the growing number of urban nonwhites.

These recommendations, of course, would not satisfy all students. Revolutionary students, for example, feel that the American university and American society *cannot change* themselves voluntarily. But the question of whether certain students would or would not be satisfied is really beside the point. What is important is the need to produce a better system of higher education in the United States.

By and large, student activists have been attempting—sometimes successfully, sometimes unsuccessfully, sometimes peacefully and with little publicity and sometimes forcefully and dramatically—to move the structure of the American university as they feel it should move in any event.

Students have been, by and large, more perceptive about the real problems of American society and higher education than have their mentors or the general public. It is the existence of this student creativity, imagination and spirit that should sustain the academic community and the American public in the difficult years which lie ahead for education.

Reflective Questions

1. Why might the more intellectual and academically oriented students be drawn to the activists position?

2. Were the student revolts that occurred at Columbia in 1965 inevitable? Explain.

3. Why have many professors been drawn to the side of the student activist?

4. Why have students selected the social sciences to suffer the brunt of curriculum criticism? Do you believe the criticism to be justifiable? Why or why not?

5. Analyze each of Woock's five recommendations for reducing student criticism. What alternatives or recommendations would appear the most promising? What additions would you contribute?

13 □ SORORITIES AND THE HUSBAND GAME

John Finley Scott

This paper probes a particular American middle-class technique of controlling mate selection among the young. Scott examines a thesis previously suggested by William Goode, which holds that social control is focused on the selection of the social circles within which youngsters are to move and thus fall in love. The sorority, according to Scott, serves to provide the college female with access to the "right kind" of potential mate. With college students encountering increased academic pressures, campus dating and courtship patterns appear to be undergoing an alteration. The change in dating practices may necessitate a drastic departure in the social activities of the sorority system. If the sorority system is unwilling or unable to adapt to the current change, its effectiveness, as a mode of mate selection, will undoubtably diminish. "When," states Scott, "parents learn that membership does not benefit their daughters, the sorority as we know it will pass into history." □

Marriages, like births, deaths, or initiations at puberty, are rearrangements of structure that are constantly recurring in any society; they are moments of the continuing social process regulated by custom there are institutionalized ways of dealing with such events.
  A. R. RADCLIFFE-BROWN, *African Systems of Kinship and Marriage*

IN MANY SIMPLE SOCIETIES, THE "INSTITUTIONALIZED WAYS" OF CONTROLLING marriage run to diverse schemes and devices. Often they include special living

Copyright © September/October 1965, by TRANS-action, Inc., New Brunswick, New Jersey. Reprinted by permission.

131

quarters designed to make it easy for marriageable girls to attract a husband: the Bontok people of the Philippines keep their girls in a special house, called the *olag,* where lovers call, sex play is free, and marriage is supposed to result. The Ekoi of Nigeria, who like their women fat, send them away to be specially fattened for marriage. Other peoples, such as the Yao of central Africa and the aborigines of the Canary Islands, send their daughters away to "convents" where old women teach them the special skills and mysteries that a young wife needs to know.

Accounts of such practices have long been a standard topic of anthropology lectures in universities, for their exotic appeal keeps the students, large numbers of whom are sorority girls, interested and alert. The control of marriage in simple societies strikes these girls as quite different from the freedom that they believe prevails in America. This is ironic, for the American college sorority is a pretty good counterpart in complex societies of the fatting houses and convents of the primitives.

Whatever system they use, parents in all societies have more in mind than just getting their daughters married; they want them married to the *right* man. The criteria for defining the right man vary tremendously, but virtually all parents view some potential mates with approval, some with disapproval, and some with downright horror. Many ethnic groups, including many in America, are *endogamous,* that is, they desire marriage of their young only to those within the group. In *shtetl* society, the Jewish villages of eastern Europe, marriages were arranged by a *shatchen,* a matchmaker, who paired off the girls and boys with due regard to the status, family connections, wealth, and personal attractions of the participants. But this society was strictly endogamous—only marriage within the group was allowed. Another rule of endogamy relates to social rank or class, for most parents are anxious that their children marry at least at the same level as themselves. Often they hope the children, and especially the daughters, will marry at a higher level. Parents of the *shtetl,* for example, valued *hypergamy*—the marriage of daughters to a man of higher status—and a father who could afford it would offer substantial sums to acquire a scholarly husband (the most highly prized kind) for his daughter.

The marriage problem, from the point of view of parents and of various ethnic groups and social classes, is always one of making sure that girls are available for marriage with the right man while at the same time guarding against marriage with the wrong man.

THE UNIVERSITY CONVENT

The American middle class has a particular place where it sends its daughters so they will be easily accessible to the boys—the college campus. Even for the families who worry about the bad habits a nice girl can pick up at college, it has become so much a symbol of middle-class status that the risk must be taken, the girl must be sent. American middle-class society has created an institution on the campus that, like the fatting house, makes the girls more attractive; like the Canary Island convent, teaches skills that middle-class wives need to know; like the *shtetl,* provides matchmakers; and without going so far as to buy husbands of high rank, manages to dissuade the girls from making alliances with lower-class boys. That institution is the college sorority.

A sorority is a private association which provides separate dormitory facilities with a distinctive Greek letter name for selected female college students. Membership is by invitation only, and requires recommendation by former members. Sororities are not simply the feminine counterpart of the college fraternity. They differ from fraternities because marriage is a more important determinant of social position for women than for men in American society, and because standards of conduct associated with marriage correspondingly bear stronger sanctions for women than for men. Sororities have much more "alumnae" involvement than fraternities, and fraternities adapt to local conditions and different living arrangements better than sororities. The college-age sorority "actives" decide only the minor details involved in recruitment, membership, and activities; parent-age alumnae control the important choices. The prototypical sorority is not the servant of youthful interests; on the contrary, it is an organized agency for controlling those interests. Through the sorority, the elders of family, class, ethnic, and religious communities can continue to exert remote control over the marital arrangements of their young girls.

The need for remote control arises from the nature of the educational system in an industrial society. In simple societies, where children are taught the culture at home, the family controls the socialization of children almost completely. In more complex societies, education becomes the province of special agents and competes with the family. The conflict between the family and outside agencies increases as children move through the educational system and is sharpest when the children reach college age. College curricula are even more challenging to family value systems than high school courses, and children frequently go away to college, out of reach of direct family influence. Sometimes a family can find a college that does not challenge family values in any way: devout Catholic parents can send their daughters to Catholic colleges; parents who want to be sure that daughter meets only "Ivy League" men can send her to one of the "Seven Sisters"—the women's equivalent of the Ivy League, made up of Radcliffe, Barnard, Smith, Vassar, Wellesley, Mt. Holyoke, and Bryn Mawr—if she can get in.

The solution of controlled admissions is applicable only to a small proportion of college-age girls, however. There are nowhere near the number of separate, sectarian colleges in the country that would be needed to segregate all the college-age girls safely, each with her own kind. Private colleges catering mostly to a specific class can still preserve a girl from meeting her social or economic inferiors, but the fees at such places are steep. It costs more to maintain a girl in the Vassar dormitories than to pay her sorority bills at a land-grant school. And even if her family is willing to pay the fees, the academic pace at the elite schools is much too fast for most girls. Most college girls attend large, tax-supported universities where the tuition is relatively low and where admissions policies let in students from many strata and diverse ethnic backgrounds. It is on the campuses of the free, open, and competitive state universities of the country that the sorority system flourishes.

When a family lets its daughter loose on a large campus with a heterogenous population, there are opportunities to be met and dangers to guard against. The great opportunity is to meet a good man to marry, at the age when the girls are most attractive and the men most amenable. For the girls, the pressure of time is urgent; though they are often told otherwise, their attractions are in fact primarily physical, and they fade with time. One need only compare the relative handicaps in the marital sweepstakes of a 38-year old single male lawyer and a single, female teacher of the same age to realize the urgency of the quest.

The great danger of the public campus is that young girls, however properly reared, are likely to fall in love, and—in our middle-class society at least—love leads to marriage. Love is a potentially random factor, with no regard for class boundaries. There seems to be no good way of preventing young girls from falling in love. The only practical way to control love is to control the type of men the girl is likely to encounter; she cannot fall dangerously in love with a man she has never met. Since kinship groups are unable to keep "undesirable" boys off the public campus entirely, they have to settle for control of counter-institutions within the university. An effective counter-institution will protect a girl from the corroding influences of the university environment.

There are roughly three basic functions which a sorority can perform in the interest of kinship groups:

- It can ward off the wrong kind of men.
- It can facilitate moving-up for middle-status girls.
- It can solve the "Brahmin problem"—the difficulty of proper marriage that afflicts high-status girls.

Kinship groups define the "wrong kind of man" in a variety of ways. Those who use an ethnic definition support sororities that draw an ethnic membership line; the best examples are the Jewish sororities, because among all the ethnic groups with endogamous standards (in America at any rate), only the Jews so far have sent large numbers of daughters away to college. But endogamy along class lines is even more pervasive. It is the most basic mission of the sorority to prevent a girl from marrying out of her group (exogamy) or beneath her class (hypogamy). As one of the founders of a national sorority artlessly put it in an essay titled "The Mission of the Sorority":

There is a danger, and a very grave danger, that four years' residence
in a dormitory will tend to destroy right ideals of home life and
substitute in their stead a belief in the freedom that comes from
community living . . . culture, broad, liberalizing, humanizing culture,
we cannot get too much of, unless while acquiring it we are weaned from
home and friends, from ties of blood and kindred.

A sorority discourages this dangerous weaning process by introducing the sisters only to selected boys; each sorority, for example, has dating relations with one or more fraternities, matched rather nicely to the sorority on the basis of ethnicity and/or class. (A particular sorority, for example, will have dating arrangements not with all the fraternities on campus, but only with those whose brothers are a class-match for their sisters.) The sorority's frantically busy schedule of parties, teas, meetings, skits, and exchanges keeps the sisters so occupied that they have neither time nor opportunity to meet men outside the channels the sorority provides.

Marrying Up

The second sorority function, that of facilitating hypergamy, is probably even more of an attraction to parents than the simpler preservation of endogamy. American society is not so much oriented to the preservation of the *status quo* as to the pursuit of upward mobility.

In industrial societies, children are taught that if they study hard they can get the kind of job that entitles them to a place in the higher ranks. This incentive actually is appropriate only for boys, but the emphasis on using the most efficient available means to enter the higher levels will not be lost on the girls. And the most efficient means for a girl—marriage—is particularly attractive because it requires so much less effort than the mobility through hard work that is open to boys. To the extent that we do socialize the sexes in different ways, we are more likely to train daughters in the ways of attracting men than to motivate them to do hard, competitive work. The difference in motivation holds even if the girls have the intelligence and talent required for status climbing on their own. For lower-class girls on the make, membership in a sorority can greatly improve the chances of meeting (and subsequently marrying) higher-status boys.

Now we come to the third function of the sorority—solving the Brahmin problem. The fact that hypergamy is encouraged in our society creates difficulties for girls whose parents are already in the upper strata. In a hypergamous system, high status *men* have a strong advantage; they can offer their status to a prospective bride as part of the marriage bargain, and the advantages of high status are often sufficient to offset many personal drawbacks. But a *woman's* high status has very little exchange value because she does not confer it on her husband.

This difficulty of high status women in a hypergamous society we may call the Brahmin problem. Girls of Brahmin caste in India and Southern white women of good family have the problem in common. In order to avoid the horrors of hypogamy, high status women must compete for high status men against women from all classes. Furthermore, high status women are handicapped in their battle by a certain type of vanity engendered by their class. They expect their wooers to court them in the style to which their fathers have accustomed them; this usually involves more formal dating, gift-giving, escorting, taxiing, etc., than many college swains can afford. If upper-stratum men are allowed to find out that the favors of lower class women are available for a much smaller investment of time, money, and emotion, they may well refuse to court upper-status girls.

In theory, there are all kinds of ways for upper-stratum families to deal with surplus daughters. They can strangle them at birth (female infanticide); they can marry several to each available male (polygyny); they can offer money to any suitable male willing to take one off their hands (dowries, groom-service fees). All these solutions have in fact been used in one society or another, but for various reasons none is acceptable in our society. Spinsterhood still works, but marriage is so popular and so well rewarded that everybody hopes to avoid staying single.

The industrial solution to the Brahmin problem is to corner the market, or more specifically to shunt the eligible bachelors into a special marriage market where the upper stratum women are in complete control of the bride-supply. The best place to set up this protected marriage-market is where many suitable men can be found at the age when they are most willing to marry—in short, the college campus. The kind of male collegians who can be shunted more readily into the specialized marriage-market that sororities run, are those who are somewhat uncertain of their own status and who aspire to move into higher strata. These boys are anxious to bolster a shaky self-image by dating obviously high-class sorority girls. The fraternities are full of them.

How does a sorority go about fulfilling its three functions? The first item of business is making sure that the girls join. This is not as simple as it seems, because the values that sororities maintain are more important to the older generation than to college-age girls. Although the sorority image is one of membership denied to the "wrong kind" of girls, it is also true that sororities have quite a problem of recruiting the "right kind." Some are pressured into pledging by their parents. Many are recruited straight out of high school, before they know much about what really goes on at college. High school recruiters present sorority life to potential rushees as one of unending gaiety; life outside the sorority is painted as bleak and dateless.

A membership composed of the "right kind" of girls is produced by the requirement that each pledge must have the recommendation of, in most cases, two or more alumnae of the sorority. Membership is often passed on from mother to daughter—this is the "legacy," whom sorority actives have to invite whether they like her or not. The sort of headstrong, innovative, or "sassy" girl who is likely to organize a campaign inside the sorority against prevailing standards is unlikely to receive alumnae recommendations. This is why sorority girls are so complacent about alumnae dominance, and why professors find them so bland and uninteresting as students. Alumnae dominance extends beyond recruitment, into the daily life of the house. Rules, regulations, and policy explanations come to the house from the national association. National headquarters is given to explaining unpopular policy by any available stratagem; a favorite device (not limited to the sorority) is to interpret all non-conformity as sexual, so that the girl who rebels against wearing girdle, high heels, and stockings to dinner two or three times a week stands implicitly accused of promiscuity. This sort of argument, based on the shrewdness of many generations, shames into conformity many a girl who otherwise might rebel against the code imposed by her elders. The actives in positions of control (house manager, pledge trainer or captain) are themselves closely supervised by alumnae. Once the right girls are initiated, the organization has mechanisms that make it very difficult for a girl to withdraw. Withdrawal can mean difficulty in finding alternative living quarters, loss of prepaid room and board fees, and stigmatization.

Sororities keep their members, and particularly their flighty pledges, in line primarily by filling up all their time with house activities. Pledges are required to study at the house, and they build the big papier-mache floats (in collaboration with selected fraternity boys) that are a traditional display of "Greek Row" for the homecoming game. Time is encompassed completely; activities are planned long in advance, and there is almost no energy or time available for meeting inappropriate men.

The girls are taught—if they do not already know—the behavior appropriate to the upper strata. They learn how to dress with expensive restraint, how to make appropriate conversation, how to drink like a lady. There is some variety here among sororities of different rank; members of sororities at the bottom of the social ladder prove their gentility by rigid conformity in dress and manner to the stereotype of the sorority girl, while members of top houses feel socially secure even when casually dressed. If you are born rich you can afford to wear Levi's and sweatshirts.

Preliminary Events

The sorority facilitates dating mainly by exchanging parties, picnics, and other frolics with the fraternities in its set. But to augment this the "fixer-uppers" (the American counterpart of the *shatchen*) arrange dates with selected boys;

their efforts raise the sorority dating rate above the independent level by removing most of the inconvenience and anxiety from the contracting of dates.

Dating, in itself, is not sufficient to accomplish the sorority's purposes.

GLOSSARY OF MARRIAGE TERMS

Endogamy: A rule or practice of marriage within a particular group.

Exogamy: A practice or rule of marriage only between persons who are *not* members of a well-defined group, such as one based on family or locality.

Hypergamy: The movement of a woman, through marriage, to a status *higher* than that to which she was born.

Hypogamy: The movement of a woman, through marriage, to a status *lower* than that to which she was born.

Polygyny: The marriage of one husband to two or more wives. It is not the same as *polygamy,* which simply means a plurality of mates irrespective of sex.

Dating must lead to pinning, pinning to engagement, engagement to marriage. In sorority culture, all dating is viewed as a movement toward marriage. Casual, spontaneous dating is frowned upon; formal courtship is still encouraged. Sorority ritual reinforces the progression from dating to marriage. At the vital point in the process, where dating must be turned into engagement, the sorority shores up the structure by the pinning ritual, performed after dinner in the presence of all the sorority sisters (who are required to stay for the ceremony) and attended, in its classic form, by a choir of fraternity boys singing outside. The commitment is so public that it is difficult for either partner to withdraw. Since engagement is already heavily reinforced outside the sorority, pinning ceremonies are more elaborate than engagements.

The social columns of college newspapers faithfully record the successes of the sorority system as it stands today. Sorority girls get engaged faster than "independents," and they appear to be marrying more highly ranked men. But what predictions can we make about the system's future?

All social institutions change from time to time, in response to changing conditions. In the mountain villages of the Philippines, the steady attacks of school and mission on the immorality of the *olag* have almost demolished it. Sororities, too, are affected by changes in the surrounding environment. Originally they were places where the few female college students took refuge from the jeers and catcalls of men who thought that nice girls didn't belong on campus.

They assumed their present, endogamy-conserving form with the flourishing of the great land-grant universities in the first half of this century.

ON THE BRINK

The question about the future of the sorority system is whether it can adapt to the most recent changes in the forms of higher education. At present, neither fraternities nor sororities are in the pink of health. On some campuses there are chapter houses which have been reduced to taking in non-affiliated boarders to pay the costs of running the property. New sorority chapters are formed, for the most part, on new or low-prestige campuses (where status-anxiety is rife); at schools of high prestige fewer girls rush each year and the weaker houses are disbanding.

University administrations are no longer as hospitable to the Greeks as they once were. Most are building extensive dormitories that compete effectively with the housing offered by sororities; many have adopted regulations intended to minimize the influence of the Greeks on campus activities. The campus environment is changing rapidly: academic standards are rising, admission is increasingly competitive and both male and female students are more interested in academic achievement; the proportion of graduate students seriously training for a profession is increasing; campus culture is often so obviously pluralist that the Greek claim to monopolize social activity is unconvincing.

The sorority as it currently stands is ill-adapted to cope with the new surroundings. Sorority houses were built to provide a setting for lawn parties, dances, and dress-up occasions, and not to facilitate study; crowding and noise are severe, and most forms of privacy do not exist. The sorority songs that have to be gone through at rushing and chapter meetings today all seem to have been written in 1915 and are mortifying to sing today. The arcane rituals, so fascinating to high school girls, grow tedious and sophomoric to college seniors.

But the worst blow of all to the sorority system comes from the effect of increased academic pressure on the dating habits of college men. A student competing for grades in a professional school, or even in a difficult undergraduate major, simply has not the time (as he might have had in, say, 1925) to get involved in the sorority forms of courtship. Since these days almost all the "right kind" of men *are* involved in demanding training, the traditions of the sorority are becoming actually inimical to hypergamous marriage. Increasingly, then, sororities do not solve the Brahmin problem but make it worse.

One can imagine a sorority designed to facilitate marriage to men who have no time for elaborate courtship. In such a sorority, the girls—to start with small matters—would improve their telephone arrangements, for the fraternity boy in quest of a date today must call several times to get through the busy signals, interminable paging, and lost messages to the girl he wants. They might arrange a private line with prompt answering and faithfully recorded messages, with an unlisted number given only to busy male students with a promising future. They would even accept dates for the same night as the invitation, rather than, as at present, necessarily five to ten days in advance, for the only thing a first-year law student can schedule that far ahead nowadays is his studies. Emphasis on fraternity boys would have to go, for living in a fraternity and pursuing a promising (and therefore competitive) major field of study are rapidly becoming mutually exclusive. The big formal dances would go (the fraternity boys dislike them now); the football floats would go; the pushcart races would go. The girls would reach the hearts of their men not through helping them wash their sports cars but through typing their term papers.

But it is inconceivable that the proud traditions of the sororities that compose the National Panhellenic Council could ever be bent to fit the new design. Their structure is too fixed to fit the changing college and their function is rapidly being lost. The sorority cannot sustain itself on students alone. When parents learn that membership does not benefit their daughters, the sorority as we know it will pass into history.

Reflective Questions

1. How may sororities be considered analogous to social-control techniques used in some "simple societies"?

2. How do sororities function to provide the "right men" for its members?

3. In what manner have campus dating practices been modified during the past decade?

4. What does the future appear to hold for the sorority system? How might sororities adapt to the changing social environment?

14 □ Making It in America

John P. Sisk

One of the most persistent challenges confronting American citizens is the ethic that one should be successful or "make it." In a literary fashion, John P. Sisk analyzes the ramifications of the "making it" orientation. Ambition, to the author, is a universal feeling. Equally universal, however, is the fear of not "making it." Making it in America is not an unmitigated blessing, since it implies contamination by a value system that may threaten one's integrity, that implies selling out to the "Bitch Goddess." In the whole process, Sisk feels that a writer faces the dilemma of being torn between truth, virtue, and purity and the impulse to gain affluence. One of the unresolved issues in an affluent competitively oriented system is the relation between success (money, power, fame, and the like) and intellectual honesty. Although one of the political consequences of "making it" implies determination by bourgeois values, Sisk claims that America is equally threatened by tyrannies of "virtue" from the left and the right. □

"Wherever the American writer goes, he finds before him the temptation to try to 'make it'," and his fear of doing so can be compulsive and crippling. The wages of ambition and success may be deplorable, according to the author of this essay, but the same can be true of "tyrannies of virtue," whether they emanate from literary critics, or from George Wallace on the right or Herbert Marcuse on the left.

Though neither seems to have been aware of the other's existence, Norman Podhoretz and James D. Watson were at Cambridge at the same time

From *The Atlantic Monthly,* December 1969, pp. 63–68. Copyright © 1969 by The Atlantic Monthly Company, Boston, Mass. Reprinted with permission.

during the early 1950s—two highly talented young Americans eager to reverse the legendary pattern by making it big in the Old World. Each succeeded spectacularly: Podhoretz at twenty-one published a critical essay on Lionel Trilling in *Scrutiny*, "the notoriously hardest nut to crack of all the magazines of its kind in the world." Watson at twenty-three discovered (with the assistance of Francis Crick and Maurice Wilkins) the structure and method of reproduction of the DNA molecule. When in 1962 Watson received the Nobel Prize for this achievement, Podhoretz, now just over thirty, was established as the successful editor of the new *Commentary*. A half dozen years later they were to publish, with *Making It* and *The Double Helix*, unexpectedly frank accounts of their ambition for success. In a foreword to the latter, Sir Lawrence Bragg warned that "those who figure in the book must read it in a forgiving spirit." Not everyone did; there was even talk of legal action on the part of Crick to enjoin the book. As might have been predicted, however, Watson was neither as widely blamed nor as slow to be forgiven as Podhoretz, who knew as he wrote that in confessing to a "dirty little secret" he was placing himself beyond forgiveness in some quarters.

And yet *Making It* is in a thoroughly respectable American tradition—that of the exemplary confession of the successful man. The first great example in our literature is Benjamin Franklin's *Autobiography*. It is not an easy book to get into focus, partially because we come at Franklin by way of later versions of the success story that have the effect of diminishing him, partially too because people like D. H. Lawrence have so fouled the air around Franklin that clear vision is impossible. In any event, Franklin is likely to come through to us as a smug, hypocritically venal, and meanly rational person who took snuff and "used" venery; if we catch any sense of the exemplary in his book, we are likely to hold that against him also, since we find it hard to understand how a man can be genuinely honest and at the same time aware of his own exemplary qualities.

Podhoretz' book is exemplary, too, but he is much more self-conscious about the issue of material success. Franklin is able to be at ease with it because he writes in a world that sees no necessary contradiction between the selfish and the altruistic. Everyone remembers his famous footnote: "Nothing so likely to make a man's fortune as virtue." Probably there is irony in the remark, but the whole book proves that Franklin also means it seriously.

And even a transcendentalist like Emerson, who was quite aware of the menace of State Street, could sound very much like Franklin on the subject of making it. Thus, writing of the dead Thoreau, and remembering that "he seemed born for great enterprise and command," Emerson could not

help counting it a fault in him that he had no ambition. Wanting this, instead of engineering for all America, he was the captain of a huckleberry party. Pounding beans is good to the end of pounding empires one of these days; but if, at the end of years, it is still only beans!

Emerson here is giving expression to the American fear of the missed opportunity to develop a potential to the fullest possible extent and in a manner sufficiently public so that there can be no doubt about the matter. Of course we have learned to say that Emerson had it all wrong, that Thoreau pounding his beans made it colossally, after all, without any of Emerson's vulgar ambition. But if one goes along with the late Perry Miller (see his *Consciousness in Concord*), Thoreau was no stranger to this fear of the missed opportunity; he knew himself born for great enterprise and command, and after the failure of *A Week on the Concord and Merrimack Rivers,* and later of *Walden,* had to confront (with what contained despair?) the "defeat of high expectations" and the realization that he was going to have to make it, if at all, in the isolation of his *Journal.* So we get that chilling image of him in the last year of his life packing the thirty-nine notebooks of that *Journal* into a yellow pine box, not comforted by the knowledge that he would ultimately become "our" Thoreau and so make it as few Americans have.

We do the same thing for Melville: extend what is for us the triumph of *Moby Dick* back into Melville's life, as if the ultimate certainty of that triumph more than compensated for the growing sense of failure after high expectations that must have been the preliminary to his final nineteen years of obscurity as a customs inspector. And who would have been better placed to appreciate the bitter irony and the coffinlike confinement of that yellow pine box than the man who created Ishmael?

In America, as Tocqueville observed, ambition is the universal feeling, and one might add the obvious corollary that the fear of not making it is no less universal. Certainly to be a writer in America is to be hounded by this fear, confronted as he is with the evidence that his society places a relatively low value on activities that do not make it. And his fear of not making it is in relation to his dream of making it—a relationship that helps to explain why it was that, at a time when Fitzgerald was making it big, all the stories that came into his head had that "touch of disaster" in them. The man who packed away the thirty-nine notebooks and the man who created Ahab must indeed have had Gatsby-like dreams, and their experiences of failure must have been correspondingly painful. Unlike Gatsby, they had to live on after their discoveries of illusion. Dreiser tells their story in *Sister Carrie:* Hurstwood is the dramatic analogue of the writer who, having been given every reason to expect success as his due, must then live with failure. Hurstwood's declension from the glamorous affluence of the Chicago nightclub to a pauper's suicide repeats Melville's long decline into the oblivion of the New York customs; as he turns on the flophouse gas one hears Thoreau nailing the top on that yellow pine box, and perhaps between blows of the hammer catches an echo of that shot in Ketchum, Idaho, that rang around the world.

But if the writer in America is afraid of not making it, he is at least as afraid of making it, since to make it in America is to risk contamination by a value system that appears to threaten his integrity as a writer—and his chance to make it in a more enduring way. The ways of the Bitch Goddess are subtle: she even tempted Henry James (and who can say that if he had known how to sin he might not have fallen?). The Bitch Goddess means kitsch, and kitsch, as Clement Greenberg pointed out in his essay "Avant-Garde and Kitsch," is not only virulent but irresistibly attractive. Its traps are laid in the preserves of genuine culture; it exists deceptively on many levels, some of them "high enough to be dangerous to the naïve seeker of true light."

Greenberg's thirty-year-old *Partisan Review* essay is useful background reading for Podhoretz' book, concerned as the book is with the connection between the study and production of literature and that contempt for success that is the strong underside of the fear of making it. This is especially true given the part *Partisan Review* played in inducing in American literary intellectuals a pathology about kitsch that anticipated the Birchers' pathology about Communism. Of course, to get the lines straight one must go back farther than this—at least all the way to Romanticism, with its glorification of the artist's private and ascetically won vision and its discovery (in part creation) of the unbridgeable gap between the artist and the kitsch-hungry public that this vision entailed. But if we go back only to 1856 and Baudelaire on Poe we find this:

All the documents that I have read lead to the conviction that for
Poe the United States was nothing more than a vast prison which he
traversed with the feverish agitation of a being made to breathe a
sweeter air—nothing more than a great gas-lighted nightmare—and that
his inner, spiritual life, as a poet or even as a drunkard, was nothing
but a perpetual effort to escape the influence of this unfriendly
atmosphere.

This sounds very much like a mid-twentieth-century American writer (say James Baldwin, John Cheever, or Norman Mailer at an *Esquire*-sponsored symposium earlier in this decade) on the subject of the corruptions of the environment in which, and in part because of which, he has been able to make it.

The American writer in this mood may sound hypocritical, or at least downright ungrateful, to some of his supporting public, but his fear of being corrupted is nevertheless genuine enough, particularly given the extent to which he is compelled by the modernist tradition that requires the artist to serve beauty and truth with the same ascetic purity with which the Desert Fathers served God. He keeps his discipline at the cost of eternal vigilance, and yet ironically the always likely end of discipline (for a Hemingway no less than his Puritan forebears) is success and corruption. Affluence and ease make him doubt his identity and authenticity, for they are what he traditionally defines himself as against, the means he uses to experience his own virtue and authority. The Desert Fathers made a similar use of their image of a godless civilization and its tantalizing, discipline-destroying lusts.

When discipline goes, the artist, like the saint, is threatened by the most enervating of dreams—that of joy separated from anguish. In proportion as the artist allows this pair to separate he is left naked to adversity, which is how A. E. Hotchner represents Hemingway in their conversation outside the Mayo Clinic. In response to the question, "Papa, why do you want to kill yourself?" Hemingway answers "in his old deliberative way":

What do you think happens to a man going on sixty-two when he
realizes that he can never write the books and stories he promised
himself? Or do any of the other things he promised himself in the
good days?

Toward the end of his confession Podhoretz recounts his four-day experience at Paradise Island, Huntington Hartford's plush Carribbean resort. Here he begins to discover that

in an affluent society and a post-middlebrow culture, not to expect was a
way of not demanding *what was now there to be had,* and that not
demanding was the surest way of not getting. I left Paradise Island
resolving to demand.

No discovery could be more in the American grain or in the Alger tradition. The trouble for many of Podhoretz' readers, however, is not that he makes this discovery, but that it isn't followed by the expected further discovery: the ultimate illusion of the first one. What is unforgivable to them is that *Making It* doesn't turn out to be a latter-day version of Fitzgerald's "Crack-Up."

For some of his contemporaries the four confessional essays Fitzgerald published in *Esquire* and *American Cavalcade* between February, 1936, and October, 1937, were just as objectionable as *Making It* is now, if for not quite the same reasons. There was no "new honesty" to support Fitzgerald. His story, nevertheless, has become the classic statement of what we expect from the writer who has attempted to make it; and its central message is that behind the green light on Daisy Buchanan's dock, there is nothing (the man who wrote *The Great Gatsby* knew better than this). The writer's fear of making it is in part a protection against this discovery, as though he couldn't trust the

Jay Gatsby in himself out of his sight. Podhoretz may seem to be saying that we ought to have more faith in the green light; actually he is saying that in our nervousness about making it we have made the green light into a negative idol. It is easy to envy the world of James Watson's *Double Helix;* it is apparently little troubled with green dock lights.

The writer-intellectual's ambivalence about the ambition for success makes the recent work of George Plimpton especially interesting. For Podhoretz, the significant thing about Plimpton was that in the waning hours of the fifties he

brought writers and intellectuals into contact with the rich, the
powerful, and the fashionable for the first time in any of their lives,
and thereby did much to increase the standing and power of the
former, if not the comfort and happiness of the latter.

This reading casts Plimpton in the role of a two-culture bridger, and would probably give Podhoretz' old mentor, F. R. Leavis, as little comfort as C. P. Snow's famous lecture did. But Plimpton functions much more significantly as a tension-reliever for problems peculiar to the American writer. His three "out of my league" books, of which *Paper Lion* is something of a classic, are confessions of the writer-intellectual's failure to make it in a world where the attention of participants and spectators is fiercely concentrated on making it in terms highly acceptable to the American public.

Plimpton (or that somewhat fictive version of him that appears as the "hero" of the series) reconciles in a comic context the writer's sharply opposed fears of making it and not making it. Because by accident of birth he already has it made, he can afford the therapeutic and ironic game of turning the Alger-Franklin legend upside down; and since in the end he succeeds, as a writer, by failure, his story is both revenge on that legend and a comic version of what has so often been the grim historical case with the writer. At the same time he is himself a comic and relaxing version of a figure especially compelling to the modern writer: the hero who throws himself intrepidly into experience for which he has little or no preparation out of a conviction that to do otherwise is to risk spiritual death. He courts failure as Perry Miller helps us to see that Thoreau did, yet he does not fail as Thoreau did (although he will probably not succeed as Thoreau did either).

Podhoretz announces as the second purpose of his confession a diagnosis "of the curiously contradictory feelings our culture instills in us toward the ambition for success, and toward each of its various goals: money, power, fame, and social position." So far as his diagnosis goes it is accurate, but in the end it is not sufficiently ecological. It is dominated by the image of a conflict between the writer and a society whose values threaten literature. This is a maplike view of the relationship; the territorial fact is much more complex. For if, as

Greenberg says, "the avant-garde remained attached to bourgeois society precisely because it needed its money," that society remains attached to the avant-garde because it is afraid of what will happen to it if it is cut loose from avant-garde values.

Podhoretz more than once reminds his readers that there are other ways of losing one's purity than by pursuit of monetary profit; nevertheless, in America, the Bitch Goddess means money more than she means anything else. In American literature the good man is conventionally and hyperbolically defined by his disregard of money and his determination by some self-transcending commitment, usually love. Huckleberry Finn, with his utter carelessness about his six-thousand-dollar reward and his utter devotion to one of the wretched of the earth, acts out Thoreau's intransigent formula: "Absolutely speaking, the more money the less virtue." It is money that has corrupted the worlds in which we find Carrie Meeber, Clyde Griffiths, George Willard, George Babbitt, Nick Carraway, Dick Diver, Ike McCaslin, and Holden Caulfield. It is the rich with their belief "that every day should be fiesta" who break into the world of Hemingway's *A Moveable Feast* to corrupt both the love and the writing. Therefore the writer as good man in the bad world will turn his back as dramatically on money as Sherwood Anderson represents himself turning his back on his money-making paint factory, risking all to save his soul. That Anderson's account may be as much heroic fiction as history is beside the point; it is his version of the writer's salvation story, his midrash, and it is an important means for maintaining the writer's morale (of course it is also a powerful device for suppressing Podhoretz' dirty little secret).

At the same time, the Huck Finn-Thoreau hard line about money is no less admired in the world of popular culture, in which the good man tends similarly to be defined by his willingness to put love or a commitment to some self-transcending value ahead of money. Alger's heroes, for instance, always put virtue ahead of money; it is simply that the virtues they take a stand on are the ones that make money in Alger's context (in Hemingway's context many of the same virtues are on heroic display, but they are much less profitable—except for the author). In conventional American romantic comedy true lovers define themselves by their saintlike rejection of money, as a consequence of which it is generally made clear that money will never be a problem: Cupid simply turns out to be Daddy Warbucks in disguise. The "business" fiction of the late Cameron Hawley was successful in part because it was able to update Alger's subordination of acquisitiveness to virtue. Ayn Rand's fictional world reeks of virtue, for all its emblematic dollar signs.

This "virtuous" disdain of money by a culture passionately devoted to its acquisition and accumulation strikes the writer-intellectual as the most palpable hypocrisy, one more sign of the corruption of the culture that threatens him on all sides. But there is more than hypocrisy in the popular disdain of money.

There is exactly that effort to hold before itself exemplary models of the virtue most likely to protect it from dangerous excess that one would expect in an acquisitive society. Highbrow, lowbrow, and middlebrow approve of Huck's carelessness about the reward money; the consequences of ceasing to give at least lip service to this carelessness are too frightening.

This ambivalence about money is repeated in the public's ambivalence about the writer-intellectual. In so far as the latter attacks the Bitch Goddess, he attacks an idol intricately involved with public pieties and comforts; but at the same time there is a real public awareness, however unarticulated, of the writer's necessary cybernetic function. Along with Hippies, Yippies, and Black Panthers, he is not only a luxury the culture can afford (a luxury which will be dispensed with when the public becomes convinced that it is too expensive) but an absolute necessity if the culture is to keep itself under some kind of control and to mitigate the effects of the hypocrisies and self-delusions it is prone to while striving mightily to make it.

Part of the truth, then, is that the avant-garde is always a function of the bourgeois: its conscience, to put it in conventional terms, as well as an expression of its anxiety about order and the consequences of excessive specialization. The cultural assignment of the writer in America is to counter the culture lest it destroy itself, deny itself too much life, in the pursuit of dangerously limited ends. The culture even demands an exemplary purity in the writer, which he is inclined to think of as strictly a matter of his own heroic choice, just as earlier cultures needed and demanded the purity of troglodytes and pillar-dwelling ascetics. In the grossest economic terms, this means that the public still derives great comfort from the image of the writer starving in a garret to bequeath to the world immortal manuscripts. Few of us can live without some kind of assurance that it is possible to make it in terms more permanent than those that immediately rule our lives. We need to believe that it is ultimately possible to walk out of the paint factory to a larger life.

The writer accepts this cultural assignment somewhat less meekly than Christ accepted his cross. In a way he is a trapped man; he cannot reject the assignment, however mixed his feelings about making it may be, for the disjunctive terms—either accept or be damned—are after all his own. How much of the virulence in the traditional avant-garde attack on kitsch, then, in an expression of his frustration at this entrapment and a desire to be revenged on the responsible forces? How much of Mark Twain's eruption was actually rage at the predicament his authentic talent had gotten him into? It is, after all, the predicament not only of the writer but of the American, who is torn between his historic impulse to travel, however Spartanly, toward the light, and his impulse to affluence. When a writer makes this predicament his subject, as Fitzgerald does, he endlessly fascinates us.

In any event, the really subversive thing about *Making It* is Podhoretz' refusal to be caught any longer in the trap of the traditional assignment, even though the full context of this refusal isn't in the book. His own exemplary figure for this refusal is Norman Mailer, whom Podhoretz sees as performing an experiment on himself in public:

> ... trying to prove that the best way for an American to deal with the ambition for worldly success—an ambition the American male can as easily escape as he can get away with not going to school—was to throw himself unashamedly into it in the hope of coming up again on the other side.

This is a romantic formula, and it suggests Stein's paradoxical philosophy in Conrad's *Lord Jim:* "The way is to the destructive element submit yourself, and with the exertions of your hands and feet on the water make the deep, deep sea keep you up." But long before Conrad and Podhoretz the Fathers of the Desert had their own version (I quote from Helen Waddell's *Desert Fathers*): "If temptation befall thee in the place thou dost inhabit, desert not the place in the time of temptation: for if thou dost, wheresoever thou goest, thou shalt find what thou fliest before thee." Wherever the American writer goes he finds before him the temptation to try to make it. Stein and Mailer may be right: one can easily waste one's energies simply removing obstacles or fighting temptation, and then be forced to dignify this waste by making an idol out of one's discipline. Sisyphus interminably rolling his stone can be put into a context where he is a figure of futility: a man bound forever to a preliminary action. Avant-garde writing has always been cursed with its preoccupation with the preliminary action of trying not to make it in the vulgar bourgeois world, just as the Fathers were cursed with the preliminary action of fighting off lustful thoughts in the interest of safeguarding an image of purity so extreme that it could only predispose them to lustful thoughts.

The melodramatic intensity of this conflict of lust and virtue (the conflict may now appear to have been much more clear-cut when Greenberg wrote his essay) is responsible for the "critical overkill" about which Podhoretz complains: the intransigent measurement of contemporary literature against impossible standards of purity in order to find it sadly wanting—especially if that literature makes it with the large audience, as Mailer's fiction has. It is hard to distinguish critical overkill from the proper application of uncompromising standards (which, for instance, was Podhoretz' own unfavorable but attention-getting review of Bellow's *Herzog?*). One important difference, however, is that critical overkill, like other forms of overreaction, is strongly determined by factors behind the scene for which the apparent subject of criticism is a convenient metaphor (as T. S. Eliot's work has become a convenient metaphor for over-killers like Karl Shapiro). Criticism of the sort that Podhoretz complains about is damaging to contemporary writers because it insists on treating them as preliminary to a crucial issue: the traditional necessity to hold the line against threatening lusts. The writer is in effect kept subordinated to the exigencies of a national cultural melodrama—and God help him if he happens to come on the scene at a moment when the villain is particularly menacing. Perhaps it was the pressure of such a moment that explains Greenberg's observation to Podhoretz that *Commentary* had from the beginning been a middlebrow magazine.

In proportion as the writer is himself caught up in this melodrama he tends to be a compelled ascetic, overdetermined and perhaps driven half mad by the lusts of an affluent society; and the larger action he is part of inclines him to court failure as a sign of salvation. The ideal writer in this melodrama, the artist-saint, would have lived a completely anonymous life, so that when his yellow pine box is opened after his obscure death the rarefied contents can be valued in complete isolation from any contaminating historical context, since any conceivable historical context is bound to be unworthy of it. Flaubert must have had such an ideal in mind when he wrote to his mistress, Louise Colet, about his dream of a "book dependent on nothing external . . . which would have almost no subject" since the finest works "are those that contain the least subject matter." At this extreme, art is an act of mortification, the perfect image of which we find in Miss Waddell's book. Here the Abbot Paul labors daily to fill his cave with salable merchandise woven out of palm leaves, then at the end of the year burns all that he has carefully wrought and starts over. Thoreau, who was intrigued with the idea of a periodic burning, and who once almost burned up Concord, would have understood and applauded the act.

Art, the product of the heroically isolated and alienated artist, turned in upon itself in pursuit of Flaubert's ideal; it became abstract, "pure," technique-conscious, arcane; and its compelling symbol became, as Frank Kermode points out in *Romantic Image,* the female dancer whose face was utterly devoid of intellectual meaning and human expression. This was the extreme, of course, and few avant-garde writers could be this extreme since they had to survive as writers. Hence a favorite strategy involved not so much an avoidance of subject matter as a self-conscious avoidance of the subject matter the corrupt bourgeois world expected them to work with. It also involved an exploitation of subject matter calculated—because of its eccentricity, ugliness, morbidity, violence, or perversity—to shock bourgeois readers, and eventually to develop in them tastes that could be catered to profitably by both avant-garde and kitsch writers. One consequence is the void about which Irving Kristol speaks: a void into which "spills a debased version of avant-garde culture." So we have our present confusion. Is Andy Warhol a jet-age Da Vinci or a hoax which we use the media to perpetrate on ourselves? Is Gore Vidal's *Myra Breckinridge* kitsch or a mockery of the efforts of kitsch to be avant-garde? Is Truman Capote's *In Cold Blood* kitsch trying to be avant-garde or avant-garde trying to be kitsch?

It is unlikely, at any rate, that either Vidal or Capote is much bothered by what Kermode calls "the twin concepts of the isolated artist and the supernatural image." Here Thoreau is still our greatest champion. This is why, as Perry Miller makes clear, he came so close to having no subject. "He told himself," says Miller, "that a man was fortunate who could get through life with no reputation." But in the last years, Miller continues, "these exclamations on the bigness of the little become a nervous tic, cease to carry any conviction." Hence Miller is led to wonder what would have become of Thoreau had he achieved at least such a modest success as Emerson did. Perhaps, captivated as he was by the image of himself as Apollo laboring in the fields of Admetus, he did not dare risk the effort, since any success less than that of a god would have been as intolerable as the attempt to realize it would have been self-destructive. And Miller's point is really Podhoretz': the American writer's fear of making it can be compulsive and crippling.

It can also have disturbing political consequences in a democracy in which making it always implies some determination by bourgeois values. Democracy provides an enclave in which a Thoreau can exist; nevertheless, as everyone knows, Thoreau occupies that enclave with a dim view of democracy, indeed of all political activity. He is as intransigent about politics as he is about making it, and so perhaps gives expression to democracy's doubts about itself. His political position is not so much anarchist as Olympian and aristocratic. In fact, about the time that *Walden* was in the process of failing as a publishing venture, Baudelaire, outraged at Poe's fate, was writing "that it must be difficult to think and write readily in a country which has millions of rulers, a country without a great capital and without an aristocracy."

The frank expression of a bias against democracy is hardly an available option to the American writer-intellectual: at this point in the twentieth century all namable alternatives to democracy have been too thoroughly discredited or appropriated by the right. His standing temptation, however, is to suspect that a society which so vigorously produces, consumes, and profits from kitsch cannot be trusted with political power. The negative attitude toward making it, and toward popular culture, which Podhoretz first encountered at Columbia, is one expression of this suspicion. It is inevitable than that his attempt to expose the dirty little secret should turn out to have a political dimension that becomes clearer as the book goes along and that culminates in the next to last chapter. Here Podhoretz defines his own attitude toward America against the uncompromising austerities of the *New York Review,* which he sees as mainly serving the "objective of proving how dreadful the United States was."

Podhoretz is really making the point that too often the writer-intellectual's preoccupation with the dreadfulness of an America in which material success is the overriding interest is the expression of a crippling concern with his own virtue. It is also an expression of the breakdown of the traditional distinction between highbrow, middlebrow, and lowbrow that once made the world of the writer-intellectual so coherent. Kristol, like Susan Sontag, is convinced that these distinctions have ceased to be meaningful. Perhaps, however, it would be more accurate to say that the old distinctions have been transmuted, with some desperation, into political terms so that the ancient enemy can be attacked as intransigently as ever.

One of the virtues of *Making It* is its ironic awareness that an intransigent virtue, whether in art or politics, is tyrannous and therefore a vice. The book is written in the awareness that America, not simply culture, is threatened by tyrannies of virtue from the left and the right: from Jerry Rubin and Herbert Marcuse no less than from Robert Welch and George Wallace. Podhoretz is in the position of St. Augustine, who, knowing all too well how the lusts of civilization might drive one to the virtues of the desert, still resisted the lure of the desert as a distraction he could not afford. Podhoretz has come to believe that the dirty little secret hides a similar distraction. We really do not have to choose between Huntington Hartford's Paradise Island and a cabin at Walden Pond, he seems to be saying, and the traditional conviction that we do have to choose disturbs our politics, our literature, and our private lives.

Reflective Questions

1. How does the competitive struggle for success generate human casualties?

2. Do positive benefits come from a competitive struggle and materialistic orientation?

3. Can an emphasis on success exert strains toward illegitimate and nonconforming behavior?

4. Against what standards might one best evaluate the adequacy or worthiness of his life?

15 □ PSYCHEDELICS AND RELIGION: A SYMPOSIUM

Raziel Abelson □ Allen Ginsberg □ Michael Wyschogrod

The following article, edited by Raziel Abelson, is drawn from a symposium on drugs held in 1967 at New York University. The primary purpose of this article, as described by Abelson, "is to discuss the religious and philosophical aspects of the so-called 'consciousness expanding' drugs." Allen Ginsberg argues the value of using hallucinogenic drugs in seeking a more intense religious experience, while Michael Wyschogrod describes drug use, in a religious context, as an attempt to develop instant mysticism. Wyschogrod's argument is not based on the morality or legality of drug use, but on the artificiality of religious experience stemming from psychedelic drugs. Abelson provides, in his post mortem, a very careful critique of the positions taken by Ginsberg and Wyschogrod. □

INTRODUCTION □ Raziel Abelson

THE PURPOSE OF THIS SYMPOSIUM IS TO DISCUSS THE RELIGIOUS AND philosophical aspects of the so-called "consciousness expanding" drugs, particularly LSD and marijuana. It occurs to me that the title of this symposium is much too pretentious and stuffy; I would prefer to call it something simpler and more cozy. I suggest we call this a "Trip-in," for a reason not quite what you would naturally think. My reason is a personal one: it has to do with various trips I have made recently and a new one I am reluctant to take until I can see a good reason for it.

I am particularly interested in the subject of our discussion because of my feeling of closeness to the generation that has made it an issue, the generation

This article first appeared in THE HUMANIST, September/December 1967, and is reprinted by permission.

that came of age or will come of age in the 1960's. I consider it an extraordinarily interesting generation, the most exciting that I have had contact with. My own generation of the 40's was, I think, not a bad one; it was interested in its fellowmen, it was dynamic and hard working, it fought a world war against barbarism, but it was not as free as the present one because it was enslaved to ideologies. For the conservative prejudices of our parents we substituted the radical and neo-Puritanical prejudices of Marxism and Freudianism. I began to teach in the 1950's, and the generation of students who attended my lectures in that decade was, I think, the dullest, most boring of my time. It was enslaved to things far worse than ideologies: to chrome-plated Cadillacs, large houses, good jobs and social status. Its heroes were McCarthy on the "right" and Eisenhower on the "left." I first began to enjoy teaching in the 60's, because only then did I feel a rapport with students, whom I found so remarkably free that I felt myself liberated by them—free of pretentious ideology, free of mechanical rules of grammar, spelling, etiquette and sexual behavior, free of parental authoritarianism, of superstitions and phobias, willing to explore and appreciate any kind of human experience, able to say, like Marsiglio of Padua: "Nothing human is alien to me." Unfortunately, my age disqualifies me from full, card-carrying membership in this new generation, but, unlike Lewis Feuer and Ronald Reagan, I recognize its superiority to my own and I would like to be at least an honorary or associate member. For this reason, I have tried to share its experience by taking various "trips" with it. In 1963 I took a trip on a rickety old school bus at four in the morning, to the Washington March for civil rights legislation. The following summer I took a trip to Mississippi to observe the Freedom Schools and voter registration drive; although I wasn't there long, I did get a taste of the "agony and the ecstasy" of the students who fought non-violently and valiantly for reason and decency. I believe that summer of 1964 was the most glorious moment in the history of American youth; it was the moment at which the older generations began to look to the youth for the leadership they did not have the courage to assume. Two summers later I took another trip on a rickety old school bus, full of students, to march on Washington to end the war in Viet Nam, and this year I marched with them in New York, surrounded by Viet Cong banners and hippies with bananas, flowers, and electric guitars. Up to that point, the generation of the 60's had always turned me on. their skeptical rebelliousness and their intense social involvement seemed to me to promise a far better world when they would take control. But something very disturbing has been happening in the last two years. This generation, that created in me and many others so much hope for the future, has itself lost hope and nerve, and has turned from social concern inward toward its own private experience: it has turned from iconoclasm to quietism, from humanistic liberalism to passivity and drugs. The revolutionary generation is "copping out."

The "trips" I had taken with it were all outward, other-centered, and to get thing done that needed doing. Now, if I listen to the proselytes of Liberation Through Drugs, I am to take a trip in the exact opposite direction—inward, toward passivity, hallucination, inconsequence. Maybe I can understand the motives for this shift into reverse gear—disappointment at the snail's pace of social reforms, moral revulsion and despair about the abominable, uncontrollable and endless war in Viet Nam—but motives are not reasons, and I would like to know the *reason* why, before I take this trip backward into darkness. I am in search of enlightenment: why are drug induced fantasies better than the light of cool reason; why is sensual over-stimulation more worthwhile than the pursuit of rational social ideals? I look to two extremely well-qualified experts to enlighten me on these questions. From Mr. Ginsberg I hope for a clear answer to the question, "Why?" and from Professor Wyschogrod, an equally clear explanation of "Why not?"

Turning on With LSD and Pot □ Allen Ginsberg

I would like to begin by introducing some data from comparative religion. Those who have done any dilettanting around in Tantric Hinduism or its esoteric erotic sexual practices will no doubt know of the book, *The Serpent Power,* by Arthur Avalon. It is a translation of an ancient Hindu text, the *Mahanirvana tantra,* one of the older, more conservative texts of the Shaivite school of Hinduism. This text deals with ritual, prayer, and the formal religious use of marijuana. If one reads just a few sentences from the text, he can get an appreciation of the importance of the use of marijuana in the religious rituals. One who engages in mantra prayer and chanting will use this narcotic hemp in his ceremonies.

I should point out that I am a formally initiated member of the Shiva sect, and I assume that my presentation of its rituals is protected by the First Amendment of the U. S. Constitution. Since I have a central preoccupation within my heart with religious matters, I wish to stay off legal problems and to focus upon the actual subject matter on a more realistic level, without worrying about whether it's going to be against the law, whether it's moral or immoral to break the law, whether you'll go mad or you won't go mad. I want to deal with the phenomenology of LSD and pot and their philosophical implications. Professor Elia Rubichek of Prague, who has done a lot of work on LSD, defines it in Pavlovian and Marxian terminology, the terminology the "Iron Curtain" would use in dealing with the effects of LSD. The phraseology is really interesting. What he said was, "It inhibits conditioned reflexes." Now that's a big deal out there in Russia where there's a Pavlovian conception of consciousness, because it means that there is a way or reversing or wiping out the conditioning

Drawing by
Rez Williams

that would make a member of the former upper class no longer eligible to be condemned by the bureaucrat. Anybody could take LSD and say that he had his conditioned reflexes wiped out and was now just as good as the proletariat.

What it means in terms of our country is something you have been digging lately—Marshall McLuhan's generalizations about the effects of the conditioning of our technology on our consciousness. He's saying that the media or environment we have created around us is a giant conditioning mechanism, a giant teaching machine. We are hardly aware of it as a teaching machine. We are hardly aware of its effect. We are hardly aware that consciousness is not necessarily a conceptual or verbal matter, that there are other levels of consciousness, depths of consciousness, that there is feeling consciousness, that there is touch consciousness, that there is smelling, seeing, hearing, and levels of memory consciousness that we are not generally aware of. But McLuhan has been saying recently that the verbal and language consciousness that we have been conditioned to over the last centuries has atrophied our other senses. That is, the universe into which we have projected ourselves and developed has atrophied our other senses —smell, touch, taste—in a way that he could even quantify. McLuhan hold me that he wanted to work out a way to quantify in scientific terminology the difference caused by our preoccupation with visual consciousness; that is, the difference caused to the other senses. There is a quantitative mode of measurement that he could apply. What has this to do with LSD? McLuhan didn't know the connection because he hasn't taken LSD or read much about it. Yet given a chemical which can reverse conditioning, we have a kind of open consciousness which receives almost all of the data present to us and takes account of it all, as if that which we usually are not aware of or is unconscious within us is presented to our awareness during the time that we are high on LSD. This goes on without any screening structure—something that Leary has been saying over and over—to the point where something is either understood and is boring or is not understood and is still a koan for people to solve.

What good is that kind of consciousness? I don't know if I have presented it clearly enough to have any value for you. It involves a consciousness that is not socially conditioned (though conditioned by our bodies surely), a consciousness where the social conditioning is reversed, and where we had eight hours to look around us as newborn babes to see our bodies, to see our relationships, to see our architecture around us, to see our relationships to other forms of life. It involves eight hours of experience of ourselves as mammalian sentient beings. Is that a socially useful experience?

I think it always has been considered a socially useful experience. I think that the LSD experience approximates the mystical experience, as it is called, the religious experience, or the peak experience, as Maslow calls it. It approximates the kind of experience that one reads about in William James's *The Varieties of Religious Experience*. I'm not sure it's identical with what people would call the classical religious experience, but then in William James one also finds that very few of those experiences are identical experiences. Their common quality is that there is a break in the normal mode of consciousness, an opening up of another universe of awareness, so that from one description to another in any of the books describing mystical experiences the forms are not the same. One thing that everybody cries out in delight at is that the universe they had taken for granted had suddenly opened and revealed itself as something much deeper and fuller, much more exquisite, something more connected with a divine sense of things—a Self perhaps. So I would say that the LSD experience does approximate what we humans have been recording over millenia as a flight of higher imagination or a flight of higher awareness. Now that experience has always been accorded a very honored status in society. A few people have been burned at the stake or crucified for attempting to manifest the insights that they've experienced. But at least in the academies, in religion, in the church, and even among truck drivers, there is a respect for the non-conditioned, non-verbal, non-conceptual opening up of the mind to all of the data of experience flooding in at once, newly perceived, or perceived as a newborn babe or early child.

Its usefulness in our society is extra. That's why I began talking about McLuhan, inasmuch as we have arrived at sort of a Buck Rogers space age, science-fiction society in which everybody is electronically intercommunicated, in which visual images and verbal images are multiplied, stereotyped and implanted in everybody's brain so that it is very difficult to escape the automatic, mechanistic forms that are constantly being played on our bodies by radio, television, newspapers, by our own university, or by our own parents.

In a world now facing apocalypse, in the sense that America, the largest world power, is perhaps preparing for a war on the Asiatic life form, it becomes important not only to see what we have in common with the Asiatic life form and what we actually have distinct and separate from it but also to find those points, to control the angers built up in us, to measure the actual universe around, to lose the conditioning that brought us to this path of anger, fear and paranoia, to experience what is original in our nature as distinct from what has been educated into our nature since our birth. The problem, however, that still arises, particularly when people have had religious experience and have not had LSD experience, is this question: "Is this experience like an evil specter or is it something that can be reconciled with the older religious experience? Does it have any relationship to the norms of human experience, or at least the high norms of human experience, that are described in the religious books?

Of these we have neither enough experiments nor enough data. My own experience is as follows: When I was younger (when I was about 28) I had a series of visionary or religious or illuminative experiences which are best categorized as the aesthetic experience, since they became catalyzed by reading poems of Blake. I had an auditory hallucination of Blake's voice and also experienced a number of moments of guilelessness about the world around me and feeling that the father of the universe had existed all along but I had not realized it, that the father of the universe loved me and that I was identical with the father. So this was an experience of bliss. I realized that I had my place in the universe. I tried to describe this a few times in poetry or in prose but it's very difficult to describe. At the time that I had it (it was about in 1948) this kind of experience was, at least in the circles where I ran (Columbia University), an experience which was practically unknown and was considered madness. I remember that when this happened I went to Lionel Trilling and said, "I've seen light." And he looked at me and seemed to be wondering, "What am I going to do with this?" He looked as if he wondered where I was going to wind up. There were two people at Columbia at the time who had enough inner experience to be able to understand, to talk to me, to reassure me. One was Raymond Weaver who had been the first biographer for Herman Melville and who had lived in Japan and was for those at Columbia in the forties *the* great light, a secret light because he was a cranky cat. He used to know Hart Crane and Wanda Landowska. He was the most eminent professor at Columbia. He shared an office with Mark Van Doren. Weaver could deal with this kind of experience without slipping out and becoming anxious. Mark Van Doren also could deal with it. When I went to him in an overexcited and totally disoriented state and said, "I have seen some light, I heard Blake's voice!" He said, "What kind of light was it?" Then he began questioning me about the quality of the experience, asking for data. Everybody else thought I was nuts. However I am what I am. So I'll stand in my own body and believe my own senses and experiences.

Later I found that LSD catalyzed a variety of consciousness that was very similar to the natural experience. I've used a variety of other hallucinogenics—maybe about thirty times over a fifteen-year period. This is very small actually compared to the usage now being made by the younger people. I found that there has not been any contradiction between the kind of consciousness I had under LSD and my height of rapture of consciousness in natural moments. I also found that I faced the same difficulties with LSD as I had faced with my original visionary experience. Those difficulties were that, having gotten into a state of high perception, how to maintain my normal life, my awareness on a higher level, incorporating in my daily experience some of the concrete perceptions that I had in a moment of ecstasy. Specifically I had had a non-drug vision in the Columbia book store. I'd gone in there for years, and I went in there this day and suddenly I saw that everybody looked like tortured animals. I was reading Blake's poem about—

I wander through London's chartered streets
Near where the chartered Thames doth flow
On every face I meet I see
Marks of weakness
Marks of woe

Well, in those moments I saw marks of suffering on the faces of the bookstore clerks, the enormous-like mammalism sexual deliciousness of their being and the contrary stultified, rigid, unsexualized, non-feeling, day-to-day commerce over the books with a few camp jokes mixed in to refer to the unknown. I asked, How, in coming down to a day-to-day dealing with the bookstore people or anyone on the campus, how to deal with such persons, such deep persons as exist in everybody? And that took very slow practice and continuous awareness of the fact that everyone was a deep person and a divine mammal rather than a bookstore clerk. The same problem exists in relation to LSD. Having had a vision on LSD of either your parents or your own role, how do you manifest that in your school life or whatever life you are pursuing? Henri Michaud, a great French poet who did a lot of early experiments, finally told me that he had concluded that what was important was not the visions, but what people did with the visions afterward, and how they manifested them in their daily life. I think that the really basic practical problem to be faced is the problem common to all mysticism. How is one in day-to-day life to keep continuous high consciousness of the eternal which he had experienced in separated moments of a larger consciousness? What good is it if they are separated moments; if they are not totally, distinctly integrated into every day life? Having experienced only separated moments of divine consciousness without drugs, I find that the drugs do make possible a return to more native awareness which is useful when I have to take stock of my activities. For instance, a year and a half ago I was involved in the Viet-Nam

Day Committee in Berkeley. There was a great deal of anger and outrage about the war. I found myself being swept along into that outrage and vowing vengeance on the murderers of innocent children; and my wits were astray because of all of that senseless tumult; and I all but cried for vengeance on the murderers. I took some LSD the day the President went for his gall bladder operation and I realized that he was another suffering deep person, perhaps one almost ignorant of his own state of consciousness and so suffering a great deal more because of that ignorance, one however entering the valley of the shadow. My hatred simply disappeared. What was left was a funny kind of compassion for him in his ignorance, a prayer for him for his return from the valley of the shadow. In a state of awareness, less hostile, less fearful, less paranoid than his entrance, I found myself praying for him, praying for his own understanding. The thing that I did realize was that my piling up my own hatred on top of the general hatred of the Pentagon and the *New York Daily News* and the military and industrial complex only added to the anti-Vietnam War reaction. Piling up my hatred and my curses and my magic on top of that was going to make the situation worse. I wanted to move to liquidate the anger hallucination that was controlling everybody.

Finally, we have a few other details that might interest you. A poet friend of mine was worked for ten years in Zen monasteries, has done formal meditation, and is an accomplished Zen student. He was here in America a few months ago, and we had several long conversations about the rising LSD culture and the Haight-Asburys. He felt that the LSD experience was not contradictory to the experience of Satori as described by Zen. The younger, qualified, completely trained Zen masters in Japan who had tried LSD, were interested in it and considered it a useful tool for education in relation to their own discipline. They were not against its use and were themselves beginning to employ it. The Roshi Suzuki—Roshi means master—who is the head of the meditation sect in San Francisco, said that he felt the LSD experience is not the same as Zazen sitting meditation. However he finds that most of the meditators in his group are people who are originally turned on by LSD. As far as he can see, it does open people up to a widening area of consciousness, which can then be worked in with other disciplines. I find the same report coming in now from the schools of Tibetan Buddhism. There is a Geshe who has a monastery in New Jersey. He has some American disciples who have been equally experienced in Tibetan meditation and psychedelics. Wanga and his disciple, Tenjin, who is an ex-Harvard student have prepared translations of old Tibetan meditation texts and are preparing them for publication with the foreword note that the Tibetan prayers, methods and procedures may be found useful in collaboration with psychedelic experiments. Thus it seems clear to me that there is a close relationship between psychedelic drugs and mystical experience.

Instant Mysticism □ Michael Wyschogrod

I think the point of view expressed by Allen Ginsberg is a very good one—an attitude of reason, of peace, of affection, of understanding, and therefore, I am not in a polemical spirit. I do not wish to disagree, to forbid, to outlaw, or to consider LSD and marijuana evil or immoral. They exist like many other things in the world, and it's very superficial to take a simple "no" attitude to what one finds in the world.

Nevertheless there are a number of issues that deserve deeper analysis. I think the two issues we do not want to discuss are these: first, I think it a mistake to approach this problem from the point of view of the dangers involved. The dangers, of course, are not irrelevant. I think anyone who contemplates taking psychedelic drugs deserves to have all of the knowledge necessary so that he can make an intelligent choice as to just what risk is involved; but that is not a final word because many things in life involve risk and yet we don't shun them. In this country the automobile kills forty thousand people a year, and yet I have not heard anyone advocate the abolition of the automobile. For some reason we feel that the advantages of the automobile outweigh the disadvantages. In any case if the psychedelic substances have substantial spiritual and religious advantages, then I would be prepared to say that this outweighs a great many perils and disadvantages. So the element of peril, though relevant, in my opinion is not crucial and is not the final consideration. Secondly, I think that this problem ought not to be approached essentially from the legal point of view, because whether we ought or ought not to outlaw something is again a secondary question.

The first consideration is, is this a good thing or a bad thing? Outlawing is only secondary. Even if we decide that this is a bad thing, it does not necessarily follow that it ought to be outlawed. The heart of the matter is the question: what good are these drugs? And the moment we ask this question we are in the religious realm. My thesis can be stated very simply: it's a thesis of wonder and surprise. I find that the younger generation to which Professor Abelson referred senses that there is something wrong with the technological mode of existence into which we have been projected in the middle of the twentieth century. There is something wrong with the artificiality of our existence. We no longer experience reality. We live through artificial media such as the television and radio, which have a life of their own and stand as a screen between man and reality. Life in our times is in essence artificial. And because it is artificial there are those people who want to break through this artificiality on all levels, who want to live as a man ought to live and was intended to live, in serenity and peace, with direct contact with reality, not in a life of instant coffee, instant pudding, instant bake mixes, and instant this and that and the other thing—but a wholesale life of cooking vegetables as they grow and taking flour and using it for baking, of brewing coffee, instead of getting it out of an instant mix. Our lives are nightmares of instant experiences. And this, of course, is a profound truth. But then something amazing has happened and I am genuinely amazed—suddenly there is instant mysticism, there is technological mysticism, instead of patience, serenity, humility and waiting for enlightenment and praying for it and loving our fellow man. Instead we look to chemistry: "better living through better things through chemistry."

It seems to me that the genuinely religious person cannot want to buy his relationship to God in a sugar cube, a bottle, or a chemical. It is true that these substances are not yet mass-produced by the pharmaceutical companies. But perhaps that won't take long, if this thing catches on and if people go for it. I assure you that in a few years *Life* and *Time* will be full of ads and every drug company will be selling the stuff and holding out the hope of a quick road to God. And there will be competition, there will be the jingles. I don't want that. I think that would be a travesty on genuine religion, genuine mysticism, and genuine religious experience.

The real thing is always harder and more difficult to achieve than the imitation. And with the real thing you run the risk of never quite making it. There is one element and thought that is universally agreed on among scholars of religion, and that is this: there is a profound distinction between magic and religion. The distinction is simple: Magic is power; religion is prayer. The magician is of the opinion that there is some secret formula which, when discovered, gives him power over the spirit. Once he has that, the spirit cannot refuse his demands. The spirit of magic and the spirit of modern technology are very close indeed because both see man in the driver's seat. Both see man as the power that controls the world around him, and human destiny as a destiny with ever greater control over human existence. Just as through technology we control our environment, the heat and the cold, and the world around us, so by means of magic was the same attempted. The only difference was that we think that science works better than magic. But the spirit is the same; and against science and against magic stands genuine religion. Genuine religion is prayer. Prayer is asking God, and he can say "no."

There is the story of the little kid who prayed; and his cynical uncle said, "Well God didn't answer you, did he?" And the little kid answered, "Yes, he did. He said, 'No.'"

This is the spirit of true religion. In genuine religion we hand ourselves over to the greater spirit, whether one calls it "God," "the Father," or "the spirit of the universe." Fundamentally it doesn't matter. But you see yourself as worshipping that being, that spirit, loving Him. He loves you in return. And you live in peace and union with Him.

Drug mysticism is the conversion of mysticism into magic. It is the illusion that man can have power over the spirit; and this never has happened and never will happen. What comes in a bottle or in a chemical is not the spirit of God. What comes in a bottle or a chemical is an illusion. It is the epitome of just that technological threat against which well-meaning people are fighting and succumbing to through drug and narcotics. It is the victory of the slogan of the chemical industry, and I don't want to see that happen.

Ginsberg Replies to Wyschogrod

For all I know perhaps Professor Wyschogrod is right! I have no idea about the victory of the chemical industry, or victory of artificial madness, or black magic technology. Burroughs, a former teacher of mine and someone I respect a great deal, has had considerable experience with hallucinogens and has stopped using them. Occasionally he turns on; but lately he has taken to saying, "No, I'd better watch out. The Pentagon is going to poison us all. Things have gotten too Orwellian."

As to religious reality, I don't agree with Professor Wyschogrod as to what constitutes a valid religious experience. The spirit of religion is investigation and practice, of which prayer is only an element. But there isn't a pre-supposition, or what I call a hang-up on a Jehovah, that you've got up there that you've got to be humble to, that you've got to pray to, or to be said "no" by. Jehovah is within in Buddhism and Hinduism and in some aspects of Christianity and actually in some Hebraic traditions also. The external Jehovah is just high camp. In some schools that sense of an external authority is not relied on, certainly not in Buddhism where one of the major koans is that Buddha is not a divine being to be worshipped. The saying is that, "If you meet the Buddha on the way to enlightenment and he bars your way, cut him down!"

As to LSD coming in a bottle and whether or not it is the spirit of God, it all depends on the way we are using the term "god." If there were a Jehovah I wouldn't put it past him to come through a bottle any way. Certainly it would be within his power. Certainly a God would see it as equally charming to come through a bottle as through prayer. So I don't think there is anything to be feared in that sense. What might be feared is dependence on the drug and lack of ritual or lack of prayer or lack of humility or lack of earnestness in the yoga of the drug. I tried to provide the suggestions for ritual, the suggestions for prayer, the suggestions for the application of the drug vision to daily life. But I think that purely verbal terminologies are a bit over-dramatized in speaking of LSD as merely "magic" as opposed to religion. I think those are verbal distinctions. I think they are basically stereotypes of thought. I don't think they fit the enormity and eloquence of the experience which many of us have felt.

Wyschogrod Replies to Ginsberg

I agree with Mr. Ginsberg that these are very serious matters and it's presumptuous for anyone to say what is the case and what is not the case. Yet each of us talks from his own experience. I do not speak out of LSD experience but I talk out of religious experience and I think that I am reporting what I see. I don't think that I have the last word. I don't think that I am right, but I do feel deeply that there is profound danger here.

I would add just one word. I don't know much about eastern religion. I deeply respect it. I have an intuitive sense that there is something very real and very deep there, but I'm not a Japanese, Chinese or a Far Easterner. I'm a Westerner. What goes on in the Far East in the setting of that civilization over the thousands of years of art, poetry, and history, and what has gone into the development of those religions I cannot enter into. Therefore I think it is spiritually dangerous for men of New York, for example, to take one aspect of foreign or eastern civilization and transport it here and to think that we have the same thing here that they have. We are Jews or Christians and there is very much to Judaism and Christianity, and we must be what we are. I think there is something very sad about a person trying to be something that he is not and never can be.

Mr. Ginsberg advises people to take pot and LSD. Now I grant an individual the full freedom to act as he wishes and to be what he wishes and I'd be the last person to take that away. But at the same time I must express my convictions. Life poses a peculiar problem: to become what you are. Now this sounds paradoxical, because if you are what you are, why do you need to become what you are? Here there is always tension between becoming what you are, and becoming what you are meant to be. And that's the job for each of us to find. All I can do for you is to say, Look once more before you embark on this strange new path of psychedelic religion. Look once more at your heritage. Just give it a second look and after that you're on your own.

Post Mortem □ Raziel Abelson

I must confess that I do not feel I have received the enlightenment I had hoped for—I am not exactly in a state of Satori. The trouble with this discussion is that both participants have assumed something to be the case which, it seems to me, is even more doubtful than the qualities of the drugs they have argued about. Both Ginsberg and Wyschogrod have assumed that religious experience is necessarily good, and I do not see any reason for accepting that assumption. Ginsberg has argued that, because religious experience is always good, and (he claims) LSD and marijuana help produce religious experience, these drugs are very good and useful things. Wyschogrod has argued, to the contrary, that drugs cannot *possibly* (later he modified his claim to the effect that they do not, so far as he can see) produce genuine religious experience, but only spurious, synthetic, "instant," "bottled," in a word, *illusory* religious experience. Thus he takes it for granted that there is a clear distinction between illusion and reality in religious experience. On this point, it seems to me, Ginsberg has much the better of the argument. To Wyschogrod's claim, "You can't get God out of a bottle" Ginsberg replied, very sensibly, "Why not?"

Why not, indeed? I am reminded of Philip Roth's story, *The Conversion of the Jews,* in which the Rabbi pontificates to his Hebrew school class that Christianity is more irrational than Judaism, because it (Christianity) claims that Jesus was born without sexual intercourse; and little Ozzie then demands to know why an omnipotent God, who can divide the Red Sea and send plagues over Egypt, cannot make a woman become pregnant without sexual intercourse. Once we begin talking about the transcendental (a fancy word for supernatural) anything goes—each one makes up his own rules. One says you can't find God in a bottle, but you can in a burning bush; another says God can't make a woman pregnant without intercourse but that the Holy Ghost in the form of a dove can. How adjudicate such theological claims, and why bother? How one can find God depends very much on just what one means by "God," and it is not at all clear what either Ginsberg or Wyschogrod means, and still less clear whether whatever they mean exists. And if He doesn't exist, you can no more find Him through prayer than through drugs or in a bottle.

Now it seems to me that the distinction between real and unreal, whether it is applied to religious experience, to God, or to the beauty and goodness allegedly revealed by psychedelic drugs, is crucial to this discussion. And my own objection to the claims made for such drugs is on the philosophical ground that this distinction is being applied to a type of experience to which it cannot properly be applied, because there are no established criteria for making the distinction. Indeed, the experience, being hallucinatory, is such that there cannot possibly be criteria for distinguishing the real from the apparent. Mr. Ginsberg made this clear in describing how, under LSD, he felt compassion for everyone and anything, for President Johnson and (he said to me later) for Adolph Hitler. Now what sense is there in compassion that does not distinguish the executioner from his victims? How can one have real compassion for the sufferer without hating the agent who makes him suffer? What good is such compassion; indeed, is it really compassion, or is this feeling of compassion not as hallucinatory as everything else in the state of being drugged? To be more exact, the trouble here is that there is no objective way of distinguishing what is real from what is imaginary, hallucinatory, apparent, spurious, or in any sense unreal. The psychedelic experience is one that, by its very nature, leads one beyond (or below) all criteria of reality. One can, of course, easily say that it leads one to a "higher reality," but this verbalism is empty because "real" makes no sense where it cannot be distinguished from unreal. And this breakdown of the distinction is, of course, typical of all modes of irrationality, including religious mysticism. Consequently, it is impossible to judge whether psychedelic experience and religious experience are the same or different. All we can say is that they are equally hallucinatory. Why the speakers should assume that that is a very good thing is still a mystery to me.

In effect, Mr. Ginsberg has made two claims: first that psychedelic drugs are good in an instrumental sense because they have beneficial effects on one's personality and abilities, and second, that the experience they induce is intrinsically good. The first claim, it seems to me, cannot be authoritatively established by Mr. Ginsberg or anyone else who testifies only from personal experience, any more than the therapeutic value of psychoanalysis can be established by brainwashed patients who have been persuaded by their analyst that they are much improved (when no one else can see any difference in their behavior.) Such a claim can only be proved by carefully controlled scientific studies, and no conclusive studies have yet been made. So I would discount this claim completely, just as anyone with sense would discount the claims made by Krebiozin enthusiasts, and just as Freud came close to discrediting himself as a doctor when he made premature claims for the therapeutic value of cocaine.

The second claim, that the psychedelic experience is intrinsically good, is more difficult to assess, for the reason that its value has to be judged within the experience (I am frequently rebuked by students when I question the value of taking drugs. I am told I haven't tried them, so I can't possibly know whether they are good or bad). Yet the experience is such that within it, all established criteria of good or bad are dissolved, just as, in a dream, the criteria for distinguishing real from apparent cease to apply. One dreams that something is real and something else is not, but this distinction is itself dreamt, and therefore ineffectual. Consequently, it makes no more sense to say that what one experiences is bad than to say that it is good. We simply have no standards for evaluating the hallucinatory objects of a psychedelic experience, for we have no standards for evaluating any hallucinatory objects. So far, the human race is a reality-oriented species. If enough people take drugs, this may change, and then the philosophical premises of a discussion such as this will be different, but it is as useless to speculate on such a state of affairs as to try to imagine what the world would be like if the laws of physics ceased to hold.

I do not mean to question the right of anyone, including Mr. Ginsberg, to express a preference for any type of experience he chooses to enjoy. If someone likes to smoke pot or take acid, and injures no one else in doing so, that, so far as I am concerned, is his affair; and I no more support legislation against such activities than I support legislation against suicide. But to say that one likes something is not the same as to say that that something is good. I do very strongly object to the proselytizing of drugs, because, as I have tried to explain, there are no objective grounds for making a claim either to intrinsic value or to instrumental value with respect to such drugs. I still see one rather compelling reason not to take them, a reason that I tried to indicate in my opening remarks. To steep onself in illusion is to escape from the irksome necessity to distinguish illusion from reality—in a word, to cop out. My conclusion from this discussion is: there's a lot of work to be done in the real world, and a lot of real beauty to enjoy—let's get on with it.

Reflective Questions

1. What are the grounds for Abelson's position that "the revolutionary generation is 'copping out' "?

2. What are the primary arguments, presented by Ginsberg, for drug use in seeking a religious experience?

3. In what context does Wyschogrod discuss the connection between science and magic? Is the "real" question magic versus religion?

4. What does Abelson see as the chief weaknesses of the arguments presented by Ginsberg and Wyschogrod?

5. What changes, if any, would you anticipate in organized religion if hallucinogenic drugs become widely used in the search for a religious experience?

16 □ THE PRICE OF WAR

Bruce M. Russett

The propositions that war has a dysfunctional and devastating impact on the production and utilization of social and economic resources, that universal peace is related to human progress, and that war is one of the major creators of dependency in the contemporary world, are frequently asserted and reasonably shared by humanistically oriented citizens throughout the world. Bruce Russett's article, while not sociologically oriented presents a rather penetrating statistical analysis of the costs and economic consequences of war. He documents the idea that defense spending comes at the expense of something else. Consumer durables; investment; international balance of payments; and education, health, and welfare are shown to be among the most apparent casualties of an economy bent on war and high military spending. Particularly acute is the effect that defense spending has on the creation of new programs and priorities. Similarly, Russett is not unmindful of the unequal distribution of the "burdens" of defense spending and its relation to the nation's future. □

"PEACE" STOCKS ARE UP; "WAR" STOCKS ARE DOWN; CONGRESSMEN SCRUTINIZE Pentagon expenditures with newly-jaundiced eyes. Any (New Left) schoolboy can rattle off a list of the top ten defense contractors: General Electric, Boeing, General Dynamics, North American Aviation.... Scholars and journalists have worked hard lately, and now almost everyone knows who *profits* from defense spending. But who knows who *pays* for it?

Nothing comes free, and national defense is no exception. Yet curiously little attention has been paid to the question of which segments of American society and its economy are disproportionately sacrificed when defense spending rises. Despite some popular opinion to the contrary, our economy is a good deal less than infinitely expansible. Something has to give when military expenditures

Copyright © October 1969, by TRANS-action, Inc., New Brunswick, New Jersey. Reprinted by permission.

take larger bites out of the pie. But when this happens, what kinds of public and private expenditures are curtailed or fail to grow at previously established rates? What particular interests or pressure groups show up as relatively strong or relatively weak in maintaining their accustomed standards of living? And which of them are better able to seize the opportunities offered when international conflict cools off for awhile?

The questions, of course, are implicitly political, and they are important. But the answers have to be sought within economic data. What we want, in a sense, is a "cost-benefit" analysis of war or the preparations for war, an analysis that will tell us not only who most profits from war, but who most bears its burden. Apart from the direct costs in taxation and changes in wages and prices, which I will not go into here, there are the equally significant costs in social benefits, in opportunities foregone or opportunities postponed.

What I want to do here is to examine *expenditures*—by categories of the Gross National Product, by their function and by governmental unit—to see what kinds of alternative spending suffer under the impact of heavy military spending. The necessary data are available for the period 1939–1968, and they allow us to see the effects of two earlier wars (World War II and the Korean War) as well as the burdens of the current Vietnam venture.

First, however, an overview of the changing level of defense expenditures may be helpful. For 1939, in what was in many ways the last peacetime year this nation experienced, defense expenditures were under $1.3 billion. With the coming of war they rose rapidly to a still unsurpassed peak of $87.4 billion in 1944. The 1968 figure was by contrast around $78.4 billion, reflecting a build-up, for the Vietnam war, from levels of about $50 billion in the first half of this decade. The raw dollar figures, however, are deceptive because they reflect neither inflation nor the steady growth in the economy's productive capacity that makes a constant defense budget, even in price-adjusted dollars, a diminishing burden.

The graph shows the trend of military expenditures as a percentage of Gross National Product over the past thirty years.

We immediately see the great burdens of World War II, followed by a drop to a floor considerably above that of the 1930's. The Cold War and particularly the Korean action produced another upsurge in the early 1950's to a level that, while substantial, was by no means the equal of that in the Second World War. This too trailed downward after the immediate emergency was past, though again it did not retreat to the previous floor. In fact, not since the beginning of the Cold War has the military accounted for noticeably less than 5 percent of this country's G.N.P.; not since Korea has it had as little as 7 percent.

This repeated failure to shrink the military establishment back to its prewar level is a phenomenon of some interest to students of the dynamics of international arms races and/or Parkinson's Law. It shows up even more clearly in the data on military personnel, and goes back almost a century to demonstrate the virtual doubling of the armed forces after every war. From 1871 to 1898 the American armed forces numbered fewer than 50,000; after the Spanish-American War they never again dropped below 100,000. The aftermath of World War I saw a leveling off to about 250,000, but the World War II mobilization left 1,400,000 as the apparent permanent floor. Since the Korean War the United States military establishment has never numbered fewer than about 2,500,000 men. Should the post-Vietnam armed forces and/or defense portion of the G.N.P. prove to be higher than in the early and mid-1960's, that will represent another diversion from private or civil public resources and a major indirect but perhaps very real "cost" of the war.

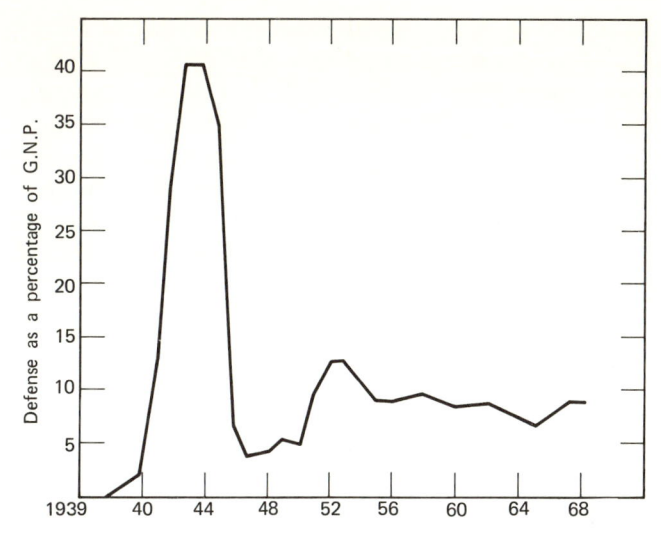

Returning to the graph, we see the effect of the Vietnam build-up, moving from a recent low of 7.3 percent in 1965 to 9.2 percent in 1968. This last looks modest enough, and is, when compared to the effects of the nation's two previous major wars. At the same time, it also represents a real sacrifice by other portions of the economy. The 1968 G.N.P. of the United States was well in excess of $800 billion; if we were to assume that the current war effort accounts for about 2 percent of that (roughly the difference between the 7.3 percent of 1965 and the 9.2 percent of 1968) the dollar amount is approximately $16 billion. That is in fact too low a figure, since some billions were already being devoted to the war in 1965, and direct estimates of the war's cost are typically about $25 to $30 billion per year. The amounts in question, representing scarce resources which might be put to alternative uses, are not trivial.

I assume that defense spending has to come *at the expense* of something else. In the formal sense of G.N.P. proportions that is surely true, but it is usually true in a more interesting sense as well. Economics is said to be the study of the allocation of scarce resources; and, despite some periods of slack at the beginning of war-time periods (1940–41 and 1950), resources have generally been truly scarce during America's wars. Major civilian expenditures have not only lost ground proportionately (as would nevertheless happen from a military spending program financed entirely out of slack) but they have also failed to grow at their accustomed rates, they have lost ground in constant dollars as a result of inflation, or they have even declined absolutely in current dollars. During World War II, for example, such major categories as personal consumption of durable goods, all fixed investment, federal purchases of non-military goods and services, and state and local expenditures all declined sharply in absolute dollar amounts despite an inflation of nearly 8 percent a year.

Some observers argue that high levels of military spending are introduced to take up the slack and maintain demand in an otherwise depression-prone economy. If this were the case, opportunity costs would be minimal. But there is little evidence for that proposition in the American experience of recent decades. Certainly the Vietnam experience does not support it. I assume, *pace* "Iron Mountain," that with the demonstrable public and private needs of this society, and with modern tools of economic analysis and manipulation, full or near-full employment of resources would be maintained even in the face of major cuts in military spending. Because of the skill with which economic systems are now managed in modern economies, defense expenditures are much more likely to force trade-offs than they were some thirty years ago. Hence the point of my original question, "Who pays for defense?"

I do not argue that defense expenditures are necessarily without broader social utility. Spending for military research and development produces important (if sometimes overrated) technological spill-overs into the civilian sector. The education, skills and physical conditioning that young men obtain during service in the armed forces are likely to benefit them and their society when they return to civilian life. Nevertheless the achievement of such benefits through spill-overs is rarely the most efficient way to obtain them. While scientific research may be serendipitous, the odds are far better that a new treatment for cancer will come from medical research than from work on missile systems. Therefore we must still consider as real costs the trade-offs that appear when defense cuts deep into the G.N.P., though they are not quite so heavy as a literal interpretation of the dollar amounts would imply.

One must also recognize that some civilian expenditures—for health, for education and for research—have been stimulated by Cold War and ultimately military requirements. Such were various programs of the 1950's, when a greater need was felt for a long-run girding of the loins than for more immediate military capabilities. Still, to concede this is far from undercutting the relevance of the kind of question we shall be asking. If civilian and military expenditures consistently compete for scarce resources, then the one will have a negative effect on the other; if both are driven by the same demands, they will be positively correlated. If they generally compete but are sometimes viewed as complementary, the negative correlation will be fairly low.

An evaluation of the relationship of defense and alternative kinds of spending in this country requires some explicit criteria. There is room for serious argument about what those criteria should be, but I will suggest the following:

1. It is bad to sacrifice future productivity and resources for current preparation for war or war itself; insofar as possible such activities should be financed out of current consumption. Such an asumption might be easily challenged if it were offered as a universal, but for the developed countries of North America and Western Europe in recent years it seems defensible. All of them are now, relative to their own past and to other nations' present, extremely affluent, with a high proportion of their resources flowing into consumption in the private sector. Furthermore, for most of the years 1938–1968, the demands of defense have not been terribly great. Since the end of World War II, none of these countries has had to devote more than about 10 percent of its G.N.P. to military needs, save for the United States during the Korean War when the figure rose to just over 13 percent. It is surely arguable that such needs rarely require substantial mortgaging of a nation's future.

(a) By this criterion one would hope to see periodic upswings in defense requirements financed largely out of personal consumption, with capital formation and such social investment in the public sector as health and education being insensitive to military demands.

(b) Another aspect of this criterion, however, is that one would also anticipate that in periods of *declining* military needs the released resources would largely be *kept* for investment and education rather than returned to private consumption. In a strong form the criterion calls for a long-term increase in the proportion of G.N.P. devoted to various forms of investment, an increase that would show up on a graph as a fluctuating line made up of a series of upward slopes followed by plateaus, insensitive to rising defense needs but responsive to the opportunities provided by relaxations in the armament pace.

2. Another point of view, partially in conflict with the last comment, would stress the need for a high degree of *insulation from political shocks*. A constant and enlarging commitment to the system's social resources is necessary for the most orderly and efficient growth of the system, avoiding the digestive problems produced by alternate feast and famine. Some spending, on capital expenditures for buildings for instance, may be only temporarily postponed in periods of fiscal stringency, and may bounce back to a higher level when the pressure of defense needs is eased. To that degree the damage would be reduced, but not

eliminated. In the first place, school construction that is "merely" postponed four years will come in time to help some students, but for four years a great many students simply lose out. Secondly, boom and bust fluctuations, even if they do average out to the socially-desired dollar level, are likely to be inefficient and produce less real output than would a steadier effort.

Guns, Butter and Structures

Calculation of a nation's G.N.P. is an exercise in accounting; economists define the Gross National Product as the sum of expenditures for personal consumption, investment or capital formation, government purchases of goods and services and net foreign trade (exports minus imports). Each of these categories can be broken down. Private consumption is the sum of expenditures on durable goods (e.g., automobiles, furniture, appliances), nondurables (e.g., food, clothing, fuel) and services (airline tickets, haircuts, entertainment); investment includes fixed investment in non-residential structures, producers' durable equipment (e.g., machinery), residential structures and the accumulation or drawing down of stocks (inventories); government purchases include both civil and military expenditures of the federal government and spending by state and local units of government. Except for inventories (which fluctuate widely in response to current conditions and are of little interest for this study) we shall look at all these, and later at a further breakdown of public expenditures by level and function.

In Table 1 the first column of figures—the percentage of variance explained—tells *how closely* defense spending and the alternate spending category vary together—how much of the changes in the latter can be "accounted for" by defense changes. The regression coefficient tells *the amount in dollars* by which the alternate spending category changes in response to a one dollar increase in defense. The proportionate reduction index shows the damage suffered by each category relative to its "normal" base. It assumes for illustration a total G.N.P. of $400 billion, an increase of $25 billion in defense-spending from the previous period, and that the alternative expenditure category had previously been at that level represented by its mean percentage of G.N.P. over the 1946–67 period. This last measure is important for policy purposes, since the *impact* of the same dollar reduction will be far greater to a $100 billion investment program than to a $500 billion total for consumer-spending.

Looking at the table, one can see that, in general, the American experience has been that the consumer pays most. Guns do come at the expense of butter. Changes in defense expenditure account for 84 percent of the ups and downs in total personal *consumption,* and the regression coefficient is a relatively high —.420. That is, a one dollar rise in defense expenditures will, all else being equal, result in a decline of $.42 in private consumption.

Of the subcategories, sales of consumer durables are most vulnerable, with

TABLE 1 □ THE EFFECT OF DEFENSE SPENDING ON CIVILIAN ACTIVITIES IN THE UNITED STATES, 1939–68

	Percent of Variation	Regression Coefficient	Index of Proportionate Reduction
PERSONAL CONSUMPTION			
TOTAL	84	−.420	−.041
Durable goods	78	−.163	−.123
Nondurable goods	04	−.071	−.014
Services	54	−.187	−.050
FIXED INVESTMENT			
TOTAL	72	−.292	−.144
Nonresidential structures	62	−.068	−.140
Producers' durable equipment	71	−.110	−.123
Residential structures	60	−.114	−.176
Exports	67	−.097	−.115
Imports	19	−.025	−.037
Federal civil purchases	38	−.048	−.159
State & local gov't consumption	38	−.128	−.105

78 percent of their variations accounted for by defense. Spending on services is also fairly vulnerable to defense expenditures, with the latter accounting for 54 percent of the variance. But the negative effect of defense spending on nondurables is not nearly so high, with only 4 percent of the variance accounted for. This is not surprising, however, as needs for nondurables are almost by definition the least easily postponed. Moreover, during the World War II years new consumer durables such as automobiles and appliances were virtually unavailable, since the factories that normally produced them were then turning out war material. Similarly, due to manpower shortages almost all services were expensive and in short supply, and long-distance travel was particularly discouraged ("Is this trip necessary?"). Hence, to the degree that the consumers' spending power was not mopped up by taxes or saved, an unusually high proportion was likely to go into nondurables.

Investment (fixed capital formation) also is typically hard-hit by American war efforts and, because it means a smaller productive capacity in later years, diminished investment is a particularly costly loss. Defense accounted for 72 percent of the variations in investment, which is only a little less than that for defense on consumption, and the reduction of $.292 in investment for every

$1.00 rise in defense is substantial. The coefficient is of course much lower than that for defense and consumption (with a coefficient of —.420) but that is very deceptive considering the "normal" base from which each starts. Over the thirty years for which we have the figures, consumption took a mean percentage of G.N.P. that was typically about five times as great as investment. Thus in our hypothetical illustration a $25 billion increase in defense costs in a G.N.P. of $400 billion would, *ceteris paribus,* result in a drop in consumption from approximately $256 billion to roughly $245 billion or only a little over 4 percent of total consumption. Investment, on the other hand, would typically fall from $51 billion to about $44 billion, or more than 14 percent. *Proportionately,* therefore, investment is much *harder* hit by an expansion of the armed services than is consumption. Since future production is dependent upon current investment, the economy's *future* resources and power base are thus much more severely damaged by the decision to build or employ current military power than is current indulgence. According to some rough estimates, the marginal productivity of capital in the United States is between 20 and 25 percent; that is, an additional dollar of investment in any single year will produce 20–25 cents of annual additional production in perpetuity. Hence if an extra billion dollars of defense in one year reduced investment by $292 million, thenceforth the level of output in the economy would be *permanently* diminished by a figure on the order of $65 million per year.

This position is modified slightly by the detailed breakdown of investment categories. Residential structures (housing) vary less closely with defense spending than do nonhousing structures or durable goods for producers, but its regression coefficient is the strongest and shows that it takes the greatest proportionate damage. Within the general category of investment, therefore, nonresidential structures and equipment usually hold up somewhat better proportionately than does housing. Doubtless this is the result of deliberate public policy, which raises home interest rates and limits the availability of mortgages while trying at the same time to maintain an adequate flow of capital to those firms needing to convert or expand into military production.

The nation's international *balance of payments* is often a major casualty of sharp increases in military expenditures; the present situation is not unusual. Some potential exports are diverted to satisfy internal demand, others are lost because domestic inflation raises costs to a point where the goods are priced out of the world market. Imports may rise directly to meet the armed forces' procurement needs—goods purchased abroad to fill local American military requirements show up as imports to the national economy—and other imports rise indirectly because of domestic demand. Some goods normally purchased from domestic suppliers are not available in sufficient quantities; others, because of inflation, become priced above imported goods. If the present situation is "typical," the

Vietnam war's cost to the civilian economy would be responsible for a loss of more than $1.5 billion dollars in exports.

The import picture is more complicated. According to the sketch above, imports should *rise* with defense spending, but in the table percentage of variance explained is very low and the regression coefficient is actually *negative.* This, however, is deceptive. The four years of World War II show unusually low importation due to a combination of enemy occupation of normal sources of goods for the United States, surface and submarine combat in the sea lanes and the diversion of our allies' normal export industries to serve *their* war needs. To assess the impact of defense expenditures on imports in a less than global war one must omit the World War II data from the analysis. Doing so produces the expected rise in imports with higher defense spending, on the order of +.060. This suggests that the current effect of Vietnam may be to add, directly and indirectly, over $1 billion to the nation's annual import bill. Coupled with the loss of exports, the total damage to the balance of payments on current account (excluding capital transfers) is in the range $2.5–$3.0 billion. That still does not account for the entire balance of payments deficit that the United States is experiencing (recently as high as $3.4 billion annually) but it goes a long way to explain it.

The Public Sector

In the aggregate there is no very strong impact of defense on *civil public expenditures.* The amount of variation accounted for by defense is a comparatively low 38 percent; the regression coefficients are only —.048 for federal civil purchases and —.013 for state and local governments. During the four peak years of World War II changes in federal civil expenditures were essentially unrelated to changes in defense spending. Samuel P. Huntington, however, notes, "Many programs in agriculture, natural resources, labor and welfare dated back to the 1930's or middle 1940's. By the mid-1950's they had become accepted responsibilities of the government," and hence politically resistant to the arms squeeze. If so, the overall inverse relationship we do find may be masking sharper changes in some of the less well-entrenched subcategories of central government budgeting. Further masking of the impact on actual programs may stem from the inability of government agencies to reduce costs for building-maintenance and tenured employees, thus forcing them in dry times to cut other expenses disproportionately.

When relating state and local government expenditures to defense some restraint is required. There really is no relationship except *between* the points above and below the 15 percent mark for defense. During World War II state and local government units did have their spending activities curtailed, but overall they have not been noticeably affected by defense purchases. Quite to the contrary, spending by state and local political units has risen steadily, in an almost unbroken line, since 1944. The rise, from 3.6 percent of the G.N.P. to 11.2 percent in 1968, has continued essentially heedless of increases or diminution in the military's demands on the economy.

When we look at the breakdowns by function, however, it becomes clear that the effect of defense fluctuations is more serious, if less distinct than for G.N.P. categories. I have chosen three major items—education, health and welfare—for further analysis, on the grounds that one might reasonably hypothesize for each that expenditure levels would be sensitive to military needs, and, for the first two, that a neglect of them would do serious long-term damage to the economy and social system of the nation.

All three are sensitive to defense spending, with *welfare* somewhat more so than the others, which is not surprising. In most of this analysis reductions in expenditure levels that are forced by expanded defense activities represent a *cost* to the economic and social system, but welfare is different. Insofar as the *needs* for welfare, rather than simply the resources allocated to it, are reduced, one cannot properly speak of a cost to the economy. Rather, if one's social preferences are for work rather than welfare, the shift represents a *gain* to the system. Heavy increases in military pay and procurement do mean a reduction in unemployment, and military cutbacks are often associated with at least temporary or local unemployment. The effect seems strongest on state and local governments' welfare spending. In fact, the inverse relationship between defense and welfare at most spending levels is *understated* at 54 percent on the chart. At all but the highest levels of defense spending achieved in World War II, the inverse relationship is very steep, with small increases in military needs having a very marked dampening effect on welfare costs. But manpower was quite fully employed during *all* the years of major effort in World War II, so ups and downs in defense needs during 1942–45 had little effect.

Both for reduction and for health and hospitals, the relationship to the immediate requirements of national defense is less powerful (less variance is explained), but nonetheless important. Furthermore, the regression coefficient is quite high for education, and since the mean share of G.N.P. going to education is only 3.5 percent for the period under consideration, the proportionate impact of reductions is severe.

A widespread assumption holds that public expenditures on *education* have experienced a long-term secular growth in the United States. That assumption is correct only with modifications. The proportion of G.N.P. devoted to public education has increased by three quarters over the period, from 3.0 percent in 1938 to 5.3 percent in 1967. But it has by no means been a smooth and steady upward climb. World War II cut deeply into educational resources, dropping the educational percentage of G.N.P. to 1.4 in 1944; only in 1950 did it recover

TABLE 2 □ THE EFFECT OF DEFENSE SPENDING ON PUBLIC CIVIL ACTIVITIES IN THE U.S., FISCAL YEARS 1938–67

	Percent of Variation	Regression Coefficient	Index of Proportionate Reduction
EDUCATION—TOTAL	35	−.077	−.139
Institutions of higher ed.	12	−.013	−.146
Local schools	34	−.053	−.125
Other ed.	19	−.014	−.265
Federal direct to ed.	16	−.013	−.309
Federal aid to state & local gov'ts for ed.	08	−.004	−.140
State & local gov't for ed.	24	−.060	−.124
HEALTH & HOSPITALS —TOTAL	32	−.017	−.113
Total hospitals	30	−.014	−.123
Fed. for hospitals	25	−.004	−.130
State & local for hospitals	29	−.011	−.120
OTHER HEALTH —TOTAL	22	−.003	−.087
Fed. for health	06	−.001	−.101
State & local for health	45	−.002	−.078
WELFARE—TOTAL	54	.019	−.128
Fed. direct for welfare	13	.003	−.493
Fed. aid to state & local gov'ts for welfare	17	−.005	−.087
State & local for welfare	30	−.011	−.134

to a level (3.6 percent) notably above that of the 1930's. Just at that point the Korean War intervened, and education once more suffered, not again surpassing the 3.6 percent level before 1959. Since then, however, it has grown fairly steadily without being adversely affected by the relatively modest rises in defense spending. Actually, educational needs may have benefitted somewhat from the overall decline in the military proportion of the economy that took place between the late 1950's and mid-1960's. The sensitivity of educational expenditures to military needs is nevertheless much more marked on the latter's upswings than on its declines. Education usually suffers very immediately when the military needs to expand sharply; it recovers its share only slowly after defense spending has peaked. Surprisingly, *federal* educational expenditures are less related (less variance explained) than is spending by state and local units of government; also, local schools at the primary and secondary levels are more sensitive than are public institutions of higher education, whose share has grown in every year since 1953.

Public expenditures for *health* and hospitals are only a little less sensitive to the pressures of defense than are dollars for education. Here again the image of a long-term growth deceptively hides an equally significant pattern of swings. Health and hospitals accounted for a total of .77 percent of G.N.P. in 1938; as with education this was sharply cut by World War II and was not substantially surpassed (at 1 percent) until 1950. Once more they lost out to the exigencies of defense in the early 1950's, and bounced back slowly, at the same rate as did education, to recover the 1950 level in 1958. Since then they have continued growing slowly, with a peak of 1.23 in 1967. Thus, the pattern of health and hospitals is almost identical to that for education—some long-term growth, but great cutbacks in periods of heavy military need and only slow recovery thereafter. In detail by political unit the picture is also much the same—despite reasonable a priori expectation, federal spending for this item is less closely tied to the defense budget than is that by state and local governments. It should also be noted that the *impact* of defense on health and hospitals is slightly less severe than on education.

It seems fair to conclude from these data that America's most expensive wars have severely hampered the nation in its attempt to build a healthier and better-educated citizenry. (One analyst estimates that what *was* done to strengthen education accounted for nearly half of the United States per capita income growth between 1929 and 1957.) A long-term effort has been made, and with notable results, but typically it has been badly cut back whenever military needs pressed unusually hard.

It is too soon to know how damaging the Vietnam war will be, but in view of past patterns one would anticipate significant costs. The inability to make "investments" would leave Americans poorer, more ignorant and less healthy than would otherwise be the case. We have already seen the effect of the war on fixed capital formation. Consumption absorbed a larger *absolute* decline in its share of G.N.P. between 1965 and 1968 than did fiscal investment—from 63.3 to 62.1 percent in the first instance, from 14.3 to 13.8 percent in the second; but given the much smaller base of investment, the *proportionate* damage is about twice as great to investment as to consumption. In most of the major categories of public social "investment," nevertheless, the record is creditable. Despite a rise from 7.6 to 9.1 percent in the defense share between 1965 and 1967, the total public education and health and hospitals expenditure shares went up 4.5 to 5.3 percent and from 1.17 to 1.23 percent respectively. And even federal spending for education and health, though not hospitals, rose. There are of course other costs involved in the inability to *initiate* needed programs—

massive aid to the cities is the obvious example. But on maintaining or expanding established patterns of expenditure the score is not bad at all.

The pattern of federal expenditures for *research and development* indicates some recent but partially hidden costs to education and medicine. From 1955 through 1966 R & D expenditures rose spectacularly and steadily from $3.3 billion to $14.9 billion. Obviously such a skyrocketing growth could not continue indefinitely; not even most of the beneficiary scientists expected it to do so, and in fact the rate of increase of expenditures fell sharply as early as 1966—the first year since 1961 when the defense share of G.N.P. showed any notable increase.

Finally, we must note a very important sense in which many of these cost estimates are substantially underestimated. My entire analysis has necessarily been done with expenditure data in current prices; that is, not adjusted for inflation. Since we have been dividing each expenditure category by G.N.P. in current dollars that would not matter *providing that price increases were uniform throughout the economy*. But if prices increased faster in say, education or health, than did prices across the board, the *real* level of expenditure would be exaggerated. And as anyone who has recently paid a hospital bill or college tuition bill knows, some prices have increased faster than others. From 1950 through 1967 the cost of medical care, as registered in the consumer price index, rose by 86.2 percent. Thus even though the health and hospital share of public expenditure rose in *current* prices, the *real share* of national production bought by that spending *fell* slightly, from one percent to about .99 percent. Presumably the difference has been made up in the private sector, and benefits have been heavily dependent upon ability to pay. Comparable data on educational expenses are less easy to obtain, but we do know that the average tuition in private colleges and universities rose 39 percent, and in public institutions 32 percent, over the years 1957–1967. This too is faster than the cost of living increase over those years (not more than 20 percent), but not enough to wipe out a gain for government education expenditures in their share of real G.N.P.

In evaluating the desirability of an expanded defense effort, policy-makers must bear in mind the opportunity costs of defense, the kinds and amounts of expenditures that will be foregone. The relationships we have discovered in past American experience suggest what the costs of future military efforts may be, although these relationships are not of course immutable. Should it be concluded that certain new defense needs must be met, it is possible by careful choice and control to distribute the burdens somewhat differently. If costs cannot be avoided, perhaps they can be borne in such a way as to better protect the nation's future.

Reflective Questions

1. In what ways is war costly to a nation and its inhabitants?

2. Is war a feasible way to handle international conflicts? What alternatives to war exist?

3. To whom is war most beneficial and to whom is it most harmful?

4. Are wars morally justifiable? If so, what types of wars?

Part Four
Individuals and Society in Crisis

The sickness of American society, in short, does not reside in the existence of problems. Nor does it reside in the existence of discontent, ferment and rebelliousness: this traditionally has been the health of our society. Our sickness resides rather in our incapacity to deal effectively with our problems—an incapacity which has begun to suffuse our nation with an ominous sense of impotence.

ARTHUR SCHLESINGER, JR.

RICHARD BALAGUR / NANCY PALMER

ONE OF THE SALIENT FEATURES OF MODERN SOCIETY IS THE PROBLEM posed by structural differentiation and collective identity. The common development of concepts such as alienation and anomie to interpret the condition of modern man attest to this fact. Whether viewed in spiritualistic or materialistic terms, the common question is: What happens to socialized man whose community with others has been broken? It is not only a matter of knowledge inadequacy or labor depersonalization, or for that matter a feeling of meaninglessness or powerlessness. In a sense, the question is also one of patterns of behavioral and attitudinal adaptation. How do we respond to problems of individual and collective identity? How do we make choices and evaluate alternatives in light of competing and contradictory norms and expectations?

In groping for answers and trying to come to terms with problems of contemporary social existence, modern man has not been undifferentiated. Some people have "dropped out" of society, as individuals and groups. Others have developed and had created in them varied forms of pathology; still others have attempted to bring about societal change through group efforts. More radical forms of change are advocated by other persons and groups of persons who feel that the system is incurably evil, cruel (but changeable), and unchangeable by traditional or reform oriented tactics.

There is a common assumption that "solutions" or responses to problems of structural change and identity are pathological in character. Such an assumption is, in part, a value judgment, which reveals more about the person who makes the claim than about the situation under investigation. It is clear that alienation is not simply an assessment of a negative nature. The modern soldier, scientist, secretary, blue collar worker, and the like, might be seen as alienated in one sense or another. This might tend to suggest that alienation is a central, generic fact of human existence. If this be the case, then perhaps we should recognize and institutionalize its significance for a new social order. Is it possible that the alienated will provide us with a new and more objective code of ethics for behavior because they are alienated, because they are detached from others—a type of self-power and self-integration undoubtedly difficult to achieve, but perhaps more in accord with social systems of the future. Could it be that pathology should be encouraged if we want to minimize racial hatred, power exclusiveness, privatization of emotions, ethnocentrism, and economic and political chauvinism? History confirms the latters' contribution to the production of problems and discontent in the world.

17 □ CHANGING PERSPECTIVES AND THE TOPICS OF DEVIANCE

John Lefland

This paper traces the evolutionary development of deviance as a sociological concept. The author presents an examination of the sociological perspectives on the topics of deviance during three diverse periods in American sociological history:

1. The pre-World War II phase is described as having a social pathological approach.
2. The orientation of the 1950's saw attention being focused on the ethically neutral, value-free position.
3. The posture of the 1960's represented an emphasis on sociological involvement and a rejection of the noncommittal perspective of the previous decade.

Lefland posits the argument that the disagreement between the various perspectives is not an attack on science, but is, rather, a sign of a healthy intellectual difference of opinion regarding the most fruitful approach to the study of deviance. □

THE TERM DEVIANCE IS A MERE INFANT COMPARED TO SUCH MAJOR AND long-standing terms as stratification, community, institution and society. Deviance is, in fact, less than twenty years of age, having "made the scene," as it were, after World War II and primarily after 1950. It and its variants, deviant, deviation and deviancy, entered the field very quickly, without eliciting much debate and almost without eliciting any reflection upon or conscious regard for what was happening. One of the lonely commentaries on this occurrence was felt by its author to merit but a footnote.

John Lefland, *Deviance and Identity*, © 1969. Reprinted by permission of Prentice-Hall, Inc., Englewood Cliffs, New Jersey, and the author.

It is remarkable that those who live around the social sciences have so quickly become comfortable with the term "deviant." . . . Just as there are iatrogenic disorders caused by the work that physicians do (which gives them more work to do), so there are categories of persons who are created by students of society, then studied by them. (Goffman, 1963a: 140.)

The unheralded advent and sweeping acceptance of deviance as a name for a subset of sociological topics pose an important question in the sociology of sociology. This question is relevant to understanding the more ideological texture and context of recent studies of a very old and standard set of topics. The coming of deviance as a sociological rubric poses, simply, the question of the conditions under which this occurred.

Sociology and the Topics of Deviance Prior to World War II

If we are adequately to understand the advent of the concept of deviance, it is necessary also to understand something of the concepts which deviance replaced. For, although the name of the sociological subfield has changed, the concrete topics of study have remained much the same. Furthermore, to understand these replaced concepts, we must also understand *who* practiced sociology in what kind of *social context*.

From the discipline's beginning in the United States at the turn of the 20th century, and for some forty years thereafter, sociologists often had a conventionally reformist-social problem-social work orientation. Many early sociologists were the products of training grounds in ideal morality, either as the result of exposure to Protestant ministerial fathers or as the result of their own earlier careers as clergymen. Others came to sociology from backgrounds in what was then called "social reform" (but has since been tamed to "social work").[1] These pioneers on the frontiers of sociology were unabashedly moral men. Their overt aim was to understand society so as to solve its problems. Although they considered themselves men of science, theirs was a science in the service of ethical ideals. Unencumbered by the doctrines of value neutrality that would make moral eunuchs of a later generation, their writing could be charmingly explicit on moral matters, as in the following passages from a popular text of the period.

Sin, vice, crime, corruption, all consciously directed antisocial forces,

[1] See Mills, 1942, to whom I am indebted for rendition of the relevant parts of pre-World War II sociology. See also Strauss, 1961 and 1968.

offer a primrose path of pleasurable activity, albeit they eventually
lead to destruction. Beguiled by clever leaders and the desires of
the moment, man is continually selling his soul for a mess of pottage.

Those unhappy creatures who offer themselves for sex hire represent
the most demoralized of all sex offenders.

Women are seldom "sold" or "forced" into lives of shame or
compelled to remain in houses of prostitution any longer than
they desire. It is a sad but valid fact that there are thousands of women
in large cities who are willing to become prostitutes voluntarily.
(Elliott and Merrill, 1934:44, 182, 188.)

Only in a world of moral certitude can "clever leaders" "beguile" the souls of "unhappy creatures" in the light of "sad but valid facts."

The more explicitly conceptual side of their work was hardly less moralistic. In place of the deviance framework of today stood such concepts as social disorganization, social pathology, and social maladjustment. All these concepts assume the existence and knowledge of standards against which polities and persons can be judged to be organized or disorganized, normal or pathological, adjusted or maladjusted. These "social pathologists"—as C. W. Mills called them—were not, however, very explicit as to the exact nature of the standards by which their judgments were made. Nonetheless, investigation into the moral backgrounds and outlooks of these men and knowledge of those objects which they conceived as disorganized, pathological or maladjusted allow one to infer their underlying standards or assumptions with some certainty.

Like millions of Americans prior to World War II, many early sociologists were of Anglo-American descent, were reared in rural Protestant areas and were migrants to the burgeoning cities. Interestingly enough, the disorganization, pathology and maladjustment they discerned were peculiarly confined to urban areas. In the early part of this century there were indeed many acute urban "problems," problems that were possibly much more acute than those now plaguing contemporary America. Successive waves of immigrants were undergoing the painful process of accommodating themselves to a new land, a land that was itself undergoing profound and rapid change. From a rural society of independent landholders, America was being transformed into the most urbanized and industrialized country in the history of the world. If the social change witnessed by the social pathologists in the cities of the time was upsetting to them, it was understandably so. For the change they witnessed was, in an important sense, something new. They were parties to the birth of a new kind of social order—a social order based on elaborate mechanization, technological innovation and occupational differentiation, a social order whose new bases were overlaying and tending to supplant the more traditional bonds of kinship, territorial anchorings and historic cultural tradition.

Because these social scientists were essentially rural persons who were also new to the big cities, they tended to view the urban complex from the perspective of their early learned conceptions or assumptions about what constituted a normal society. They had an image of a normal society as one which was small in population, compact in territory and homogeneous in cultural tradition —an image which fit the classic American small towns. Cities were exactly the opposite: large in population, sprawling in territory and heterogeneous in cultural tradition. If small towns were normal, then other places must be abnormal, pathological or disorganized. In addition, they tended to assume that a normal society was one in which people agreed about most things and did not (at least, not openly) dispute one another. The good life (i.e., the mythical utopia of small-town America) was one in which harmony characterized public and private relations. Cities, however, were arenas of conflicting groups, battling for what were thought to be scarce resources. A multitude of groups in conflict and therefore out of harmony indicated a condition of social disorganization. Furthermore, the "normal" or "adjusted" person was, in the natural order of things, a bourgeois, Sunday-go-to-meeting, stable booster of Small Town's Main Street. He was Protestant, temperate, married only once, a parent and the like. For the social pathologists,

the ideally adjusted man is "socialized." This term seems to
operate ethically as the opposite of "selfish"; it implies that the adjusted
man conforms to middle-class morality and motives and "participates"
in the gradual progress of respectable institutions. If he is not a
"joiner," he certainly gets around and into many community
organizations. If he is socialized, the individual thinks of others and
is kindly toward them. He does not brood or mope about but is
somewhat extravert, eagerly participating in his community's
institutions. His mother and father were not divorced, nor was
his home ever broken. He is "successful"—at least in a modest way—
since he is ambitious, but he does not speculate about matters too far above
his means, lest he become "a fantasy thinker," and the little men
don't scramble after the big money. The less abstract the traits and
fulfilled "needs" of the "adjusted man" are, the more they
gravitate toward the norms of independent middle-class persons
verbally living out Protestant ideals in the small towns of America.
(Mills, 1942:180.)

Woefully, cities were glutted with foreigners, workmen, Catholics, nonchurchgoers and a variety of even less savory types, such as prostitutes and hoboes, whose behavior flew in the face of the middle-class small-town ethic. Hence masses of people in the city were maladjusted or abnormal.

Sociology and the Topics of Deviance in the Fifties

It was partly with reference to and against this ideological scenery (as well as some Marxist tendencies of the thirties) that sociologists after World War II began to seek some more modern and scientific posture. This posture emerged as the doctrine of value-free sociology, the position that the work of sociologists must be purged of moral taint. Sociologists should work with ethically neutral concepts and hold themselves aloof from moral musings. The prestigious Max Weber's lecture entitled "Science as a Vocation" was the primary ideological document of this movement.[2]

The doctrine of value-free sociology is potentially revolutionary in its implication (e.g., if one is truly value-free, he avoids loyalty to the state; therefore he is disloyal), but as a matter of operating application and consequence it was conveniently congruent with and supportive of the political climate and technological developments of postwar America. The crystallization of the East-West blocs and the coming of the not-so-cold war generated considerable domestic concern over the nature and meaning of loyalty. In the period surrounding the McCarthy era, value-free sociology seemed mostly to mean politically conventional, neutral or harmless sociology. It thus helped to remove sociologists and other social scientists from too close and too continuous scrutiny or harassment by the polity. Along with this, the increasing technological complexity of the military and the economy promoted government concern over, and support of, research and development. In addition to the vast sums made available for the development of more conventional types of hardware, funds were allocated for research into the solving of "human problems," such as group morale and efficiency, mental illness and juvenile delinquency. The value-free ideology contributed to the training of moral conventionalists and amoral technicians and thus helped to ensure that social scientists would abundantly benefit from this largesse.[3]

Thus, with the coming of a belief in value-free sociology in the fifties, concepts such as social disorganization and social pathology, with their associated moral ideology, came to be thought of as inconsistent with a strictly scientific perspective. These and kindred concepts became disreputable, at least in the

---

[2] Weber, 1946:129–56 (originally published in 1922). A more detailed analysis of the fifties, upon which I have drawn, is presented in Gouldner, 1962.
[3] Although written in writhing anger, screeching voice and nasty tone, Mills' *The Sociological Imagination* (1959) is a valuable commentary on and document of sociology in the fifties. As in other matters, one must be careful not to throw the baby out with the bath.

leading universities. Their fall from grace created a conceptual vacuum. Desirous of retaining the traditional and juicy topics studied under these rubrics, sociologists needed some new concept or concepts under which the appropriate materials could continue to huddle. Enter, unheralded, the rubrics "deviance" and "deviant." Emanating primarily from Harvard and Columbia,[4] the leading centers of sociology in the fifties, the deviance framework moved quickly and quietly into a position of supremacy.

For some people a new name may offer a new lease on life. But for the topics which it was intended to designate, the new concept, deviance, seemed less helpful. Beyond some concern with anomie, the presumed discovery that people have to have opportunities to act in certain ways, and two statements on adolescent males labeled delinquent,[5] the field lay in relative quiescence. Traditional types of research studies on the topics of deviance continued, of course, at a high rate, but few of them appear to have accomplished more than a replication of prewar findings (now cast in deviance terminology) or a reiteration of the still active social pathological perspective.[6]

Dissent in the Sixties

By the beginning of the sixties an increasing number of restive musings became noticeable. In sociology generally and in deviance in particular, scholars announced doubts about sociological studies being in fact value-free.[7] Among

[4] From Harvard: Parsons, 1951:Chap. 7; and Cohen, 1955 and 1959; from Columbia: Merton, 1938, 1949 and 1957:Chaps. 4 and 5. These strangely brief treatments of the field were ubiquitously recounted, cited as major statements and read seriously by active sociologists of the time.

[5] Cohen, 1955; and Cloward and Ohlin, 1960.

[6] As T. Kuhn (1962) has noted, conceptual frameworks in science are not replaced by scientists' abandoning their former views and taking up the new. Scientists, like religionists, tend to espouse a single perspective over their entire careers. New perspectives spread, rather, through their adoption by young and relatively unknowledgeable newcomers to the field, either while in graduate training or early in their professional careers. Unencumbered by prior commitments and not understanding the orthodox very well in any case, novices more readily comprehend the new, or, if one prefers, more easily fall prey to folly.

[7] E.g., Dahrendorf, 1958; and Gouldner, 1962. Interestingly enough, pre-World War II expressions of the same theme seem to have gone into eclipse during this period, even when propounded by otherwise widely read men such as Lynd, 1939; and Myrdal, 1944:Appendix 2. Moving deep into the psychedelic sixties and into increasing involvement with questions of public policy, matters of moral stance became a prime object of dispute during which one work even put "sociology on trial" and another declared a "new sociology." The interested reader will find this diatribe conveniently chronicled in the pages of *The American Sociologist,* a magazine instituted in 1965. See also Horowitz, 1967; H. S. Becker, 1967; Tumin, 1968; and Manis, 1968. On the substantive and ideological texture of sociology more generally, see Horowitz, 1965; Lipset and Smelser, 1961; Gouldner, 1968; and Horton, 1966;

deviance scholars, Howard S. Becker's pungent distinction between conventional and unconventional sentimentality was an important expression of these doubts. Defining sentimentality as "a disposition on the part of the researcher to leave certain variables in a problem unexamined,"[8] he pointed out the conventionally sentimental tendency of deviance scholars to accept lay assumptions about the acts and qualities of "normals" and "deviants." Given their conventional sentimentality, they tended to design their studies in ways that revealed only the morally crediting aspects of normals and the morally discrediting aspects of deviants. As a consequence, much deviance research served mainly to reinforce the layman's conception of the world as divided into thoroughly "good people" and thoroughly "evil people," with perhaps a few in between. Thus studies focusing strictly on the backgrounds and psychological characteristics of people classified as criminals, for example, conveniently ignored their normal conduct, the conventional social processes in which they participated and the conventional acts and qualities of their interaction partners. Put another way, the conventionally sentimental tended to conceive their research problems in ways that overlooked the aspects of normals that were morally blemished and the aspects of deviants that were morally crediting. Expanding on Becker, we should observe that the conventional sentimentality of the fifties was more invidious than that of earlier social pathologists, because it was less naïve and less obvious, wearing as it did the facade of value-free sociology. Beneath this facade, however, lay an essentially normative—even conservative—status quo orientation.

In the same way that all perspectives tend to generate counterperspectives, a different (if not new) genre of deviance researchers arose with some force in the early sixties. Acting as both spokesman for the motif and as skeptical onlooker, Becker characterized the equally noticeable bias of this new perspective as "unconventional sentimentality," a disposition to assume that normals are less moral than typically portrayed and a disposition to assume that deviants are considerably more moral than is commonly thought. The unconventional sentimentalist "assumes . . . that the underdog is always right and those in authority always wrong."[9] As editor (1962–64) of a scholarly journal with the ironic title *Social Problems,* Becker was particularly disposed to articles of an unconventionally sentimental cast,[10] a policy that was continued by his successors. The error of the unconventionally sentimental was justified, according to

---

the works collected in Demerath and Peterson, eds., 1967; and the historical interpretation advanced by E. Becker, 1968:especially Chap. 4.
[8] H. S. Becker, ed., 1964:4.
[9] *Ibid.,* p. 5.
[10] Becker later collected many of these articles in a book he entitled *The Other Side* (H. S. Becker, ed., 1964), an overt expression of unconventional sentimentality.

Becker, because "if one outrages certain conventional assumptions by being unconventionally sentimental, a large body of opinion will be sure to tell [scholars] about it. But conventional sentimentality is less often attacked and specious premises stand unchallenged" (H. S. Becker, 1964:5–6).[11]

It needs hastily to be added that none of this controversy over value-bias is an attack on science per se. Science is only a set of procedures which disciplines the collection and analysis of data. The scientific outlook concerns itself with matters of appropriate sampling, measurement, adequate controls and comparisons, demonstrations of hypothetical associations and legitimate interpretation of data. Science cannot tell researchers what questions to ask, what problems to pose, what aspects of reality to single out for study, what concepts to employ in analyzing some situation or what assumptions to make about the nature of some problematic phenomenon. The present questions of value neutrality or tacit commitment have to do with these latter concerns. They are not issues of appropriate scientific procedure. Scholars of any value orientation can be equally scientific and yet still be at odds because they do not agree on what questions to ask or how to ask them, or, if they agree at this level, because they differ in their assessment of the fundamental characteristics of the same object. These are matters of perspective.

---

[11] There has, of course, been a concomitant, substantive shift from a focus on deviant acts and persons to a focus on "normals" and their various relations to deviance, particularly centering on the concept of labeling. The latter questions will occupy us below, especially in Part II. For histories emphasizing the substantive character of the dissent or shift, see Gibbs, 1966; Reiss, 1966; Bordua, 1967; and Douglas, 1969. See also the substantively critical statements cited in footnote 8 of Chap. 2.

Reflective Questions

1. How did the social environment during each of the three periods discussed in this paper contribute to the accepted sociological perspective of the period?

2. What are the possible consequences for scientific research on topics of deviance, with reference to each of the three perspectives?

3. How did Becker justify the perspective of "unconventional sentimentality"? Does his approach have value in the 1970's?

4. On what grounds might you argue that academic disagreement among sociologists is the real health of the discipline?

18 □ Femininity in the Lesbian Community

William Simon □ John H. Gagnon

A major limitation of many current studies on the lesbian has been the preoccupation with the "erotic" and "exotic" patterns of her sexual behavior. These studies frequently focus on the "failure" of the socialization process as an explanation of the lesbian's sexual deviation. This article examines lesbian behavior in terms of general female patterns. According to the authors, the most significant factor that serves to distinguish the lesbian from other women is the gender of the object that engages her sexuality. Simon and Gagnon argue the need to consider the lesbian not only as a deviant, but also in terms of her adaptation to conventional sex-role models. "Perhaps," suggest the authors, ". . . an understanding of homosexuality can only follow from an understanding of sexuality itself." □

FOR SOME TIME NOW IT HAS BEEN OUR CONVICTION THAT STUDIES IN DEVIANT behavior frequently have been overimpressed with the "special," or "exotic," character of the populations or groups studied. Many students of deviant behavior have been vulnerable to the temptations of a kind of intellectual "hipsterism," delighting in familiarity with esoteric argots and the ease with which they can display their "cool." One almost senses a reluctance to engage seriously more general conceptions—conceptions traditionally applied to the behavior of conforming populations—lest exotic behavior be transformed into pedestrian behavior, thus denying to the student a sense of special engagement. Consequently, for example, a good deal is known about the homosexual bar or tavern, but very little about the ways the homosexual earns a living, finds a place to live, or manages relations with his family. Similar to the larger society's reaction, there has been a tendency to be too exclusively preoccupied with the

From *Social Problems,* Vol. 15, No. 2, pp. 212–221. Reprinted by permission of The Society for the Study of Social Problems and the authors.

manifest deviance, and a failure to observe or report upon the conforming behavior which frequently accounts for the larger part of a deviant's time and energy—and provides the context for deviant performances as well as often giving meaning to such performances.

Similarly, studies of deviance tend to be overly preoccupied with failures in socialization. To be sure, deviance that becomes a major individual commitment represents, from the societal point of view, inappropriate socialization at the very least. Being homosexual, for example, is never the desired outcome of the childrearing process. The concern for explaining this undesired and unanticipated outcome, however, becomes the sociologist's version of the etiological question that too exclusively preoccupies the psychiatrist. Indeed, while the language of socialization failure or inappropriate socialization is itself appropriate, it is extremely unlikely that one can talk about total failures in socialization or socialization that is totally inappropriate. There has been a tendency to avoid the complex processes that represent the meshing of both conventional and unconventional forms of socialization resulting in an excessively narrow focus upon deviant adjustments and a corresponding neglect of conventional patterns of adjustment. Where there have been concerns with conventional adjustments, these were scrutinized simply to see how they reflect the deviant commitment; rarely is there concern with the ways in which deviant adjustments reflect conventional commitments.

The lesbian represents an excellent example of the need to integrate our understanding of both deviant and conventional developmental processes. Where, one may ask, is the research literature that reports upon the attributes and activities of the lesbian when she is *not* acting out her deviant commitment? The answer is that there is virtually none. As a result, the present paper must rely upon an exceedingly thin scientific literature,[1] an examination of the literature generated by female homophile organizations,[2] the general literature on the

---

[1] See Anonymous, "Some Comparisons Between Male and Female Homosexuals," *The Ladder*, 4, 12 (1966), pp. 4–25; Virginia Armon, "Some Personality Variables in Overt Female Homosexuality," Unpublished Ph.D. dissertation, University of Southern California, Los Angeles, 1961; Donald Webster Cory, *The Lesbian in America*, New York: Citadel Press, 1964; Helene Deutsch, "Homosexuality in Women," *International Journal of Psychoanalysis*, 14 (1933), pp. 34–56; Sylvan Keiser and Dora Schaffer, "Environmental Factors in Homosexuality in Adolescent Girls," *Psychoanalytic Review*, 36 (1949), pp. 283–295; Brian Magee, *One in Twenty. A Study of Homosexual Men and Women*, London: Secker & Warburg, 1966; Marijane Meaker (Ann Aldrich, pseud.), *We Walk Alone*, New York: Fawcett, 1955; J. D. Mercer, *They Walk in Shadow*, New York: Comet Press, 1959; Lionel Ovesey, "Masculine Aspirations in Women: An Adaptational Analysis," *Psychiatry*, 19 (1956), pp. 341–351; Joseph C. Rheingold, *The Fear of Being a Woman*, New York: Grune and Stratton, 1964, pp. 372–380; C. B. Wilbur, "Clinical Aspects of Homosexuality," in Judd Marmor, (ed.), *Sexual Inversion: The Multiple Roots of Homosexuality*, New York: Basic Books, 1965, pp. 268–281.

[2] *The Ladder*, published by the female homophile organization The Daughters of Bilitis,

processes of the development of feminine identifications and role patterns,[3] a series of exploratory, depth interviews conducted with a relatively small number of lesbians,[4] and a reanalysis of some of the data gathered by Kinsey and his associates. What follows, then, is a tentative attempt to piece together from disparate sources of information and theory an organizing perspective; its major justification is that it might serve as an effective basis for systematic research.

The lesbian differs from other women in the gender of the object that engages her sexuality. This is clearly a significant difference, one that engenders a potential for the emergence of deviant patterns in a number of aspects of social life. Indeed, the very significance of this difference tends to consume nearly all of the researcher's attention. What is generally neglected is the degree to which the lesbian's commitment to sexuality reflects general female patterns of sexuality, the difference in gender selection notwithstanding. It is the contention of this paper that in most cases the female homosexual follows conventional feminine patterns in developing her commitment to sexuality and in conducting a sexual career. This should not be particularly surprising considering that, despite the specific experiences that influenced gender selection, most lesbians are exposed to the numerous diffuse and subtle experiences and relations that generally serve to promote conventional sex-role identification in this society. Moreover, many of these experiences and relations occur prior to the emergence of sexuality as something explicit and salient and there is little reason to assume that these sources of sex-role learning are not assimilated in much the same way as occurs with females who are more exclusively heterosexual.

One of the major characteristics of female socialization in American society is the degree to which the general outlines of its processes are relatively simple and devoted to a single outcome, what Parsons has called, after Burgess, the domestic pattern.[5] Whatever the desires of females for glamor, careers, or companionship patterns, the most pervasive commitment of the society is the production of wives and mothers among all females. Much like the military's

---

is useful and often insightful reading, as is the publication of the Minorities Research Group in England, *Arena 3.*

[3] Simone de Beauvoir, *The Second Sex,* New York: Knopf, 1953; Therese Benedek, *Psychosexual Functions in Women,* New York: Ronald Press, 1953; Marie Bonaparte, *Female Sexuality,* New York: International Universities Press, 1953; Sigmund Freud, "Female Sexuality," in James Strachey, translator and editor, *Collected Papers,* Vol. 5, London: The Hogarth Press, 1950, pp. 252-272; Stephen R. Graubard, editor, "The Women in America," *Daedalus,* 93, 2 (Spring, 1964), pp. 579-808; Jerome Kagan, "Acquisition and Significance of Sex Typing and Sex Role," in M. L. Hoffman and L. W. Hoffman, editors, *Review of Child Development Research,* Vol. 1, New York: Russell Sage Foundation, 1904, pp. 137-167; Rheingold, *op. cit.*

[4] William Simon and John H. Gagnon, "The Lesbians: A Preliminary Overview," in John H. Gagnon and William Simon, editors, *Sexual Deviance,* New York: Harper & Row, 1967.

[5] Talcott Parsons, "Age and Sex in the Social Structure of the United States," *American Sociological Review,* 7, 5 (October, 1942), pp. 604-616.

inability to conceive of a soldier who is not modeled on the rifle-carrying infantryman, the society does not conceive of, nor does it train except by inadvertence, females who will have more complex roles than those of wife and mother. In the process of socialization, patterns both of aggression and assertion, as well as those of sexuality, are inhibited among female children, so that they will be labile and conforming to the needs of the male.[6] As Parsons points out, there is really no equivalent for the male term "bad boy" (except in the sexual domain during adolescence).

The single-model system of reproducing women has other basic consequences that are more discernible from the psychoanalytic literature. It is here that the enigma not only of female sexuality but of femininity and womanness is most profoundly confronted. In contrast to an author like de Beauvoir, the psychoanalyst Rheingold discusses the substantial influence that sheer biological differences play in the development of femininity and the commitments of women. As he suggests, "The denial of the body is a delusion. No woman transcends her body."[7] In addition to the biological fact of childbearing and consequently the social fact of childrearing,[8] the female is subjected to the training processes of this society focusing their energies on molding women to be "mother of the family" rather than into another role. Indeed, the alternative roles available for women, especially that of "career"—whether professional or glamorous—are almost as deviant for the society as is the role "lesbian."[9]

Previous research clearly supports the contention that the patterns of overt sexual behavior of homosexual females tend to resemble closely those of heterosexual females and to differ radically from the sexual activity patterns of both

[6] This may account for the Kinsey finding that there were no differences in the sexual patterns of females when socioeconomic status was held constant except for age at marriage and therefore age at first coitus, a fundamentally dependent variable in this case. Female sexuality is designed to conform to a relatively wide range of male sexual performance without major upset or anxiety.

[7] Rheingold, *op. cit.*, p. 215.

[8] Alice Rossi, "Equality Between the Sexes: An Immodest Proposal," *Daedalus*, 93, 2 (Spring, 1964), pp. 607–652. The author points out that for the first time in history there is a situation in which child-rearing is the full-time business of the woman rather than being simply one of her many duties as in the past.

[9] Changes in the technology and social organization of work have considerably lessened the strain of choosing between family roles and work for middle-class females. However, the problems of managing a strong career commitment, including aspirations levels appropriate for a given career, appear to remain problematic. As Mervin Freedman observed in describing his study of Vassar students: "The interviews also reveal some reluctance on the part of women to assume leadership in various professions or fields except for those which possess considerable female connotation—for example, social work. They are likely to retreat from any exceptional accomplishment which may threaten the security of men. . . . All in all, as I see it, most women today are striving to maintain the integrity of the family and, at least to some extent, the continuity of traditional sex roles." In *The College Experience*, San Francisco: Jossey-Bass, Inc., 1967, pp. 119–120.

heterosexual and homosexual males.[10] Exceptions to this generalization result either from prison experience or certain other limited group situations where the constraints operating upon sexual performances and role assignments are basically different from those observable in the rest of society.[11] The homogeneity among women (regardless of sexual object choice) and the differences between women and men begin, overtly at least, in the different introductions of males and females to sexuality. Many of the most important differences become evident when we consider the phasing of entry into sexual activity. For males the major organizing event in their sexual lives is clearly puberty. Within two years after puberty the vast majority of males have their commitment to sexuality reinforced by the experience of orgasm.[12] This is largely the result of the fact that masturbation occurs among males at fairly high rates during early adolescence. Females, on the other hand, tend to begin overt sexual activity—that is, behavior that has a reasonable probability of culminating in orgasm—much later, during late adolescence or the early years of adulthood. Moreover, for females the initial experience of orgasm is nearly as likely to occur during sociosexual activity (pre-coital petting or coitus) as it is likely to be a result of masturbatory activity. Indeed, half or more of the women who report masturbation as a source of sexual outlet "discovered" this outlet after achieving orgasm in sociosexual activity. In this pattern of male-female difference, female homosexuals do not appear to differ significantly from heterosexual females.

Two factors significant in the management of sexual life appear to derive from this differential male-female introduction into sexuality. The first of these is the fact that males usually develop commitments to sexuality prior to involvement in complicated, emotionally charged inter-personal relations—that is, prior to developing a commitment to the rhetoric of love. For females, most lesbians included, the reverse appears to be true: training in love precedes training in sexuality. As a result, sex as an interest and an activity appears to possess greater autonomy for males. It is an activity that can be engaged in with relative detachment from other areas of life. For most women—including most lesbians—the pursuit of sexual gratification as something separate from emotional or romantic involvement is not particularly attractive; indeed, for many it may be impossible. This is in part reflected in the number of sexual partners an individual reports. In the original work of Kinsey and his associates it was observed that of the lesbians interviewed only 29 per cent had sexual relations with three or more partners, and only 4 per cent had contact with ten or more partners. These figures

[10] A. C. Kinsey, et al., *Sexual Behavior in the Human Male*, Philadelphia: Saunders Co., 1948; A. C. Kinsey, et al., *Sexual Behavior in the Human Female*, Philadelphia: Saunders Co., 1953.
[11] Rose Gialombardo, *Society of Women*, New York: Wiley, 1966; D. A. Ward and Gene G. Kassebaum, *Women's Prisons: Sex and Social Structure*, Chicago: Aldine Press, 1965.
[12] A. C. Kinsey, et al., op. cit., 1953, Figures 148–150, p. 717.

are extremely close approximations of proportions for females *per se*, whether homosexual or heterosexual.[13] This is far below comparable statistics for heterosexual males and dramatically below that for male homosexuals.

The second significant factor is that differences in the early management of sexuality suggest that the repression of sexuality is an essential part of learning to be a female in our society and is learned by heterosexual and homosexual women alike. Unlike males, females during adolescence and the early adult years typically tend not to report a feeling of sexual deprivation during periods of sexual inactivity. Similarly, sexual arousal by such things as dreams, fantasy, visual stimulation, and exposure to pornography is a substantially less common experience for females than for males. Sexual arousal in females—of all indirect sources—is highest from nonpornographic fiction and movies or precisely where sex, if significant as an element, appears in the context of a legitimizing emotional setting.[14] The reported rates of sexual stimulation without emotional contexts tend to be somewhat higher for lesbians than for heterosexual women but far lower than those reported for both heterosexual and homosexual males, and far lower than one might suspect given the obviously greater salience of sexuality for the lesbian. Sexuality for the lesbian should be more self-conscious, if only because it becomes the basis for her commitment to deviant patterns; however, the more general character-molding processes of society appear to be the dominant factors. Despite a generally oversimplified and widely current image of the lesbian as a "counterfeit man," the gender of the object of her sexual desires may be one of the relatively few attributes that she shares with males.

The social careers of lesbians and, more particularly, the patterns of group life that emerge can only be understood in the light of considerations such as those that have just been raised. These considerations have substantial ramifications for an appraisal of the lesbian community when it is contrasted with the male homosexual community.

For both male and female homosexuals it is possible to talk about the existence of a community, at least in most relatively large cities.[15] In the same manner as many ethnic or occupational groups, which also can be said to have a community, this subcommunity does not require a formal character or even a specific geographical location. It is, rather, a continuing collectivity of individuals who share some significant activity and who, out of a history of continuing

---

[13] A. C. Kinsey, *et al., op. cit.,* 1953, p. 475 and Table 78, p. 336.
[14] A. C. Kinsey, *et al., op. cit.,* 1953, pp. 642–689.
[15] Studies of male homosexual communities are E. Hooker's "The Homosexual Community," in James O. Palmer and Michael J. Goldstein, editors, *Perspectives in Psychopathology,* New York: Oxford University Press, 1966, pp. 354–364; Maurice Leznoff and William Westley, "The Homosexual Community," *Social Problems,* 3 (1956), pp. 257–263; a more specialized study is Nancy Achilles' *The Homosexual Bar,* unpublished M.A. thesis, Department of Sociology, University of Chicago, 1964.

interaction based on that activity, begin to generate a sense of a bounded group possessing special norms and a particular argot. Through extensive use such a homosexual aggregate may identify a particular location as "theirs," and in almost all large cities this includes one or more taverns that cater exclusively to a particular homosexual group. In these bars the homosexual may act out more freely his or her self-definition as compared with less segregated situations. Several homophile social and service organizations have recently appeared which offer a more public image of the homosexual. These various social activities reinforce a feeling of identity and provide for the homosexual a way of institutionalizing the experience, wisdom, and mythology of the collectivity. A synonym for this community, one not untouched by a sense of the ironic, is "the gay life."

For the individual homosexual, both male and female, the community provides many functions. A major function is the facilitation of sexual union; the lesbian who finds her way to the community can now select from a population that, while differing in other attributes, has the minimum qualification of sharing a lesbian commitment. This greatly reduces what is for the isolated lesbian the common risk of "falling for a straight girl," i.e., a heterosexual. The community provides a source of social support; it is a place where the lesbian can express her feelings or describe her experiences because there are others available who have had feelings and experiences very much like hers. It is an environment in which sexuality can be socialized and ways can be found of deriving sexual gratification by being admired, envied, or desired while not necessarily engaging in sexual behavior. Lastly, the community includes a language and an ideology which provide each individual lesbian with already developed attitudes that help her resist the societal claim that she is diseased, depraved, or shameful.

Everything said about the community to this point can obviously apply to both male and female homosexual communities. Indeed, in certain ways, it is difficult to establish the fact that two separate communities exist as there is considerable overlap and sharing of facilities. However, marked differences arise when the community is examined more closely in the light of the differing sexual commitments of male and female homosexuals.

First, quite clearly, from any acquaintance with homosexual communities, the proportion of lesbians utilizing the gay world is markedly smaller than that of male homosexuals—though in both cases the visible gay world is an inadequate sampling of the respective homosexual populations. There are homosexuals of both sexes who completely avoid contact with public forms of the gay life (more true of females than males), others whose use is episodic (more true of males than females), and still others whose contact is indirect (maintaining social contact with other homosexuals who participate in the gay life). This lower rate of use by lesbians may be attributed to two related factors. One, the lesbian's sexual commitment is not as immediately alienating from the conventional society. The lesbian may mask her sexual deviance behind a socially prepared asexual role. Not all categories of women in our society are necessarily defined as sexually active. For example, spinsters are not assumed to be more sexually active than are married women by the fact of their spinsterhood. To the contrary, they are assumed to be less active sexually. In line with this, the image of two spinsters living together does not immediately suggest sexual activity between them, even when there is a public display of affection. The same is not true for men. The bachelor is presumed to be even more sexually active than the married man, and the idea of two males living together—past the years of young adulthood— strikes one as strange. This makes it more likely that the lesbian will find sources of social support or compensation in the larger society than will the male homosexual, thereby lessening her need for the subcommunity. What is involved in this socially provided asexual role for the female is society's assumption that women can manage careers of sexual inactivity with success while the male cannot.

The second factor directly involves the learning of techniques for the management of sexuality. It is possible that the same techniques of repression that lead to differences between males and females in the ages during which sexual activity is initiated allow the female to handle subsequent sexual deprivation more easily. More females than males should therefore be able to resist quasi-public homosexual behavior which increases the risks of disclosure; further, lesbians should be better able to resist relations that involve sexual exchange without any emotional investment. It is hardly a novel observation that training in the repression of sexuality is far more thorough and systematic for females than it is for males in our society. One reason for this is suggested by Rheingold when he observes that females run a double risk in the management of sexuality, while there is only a single risk for most males. "The woman's adjustment is precarious, for each new biologic event or social role evokes the fear of consequences. A man fears that he may fail; a woman fears both that she may fail and that she may succeed."[16] What is implied by success is the ability to express and pursue sexual interest and a competence in performance. This may also involve a sense of the sexual as something at least partially autonomous, as a form of behavior that need not *always* be justified in terms of service to some non-sexual end. It is the linking of sexual activity with the non-sexual that makes ours a society where both the non-sexual and fully sexual adaptations for women are viewed as deviant.

These factors should produce not only differences in the relative proportions of each sex utilizing the visible homosexual subcommunity, but also should produce differences in the quality or content of community life. Thus, camp

[16] Rheingold, *op. cit.*, p. 213.

behavior—behavior that is both outrageous and outraging—appears to be essentially a product of the male homosexual community. In terms of general social and political values the lesbian community is far more traditional—indeed, one might say conservative. There is little visible avant-gardism in the lesbian community; to the contrary, its collective taste appears highly traditional, perhaps stodgy. Partly this may be a function of the fact that lesbians are more likely to "come out"—that is, acknowledge their homosexuality—at later ages, at ages when other constraining commitments to the larger society are already established. Also, the lesbian is more likely to become available to the community only after a relatively isolated affair or series of affairs. The lesbian community, then, is far less often the scene of "coming out," and consequently less often the scene for the acting-out behavior frequently associated with this stage in the male homosexual community, where the discovery of self as homosexual and the discovery of the homosexual community more often coincide.

If two of the major functions of a homosexual community are the facilitation of sexual activity and the socialization into sexual roles, the relative emphasis given these by the two sexes should also differ. For males the emphasis upon the facilitation of sexual activity should be greater, while emphasis upon the socialization process should be greater among females. If nothing else, the lesbian community should contain a higher proportion of members existing in relatively stable, dyadic relationships, relationships that are more than sexual alliances. The use of the community by this segment of its membership is more exclusively social, providing contextual constraints against the tradition of aggressively seeking sexual partners that tends to typify the male homosexual community. However, it is possible that the extent of participation within either community may have opposite effects upon males and females. As a male homosexual becomes more integrated into the homosexual community, it becomes more possible for him to develop extensive forms of gratification that feed a homosexual identification without necessarily being sexual, while the lesbian, as she becomes more integrated into the lesbian community, may find the experience deinhibiting, freeing her somewhat from the constraints of her feminine socialization and allowing her to be sexual in more direct ways.

Both male and female homosexual communities generally share an important characteristic: both give rise to appearances that reinforce the societal image of the respective homosexualities. That is, the appearances of the male homosexual community tend to project an essentially feminine image of the male homosexual, while the appearances of the lesbian community may well reinforce the social image of the lesbian as masculine. And, of great importance, such collective appearances reinforce the notion that pseudo-masculinity or pseudo-femininity (as the case may be) are essential to the sexual commitment and performance of the homosexual. A counterargument is that, in the case of the lesbian, the community constrains *most* participating lesbians to appear more masculine than they would ordinarily desire. Firstly, this promotes a sense of group identity and participation and helps create a sense of distance between the group and the outside majority. Secondly, it reflects the activity of a relatively small proportion of lesbians for whom feminine socialization processes failed more thoroughly and/or whose sense of alienation from conventional society is fairly intense, and who self-consciously pursue a masculinized role of the "butch." It is this group that is both the most visible and, because of the extreme nature of its deviant performance, has the greatest need for the community. Thirdly, it reflects the presence of a larger proportion of lesbians who pursue a masculinized role during a limited amount of time in their homosexual careers—a stage through which many lesbians may pass, but one in which relatively few remain. This is largely a phase during which the acceptance of private homosexuality is being transformed into an acceptance of social homosexuality, a period Erikson would describe as an identity crisis with experimentation with masculinized roles being one expression of this transitional crisis.

Like many other discussions of deviant behavior, too much of the social landscape has been left out; however, it is a preliminary attempt to bring the exotic to terms with the pedestrian. One goal of this paper has been to argue the need for viewing female homosexuality in terms of both its discontinuity and continuity with conventional behavior and conventional determinants, the need to balance a sense of the degree to which the lesbian departs from standard definitions of appropriate sex-role behavior with a sense of how much of her behavior derives from the embodiment of standard definitions of sex-role behavior. Perhaps more importantly, this is an attempt to demonstrate that an understanding of homosexuality can only follow from an understanding of sexuality itself. With regard to the lesbian, we begin to come close to this when we approach more closely an understanding of the complex interweaving of sociocultural and biological forces that produce the varied forms of female sexuality.

Reflective Questions

1. What has been a result of the preoccupation with failures in socialization and studies on deviants?

2. What are the basic consequences for the female when she is subjected to the single-model system of socialization?

3. How does the sexual behavior of lesbians differ from that of both the heterosexual and the homosexual male?

4. What is the primary goal of this paper? How well is the goal achieved?

19 □ THE PENTHEUS APPROACH

Michael R. Aldrich

Michael Aldrich, a student leader of the Society for Legalization of Marijuana, has called the method by which we deal with the use of drugs and drug offenders the Pentheus Approach. To him this approach allows only two options: (1) medical use and (2) "All Other Use," called abuse, the latter being legally forbidden and punishable by harsh penalties. The idea behind the Pentheus Approach is essentially one of retribution and deterrence: the belief that the problem of drugs can be best solved by making risks so great that "rational" citizens will not use the forbidden drugs, and punishment so severe and certain for those who get caught that others will be deterred from its use. Failure in such a prohibitive approach is noted by the fact that it creates social problems worse than the ones it is designed to eliminate, such as the development of a market for organized crime; the tendency of drug enforcement agencies to exceed their authority; and illegal activity by the police. Aldrich proposes that narcotics use be treated as a health problem, that there be state, local, and federal control rather than prohibition, and that there be licensed psychedelic centers. □

WHETHER WE LIKE IT OR NOT, WE ARE IN THE MIDST OF WHAT CAN ONLY BE called a revolution in thinking. If *Life* magazine (7 July '67) is correct, 10 million Americans have smoked marijuana. Out of approximately 200 million Americans, one in every twenty people you meet has turned on—and is a criminal for doing so.

Among college students, incidence of marijuana use is even higher. Surveys on college campuses indicate that anywhere from 15 to 40 percent of the

This article first appeared in *The Humanist*, March/April, 1968, and is reprinted by permission.

average student body smokes pot; the National Institute of Mental Health estimates the figure at one out of every five students. Every fifth person you meet on campus these days is a criminal, under both state and national laws.

Whether we like it or not, and speaking only of marijuana, we are talking about an issue of considerable proportions. This is no game of statistics; we are talking about human beings whose whole lives as members of society may be at stake. Doctors, lawyers, merchants, chiefs—students, teachers, hippies, priests—are charging into the hemp field. What to do? How can we deal with this issue?

I want to tell a story that I read recently. A hippie showed up one day—longhaired, outlandishly dressed, talking religiously, carrying an unknown Dangerous Drug—in a friendly little provincial town. He was quite open about the fact that he considered himself a holy man, and he was turning a lot of people on with his strange new chemical.

The Mayor of this town was a moderate, rational, normally-calm gentleman, a bit overly prim, a bit bossy, a bit concerned with his political position. Suddenly he felt that this young hippie was a threat to him and to the town. He heard reports that the hippie and his followers were establishing a cult which encouraged people to indulge themselves in wild parties, promoting possibly erotic, possibly psychotic and surely bizarre behavior. And the Mayor felt especially unhappy when he discovered that some members of his own family were joining this cult and using this drug.

So the Mayor did what the power of his office permitted him to do; he tossed the stranger in jail. From within the hippie's cell, a voice was heard:

Kindle, flame of blazing lightning—
Burn, burn the house of Pentheus to the ground!

There was an explosion, lightning seared the jailhouse, and the hippie suddenly appeared, free. The young man offered to let the Mayor see one of these wild parties for himself, and led the official out of town. The poor Mayor was eventually torn to pieces by the hippie's followers, including the Mayor's own drug-crazed mother.

That Mayor was Pentheus; the little town was Thebes; the drug was alcohol (wine), and the strange young hippie was Dionysius. You can read all about it in Euripides' *Bacchae*.

The King of Thebes tried to use what I call "The Pentheus Approach" to drug use. Throw the deviant in jail, punish him, *put him away* from you and me, avoid him, make him a void.

The Pentheus Approach is, of course, the classic American approach to drugs. It was the approach in 1914, with narcotics; in 1918, with liquor; in 1937, with marijuana in 1965, with amphetamines, barbiturates, and hallucinogens;

and this year, with the U.S. now a signatory to the United Nations Single Convention.

The Pentheus Approach, national and international, allows only two options for drug use: the medical use in curing diseases, and All Other Use, called "abuse," legally forbidden and punishable by harsh criminal penalties. All such prohibition legislation stems from a single idea, that if there is a social problem, the best way to solve it is to prohibit the substance involved, usually indirectly, by stopping supply of it.

Ideally, this approach tries to solve the problem by making the risks involved with illicit drug use so large that normally law-abiding citizens will not use the forbidden drugs; and the severe punishment of those who do get caught is supposed to provide an example which will be further dissuasive. But the Pentheus Approach comes nowhere near meeting this ideal; it is simply a grand rationale for laws which sound as if they will work, but don't.

Prohibition has failed, is failing, and always will fail, because of one simple fact: it does not meet the problem, it does not solve the problem. It *avoids* the problems of non-medical drug use, by putting users away from us, putting the whole issue away from our social consciousness. This essential failure always becomes noticeable whenever a significant proportion of the populace ignores the law—which is what is happening with marijuana, and to a lesser extent with the hallucinogens, right now.

A second major fault of Pentheus legislation, aside from the fact that it doesn't work, is that it creates social problems worse than the ones it is designed to eliminate. Prohibition manufactures a market into which the ogre-business called Organized Crime leaps. Alcohol prohibition in the 1920's created for racketeers an ideal source of income; heroin prohibition continues to maintain them. Until recently, marijuana and LSD were not particularly strong gangland operations, since LSD was legal and much marijuana smuggling was strictly amateur. It simply wasn't lucrative enough for the syndicates to move in. But recently, they have moved into the hippie arena; student pot-dealers are getting bumped off, LSD is being cut with heroin, once amateur chemists and dealers are being rubbed out or absorbed into the Big Boys' game. Prohibition makes crime: it does not prevent crime.

Another aspect of the dangerous social situation created by the Pentheus Approach is that the agencies which enforce drug laws, especially local, state, and Federal narcotics bureaus, tend to exceed their authority, getting involved in areas far beyond law enforcement. Harry J. Anslinger, semi-retired former Narcotics Commissioner and American delegate to the U.N. Narcotics Commission, spent his years in both offices getting more and more prohibition laws, with extremely cruel penalties, passed in America and abroad.

In May of this year, only Anslinger and two other government officials (favoring prohibition) were called to testify, as the Senate considered ratification of the U.N. Single Convention, the international Pentheus Approach. No drug experts, doctors, lawyers, or sociologists were called to consider whether prohibition was the best approach to drug control in America. Anslinger testified that he favored ratification to resist the legalization of marijuana, since an enormous amount of discussion about that possibility has taken place recently in America. In effect, he urged that the law be approved so that all opinions other than his own would be stifled. That is not law enforcement, that is meglomania; he doesn't want the Federal Bureau of Narcotics to enforce the law, he wants it to dictate the law. Even under the less zealous guidance of Henry Giordano, our present Commissioner, the FBN is virtually dictator of policy over those drugs it controls. (The same is true of the FDA, whose officials are somewhat more enlightened.) Do we want such police dictatorships in America? They are not overt—the officials involved always claim to be "just doing their job"—but whoever gave the Federal Bureau of Narcotics the right to try to push *their* version of proper drug control into harsh law?

Then there is the side-issue of illegal activity by the police themselves, which exists but is usually very difficult to prove. I know of a few—that's too many—cases in which policemen, or agents sent in by the police, have planted marijuana in the homes of people they didn't like, people suspected of marijuana use. The police attitude in these instances has been—well, they were probably guilty anyway, in fact we're sure they are, so let's take them to court. And it is quite impossible for the suspect-victim to prove his innocence, since a judge and jury are automatically skeptical of such a serious claim against the police; any guilty man could make that claim. The possibility of illegal entrapment—including planting, wiretapping, and bugging—is there because of the Pentheus Approach, which deals with drug use as a criminal and police matter.

At this point we should ask why the prohibition approach, with severe criminal penalties for conviction, was established against drugs in the first place? Marijuana makes the most serious case of this, so let's go back thirty years and take a look.

Harry Anslinger, liquor-prohibition cop, was done out of his job by Repeal. The FBN was established in 1930, and Anslinger became its top banana. "An alarming increase in the smoking of marijuana reefers in 1936 continued to spread at an accelerated pace in 1937," reports Anslinger in his autobiography, *The Murderers*. A few criminals here and there try to get off charges of heinous crimes—unsuccessfully—by pleading that they'd smoked marijuana beforehand and didn't know what they were doing. Anslinger launches a two pronged campaign:

First, a legislative plan to seek from Congress a new law that would
place marijuana and its distribution under federal control. Second, on

radio and at major forums. . . . I told the story of this evil weed of the fields and river beds and roadsides. I wrote articles for magazines; our agents gave hundreds of lectures to parents, educators, social and civic leaders. In network broadcasts I reported on the growing list of crimes. . . .

Anslinger is a concerned citizen, of course; but also a man pushing for more authority for his police empire, a man using his title to arouse an enormous scare-campaign in the sensationalist news media. Anslinger's real anxiety is no excuse for manufacturing fear on the basis of conjecture, nor is it an excuse for bullheadedness on the part of a public official about the single approach that can be used to solve the problem. Why did not one consider that the disastrous prohibition approach, so recently proven a failure with alcohol, might not be the best answer to this problem? Why did no one consider that a more reasonable solution would be to punish actual criminal activities (only allegedly related to marijuana), rather than to treat the use of marijuana itself as a criminal activity?

For thirty years now, the Bureau has taken it upon itself to defend the unworking laws, gathering bits and pieces of scare-material wherever they could actually find them, selecting and distorting where they cannot, suppressing and ignoring material which offers evidence that they're wrong. Since Anslinger became a U.N. delegate, the prohibition mentality has been world-wide; but very little has actually been done to get rid of the pot in the world. The prohibitionists are so frustrated that they must resort to the sneakiest of secretive tactics, like Anslinger getting the United States to ratify the Single Convention. In open debate against more enlightened drug authorities, they haven't got a chance.

The central issue in such debate should be whether marijuana use actually contributes to crimes, or not. Virtually every objective study of pot in the last 75 years—made by agencies NOT directly or indirectly involved with law enforcement or politics—has concluded that marijuana is not the, or even *a,* major determining factor in the commission of crimes. These conclusions start with the mammoth 7-volume Indian Hemp Commission report in 1894 and run through the LaGuardia Report ('44), the Panama Canal Zone Governor's Report ('25), the White House Drug Abuse Conference report ('62), the N.Y. County Medical Society report ('66), and both reports of the President's Crime Commission last year.

I wish to make it clear that there *can* be risks involved with marijuana (or, more usually, hashish) use—like Chopra, forms of cannabis such as hashish; but the argument that marijuana use "causes" crime is not based on factual evidence. The Bureau never tires of quoting a pathetically few observers of marijuana (or, more usually, hashish) use—like Chopra, Gardikas and Wolff— to the effect that marijuana's reaction on individuals is unpredictable, leads occasionally to "fits of aggressive mania," and consequently to the commission of violent crime. All such evidence—scanty it is—provokes one serious question: did marijuana, or something else, play the determining role in the commission of the crime? *And even if it did:* why not punish the criminal behavior, the violence, instead of punishing the millions of people who do *not* commit any crimes under marijuana's influence? But the prohibitionist logic does not see the injustice in punishing millions of innocents for the crimes of the very few.

The other two-standard arguments of the Bureau—that marijuana causes insanity and leads to heroin—are equally conjectural, based on the same principal of punishing everyone because of a few proven instances, and the gaudy imaginations that bubble up from these cases. The strongest palliative against these fancies is a good strong dose of fact, fact which takes the verified risks into consideration. Here's a summary of the latest evidence for such claims, as presented by the President's Task Force on Narcotics and Drug Abuse in 1967:

Studies in India (Chopra) and North Africa (Asuni, Lambo) show that cannabis psychoses occur in association with heavy use of potent forms of cannabis. Dependency is also described, as is apathy, reduced work and social effectiveness, etc. These effects may be due, in some measure, to the vulnerability of the using population (already sick, hopeless, hungry, etc.). In the United States neither cannabis psychosis nor cannabis dependency has been described. . . .

Case history material suggests that many identified heroin users have had earlier experience with marijuana but their "natural history" is also likely to include even earlier illicit use of cigarettes and alcohol. The evidence from our college students and utopiate and news articles is clear that many persons not in heroin-risk neighborhoods who experiment with marijuana do not "progress" to "hard" narcotics.

Once again, the essential question must be asked; *recognizing* these risks, is the Pentheus Approach the best way to solve the problems? Should psychoses, "dependency" (which only means that a man *likes* what he takes, not that he's addicted to it), apathy, reduced social effectiveness, be punished as crimes? Granted that we want to reduce the possibility of anyone's getting hooked on heroin, wouldn't it be more effective to remove marijuana from the "illegal" and "narcotic" categories, since its placement in these categories is what brought marijuana and heroin into the same organized-crime circles in the first place? And most important: none of the associations between marijuana and "psychosis," and marijuana and heroin, call necessarily for total, blanket prohibition of marijuana for the millions who don't flip out or "graduate" to narcotics.

Last summer, the First National Conference on Student Drug Involvement, in College Park, Maryland, brought together more than 200 drug experts, sociologists, physicians, policemen, lawyers, college administrators and students to discuss these problems. All "sides" in the various arguments were represented. At the end of the Conference, the following resolution was passed unanimously by participant delegates:

RESOLVED, THAT (the Conference) recommends that local, state, and Federal governments stop all punitive and criminal approaches to any drug use, including use of narcotics, cannabis, and the hallucinogenic drugs; and instead, establish programs in which:

(A) narcotics use is treated as a health problem rather than as a criminal offense;

(B) 1. local, state, and Federal governments permit and encourage research into all aspects of cannabis use, including its medical applications,
2. the smoking of cannabis on private premises is allowed and no longer constitutes a criminal offense,
3. cannabis is controlled, rather than prohibited, by an *ad hoc* instrument,
4. possession and sale of cannabis is permitted and regulated, rather than prohibited, and
5. all persons now imprisoned for possession of cannabis, for allowing cannabis to be smoked on private premises, or for being present on such premises, should have their sentences commuted;

(C) psychedelic centers be licensed and established so that those who wish to use psychedelic substances can do so under safe and controlled conditions.

What we all—Pentheus lawmakers and drug-users alike—are looking for is a rational, balanced approach for society and individuals to take to the problem of drug use. The resolution's suggestions offer no panaceas, as the Pentheus Approach tries to—there will be thorny problems if a program similar to the resolution is ever implemented—but these suggestions seem more workable than the prohibition approach, with fewer resultant social evils.

Persons who get mixed up with the sad, sick narcotics scene would get some form of medical treatment, the exact program to be worked out by doctors and health officials according to individual cases.

Those who wished to take psychedelics, knowing the risks involved—meaning those who are now taking those risks with no help whatsoever—would be able to take them under conditions in which they could not hurt themselves or others physically. Since a fairly large number of people are going to take hallucinogens regardless of whether they're legal or not, it is more reasonable to set up safer conditions for such people, reducing their risks and those of society. This idea confronts the problem of LSD use head-on, rather than sweeping it under the rug into the dark world of organized crime.

The marijuana part of the resolution offers an effective program of careful regulation of marijuana, rather than complete "legalization" or the present blanket prohibition. Section 2 allows pot on private premises, which would mean that smoking pot in cars, for instance, would not be allowed. Section 3 would encourage strict regulation of legally-permitted strength of cannabis preparations, and standards of purity, which would solve two serious present problems, e.g. that pot is sometimes cut with harmful substances, and that there may be some danger in overindulgence in strong hashish preparations.

Section 4 of the resolution would replace present black-marketeering and smuggling of marijuana with government licensing and control, and a sizeable amount of revenue from taxes could accrue. Most likely, minimum age limits would be established for those who could legally purchase different brands of marijuana.

Problems would by no means disappear. Most of them would be involved with the fact that there will always be people who use drugs irresponsibly—which means immoderately, or under dangerous conditions. But we do not legislate other dangerous drugs—coffee, alcohol, tobacco—completely out of legal existence for all people, simply because some people abuse them. Some of the horrors people dream up to accompany the idea of more freely available marijuana—such as massive crime waves and more slaughter on the highways—are mostly imaginary. (Marijuana is not generally conducive to violence, and it is entirely possible to drive well while stoned, once you are familiar with your slightly-slower reaction times.) Some of the problems imagined would in fact exist; but these suggestions offer a better way of handling those problems than the present blanket prohibition. Young people would not be branded criminals, and flung into the greedy arms of organized crime or into jail.

Laws are relative: regulation of behavior should be in accord with other laws (like liquor regulation) and with current social practice, e.g. the burgeoning number of people who, for one reason or another, prefer marijuana as their choice of intoxicant. There are problems, individual and social, with drug use, but putting people in jail when they aren't hurting anybody is not an appropriate response to these problems. Present prohibition has not, and does not, deal effectively with the problems; a program like that outlined here, could. And the massive problems which have grown out of blanket drug prohibition, such as organized crime and police self-aggrandizement, would be minimized.

It is time for a change: *"Burn, burn the house of Pentheus to the ground."*

Reflective Questions

1. Should marijuana be legalized?

2. What types of regulation would you institute governing the use of morphine, heroin, and LSD?

3. What shifts in the pattern of drug use have taken place in the last 50 years?

4. Is drug use among the top five major problems in the United States? Why is it a problem?

20 □ THE FUNCTIONS OF RACIAL CONFLICT

Joseph S. Himes

Does racial conflict have system-maintaining and system-enhancing consequences for the larger American society? This is the theoretical question posed in this article. Professor Himes' answer is in the affirmative. In the black man's struggle for equality, Himes regards legal redress, political pressure, and mass action as realistic forms of conflict, that is, as rationally determined means used to achieve culturally approved ends. Racial conflict is socially functional for system maintenance and system enhancement in that it (1) alters the social structure, (2) extends social communication, (3) enhances social solidarity, and (4) facilitates personal identity. Explication of the manner in which racial conflict achieves the above functions extends our knowledge of change and corrects for an anticonflict bias in American social science. □

WHEN ONE CONTEMPLATES THE CONTEMPORARY AMERICAN SCENE, HE MAY be appalled by the picture of internal conflict portrayed in the daily news. The nation is pictured as torn by dissension over Vietnam policy. The people are reported being split by racial strife that periodically erupts into open violence. Organized labor and management are locked in a perennial struggle that occasionally threatens the well-being of the society. The reapportionment issue has forced the ancient rural-urban conflict into public view. Religious denominations and faiths strive against ancient conflicts of theology and doctrine toward unification and ecumenism. Big government is joined in a continuing struggle against big industry, big business, big finance, and big labor on behalf of the "public interest."

The image created by such reports is that of a society "rocked," "split" or

From *Social Forces*, September, 1966, pp. 1–10. Reprinted by permission of The University of North Carolina Press and the author.

"torn" by its internal conflicts. The repetition of such phrases and the spotlighting of conflict suggest that the integration, if not the very existence of the society is threatened. It is thus implied, and indeed often stated that the elimination of internal conflict is the central problem for policy and action in the society.

These preliminary remarks tend to indicate that there is widespread popular disapproval of social conflict. In some quarters the absence of conflict is thought to signify the existence of social harmony and stability. According to the human relations theme, conflict, aggression, hostility, antagonism and such devisive motives and behaviors are regarded as social heresies and therefore to be avoided. Often the word conflict is associated with images of violence and destruction.

At the same time, in contemporary sociology the problem of social conflict has been largely neglected. As Coser, Dahrendorf and others have pointed out, this tendency issues from preoccupation with models of social structure and theories of equilibrium.[1] Conflicts are treated as strains, tensions or stresses of social structures and regarded as pathological. Little attention is devoted to the investigation of conflict as a functional social process.

However, some of the earlier sociologists employed social conflict as one central element of their conceptual systems. Theory and analysis were cast in terms of a process model. Conflict was viewed as natural and as functioning as an integrative force in society.

To Ludwig Gumplowicz and Gustav Ratzenhofer conflict was the basic social process, while for Lester F. Ward and Albion W. Small it was one of the basic processes. Sumner, Ross, and Cooley envisaged conflict as one of the major forces operating to lace human society together.[2] Park and Burgess employed social conflict as one of the processual pillars of their sociological system.[3]

At bottom, however, the two analytic models of social organization are really not inconsistent. Dahrendorf argues that consensus-structure and conflict-process are "the two faces of society."[4] That is, social integration results simultaneously from both consensus of values and coercion to compliance. Indeed,

---

[1] Lewis A. Coser, *The Functions of Social Conflict* (Glencoe, Illinois: The Free Press, 1956), p. 20; Ralf Dahrendorf, *Class and Class Conflict in Industrial Society* (Stanford: Stanford University Press, 1959), chap. 5.
[2] William Graham Sumner, *Folkways* (Boston: Ginn, 1906); Edward Alsworth Ross, *The Principles of Sociology* (New York: Century, 1920); Charles Horton Cooley, *Social Process* (New York: Charles Scribner's Sons, 1918), and *Social Organization* (New York: Charles Scribner's Sons, 1909).
[3] Robert E. Park and Ernest W. Burgess, *Introduction to the Science of Sociology* (Chicago: University of Chicago Press, 1924).
[4] Dahrendorf, *op. cit.*, pp. 157–165. Arthur I. Wastow makes the same point in his concepts of "church," "state," and "government" as models of social integration. See *From Race Riot to Sit-In, 1919 and the 1960s: A Study in the Connections Between Conflict and Violence* (New York: Doubleday & Co., 1966).

in the present study it is observed that the two sources of social integration are complementary and mutually supporting.

Coser has led the revival of sociological attention to the study of social conflict. In this task he has injected the very considerable contributions of the German sociologist Georg Simmel into the stream of American sociological thought. Ralf Dahrendorf, among others, has made further substantial contributions to the sociology of social conflict. One latent consequence of this development has been to sensitize some sociologists to conflict as a perspective from which to investigate race relations. Thus race relations have been called "power relations" and it has been proposed that research should be cast in terms of a "conflict model."[5] This approach is consistent with Blumer's thesis that race prejudice is "a sense of group position" and that empirical study involves "a concern with the relationship of racial groups."[6]

In the present discussion the term racial conflict is used in a restricted and specific sense.[7] By racial conflict is meant rational organized overt action by Negroes, initiating demands for specific social goals, and utilizing collective sanctions to enforce these demands. By definition, the following alternative forms of conflict behavior are excluded from the field of analysis.

1. The aggressive or exploitative actions of dominant groups and individuals toward minority groups or individuals.

2. Convert individual antagonisms or affective compensatory or reflexive aggressions, and

3. Spontaneous outbursts or nonrationalized violent behavior.

As here treated, racial conflict involves some rational assessment of both means and ends, and therefore is an instance of what Lewis Coser has called "realistic conflict."[8] Because of the calculating of means and ends, racial con-

---

[5] Lewis M. Killian and Charles M. Grigg, *Racial Crisis in America* (Englewood Cliffs, New Jersey: Prentice-Hall, 1964), p. 18 ff.; H. M. Blalock, Jr., "A Power Analysis of Racial Discrimination," *Social Forces,* 39 (October 1960), pp. 53–59; Ernst Borinski, "The Sociology of Coexistence—Conflict in Social and Political Power Systems," unpublished, pp. 6–7; Wilson Record, *Race and Radicalism* (Ithaca: Cornell University Press, 1964); Ernst Borinski, "The Litigation Curve and the Litigation Filibuster in Civil Rights Cases," *Social Forces,* 37 (December 1958), pp. 142–147.

[6] Herbert Blumer, "Race Prejudice as a Sense of Group Position," in J. Masuoka and Preston Valien (eds.), *Race Relations* (Chapel Hill: The University of North Carolina Press, 1961), p. 217.

[7] In much authoritative literature the concept conflict in racial relations is used in various other ways. See for example, George Simpson and J. Milton Yinger, *Racial and Cultural Minorities* (New York; Harper & Row, 1965), chap. 4; Killian and Grigg, *op. cit.;* Leonard Broom and Norval D. Glenn, *Transformation of the Negro American* (New York: Harper & Row, 1965), esp. chaps. 3 and 4.

[8] Coser, *op. cit.,* pp. 48–55.

flict is initiating action. It is a deliberate collective enterprise to achieve predetermined social goals. Of necessity, conflict includes a conscious attack upon an overtly defined social abuse.

Merton has pointed out that groups sometimes resort to culturally tabooed means to achieve culturally prescribed ends.[9] Under such circumstances one might assume that if legitimate means were available, they would be employed. But, Vander Zanden has observed, "Non-violent resistance is a tactic well suited to struggles in which a minority lacks access to major sources of power within a society and to the instruments of violent coercion."[10] He goes on to add that, "within the larger American society the Negro's tactic of non-violent resistance has gained a considerable degree of legitimacy."[11] Three principal manifestations of Negro behavior fit this definition of racial conflict.

1. Legal redress, or the calculated use of court action to achieve and sanction specific group goals. Legal redress has been used most often and successfully in the achievement of voting rights, educational opportunities and public accommodations.

2. Political action, or the use of voting, bloc voting and lobby techniques to achieve legislative and administrative changes and law enforcement.

3. Non-violent mass action, or organized collective participation in overt activity involving pressure and public relations techniques to enforce specific demands.

This paper examines some of the social functions of conflict as here defined. It is asked: Does realistic conflict by Negroes have any system-maintaining and system-enhancing consequences for the larger American society? To this question at least four affirmative answers can be given. Realistic racial conflict (1) alters the social structure, (2) enhances social communication, (3) extends social solidarity and (4) facilitates personal identity. Because of space and time limitations, considerations of societal dysfunctions and goal achievements are omitted.

STRUCTURAL FUNCTIONS

H. M. Blalock has noted that within the American social structure race relations are power relations.[12] Thus, realistic social conflict is an enterprise in

---

[9] Robert K. Merton, *Social Theory and Social Structure* (Glencoe, Illinois: The Free Press, 1957), pp. 123–149.
[10] James W. Vander Zanden, "The Non-Violent Resistance Movement Against Segregation," *American Journal of Sociology*, 68 (March 1963), p. 544.
[11] *Ibid.*, p. 544.
[12] Blalock, *op. cit.*, pp. 53–59.

the calculated mobilization and application of social power to sanction collective demands for specific structural changes. Yet, because of minority status, Negroes have only limited access to the sources of social power. Robert Bierstedt has identified numbers, resources and organization as leading sources of power.[13] Of these categories, resources which Bierstedt specifies as including money, prestige, property and natural and supernatural phenomena, are least accessible to Negroes.

Perforce then, realistic racial conflict specializes in the mobilization of numbers and organization as accessible sources of power. Thus a boycott mobilizes and organizes numbers of individuals to withhold purchasing power. A demonstration organizes and mobilizes numbers of individuals to tap residual moral sentiments and to generate public opinion. Voter registration and bloc voting mobilize and organize numbers of citizens to influence legislative and administrative processes. Legal redress and lobby techniques mobilize organization to activate legal sanctions or the legislative process.

The application of mobilized social power in realistic racial conflict tends to reduce the power differential between actors, to restrict existing status differences, and to alter the directionality of social interaction. First, in conflict situations, race relations are defined unequivocally in power terms. Sentimentality and circumlocution are brushed aside. The power dimension is brought into central position in the structure of interaction. The differential between conflict partners along this dimension is thus reduced. The power advantage of the dominant group is significantly limited. In this connection and perhaps only in this connection, it may be correct to liken embattled Negroes and resisting whites to "armed camps."

Second, alteration of the power dimension of interracial structure tends to modify status arrangements. In the traditional racial structure, discrimination and segregation cast whites and Negroes in rigid and separate orders of superiority and inferiority. The limited and stylized intergroup contacts are confined to a rigid and sterile etiquette. However, in realistic conflict initiating actors assume, for they must, a status coordinate with that of the opposition.[14]

Status coordination is one evident consequence of power equalization. Moreover, it is patently impossible to make demands and to sanction them while acting from the position of a suppliant. That is, the very process of realistic conflict functions to define adversaries in terms of self-conception as status equals. Martin Luther King perceives this function of realistic conflict in the

[13] Robert Bierstedt, "An Analysis of Social Power," *American Sociological Review*, 15 (December 1950), pp. 730–738. Bierstedt argues that numbers and organization as sources of social power are ineffectual without access to resources.
[14] Thomas F. Pettigrew, *A Profile of the Negro American* (Princeton: D. Van Nostrand Co., 1964), p. 167.

following comment on the use of non-violent action and deliberately induced tension.[15]

> Non-violent direct action seeks to create such a crisis and foster such a tension that a community which has constantly refused to negotiate is forced to confront the issue. It seeks so to dramatize the issue that it can no longer be ignored.

That is, social power is used to bring interactors into status relations where issues can be discussed, examined and compromised. There are no suppliants or petitioners and no condescending controllers in a negotiation relationship. By the very nature of the case, interactors occupy equal or approximately equal positions of both status and strength.

Third, power equalization and status coordination affect the interactional dimension of social structure. The up and down flow of interaction between super- and subordinates tends to level out in relations between positional equals. That is, rational demands enforced by calculated sanctions cannot be forced into the molds of supplication and condescension.

The leveling out of social interaction is inherent in such realistic conflict mechanisms as sit-ins, freedom rides, bloc voting, voter registration campaigns and boycotts. Thus, for example, the interruption of social interaction in a boycott implies an assumption of status equality and the leveling of interaction. The relationship that is interrupted is the up and down pattern inherent in the status structure of inequality. No relationship is revealed as preferable to the pattern of supplication and condescension. Whether such structural functions of realistic conflict become institutionalized in the larger social system will depend on the extent of goal achievement of the total Negro revolution. That is, structural consequences of conflict may be institutionalized through the desegregation and nondiscrimination of education, employment, housing, recreation and the like. Changes in these directions will provide system-relevant roles under terms of relatively coordinate status and power not only for the conflict participants, but also for many other individuals. Developments in these directions will also be influenced by many factors and trends apart from the process of realistic racial conflict.

We may now summarize the argument regarding the structural functions of realistic racial conflict in a series of propositions. Realistic conflict postulates race relations as power relations and undertakes to mobilize and apply the social power that is accessible to Negroes as a minority group.

In conflict, the traditional interracial structure is modified along three

---

[15] Martin Luther King, *Why We Can't Wait* (New York: Harper & Row, 1963), p. 81.

dimensions. The power differential between interactors is reduced; status differentials are restricted; and social interaction tends to level out in directionality. Whether these structural consequences of realistic conflict become institutionalized in the general social system will depend on the extent and duration of goal achievement in the larger social structure.

COMMUNICATIONAL FUNCTIONS

It is widely claimed that Negro aggression interrupts or reduces interracial communication. Whites and Negroes are thought to withdraw in suspicion and hostility from established practices of communication. The so-called "normal" agencies and bridges of intergroup contact and communication are believed to become inoperative. Such a view of conflict envisages Negroes and whites as hostile camps eyeing each other across a "no man's land" of antagonism and separation.

It is true that racial conflict tends to interrupt and reduce traditional communication between whites and Negroes. But traditional interracial communication assumes that communicators occupy fixed positions of superiority and inferiority, precludes the consideration of certain significant issues, and confines permitted interchanges to a rigid and sterile etiquette. "The Negro," write Killian and Grigg, "has always been able to stay in communication with the white man and gain many favors from him, so long as he approached him as a suppliant and as an inferior, and not as a conflict partner."[16]

It will be evident that intergroup communication under such structural conditions is both restricted in content and asymmetrical in form. However, our analysis indicates that realistic conflict functions to correct these distortions of content and form and to extend the communication process at the secondary mass media level.

First, realistic racial conflict heightens the individual level and extends the social range of attention to racial matters. Individuals who have by long custom learned to see Negroes only incidentally as part of the standard social landscape, are brought up sharply and forced to look at them in a new light. Persons who have been oblivious to Negroes are abruptly and insistently confronted by people and issues which they can neither avoid nor brush aside. Many individuals for the first time perceive Negroes as having problems, characteristics and aspirations that were never before recognized, nor at least so clearly recognized. Racial conflict thus rudely destroys what Gunnar Myrdal aptly called the "convenience of ignorance."[17]

In *Freedom Summer,* Sally Belfrage gives a graphic personal illustration

---

[16] Killian and Grigg, *op. cit.,* p. 7.
[17] Gunnar Myrdal, *An American Dilemma* (New York: Harper & Bros., 1944), pp. 40–42.

of the attention-arresting function of realistic racial conflict.[18] In the most crowded and hottest part of an afternoon the daughter of one of Greenwood's (Mississippi) leading families walked into the civil rights headquarters. In a lilting southern voice she asked to everybody in general: "I jus' wanted to know what y'all are up to over here."

At the same time the "race problem" is brought into the focus of collective attention by realistic conflict. Negroes as well as their problems and claims insist upon having both intensive and extensive consideration. To support this contention one has only to consider the volume of scientific, quasi-scientific and popular literature, the heavy racial loading of the mass media, and the vast number of organizations and meetings that are devoted to the racial issue.

Further, realistic racial conflict tends to modify both the cognitive and affective content of interracial communication. Under terms of conflict whites and Negroes can no longer engage in the exchange of standardized social amenities regarding safe topics within the protection of the status structure and the social etiquette. Communication is made to flow around substantive issues and the calculated demands of Negroes. Communication is about something that has real meaning for the communicators. It makes a difference that they communicate. In fact, under terms of realistic conflict it is no longer possible to avoid communicating. Thus Martin Luther King argued that non-violent mass action is employed to create such crisis and tension that a community which has refused to negotiate is forced to confront the issue.[19]

In conflict the affective character of communication becomes realistic. The communicators infuse their exchanges of cognitive meanings with the feelings that, within the traditional structure, were required to be suppressed and avoided. That Negroes are permitted, indeed often expected to reveal the hurt and humiliation and anger that they formerly were required to bottle up inside. Many white people thus were shocked to discover that the "happy" Negroes whom they "knew" so well were in fact discontented and angry people.

Thus the cognitive-affective distortion of traditional interracial communication is in some measure at least corrected. The flow of understanding and affection that was permitted and encouraged is balanced by normal loading of dissension and hostility. The relationship thus reveals a more symmetrical character of content and form.

Finally, attrition of primary contacts between unequals within the traditional structure and etiquette is succeeded, in part at least, by an inclusive dialogue at the secondary communication level. The drama of conflict and the challenges of leaders tend to elevate the racial issue in the public opinion arena. The mass media respond by reporting and commenting on racial events in great detail.

---

[18] Sally Belfrage, *Freedom Summer* (New York: The Viking Press, 1965), p. 48.
[19] King, *op. cit.*, p. 81.

Thus millions of otherwise uninformed or indifferent individuals are drawn into the public opinion process which Ralph H. Turner and Lewis M. Killian have analyzed as defining and redefining the issue and specifying and solving the problem.[20]

Much obvious evidence reveals the secondary communication dialogue. Since 1954 a voluminous scientific, quasi-scientific and popular literature on the race issue has appeared. Further evidence is found in the heavy racial loading of newspapers, magazines, television and radio broadcasting and the motion pictures. The race problem has been the theme of numerous organizations and meetings at all levels of power and status. From such evidence it would seem reasonable to conclude that few if any Americans have escaped some degree of involvement in the dialogue over the race issue.

We may now summarize the argument briefly. Realistic racial conflict tends to reduce customary interracial communication between status unequals regarding trivial matters within the established communication etiquette. On the other hand, conflict tends to extend communication regarding significant issues with genuine feelings and within noncustomary structures and situations. At the secondary level both the volume of communication and the number of communicators are greatly increased by realistic conflict. These observations would seem to warrant the conclusion that communication within the general social system is extended by realistic racial conflict.

SOLIDARITY FUNCTIONS

A corollary of the claim that racial conflict interrupts communication is the assertion that conflict also is seriously, perhaps even radically disunifying. Struggles between Negroes and whites are thought to split the society and destroy social solidarity. It is at once evident that such a claim implies the prior existence of a unified or relatively unified biracial system. Notwithstanding difference of status and condition, the racial sectors are envisaged as joined in the consensus and structure of the society.

A judicious examination of the facts suggests that the claim that racial conflict is seriously, perhaps even radically disunifying is not altogether correct. On the one hand, the image of biracial solidarity tends to be exaggerated. On the other, realistic racial conflict serves some important unifying functions within the social system.

As Logan Wilson and William Kolb have observed, the consensus of the society is organized around a core of "ultimate values."[21] "In our own society,"

[20] Ralph H. Turner and Lewis M. Killian, *Collective Behavior* (Englewood Cliffs, New Jersey: Prentice-Hall, 1957), chaps. 11 and 12.
[21] Logan Wilson and William L. Kolb, *Sociological Analysis* (New York: Harcourt, Brace & Co., 1949), p. 513.

they assert, "we have developed such ultimate values as the dignity of the individual, equality of opportunity, the right to life, liberty, and the pursuit of happiness, and the growth of the free personality."

Far from rejecting or challenging these ultimate values, the ideological thrust of realistic racial conflict affirms them.[22] That is, the ultimate values of the society constitute starting points of ideology and action in racial conflict. As Wilson Record and others have observed, Negro protest and improvement movements are thoroughly American in assumption and objectives.[23]

This fact creates an interesting strategic dilemma for the White Citizens Councils, the resurgent Ku Klux Klan and similar manifestations of the so-called "white backlash." The ideology of racial conflict has preempted the traditional high ground of the core values and ultimate morality. The reactionary groups are thus left no defensible position within the national ethos from which to mount their attacks.

One consequence of realistic racial conflict, then, is to bring the core values of the society into sharp focus and national attention. People are exhorted, even forced to think about the basic societal tenets and to consider their meaning and applications. A dynamic force is thus joined to latent dedication in support of the unifying values of the society. Thus, as Coser has observed, far from being altogether disunifying, realistic conflict functions to reaffirm the core and unifying values of the society.[24] In other words the "two faces of society" are seen to be complementary and mutually supporting.

The primacy of core values in realistic racial conflict is revealed in many ways. Martin Luther King places the ultimate values of the society at the center of his theoretic system of non-violent mass action.[25] In his "Letter from Birmingham Jail" he refers to "justice," "freedom," "understanding," "brotherhood," "constitutional rights," "promise of democracy" and "truth." See how he identifies the goal of racial freedom with the basic societal value of freedom. "We will reach the goal of freedom in Birmingham and all over the nation, because the goal of America is freedom."[26]

One impact of realistic racial conflict is upon interpretation of core values and the means of their achievement. Thus, the issue is not whether or not men shall be free and equal, but whether these values are reserved to white men or are applicable to Negroes as well. Or again, the phrases "gradualism" and "direct action" depict an important point of disagreement over means to universally affirmed ends. But, it may be observed that when men agree on the ends of life, their quarrels are not in themselves disunifying.

[22] Pettigrew, *op. cit.*, p. 193.
[23] Record, *op. cit.*; Pettigrew, *op. cit.*; Broom and Glenn, *op. cit.*
[24] Coser, *op. cit.*, pp. 127–128.
[25] King, *op. cit.*, pp. 77–100.
[26] *Ibid.*, p. 97.

Further, the very process of realistic racial conflict is intrinsically functional. Participants in the conflict are united by the process of struggle itself. The controversy is a unique and shared social possession. It fills an interactional vacuum maintained in the traditional structure by limited social contacts and alienation.

At the same time, as Coser has argued, a relationship established by conflict may lead in time to other forms of interaction.[27] It is conceivable that Negroes and whites who today struggle over freedom and justice and equality may tomorrow be joined in cooperation in the quest of these values.

Conflict is also unifying because the object of struggle is some social value that both parties to the conflict wish to possess or enjoy. The struggle tends to enhance the value and to reveal its importance to both actors. A new area of consensus is thus defined or a prior area of agreement is enlarged. For example, that Negroes and whites struggle through realistic conflict for justice or freedom or equality tends to clarify these values for both and join them in the consensus regarding their importance.

"Simultaneously," as Vander Zanden observes, "within the larger American society the Negro's tactic of non-violent resistance has gained a considerable degree of legitimacy."[28] That is, conflict itself has been defined as coming within the arena of morally justifiable social action. The means as well as the ends, then, are enveloped within the national ethos and serve to enhance societal solidarity. In this respect realistic racial conflict, like labor-management conflict, tends to enter the "American way of life" and constitutes another point of social integration.

Many years ago Edward Alsworth Ross pointed out that nonradical conflicts may function to "sew" the society together.[29]

Every species of conflicts interferes with every other species in
society . . . save only when lines of cleavage coincide; in which case
they reinforce one another. . . . A society, therefore, which is ridden by
a dozen oppositions along lines running in every direction may
actually be in less danger of being torn with violence or falling to

---

[27] Coser, *op. cit.*, pp. 121–122.
[28] Vander Zanden, *op. cit.*, p. 544.
[29] Ross, *op. cit.*, pp. 164–165. Dahrendorf, *op. cit.*, pp. 213–215, argues that conflicts tend to become "superimposed," thus threatening intensification. "Empirical evidence shows," he writes, "that different conflicts may be, and often are, superimposed in given historical societies, so that the multitude of possible conflict fronts is reduced to a few dominant conflicts . . . . If this is the case, (class) conflicts of different associations appear superimposed; i.e., the opponents of one association meet again—with different titles, perhaps, but in identical relations—in another association." (Pp. 213–214.) Such an argument, however, fails to recognize that conflicts may superimpose along religious, regional, ethnic or other fronts and thus mitigate the strength of the class superimposition.

pieces than one split just along one line. For each new cleavage contributes to narrow the cross-clefts, so that one might say that society is sewn together by its inner conflicts.

In this sewing function, realistic racial conflict is interwoven with political, religious, regional, rural-urban, labor-management, class and the other persistent threads of struggle that characterize the American social fabric. What is decisive is the fact that variously struggling factions are united in the consensus of the ultimate societal values. The conflicts are therefore nonradical, crisscrossing and tend to mitigate each other.

The proposition on the solidarity function of realistic racial conflict can now be formulated briefly. The claims that racial conflict is disruptive of social solidarity, though partially true, tends to obscure other important consequences. Conflict not only projects the combatants into the social consensus; it also acts to reaffirm the ultimate values around which the consensus is organized. Moreover, conflict joins opposing actors in meaningful interaction for ends, whose importance is a matter of further agreement. From this perspective and within a context of multifarious crisscrossing threads of opposition, realistic racial conflict is revealed as helping to "sew" the society together around its underlying societal consensus. We now turn to a consideration of certain social-psychological consequences of realistic racial conflict.

Identity Functions

The fact is often overlooked that realistic racial conflict permits many Negroes to achieve a substantial measure of identity within the American social system. This function of racial conflict is implied in the foregoing analyses of communication and solidarity. However, the analysis of the identity function of racial conflict begins with a consideration of the alienation of the American Negro people. Huddled into urban and rural slums and concentrated in menial and marginal positions in the work force, Negroes are relegated to inferior and collateral statuses in the social structure. Within this structural situation discrimination prevents their sharing in the valued possessions of the society. Legal and customary norms of segregation exclude them from many meaningful contacts and interactions with members of the dominant group.

Isolated and inferior, Negro people searched for the keys to identity and belonging. The social forces that exclude them from significant participation in the general society also keep them disorganized. Thus identity, the feeling of belonging and the sense of social purpose, could be found neither in membership in the larger society nor in participation in a cohesive racial group. Generation after generation of Negroes live out their lives in fruitless detachment and personal emptiness. In another place the alienation of Negro teenagers has been described as follows.[30]

The quality of Negro teenage culture is conditioned by four decisive factors: race, inferiority, deprivation and youthfulness. Virtually every experience of the Negro teenager is filtered through this complex qualifying medium; every act is a response to a distorted perception of the world. His world is a kind of nightmare, the creation of a carnival reflection chamber. The Negro teenager's culture, his customary modes of behavior, constitute his response to the distorted, frightening, and cruel world that he perceives with the guileless realism of youth.

Yet the search for identity goes on. It takes many forms. In the Negro press and voluntary organizations it is reflected in campaigns for race pride and race loyalty. One sector of the Negro intelligentsia invented the "Negro history movement" as a device to create a significant past for a "historyless" people. For the unlettered and unwashed masses the church is the prime agent of group cohesion and identity. The National Association for the Advancement of Colored People and other militant organizations provide an ego-enhancing rallying point for the emancipated and the aggressive. The cult of Negro business, escapist movements like Father Divine's Heaven, and nationalist movements like Marcus Garvey's Universal Negro Improvement Association, and the Black Muslims provide still other arenas for the Negro's search for identity.

Despite this variegated panorama of effort and search, the overriding experience of Negroes remains isolation, inferiority and the ineluctable sense of alienation. Whether involved in the search or not, or perhaps just because of such involvement, individuals see themselves as existing outside the basic American social system. Vander Zanden puts it this way: "By virtue of his membership in the Negro group, the Negro suffers considerably in terms of self-esteem and has every incentive for self-hatred."[31] Thus self-conception reflects and in turn supports social experience in a repetition of the familiar self-fulfilling prophecy.

In this situation, collective conflict had an almost magical although unanticipated effect upon group cohesion and sense of identity among Negroes. Group struggle, as Coser and others have pointed out, functions to enhance group solidarity and to clarify group boundaries.[32] The separations among collective units are sharpened and the identity of groups within a social system is

---

[30] Joseph S. Himes, "Negro Teen Age Culture," *Annals,* 338 (November 1961), pp. 92–93.
[31] Vander Zanden, *op. cit.,* p. 546.
[32] Coser, *op. cit.,* p. 34.

established. In the course of conflict collective aims are specified, defined and communicated. Cadres of leaders emerge in a division of labor that grows clearer and more definite. Individuals tend to find niches and become polarized around the collective enterprise. All participants are drawn closer together, both for prosecution of the struggle and for common defense.

As the racial conflict groups become more cohesive and organized, the boundaries with other groups within the American social system become clearer. The distinction between member and nonmember is sharpened. Individuals who stood indecisively between groups or outside the fray are induced or forced to take sides. The zones of intergroup ambiguity diminish. Internally, the conflict groups become more tightly unified and the positions of members are clarified and defined more precisely.

Further, conflict facilitates linkage between the individual and his local reference group as the agent of conflict. The individual thus achieves both a "commitment"[33] and a "role" as a quasi-official group representative in the collective struggle. Pettigrew writes:[34]

> Consider the Student Non-Violent Coordinating Committee (SNICK),
> ... The group is cohesive, highly regarded by Negro youth, and
> dedicated entirely to achieving both personal and societal racial
> change. Recruits willingly and eagerly devote themselves to the group's
> goals. And they find themselves systematically rewarded by
> SNICK for violating the 'Negro' role in every particular. They
> are expected to evince strong racial pride, to assert their full rights
> as citizens, to face jail and police brutality unhesitatingly for the
> cause .... Note, ... that these expected and rewarded actions all
> publicly commit the member to the group and its aims.

In the general racial conflict system individuals may act as leaders, organizers and specialists. Some others function as sit-inners, picketers, boycotters, demonstrators, voter registration solicitors, etc. Many others, removed from the areas of overt conflict, participate secondarily or vicariously as financial contributors, audience members, mass media respondents, verbal applauders, etc.

In the interactive process of organized group conflict self-involvement is the opposite side of the coin of overt action. Actors become absorbed by ego and emotion into the group and the group is projected through their actions.

---

[33] Amitai Etzioni employs the concept "commitment" to designate one dimension of cohesiveness and operational effectiveness in complex organizations. See his *Complex Organizations: A Sociological Reader* (New York: Henry Holt Co., 1961), p. 187; and *A Comparative Study of Complex Organization* (Glencoe, Illinois: The Free Press, 1961), pp. 8–22.

[34] Pettigrew, *op. cit.*, pp. 165–166.

This linkage of individual and group in ego and action is the substance of identity.

Paradoxically, the personal rewards of participation in conflict groups tend to support and facilitate the larger conflict organization and process. Edward Shils and Morris Janowitz have noted this fact in the functions of primary groups in the German Army in World War II.[35] That is, for the individual actor the sense of identity is grounded and sustained by gratification of important personal needs.

In the case of realistic racial conflict, group-based identity functions to facilitate sociopsychic linkage between the individual and the inclusive social system. It was shown above that racial conflict is socially unifying in at least two ways. First, the conflict ideology identifies parties to the conflict with the core values of the social heritage. Thus sit-inners, and demonstrators and boycotters and all the others in the drama of racial conflict conceive themselves as the latter-day warriors for the freedom, justice and equality and the other moral values that are historically and essentially American. For many Negroes the sense of alienation is dispelled by a new sense of significance and purpose. The self-image of these embattled Negroes is consequently significantly enhanced.

Second, the conflict process draws organized Negroes into significant social interaction within the inclusive social system. Some of the crucial issues and part of the principal business of the society engage Negroes of all localities and stations in life. Though often only vicariously and by projection, life acquires a new meaning and quality for even the poorest ghetto dweller and meanest sharecropper. The sense of alienation is diminished and the feeling of membership in the inclusive society is enhanced.

We may now formulate the argument as follows. Intense alienation kept alive the Negro's quest for identity and meaning. Miraculously almost, realistic racial conflict with its ideological apparatus and action system functions to alleviate alienation and to facilitate identity. Conflict enhances group solidarity, clarifies group boundaries and strengthens the individual-group linkage through ego-emotion commitment and overt action. In-group identity is extended to the larger social system through the extension of communication, the enlargement of the network of social interactions and ideological devotion to national core values. It may be said, then, that through realistic racial conflict America gains some new Americans.

[35] Edward A. Shils and Morris Janowitz, "Cohesion and Disintegration in the Wehrmacht in World War II," *Public Opinion Quarterly,* 12 (Summer 1948), p. 281.

Reflective Questions

1. Is conflict present in all groups?

2. Should conflict that leads to open warfare and violence be regarded as "realistic" conflict?

3. In comparison with cooperation, how effective is conflict in reducing interracial tension and hostility?

4. Design a model of a social system in which racial conflict is nonexistent. Do you know of any social systems or nations in which racial problems and conflicts do not exist?

21 □ BLACK PANTHERS

Nora Sayre

This paper presented the results of interviews with leaders and critics of the Black Panthers. The author contends that the Panthers provide the first nationwide black political movement. Initially, the organization was seen as an organ of self-defense for the black community; however, it has a platform and an ideology. The archenemy is capitalism, with its emphasis on property above human life. Capitalism is intertwined with racism. Panthers feel that improvement in the lives of black people will come through education. A Panther will not attack anyone first, but he will "wipe out" the aggressor if attacked. Among other goals, the Panthers seek freedom from the military, full employment, humane housing, education about the racist history of America, community control, an immediate end to police brutality, and freedom for all black men held in jails and prisons. □

> *We need a Boston Tea Party from one end of this country to the other. You'd better get ready, because the pigs are ready. And if whites are not yet ready, niggers are going to create a situation where you'll have no choice: you'll have to move for your liberation, or get into the pigpen with the oinks. Today, you're either part of the solution or part of the problem.*
> ELDRIDGE CLEAVER, *speaking at New York University, October 1968*

FIVE HUNDRED DOLLARS WAS MADE ON THE SALE OF THE FIRST SLAVE: RACISM began as an economic program. Malcolm X said that "History rewards all research." But black and white America hardly agree about history—as well as a

From *The Progressive*, July, 1969, pp. 20–23. Copyright © 1969 by The Progressive, Inc. Reprinted with permission.

few other points. Even many of the young white radicals recoil from historical references. They suspect that history and "funky old things" will impede their momentum, sidetrack the precious "dialogue," make coping with the present more complex. And, for many whites, it is difficult to feel any urgent identification with the American past; as for the American Revolution, one is sympathetic, but it is remote. However, black people can and do feel extremely close to the experience of their forebears: because the hatred and cruelty, the random killings and living deaths, are so similar to what they know today. For them, the past tastes like the present.

Grubbing back to our origins, we recall that the Declaration of Independence might have read, "life, liberty, and the pursuit of property" (instead of "happiness") if Jefferson had not corrected John Locke's phrase. "Property" would have been more honest—and it explains some of the ugliness that boils in our soup today. Naturally, slaves were property; stealing another man's slave was a crime against property. Now, blacks and whites who hate the sanctity of ownership and goods are challenging the code which rates property over human life. (Mayor Daley's "shoot to maim or cripple" order in Chicago last year was aimed at looters.) Footnotes to garbled history are infinite, but one more is crucial: Those who included "the right to bear arms" in the Second Amendment to the Constitution did not foresee that blacks as well as whites might bear them. The amendment was inserted to protect citizens from tyrannical actions by their own government.

When you comb out U.S. history, one fact is as clear as killing: Democracy never included blacks. Most of those who were against slavery were also against equality for the freed slaves. Last winter, at a bail-raising Black Panther dinner, I asked a member if I could talk to him later, when he was free. "When I'm *what?*" he cried—unleashing a large laugh for a few of us, amidst the soul food and champagne.

The Black Panther Party was organized in October, 1966, in Oakland, California, by Huey Newton (now in jail, despite great black and white public protest that he was unjustly charged with killing a policeman) and Bobby Seale (on probation for a "gun law violation"). Eldridge Cleaver joined them in 1967. The inspiration was self-defense: Armed black patrols followed the police, acting as witnesses to brutality, informing accosted citizens of their rights. The Panthers' motto is the famous quotation from Mao: *"We are advocates of the abolition of war; we do not want war; but war can only be abolished through war; and in order to get rid of the gun it is necessary to pick up the gun."* Cleaver, in an interview published in *Playboy,* spoke as one who has often seen the wrong end of a gun: "I don't dig violence. Guns are ugly... But there are two forms of violence: violence directed at you to keep you in your place and violence to defend yourself against that suppression and to win your freedom."

The Panthers now have chapters all over the United States. Their numbers are swelling, and their appeal to the young is enormous, especially in our ravaging ghetto high schools. The Panthers have been called "the vanguard of the North American revolutionary movement;" they call themselves "the children of Malcolm." Many of their ideas were developed from those which Malcolm X arrived at in his later years, such as the readiness to work with whites—an attitude which the press often ignores. Since many whites were tossed out of certain civil rights groups a few years ago, some do not yet realize that the Panthers have welcomed them back. Cleaver has often explained that the Panthers are not seeking vengeance, that they do not object to white skin, but to the actions of white racists. However, the press concentrates on the guns and berets and the black leather jackets—which few Panthers now wear, since the uniform often means instant arrest.

Armed white vigilante groups, which sometimes threatened moderate civil rights workers, existed several years before the Panthers were organized. In the late Fifties and early Sixties, it was whites who rioted to protest against black students entering Southern universities and schools. The white policeman hardly protects the black ghetto; the law has not shielded blacks from attacks by whites.

But when the Panthers stress self-defense, it is often (conveniently or ignorantly) forgotten that so many blacks are dying—now. From malnutrition to murder, from the diseases of poverty to provoked shoot-outs, from lead poisoning in slum tenements to inadequate hospital care, the death rate for black people is unacceptable to the Panthers. Their symbol is apt: "Because it is not in the panther's nature to attack anyone first, but when he is attacked and backed into a corner, he will . . . wipe out the aggressor."

Bewilderment, panic, incomprehension ossified by anger: Much of this white response is filtered through the prism of confusion. Yet, where we are now seems almost inevitable. It is hard to remember that only five years ago civil rights legislation, sit-ins, marches, and poverty programs suggested a solution. A Panther said, "That was like putting a Band-Aid on cancer." For many, liberalism lost its legs because it came to mean hypocrisy: the promises of "economic advancement" followed by projects that were only miserably funded, plus the notion that the Vietnam war is a moral exercise, and above all, the ability to rationalize: "to see all sides of the question, and then walk away." (A Panther added, "The liberal really is a threat—because he can rationalize *anything*: like overkill.") And—as throughout much of the United States—there is the supreme disillusionment with professional politicians and parties. Many blacks felt that whoever became President could make no difference in their lives. As a Panther told me, "One of the myths that's died is that things are getting better for black people." (The recent sequel to the 1968 Kerner Commission report tragically confirms this.) Another Panther said, "The melting pot's a joke, you know. It didn't melt."

The Panthers provide the first nationwide black political movement—as distinguished from the religious or apolitical groups of the past. For the Panthers, the "archenemy" is capitalism, which they see as intertwined with racism: "You cannot have a democracy with capitalism. And we don't." (The "black capitalism" encouraged by Mr. Nixon raises a snort.) Eventually, they wish for the establishment of some form of socialist state—and a total redistribution of wealth.

However, some are critical of socialism because, as one Panther remarked, "a welfare state proclaims equality—and that lets people dodge the issue of racism. Socialism takes care of your body, but it doesn't protect you from what other people feel about you—and what they do to you." (Britain was given as an example. Also, they are critical of the Russians as "jive revisionists.") Although they are studying Lenin, it is noted that "he didn't take racism into account."

Since blacks have been used as free or cheap labor for 400 years, the Panthers repeat that racism is oiled by colonialism, through the white businessmen and landlords who profit from the ghettos "and take all the bread home at sundown." They find that "taxation without representation" still applies to them, and they feel that colonialism will end only when white businesses are forced to leave the ghettos. (They are talking about cooperatives as an alternative.) Moreover, the Panthers assert that they must work for unity with colonized peoples throughout the world: "the victims of imperialism." They have asked the United Nations for "non-governmental status" for black Americans. (This category is for colonials who are not self-governing.) One Panther said, "There's no doubt that we're conspiring to liberate our people. The pig power structure calls it conspiring to overthrow the government. Yes, we're guilty—of wanting to improve the lives of our people."

Education is the theme; the Panthers hold classes for members and work with black high school groups. Detailing the styles of oppression, they also study liberation movements. They particularly stress the contradictions and the fantasies throughout American history—especially the fiction of equal opportunity. Even at times of glittering prosperity, there has always been an economic depression for blacks.

Black students are being educated about the draft: "You're programmed to fight their dirty wars, so that people can get rich on the war machine. . . We're fighting abroad to give people the American way of life—when so many *here* don't want it." (The current concept of a volunteer army may well not attract so many blacks as some of Nixon's advisers seem to hope.) Moreover, "We believe that all black men should be exempt from military service. It's absurd for us to fight the white man's war against people of other colors. We tell students that they have no real squabble with Ho." (Last fall, Cleaver said,

"We should give the man a deadline for stopping that war" by a definite date, "or we start a second front here.") All in all, black awareness is expanding far more swiftly than many whites imagine.

As well as freedom from the military, the goals of the Panther Party include full employment (or guaranteed income) plus humane housing for blacks, education based on historical fact (about "the true nature of this decadent, racist society," which has forced blacks to accept their characterization—as inferior and even evil—from whites, hence the need for new self-definition), release for all blacks in jails (to be retried by all-black juries), the end of white economic "robbery" in ghettos, and of police brutality. Community control is the demand. The Panthers have filed a suit with the Supreme Court aimed at decentralizing police departments, requiring that all policemen be recruited from the neighborhood areas they patrol: "Then they'd be less savage."

As for a separate black state in the United States, the Panthers feel that all blacks in the country should vote on the question, that it should be decided through a United Nations plebiscite, and that those who want it should be given land—perhaps for building new communities in the rural South where there are facilities for feeding large numbers of people. The Panthers emphasize that no one organization can represent all black people, and that varying programs must exist for those who want different ways of life. They say that the Government owes them some land: They feel it has been earned by centuries of the enslaved black labor that helped to build the United States.

The Panthers say they know that change occurs in stages. In functioning as "a service organization" for black communities, they organize around local issues, from supporting the demand for more black and Puerto Rican doctors and administrators for a neighborhood hospital to working closely with welfare rights groups, instructing recipients about what is due them under the law—something many are unlikely to learn from apathetic social workers. Last summer, in Harlem, the Panthers led some successful rent-strikes; they united tenants and occupied the buildings until the (often tardy) city housing investigators finally came to make inspections; 700 violations were found in two buildings alone. In New York City, the Panthers are planning a hot breakfast program for underfed public school children; Oakland already has one.

Meanwhile, the Government views the Panthers with alarm; the Senate plans an investigation. A white lawyer for the Panthers said, "They're a national myth—and the Feds have bought it." The FBI works closely with all local police departments; the Panthers have been constantly arrested (often for mere "misdemeanors"), and held for mammoth bails.

In New York, some Panthers—who had been charged with holding a rally without a permit—were beaten up in the hall of the Brooklyn courthouse by 150 white policemen who were off duty. (Although nine months have passed, no charges or indictments have been brought against these policemen.)

For several months, the Panthers and their lawyers kept telling me that there would be an effort to eliminate the party. On April 2, twenty-one New York Panthers were charged with a "conspiracy" to bomb midtown department stores, railway tracks, and a police station the next day. They pleaded not guilty; and their lawyers called it "a frame-up." The initial evidence was ethereal, to put it mildly—and no tangible proof of how the "plot" was uncovered was released. The Panthers have known that they were infiltrated by the police since the New York party was founded. As one lawyer said, it is "easy to create a situation which could bring about an indictment." The bails of $100,000 each kept twelve defendants in jail for several months while awaiting trial. From their national headquarters, the Panthers issued a statement which stressed that "the party would not blow up railway stations and department stores simply because some of our own poor people would be killed"—a sensible point which was disregarded by the press. Many were automatically ready to believe in the Panthers' guilt, without even reflecting on the impracticalities of the alleged plan.

Meanwhile, the Panthers are studying "preventive detention." In 1950, despite President Truman's veto, Title II of the McCarran Act was passed. Called the "Emergency Detention Act," it can be evoked by the President in case of "(1) Invasion of the territory of the United States or its possessions, (2) Declaration of war by Congress, or (3) Insurrection within the United States in aid of a foreign enemy." Considering the third point, anti-war groups have worried that peace demonstrations or draft-resistance could be met by Title II, which authorizes placing citizens in detention camps. Black people have been talking about the camps for several years. When liberals deride the possibility— as they do—they should remember that thousands of Japanese-Americans were confined in West Coast camps during World War II because it was feared that they might perform as enemy agents. (There is no evidence that a single one ever did.)

Title II enables the Attorney General to confine "all persons as to whom there is reasonable ground to believe that such person probably will engage in or probably will conspire with others to engage in acts of espionage and sabotage." (The word "probably" does sound like a siren.) However, the Attorney General is not "required to furnish information . . . which would disclose the identity or evidence of Government agents or officers which he believes it would be dangerous to national safety and security to divulge." In short, proof of guilt would not be needed.

The House Committee on Un-American Activities, in its May 1968 report on "Guerrilla Warfare Advocates in the United States," detailed a plan for controlling ghetto upheavals, including the proposition that "the police agencies would be in a position to make immediate arrests, without warrants, under suspension of guarantees usually provided by the Constitution." Many lawyers feel that President Nixon's law-and-order proposals are moving towards the use of Title II—above all, for the pre-trial jailings of black people, simply because of "what they might do."

The detention camps were established by the Attorney General in 1952 at Allenwood, Pennsylvania; El Reno, Oklahoma; Florence and Wickenburg, Arizona; and Tule Lake, California. Several were prisoner-of-war camps during World War II. A couple of them are considered ready for use; others could be swiftly rehabilitated. Meticulous research on the state of the camps has appeared in a series of articles by Charles R. Allen, Jr. (which were published in the *New Statesman* and *The Nation* in 1952). He also revisited the camps three years ago and published an updated version of "Concentration Camps U.S.A." Otherwise, aside from a *Look* article a year ago, little has been published about them. As one civil rights lawyer remarked, "Even if the camps are never used, the statute is on the books. You can say that they're already successful—as a threat."

The Panthers have repeated, "Black people are not going to play Jews"— meaning that they will not go docilely to camps. Many blacks are prepared for the possibility of "prolonged struggle"—which could last for decades. In New York, Cleaver said, "The future of the world depends on whether this country moves to the left or the right. It ain't going to stay where it is. But we will destroy it before we let it move to the right."

Cleaver has since emphasized that "war will come only if [the] basic demands are not met." He told *Playboy*, "Perhaps if enough people recognize how possible [violence] is, they'll work all the harder for the basic changes that can prevent it." When he lectured about the possibility of genocide for blacks, he reflected that "we may be wrong"—and added that it would be wonderful to be wrong. Throughout, he has asked people to *listen;* again and again, he said, "I appeal to your humanity."

Currently, it is tempting to spit when New York literary persons chat brightly over cocktails about revolution; few indoor natives have any conception of the word. At the same time, many refuse to believe that internal warfare *or* detention camps are possible. But for many black people—plus the expanding numbers of young whites who have joined them—racism is literally worth fighting, as well as the capitalism and imperialism which perpetuate it.

Most affirm that they want no more ghetto riots—"We're not masochists" —and militants have helped to prevent them on several occasions. (A Watts leader said last year, "The brother is too busy getting his thing together to think about riots. Whitey's funny; he worries like hell when we riot and he worries like hell when we don't.") But we are in a state where "pre-revolutionary churnings" occur. Since "capitalism won't just fade away by itself," the target would be the economic system.

Although yards have been written about the impossibility of revolution in the United States, one can imagine how organized disruption could indeed sap the economy. As a Harlem militant said, "We are the virus in the belly of the beast. The virus can weaken the body. So we're in an ideal situation."

Some have accused the Panthers of romanticism; others have angrily charged that their young white collaborators are being romantic about blacks getting killed. But there were no echoes of romance in any of the conversations I had with Panthers; the country's moral issues—and their own—are just too serious. Decades of nonviolence did not work; now, many are prepared to die for what they believe. The national ether crackles so frantically that people feel they must make extreme statements or take urgent action to catch anyone's attention; few are listening, as Cleaver asked them to—except the FBI. In this antiverbal age, not only are words ignored, but ears are waxed. Hence the new physical styles of expression.

Pickets and marches were symbolic statements, which were noticed less as the public grew more accustomed to them; now, death itself may become a form of speech: a way of asking to be heard. As a radical in Chicago said, "If you had a sane society, no one would be talking death—or dying. How sweet that would be." Meanwhile: "Many of us die all the time," said a woman Panther. "That's not new for us. But the *purpose* for it: That's what we have now. A new strength. People are becoming hopeful in a new way. By knowing that you're part of something so powerful that it will continue after your death."

The concept of revolution is still in a wingless, larval state; most of those who discuss it are talking well into the future, "if things do not change." But others who shrink at the thought of insurrection should find some answers for those who think it will come. And the answers are almost impossible, considering the toll of today. If you argue that the innocent will suffer, you are reminded that the innocent are suffering now—from the six black babies who die for each white one, to the Vietnamese, and the throngs of blacks who die from the nature of ghetto life.

If you object that devastating retaliations and repressions will overwhelm any shape of revolt, you are told that "more people will join in as blacks are killed off. They won't just stand back and watch it happen." But—in a frightened, conservative society—that is exactly what one fears. It would be acutely cheering to share Cleaver's confidence in large numbers of whites supporting the blacks —to believe that a majority would defend a minority against suppression. But that would indeed require a revolution—inside the skulls of whites.

Reflective Questions

1. What is it about the Black Panthers that makes it different from other civil rights organizations and black groups?

2. What are the prospects of the Panthers forming a large-scale revolutionary coalition with militant white and third-world organizations?

3. Do you feel that there is a systematic attempt to "wipe out" the Panthers by police and other law-enforcement agencies?

4. What is the likelihood that militant groups, in the event of riots and revolts, will be placed in emergency detention camps as enemy agents, such as was implied in Title II of the 1950 McCarran Act?

22 □ Racism and Anti-Feminism

Shirley Chisholm

In 1968, Shirley Chisholm became the first black woman elected to the Congress of the United States. A fighter for both black and women's liberation, she sees parallels between racism and antifeminism. She states that America is both racist and antifeminist. Women are paid less than men for the same work. Young girls are counseled to follow "natural" careers, just as the racist counselor advises black youth to seek service-oriented occupations. Women must become revolutionaries, says Congresswoman Chisholm. She asserts that the harshest discrimination she has encountered in the political arena was antifeminism, not simply from males, but from brainwashed "Uncle Tom" females as well. In an address before a group of women, she offered the following challenge:

I want you to go home and work for—fight for—the integration of male and female—human and human. Franz Fanon pointed out in *Black Skins, White Masks* that the Anti-Semitic was eventually the Anti-Negro. I want to say that both are eventually the Anti-Feminist. And even further, I want to indicate that all discrimination is eventually the same thing—Anti-Humanism. □

WOMEN TAKE AN ACTIVE PART IN SOCIETY AND IN PARTICULAR DO THEY TAKE a part in the present social revolution. And I find the question, do women dare to liberate themselves, as much of an insult as I would the question, "Are you, as a black person, willing to fight for your rights?"

From *The Black Scholar*, January/February 1970, pp. 40–45. Copyright © 1969 by Shirley Chisholm. Reprinted by permission.

America has been sufficiently sensitized as to whether or not black people are willing to both fight and die for their rights to make the question itself asinine and superfluous. America is not yet sufficiently aware that such a question applied to women is equally asinine and superfluous.

I am both black and a woman. That is a good vantage point from which to view at least two elements of what is becoming a social revolution; the American Black Revolution and the Women's Liberation Movement. But it is also a horrible disadvantage. It is a disadvantage because America, as a nation, is both racist and anti-feminist. Racism and anti-feminism are two of the prime traditions of this country.

For any individual, challenging social traditions is a giant step, a giant step because there are no social traditions which do not have corresponding social sanctions, the sole purpose of which are to protect the sanctity of the traditions.

Thus when we ask the question "Do women dare?" we are not asking if women are capable of a break with tradition so much as we are asking, "Are they capable of bearing with the sanctions that will be placed upon them?"

Coupling this with the hypothesis presented by some social thinkers and philosophers that in any given society the most active groups are those that are nearest to the particular freedom that they desire, it does not surprise me that those women most active and vocal on the issue of freedom for women are those who are young, white, and middle-class; nor is it too surprising that there are not more from that group involved in the Women's Liberation Movement.

There certainly are reasons why more women are not involved. This country as I said in both racist and anti-feminist. Few, if any, Americans are free of the psychological wounds imposed by racism and anti-feminism.

A few weeks ago while testifying before the Office of Federal Contract Compliance, I noted that anti-feminism, like every form of discrimination, is destructive both to those who perpetrate it and to their victims; that males with their anti-feminism, maim both themselves and their women.

In *Soul On Ice* Eldridge Cleaver pointed out how America's racial and sexual stereotypes were supposed to work. Whether his insight is correct or not, it bears close examination.

Cleaver, in the passage "The Primeval Mitosis," describes in detail the four major roles. There is the white female who he considers to be "Ultrafeminine" because ". . . she is required to possess and project an image that is in sharp contrast to . . ." the white male's image as the "Omnipotent Administrator . . . all brain and no body."

He goes on to identify the black female as "Subfeminine" or "Amazon" by virtue of her assignment to the lowly household chores and those corresponding jobs of tedious nature. He sums up the role of the black male as the "Supermasculine Menial, all body and no brain," because he was expected to supply society with its source of brute power.

What the roles and strange interplay between them have meant to America, Cleaver goes on to point out quite well.

What he does not say and what I think must be said is that because of the bizarre aspects of their roles and the influence that non-traditional contact among them has on the general society, blacks and whites, males and females, must operate almost independently of each other in order to escape from the quicksands of psychological slavery. Each—black male and black female, white female and white male—must escape first from their own historical trap before they can be truly effective in helping others to free themselves.

Therein lies one of the major reasons that there are not more women, involved in the Women's Liberation Movement. Women cannot, for the most part, operate independently of males because they often do not have sufficient economic freedom.

In 1966 the median earnings of women who worked full-time for the whole year was less than the median income of males who worked full-time for the whole year. In fact, white women workers made less than black male workers, and of course, black women workers made the least of all.

Whether it is intentional or not women are paid less than men for the same work, no matter what their chosen field. Whether it is intentional or not, employment for women is regulated still more in terms of the jobs that are available to them. This is almost as true for white women as it is for black women.

Whether it is intentional or not, when it becomes time for a young high-school girl to think about preparing for her career, her counselors, whether they be male or female, will think first of her so-called "natural" career—housewife and mother—and begin to program her for a field with which marriage and children will not unduly interfere.

That is exactly the same as the situation of the young blacks or Puerto Ricans whom the racist counselor advises to prepare for service-oriented occupations because he does not even consider the possibility of their entering the professions.

The response of the average young lady is precisely the same as the response of the average young black or Puerto Rican—tacit agreement—because the odds do seem to be stacked against them.

This is not happening as much as it once did to young minority-group people. It is not happening because they have been radicalized and the country is becoming sensitized to its racist attitudes and the damage that it does.

Young women must learn a lesson from that experience!

They must rebel—they must react to the traditional stereo-typed education mapped out for them by the society. Their education and training is programmed and planned for them from the moment the doctor says, "Mr. Jones, it's a beautiful baby girl!", and Mr. Jones begins deleting mentally the things that she might have been and adds the things that society says that she *must* be.

That young woman (for society begins to see her as a stereotype the moment that her sex is determined) will be wrapped in a pink blanket (pink because that is the color of her caste) and the unequal segregation of the sexes will have begun.

Small wonder that the young girl sitting across the desk from her counselor will not be able to say "No" to educational, economic, and social slavery. Small wonder, because she has been a psychological slave and programmed as such since the moment of her birth!

On May 20th of last year I introduced legislation concerning the equal employment opportunities of women. At that time I pointed out that there were three and one-half million more women than men in America but that women held only two percent of the managerial positions; that no women sit on the AFL-CIO Council or the Supreme Court; that only two women had ever held Cabinet rank and that there were at that time only two women of Ambassadorial rank in the Diplomatic Corps. I stated then as I do now that this situation is outrageous.

In my speech on the Floor that day I said:

> It is true that part of the problem has been that women have not been aggressive in demanding their rights. This was also true of the black population for many years. They submitted to oppression and even co-operated with it. Women have done the same thing. But now there is an awareness of this situation, particularly among the younger segment of the population.
>
> As in the field of equal rights for blacks, Spanish-Americans, the Indians and other groups, laws will not change such deep-seated problems overnight. But they can be used to provide protection for those who are most abused, and begin the process of evolutionary change by compelling the insensitive majority to re-examine its unconscious attitudes.

The law cannot do it for us, we must do it ourselves. Women in this country must become revolutionaries. We must refuse to accept the old—the traditional—roles and stereotypes.

We must reject the Greek philosopher's thought, "It is thy place women, to hold thy place and keep within doors." We must reject the thought of St. Paul who said "Let the woman learn in silence." And we must reject the Nietschzian thought "When a woman inclines to learning, there is something wrong with her sex apparatus."

But more than merely rejecting we must replace those thoughts and the concepts that they symbolize with positive values based on female experience.

A few short years ago if you called most Negroes black it was tantamount to calling them niggers. But now black is beautiful and black is proud. There are relatively few people, white or black, who do not recognize what has happened.

Black people have freed themselves from the dead weight of the albatross of blackness that once hung around their neck. They have done it by picking it up in their arms and holding it out with pride for all the world to see. They have done it by embracing it—not in the dark of the moon but in the searing light of the white sun. They have said "Yes" to it and found that the skin that was once seen as symbolizing their shame is in reality their badge of honor.

Women must come to realize that the superficial symbolisms that surround us are negative only when we ourselves perceive and accept them as negative. We must begin to replace the old negative thoughts about our femininity with positive thoughts and positive actions affirming it and more.

But we must also remember that that will be breaking with tradition and we must prepare ourselves—educationally, economically and psychologically—in order that we will be able to accept and bear with the sanctions that society will immediately impose upon us.

I am a politician. I detest the word because of the connotations that cling like slime to it but for want of a better term I must use it.

I have been in politics for twenty years and in that time I have learned a few things about the role of women in politics.

The major thing that I have learned is that women are the backbone of America's political organizations. They are the letter-writers and envelope-stuffers, the telephone-answerers; they are the campaign-workers and organizers. They are the speech writers and the largest numbers of potential voters.

Yet they are but rarely the standard-bearers or elected officials. Perhaps it is in America, more than any other country, that the inherent truth of the old bromide "The power behind the throne is a woman" is most readily apparent.

Let me remind you once again of the relatively few women standard-bearers on the American political scene. There are only ten United States Representatives. There is only one Senator and there are no Cabinet members who are women. There are no women on the Supreme Court and only a small percentage of lady judges at the Federal Court level who might be candidates.

It is true that at the state level the picture is somewhat brighter just as it is true that the North presents a surface that is somewhat more appealing to the black American when compared with the South. But even though in 1967 there were 318 women in various state legislatures, the percentage is not good when compared with the fact that in almost all fifty states there are more women of voting age than there are men; and that in each state the number of women of voting age is increasing at a greater rate than the number of men. Nor is it an encouraging figure when compared with the fact that in 1966 there were not 318 but 328 women in the state legislatures.

Secondly I have learned that the attitude held by the high school counselors that I mentioned earlier is a general attitude held by political bosses. A few years ago a politician remarked to me about a potential young female candidate, "Why invest all the time and effort to build up the gal into a household name when she's pretty sure to drop out of the game to have a couple of kids at just about the time we're ready to run her for mayor?"

I have pointed out time and time again that the harshest discrimination that I have encountered in the political arena is anti-feminism—both from males and brain-washed "Uncle Tom" females.

When I first announced that I was running for the United States Congress last year, both males and females advised me, as they had when I ran for the New York State Assembly, to go back to teaching, a woman's vocation, and leave the politics to the men.

One of the major reasons that I will not leave the American political scene —voluntarily, that is—is because the number of women in politics is declining.

There are at least two million more women than men of voting age but the fact is that while we get out the vote we often do not get out *to vote*. In 1964, for example, 72 percent of registered males voted while only 67 percent of registered females voted. We seem to be a political minority by choice.

I believe that women have a special contribution to make to help bring order out of chaos because they have special qualities of leadership which are greatly needed today. These qualities are the patience, tolerance and perseverance which have developed in many women because of their suppression. If we can add to these qualities a reservoir of information about techniques of community action we can indeed become effective harbingers of change. Women must participate more in the legislative process because, even with the contributions that I have just mentioned, the single greatest contribution that women could bring to American politics would be a spirit of moral purpose.

But unfortunately women's participation in politics is declining, as I have noted. Politics is not the only place that we are losing past gains, though. Columnist Clayton Fritchey in a column *Woman In Office,* noted that "although more women are working, their salaries keep falling behind men's. Some occupations are (still) closed by law to women. Key property laws favor men. In 1940 women held 45 percent of all professional and technical positions as against 37 percent today."

The decline is a general one. But it is because it is a decline that I believe that the true question is not whether or not women dare to move. Women have always dared! The question which now faces us is "Will women dare move in numbers sufficient to have an effect on their own attitudes toward themselves and thus change the basic attitudes of males and the general society?"

Women will have to brave the social sanctions in great numbers in order to free themselves from the sexual, psychological, and emotional stereotyping that plagues us. Like black people we will have to raise our albatross with pride.

It is not feminine egoism to say that the future of mankind may very well be ours to determine. It is simply a plain fact. The softness, warmth, and gentleness that are often used to stereotype us are positive human values; values that are becoming more and more important as the general values of the whole of mankind slip more and more out of kilter.

The strength that marked Christ, Gandhi, and Martin Luther King was a strength born not of violence but of gentleness, understanding and genuine human compassion.

We must move outside the walls of our stereotypes but we must retain the values on which they were built.

No, I am not saying that we are inherently those things that the stereotypes impute that we are; but I am saying that because of the long-enforced roles we have had to play we should know by now that the values are good ones to hold and I am saying that by now we should have developed the capacity to not only hold them but to also dispense them to those around us.

This is the reason that we must free ourselves. This is the reason that we must become revolutionaries in the fashion of Christ, Gandhi, King and the hundreds of other men and women who held those as the highest of human values.

There is another reason. In working toward our own freedom we can also allow our men to work toward their freedom from the traps of their stereotypes.

We are challenged now as we never were before. The past twenty years, with its decline for women in employment and government, with its status quo attitude toward the preparation of young women for certain professions, makes it clear that evolution is not necessarily always a process of positive forward motion. Susan B. Anthony, Carrie Nation and Sojourner Truth were not evolutionaries. They were revolutionaries, as are many of the young women of today. More women and more men must join their ranks.

New goals and new priorities, not only for this country, but for all mankind, must be set. Formal education will not help us do that. We must therefore depend on informal learning.

We can do that by confronting people with their own humanity and their own inhumanity. Confronting them wherever we meet them—in the church, in the classroom, on the floors of Congress and the state legislatures, in bars and on the streets. We must reject not only the stereotypes that others hold of us but also the stereotypes that we hold of ourselves and others.

In a speech made a few weeks ago to an audience that was predominantly white and all female I suggested the following if they wanted to create change:

You must start in your own homes, your own schools and your own
churches . . . I don't want you to go home and talk about integrated
schools, churches or marriages when the kind of integration you are
talking about is black with white.

"I want you to go home and work for—fight for—the integration of male and female—human and human. Franz Fanon pointed out in *Black Skins, White Masks* that the Anti-Semitic was eventually the Anti-Negro. I want to say that both are eventually the Anti-Feminist. And even further, I want to indicate that all discrimination is eventually the same thing—Anti-Humanism.

That is my challenge for us today, whether we are male or female.

Reflective Questions

1. What differences do you find between women's fight for equality and that of blacks?

2. Are there any types of discrimination that are not antihumanist, but are legitimate and approved?

3. Is positive discrimination or preferential treatment necessary to solve the problems of inequality by sex and race in America?

4. Do you feel that the principal role of a woman should be that of housewife and mother?

23 □ Master Slave Clashes as Forerunners of Patterns in Modern American Urban Eruptions

Richard S. Sterne □ Jeane Loftin Rothseiden

In this timely article, Sterne and Rothseiden remind us that violence is institutionalized in America; that is, it has historically been a continuing aspect of the American culture. This view contrasts vividly with the one that sees contemporary racial violence as discontinuous and new. The authors remind us that racial violence occurred in American cities prior to the Revolutionary War and before and after the Civil War, and it has continued as part of an American tradition. They contend that blacks have accepted the American tradition of using violence to solve problems related to the significance that race has come to occupy in contemporary American life. The authors do not believe that pursuit by blacks of this tradition of violence can be avoided unless massive programs are instituted to alter their conditions. □

THE ERUPTIONS THE UNITED STATES IS UNDERGOING IN ITS CITIES REFLECT A culture of violence. Violence, as the public now is increasingly admitting to itself, is an established form of behavior which colors American life in many arenas. Criminals practice violence, as do the police in suppressing them. Citizens practice violence in war, industrial conflicts, religious disputes, class competition, ethic battles, race riots and in many additional ways. Politics and civic life have recently been heavily infected by this component of American civilization,

From *Phylon*, Fall 1969, pp. 251-260. Reprinted by permission of *Phylon* and the authors.

as assassinations and riots mount. Violence is part of the American culture, it is not a subculture. It is a tool of action employed by all segments of society when it seems the appropriate means. If not all men are its agents, most support it, condone it, encourage it. Matza and Sykes point to the confluence of the criminal culture and the general culture, saying that for the latter, "disclaimers of violence are suspect not simply because phantasies of violence are widely consumed, but also because of the actual use of aggression and violence."[1]

How did Americans learn to be violent? This paper will discuss one important piece of history through which violence was built—the erection of American slavery. As this institution was hewn, it helped to make violence legitimate, and the present-day culture exhibits the product.

Space forbids more than an outline of the routes by which violent practices traveled to the cities as they were becoming urbanized. The earlier times only are discussed in detail, yet what was established then continues in a derivative form today.[2]

Building one of the nation's institutions—slavery—by violence painted a band of lawlessness across the American way of life, a streak which James Truslow Adams has called our "lawless heritage."[3] Again and again this lawless heritage has been a crashing theme in American history. The erection of the Baltimore Railroad, which was begun in 1828, was punctuated by riots, Adams says. In 1834 a race riot erupted in Philadelphia, thirty houses were sacked or destroyed and several persons killed. Many minorities have suffered this havoc. In 1834, the Ursuline Convent near Boston was pillaged and razed by anti-Catholics. In 1833, before Mormons embraced polygamy, Missourians destroyed their houses, beat and killed men and mutilated their bodies.[4] The sample citations of early nineteenth century conditions illustrate extensive documentation provided by Adams and by Allen D. Grimshaw.[5]

Violence, habitually used, destroys patience with tidy rules. The bounds which define what portion of force is legitimate in a society become indistinct. Men who do not trust the law to take its course come to honor illegal and

---

[1] David Matza and Gresham M. Sykes, "Juvenile Delinquency and Subterranean Values," *American Sociological Review,* XXVI (October, 1961), 712-19.
[2] Material presented here and elsewhere in this article is drawn from a study to be published in the near future. Because of the need to shorten the text for the current presentation, it has not been possible to document all statements in detail, nor to give credit in some cases to authors whose ideas are reflected.
[3] James Truslow Adams, "Our Lawless Heritage," *Atlantic Monthly,* CXLII (December, 1928), 732-40.
[4] *Ibid.*
[5] *Ibid.*, and Allen D. Grimshaw, "Lawlessness and Violence in America and Their Special Manifestations in Changing Negro-White Relationships," *Journal of Negro History,* XLIV (January, 1959), 52-72.

forcible action,[6] and civil discipline is destroyed.[7] Lawlessness becomes a tradition. At the least, official rules become discretionary.

De facto law is established by such a process, creating new laws with as much, perhaps more, effect than those achieved through formal political processes. The persons who lead these revisions are, in effect, legislators, and other segments of society ratify their decisions when they condone the new codes merely by inert acceptance (perhaps even while pronouncing overt disapproval of illegal behavior). The custom of riots in which white mobs have punitively invaded Negro neighborhoods has been such a "law," forays which Dawson and Gettys compare to European pogroms.[8] Another "law" which the mores have justified has been lynching. It has become lynch-law and the Ku Klux Klan a "law" body.

Extra-legal practices command conformity. In communities where there is strong opposition to social and political equality for Negroes, no ordinance can be found which requires that they be shot, discharged from their jobs, or that their houses be burned down when they rebel against their position. Yet, true believer whites in Northern and Southern communities have believed in this violence against infractors of the caste system.

Negroes were also true believers—but not in the caste system. They were punished for that. But to violence they cleaved. Negroes who engaged in counter-aggression in pre-Civil War days, and who are exploding in ghettos one hundred years later, show that they have believed in the American way. It has been only one part of American culture—the caste system—which they have rejected; in their use of violence they are and have been thoroughly American.

"It is needless to say," Adams declares, "that we are not going to be able to shed this heritage quickly or easily. In fact we have gone so far on the wrong road that it is by no means certain that we can ever get back on the right one even with the best of intentions."[9]

There were no laws authorizing or condoning slavery in the virginial American colonies. The status of black men was an anomaly in the American social system. Slavery defied the values for which whites shed their own blood to achieve their own freedom. For these values they bleed today in the hope of destroying the dominance of man over man abroad. These values are in the American creed which enounces "a perfect Union, one and inseparable; established upon those principles of freedom, equality, justice and humanity for which American patriots have sacrificed their lives and fortunes." Henry Tyler

---

[6] See Hans Gerth and C. Wright Mills, *Character and Social Structure* (New York, 1953), p. 263.

[7] Seymour M. Lipset, "The Sources of the 'Radical Right,'" chap. xiii, in *The Radical Right*, ed. by Daniel Bell (Garden City, 1963), p. 320.

[8] C. A. Dawson and W. E. Gettys, *An Introduction to Sociology* (New York, 1929), p. 382.

[9] Adams, *op. cit.*

Page set forth those words in 1917, when Americans sailed to foreign shores to fight "to make the world safe for Democracy."

Long before the First World War, colored men came to the shores of the land of the Union, but their transoceanic voyages were not voluntary. They came as merchandise ordered by whites with challenging New World enterprises. Hundreds of thousands of children, women and men traveled in fetters, delivered to buyers who had use for captive hands and backs.

New England traders made enormous profits from slavery. Goods and rum were carried from the home port to the coast of Africa where they were bartered for slaves, who were taken to the Americas and were traded for sugar, molasses, rice or tobacco, with which the boats proceeded homeward. Many black people died on the way, but the shippers grew rich.[10] Of the unwilling passengers, Harvey Wish says:

> The captives displayed a profound dejection and sought many devices to commit suicide. Sometimes they would jump overboard if the crew did not take every precaution to prevent this. Self-imposed starvation was common. One witness, testifying before a parliamentary committee, declared that compulsory feeding was used on every slave ship with which he was familiar. Sick Negroes would refuse medicines, declaring that they wished only to die. Characteristic of many slavers was a "howling melancholy noise" with the women occasionally in hysterics. Sometimes the slaves were convinced that they were to be eaten.[11]

The impulse of self-destruction was, according to inquiry, the disruption of family and tribal bonds. Black people simply preferred death to separation from their spouses and families.

Slavery as Americans know it was the product of early colonial enterprise; yet America was not the first country to employ forced labor. Portuguese mariners brought the custom to Europe before Columbus sailed to America. In Portugal, Negro *escravos* labored in houses, ports and fields. As Latin colonies rose in South America, the supply of freemen fell short of the manpower needs. Native Indians were forced into service but, in about 1510, Latins transported to the New World the custom of using Negroes, who replaced other slave types.[12]

Anglo-Saxon colonists followed the steps of the Latins and also attempted to make slaves of the Indians. Red men ran away or rebelled and, for decades,

---

[10] John Hope Franklin, *From Slavery to Freedom* (New York, 1947), pp. 56–58, 102; Mary Wilhelmine Williams, "Slavery, Modern-General," *Encyclopedia of the Social Sciences*, XIV (New York, 1934), 81–82.
[11] Harvey Wish, "American Slave Insurrections Before 1861," *Journal of Negro History*, XXII (July, 1937), 299. Used by permission.
[12] Williams, *op. cit.*, pp. 80–81.

white indentured servants from Britain and elsewhere in Europe made up the slave labor force, so states historian Ulrich B. Phillips (who believed Negroes were better suited to slavery by virtue of their "natural" docility and obedience).[13]

At first Negroes were only another group of the bonded. This anonymous status was soon lost. The cheap price of Negroes and their seemingly inexhaustible supply were one thing; but equally important was their skin color, which made them visible, easy to see, to locate, to seize, and to punish when they ran away. During the first years of slavery in America it was believed that because Negroes were heathens their Christian masters had no humanitarian obligation to them. This served as an excuse for brutality. Negroes adopted the religious practices of their owners and the rules of the game were changed. Color alone and not belief in the Christian religion served as justification for enslavement.[14] Negroes were therefore slaves for life—as long as they were black. Race became the rule for the division of labor and Negroes were stripped of all rights belonging to other men. E. B. Reuter declares that the principle that controlled the allocation of plantation work was naked power. Mean work went to the slaves, other work to the owners. The duties of Negroes were determined in the same way as those of the livestock.[15] Those who resisted were beaten and whipped. As valuable property, less frequently were they hanged or shot.

Though profiting from the shipment of slaves, Northerners actually used fewer for themselves than did their Southern customers. This difference has been laid to the terrain which it is said made it impossible to establish large plantations with herds of unskilled captive workers. It has also been said that economic and ideological factors prevented Northerners from preserving their own system of slavery.[16]

It is not to be assumed that Northerners came to like blacks. They opposed slavery only in their midst and part of their opposition was based upon hatred. The lower classes viewed blacks as intolerable competitors. Similar competition with freedmen later produced riots. The upper classes came to hate slaves for a different reason. Uprisings of enraged slaves frightened the slaveholders. One took place in 1712 in New York, for example, and another in 1741. The combined effects of the forces of economics, abolitionism and fear produced the

---

[13] Ulrich B. Phillips, "Slavery, Modern-United States," *Encyclopedia of the Social Sciences*, XIV (New York, 1934), 84.
[14] E. Franklin Frazier, *The Negro in the United States* (New York, 1949), pp. 22–28; also, Franklin, *op. cit.*, pp. 48–49.
[15] Edward B. Reuter, "Competition and the Racial Division of Labor," *Race Relations and the Race Problem*, ed. by Edgar T. Thompson (Durham, North Carolina, 1939), chap. ii, pp. 55–56.
[16] See for example, Edward R. Turner, *The Negro in Pennsylvania* (Washington, D. C.: The American Historical Association, 1911), pp. 14–15.

extinction of slavery in Northern states; by 1790 it was dwindling and by 1840 had largely disappeared.[17]

William Renwick Riddell describes the New York insurrections:

The so-called conspiracy of slaves or Negro insurrection was officially reported to the Lords of Trade by Governor Robert Hunter in his Despatch from New York, June 23, 1712. Describing the "bloody conspiracy of some of the Slaves of this place to destroy as many of the inhabitants as they could . . . to revenge themselves for some hard usage they apprehended to have received from their Masters," the Governor says: "They agreed to meet in the orchard of Mr. Crook, the middle of the Town, some provided with firearms, some with swords and others with Knives and hatchets . . . the sixth day of April . . . about twelve or one o'clock at night . . . three and twenty of them were got together, one coffee and negroe slave to one Vantilburgh set fire to an outhouse of his Master's and then repairing to the place where the rest were they all sallyed out together with their arm's and marched to the fire: by this time the noise of the fire spreading through the town the people began to flock to it: upon the approach of severall the slaves fired and killed them . . . some escaping their shot soon published the cause of the fire which was the reason that not above nine Christians were killed and about five or six wounded. . . . I order'd a detachment from the Fort . . . to march against them but the Slaves made their escape into the woods by the favour of the night." By placing sentries and having the Militia of New York and the County of West Chester "drive the Island" "we found all that put the design in execution, six of these having first laid violent hands on themselves, the rest were forthwith brought to their tryal before ye Justices. . . . In that Court were twenty-seven condemned whereof twenty one were executed—one being a woman with child, her execution by that means suspended— some were burnt, others hanged, one broke on the wheele and one hung alive in chains in the town. . . ." Compensation for the nineteen Negroes actually executed for this conspiracy and the cost of prosecution should have been paid by an assessment levied on all the slave owners of the Town; but it was thought reasonable that these amounts should be paid from the funds of the Province.

Accordingly, in December, 1717, an Act was passed by the Assembly providing for the payment of these sums with many other claims and for raising the money by Bills of Credit. . . .

[17] See Franklin, *op. cit.*, pp. 144–45; and U. S. Department of Commerce, Bureau of the Census, *A Century of Population Growth* (Washington, D. C., United States Government Printing Office, 1909), p. 133.

Provision was made for payment at the rate of fifty ounces of "Sevil Mexico or Pillar Plate" for each "Negro so as aforesaid executed."

In March, 1741, occurred a very great fire destroying the Fort and some of the records. This was followed by many in the Town, sometimes four a day and some apparently kindled by design. General consternation followed. Lieutenant Governor George Clarke offered a reward and strong suspicion arose that the fires were the result of a Negro plot. Many Negroes were imprisoned on suspicion and all denied knowledge of plot or cause of the fires. At length a Negro called Quack, who set fire to the Fort, confessed, and this, joined to the evidence of other witnesses, convinced the authorities that the fires were kindled "in the execution of a horrid Conspiracy to burn . . . the whole town and to Massacre the people," that there were "not many innocent Negroes" and that "some Negroes of the Country were accomplices. . . ."

A Trial was had . . . in all there were "executed three whites and twenty-nine Negroes; the authorities pardoned one white woman, namely, Huson's daughter, and pardoned and transported eighty Negroes besides eight Negroes not indicted but accused and strongly suspected to be guilty. Their Masters consented to transport them."

This plot does not seem to have created the alarm of the former one in 1712, which was practically contemporaneous with an attempted revolution by the Negro slaves in South Carolina whose number had been largely increased owing to the manufacture of pitch and tar. This attempt, however, led to a duty of £30 on every Negro imported.[18]

Frightening events such as these helped cool the fervor toward keeping slaves in the North; they reveal, also, that American patterns of violence were already forming and that cities even then were experiencing their effects.

The South was taking a different road. The Revolutionary War, declares E. Franklin Frazier, stimulated an interlude of idealism.[19] There is a belief that although the nerve of slavery was failing at that time, there was still a demand for the continuation of that institution. Earlier crops had exhausted the soil and had left many Virginians with surplus and profitless manpower inventories. Not even this fact, avers Robert McColley, could have induced these American aristocrats to have abandoned the status of masters.[20] It cannot be determined what they might have paid to have continued as lords over Negroes and poorer whites. If there ever was a question that slavery meant profit,

---

[18] William R. Riddell, "The Slave in Early New York," *Journal of Negro History*, XIII (January, 1928), 53–86. Used by permission.
[19] Frazier, *op. cit.*, pp. 34–36.
[20] Robert McColley, *Slavery and Jeffersonian Virginia* (Urbana, Illinois: University of Illinois Press, 1964), pp. 54 and 182 ff.

the invention of the cotton gin answered it in 1793. Wide territories were opened up to the cultivation of short staple cotton and, thus, to the unskilled labor of slaves in the fields. The use of slaves quickly expanded and spread and opposition and Revolutionary idealism vanished.

Benjamin Franklin declared before the Revolution that any rational man could tell that slavery did not make a profit.

Any one may compute it. Interest of money is in the colonies from six to ten per cent. Slaves, one with another, cost thirty pounds sterling per head. Reckon then the interest of the first purchase of a slave, the insurance or risk on his life, his clothing and diet, expenses in his sickness and loss of time, loss by his neglect of business. . . .[21]

Franklin was wrong, at least in the case of the South. Reanimated Southern slavery made real money up to the moment that it was abolished after the Civil War. Kenneth Stampp states, "There was no evidence in 1860 that bondage was a 'decrepit institution tottering toward a decline'—and indeed, if the slaveholder's economic self-interest alone were to be consulted, the institution should have been preserved."[22]

The profit of cotton produced a renewed belief in the value of slavery, a belief which stood all onslaughts. Similar to the North, the South had its Negro revolts and terrors; however, uprisings in the South did not cause the system to be thrown out. Southerners increased their controls; their attitude toward the value of slavery stiffened. If rebellion were indeed a risk to business, they would see that this risk was destroyed.

Whites perfected dominance, relying upon force in the final test; but blacks were never the docile lambs that whites would have liked them to be. They did not willingly accept their destination, and many slew their masters on the foreign soil. There were years of such conflict before and during the Civil War; these are described by Harvey Wish.

The romantic portrayal of *ante-bellum* society on the southern plantation, which depicts the rollicking black against a kindly patriarchal background, has tended to obscure the large element of slave unrest which occasionally shook the whole fabric of the planter's kingdom. Even the abolitionist, eager to capitalize upon such material, could make only vague inferences as to the extent of Negro insurrections in the

---

[21] The Works of Benjamin Franklin, *Correspondence*, VII, 201–02. Reprinted in *Journal of Negro History*, IV (January, 1919), 42.
[22] Kenneth M. Stampp, *The Peculiar Institution* (New York, 1956), pp. 417–18. See also William L. Miller, "Slavery and the Population of the South," *Southern Economic Journal*, XXVIII (July, 1961), 46–54.

South. The danger of inducing general panic by spreading news of an insurrection was a particularly potent factor in the maintenance of silence on the topic. Besides, sectional pride, in the face of anti-slavery taunts, prevented the loyal white Southerner from airing the subject of domestic revolt in the press. "Last evening," wrote a lady of Charleston during the Denmark Vesey scare of 1822, "twenty-five hundred of our citizens were under arms to guard our property and lives. But it is a subject not to be mentioned; and unless you hear of it elsewhere, say nothing about it." Consequently, against such a conspiracy of silence the historian encounters unusual difficulties in reconstructing the true picture of slave revolts in the United States.[23]

The text of the comprehensive reviews by Wish of these rebellions cannot be reproduced here, but it is clear that slave owners had to use increasing force to preserve the profitable institution. Upon emancipation, release or escape from the status of slaves, many flew to the Union armies. Some killed their erstwhile masters, which gave other masters new reasons to fear their long-held captives. The stereotype of the passive slave is indeed a most erroneous American myth; docility was only superficial and was based upon fear.

White masters perfected the culture of violence and, therefore, created eager black pupils who desired to practice their lessons. Nat Turner led the most frightening revolt, which was outstanding for its violence. Turner's bloody insurrection was a reflex to the cruelties of slavery; but it shocked the spine of Southerners, so that the "Black Laws" were tightly closed on any further insubordination among Negroes. Turner raised a flurry of speech in Virginia over the rightness of slavery—a question settled on the side of owners with police power and resolute determination.[24] Whatever violence was needed would be used to preserve slavery.

Nat Turner was hung in Jerusalem, Virginia, but the massacre helped lead to the Civil War. When the War was over, slavery was officially destroyed; however, Southern whites surmounted the obstacle by reestablishing dominance through other means, while Northern whites lost interest in the status of black men and acquiesced to the reversion of their position. White supremacy replaced slavery, a substitution executed through brutal assaults and new laws. Blacks were forced to conform under pressure of whippings, lynchings, riots and other types of violence. What force Negroes could muster was weak and the repression

---

[23] Wish, *op. cit.* Used by permission. See also Harvey Wish, "Slave Disloyalties under the Confederacy," *Journal of Negro History,* XXIII (October, 1938), 435-50.

[24] John W. Cromwell, "The Aftermath of Nat Turner's Insurrection," *Journal of Negro History,* V (April, 1920), 203-34.

they feared seemed unassailable. As most of them lived on Southern plantations or in small towns, they found it difficult to escape surveillance by whites.[25]

One effect of violence was to cause blacks to move into Southern metropoli where jobs were becoming available as the cities industrialized.[26] Further, the boll weevil traversed the cotton states between 1890 and 1921; cotton lost its crown and thousands of fieldhands were without work.[27] In cities, Negroes found jobs as laborers, menials and servants, which relieved some of the obsolete slave-like status that was still preserved in closer face-to-face contacts on the farms. Nevertheless, many whites who also had left the countryside were not willing to compete with Negroes as people. The lot of all citizens improved in time in Southern cities but avenues of upward mobility for black men remained segregated and limited. Blacks usually were allowed only those advances which were convenient to whites or which were won and kept by great struggle. Negroes proliferated class differences among themselves, establishing fortunes beyond the meager existences of antebellum freedmen, or the protected stations of favored house slaves; yet when blacks "got out of line" they were pushed back into their "place" by violent means. The differing social achievements of blacks in 1906 offered two neighborhoods of attack in Atlanta;[28] in Tulsa, in 1921, on the other hand, all classes were penned in "Little Africa" and were attacked together.[29] Although Negroes defended themselves by return fire, they were relatively helpless since a white mob force was superior.

Negroes fled North; violence did not altogether keep Negroes from Atlanta or other cities of the South, but during fifty years (1910-1960), 4,252,600 Negroes left Dixie.[30] So great was the emigration that Southern states sought to halt it. Plantations still needed labor despite changes in crops, and communities barred Northern industrial recruiting agents, who were extremely active in the South, or demanded license fees as high as $1,000. Servants and workers became hard to get. Negroes were threatened if they wanted to move and were

---

[25] This material and that following are described more fully in the forthcoming book by the authors.
[26] Frazier, *op. cit.*, pp. 190–91.
[27] Gunnar Myrdal, *An American Dilemma* (New York, 1944), pp. 234–35; also, Calvin L. Beale, "The Negro in American Agriculture" in *The American Negro Reference Book*, ed. by John P. Davis (Englewood Cliffs, 1966), chap. iii, pp. 161–204. See also pp. 164–67.
[28] See Ray Stannard Baker, *Following the Color Line* (New York, 1908) Chap. i.
[29] See Walter F. White, "The Eruption of Tulsa," *The Nation*, CXII (June 29, 1921), 309–10.
[30] Population figures cited here and in the following paragraph are based upon or estimated from Karl E. Taueber and Alma F. Taueber, "The Negro Population in the United States," in *The American Negro Reference Book*, Davis, *op. cit.*, pp. 96–160. See also pp. 104, 106–07, 110, 119, 122.

encouraged by newspapers to stay.[31] Some migrated to the Midwest, some migrated from town to town or county to county within a region, some went to Canada, some to Mexico, but for the greater part migration proceeded from the rural South to the Northern urban centers—the big cities, where they hoped to board the American mainstream.[32]

City areas in the North and the West swelled to over 7,000,000 population, increasing eightfold between 1910 and 1960. There was an actual drop of nearly one third in the overall Negro proportion in the South during these fifty years; in 1960 it was only 20.6 percent. The reception north of the Mason-Dixon line was not all that Negroes might have dreamed it would be. In the North and West, whites gave half of what Negroes desired, denied half, leading to violent clashes. The New York Draft Riots in 1863 presaged the reception Negroes would actually receive in the North in the twentieth century. During the Civil War poor whites feared the competition of freed slaves as they had feared slave competition in pre-bellum years and as they fear competition today from Negroes. In the 1900's, blacks were assaulted by competitors in the Tenderloin Riot; in Chicago in 1919; in Detroit in 1943.[33] These are bare samples of the white men's attacks upon Negroes, attacks built upon the culturally established pattern of pushing Negroes into the position of slaves or a slave-like status, in order to further the interests of whites.

Yet, Negroes have always shown that they too are Americans. They have been as violent as whites when given the opportunity. The philosophy of the Beatitudes has never been followed by any mass of American citizens. Martin Luther King, Jr., now dead, was trying to teach Americans an alien creed. Therefore, as long as whites choose to exclude visible Negroes from the black men's choice of competitive accomplishment, Americans may expect race violence. Negroes have carried their resentment from the Southern fields and have met white men on the urban ground, where both act out the tradition of lawlessness. A thin layer of upper-class Negroes is joining the white society, being accepted as a kind of exotic minority. Some are mayors, yet the population shifts through which whites are abandoning cities to blacks mainly account for the elections of these mayors.[34]

[31] Franklin, *op. cit.,* p. 465, and Myrdal, *op. cit.,* pp. 248–49.
[32] It is to be noted that despite the extended years of migration, 54.1 percent of Southern Negroes still lived in small towns or on farms by 1960, representing nearly three tenths of all American Negroes.
[33] References to particular incidents in this section are not footnoted, since they are well-known, or are currently in the news; citations will be provided, however, in the fuller exposition of which mention has been made.
[34] In Cleveland, for example, Negroes formed 38 percent of the population, but captured the mayorship by a strong bloc vote. Similar factors prevailed in Gary, Indiana. See Jeffrey K. Hadden, Louis H. Masotti and Victor Theissen, "The Making of Negro Mayors 1967," *Transaction,* XV (January-February, 1968), 21–30.

In the metropoli, poor black men, whether in the minority or the majority, have expressed strong feelings in some of the larger cities such as Detroit, Newark, Philadelphia and Los Angeles. These events represent a mere sample of a vast universe of recent disorders. Blacks of less dispossessed groups are found to sympathize with the rioters, even though middle-class Negroes are scorned by the many poorer blacks who are more typical of the mob members.[35] Their actions, in the eyes of many white people, are "senseless"; but these Negroes express, in the American way, the feelings of people deprived of rights to which as Americans they are entitled, and they are determined to either seize power by force or destroy the system so far as they can.

Only a massive program to undo past patterns could forestall further eruptions, unless the white majority is to continue the tradition of violence in an amplified form, so that there will be not merely isolated conflicts but war. This may take the form of mob repression or totalitarian police repression, but tradition has led Americans to the point where such a choice is necessary.

[35] See for example, Nathan E. Cohen, "The Los Angeles Riot Study," *Social Work,* XII (October, 1967), 14–21, and National Advisory Commission on Civil Disorders Report (New York: Bantam Books, 1968), pp. 111, 128–29, 130–32, 134 for discussion of the characteristics and attitudes of black rioters in Newark and Detroit, and comparison to the poorer and to the middle-class blacks.

Reflective Questions

1. What alternatives to racial violence exist in American culture? What is the likelihood that they will be effectively utilized to avert further violence?

2. If massive social programs are instituted, what assurances exist that racial violence will automatically cease to exist?

3. Given the legitimation and rationale for violence by groups, what is the likelihood of an increase in political repression and curtailment of civil liberties in the American social order?

4. Is there any historical or psycho-biological basis for assuming that man is by nature violent or nonviolent?

24 □ What Looting in Civil Disturbances Really Means

Russell Dynes □ E. L. Quarantelli

Professors Dynes and Quarantelli offer a definition of looting and then proceed to distinguish between types of looting. In order to examine the differences between looting after disasters and looting in civil disturbances, the authors offer an analysis of what happens to private property during natural disasters, and then contrast this with the acquisition of property that occurs during civil disorders. Widespread looting in civil disturbances may, according to their view, be interpreted as a kind of mass protest against the traditional American conceptions of property rights. They claim that looting in civil disturbances is a plea for a redistribution of property. The fate of our urban centers may depend on the ability of key political figures to interpret the underlying motivation of looters, and to act in such a manner so as to resolve the gross inequalities which are now present. □

IN MARCH AND APRIL OF THIS YEAR, THERE WERE CIVIL DISTURBANCES IN Memphis, Tenn., Washington, D.C., Chicago, Pittsburgh, and Baltimore. Many films and photographs were taken of people looting other people's property. These looting incidents conformed to the pattern, for according to many reports people may be found looting when a community is having certain kinds of crises. One of these crises is caused by a natural disaster—a flood, hurricane, and so forth. And the other is caused by a civil disturbance, like the ones that have hit American cities every summer since the Watts outbreak of August 1965.

Copyright © May 1968, by TRANS-action, Inc., New Brunswick, New Jersey. Reprinted by permission.

Natural disasters and civil disturbances give people a chance to help themselves to other people's goods. Yet there are important, fascinating differences between what happens in these two crisis situations. For example, looting is far more common in civil disturbances than in disasters. Then too, the *kinds* of goods taken during these two crises are different. And public disdain for the act varies. Sometimes taking other people's property during a community crisis is not even considered looting!

In order to examine the differences between the two crisis situations, let us analyze what happens to private property during natural disasters, and then contrast this with the transfers of property that take place during civil disorders.

The word "looting" has military roots. It implies that invading armies take property by force, generally when the rightful owner cannot protect it. Similarly, in civil disturbances "invading armies" plunder property left unguarded when the owner is forced out by violence or the threat of violence. During disasters, according to common belief, "invading armies" of opportunists take property left unguarded when the owner is forced out by the disaster.

The looting that takes place in these situations is usually interpreted as evidence of human depravity. In periods of natural or civil chaos, goes the explanation, the human animal is stripped of his usual social controls. Without them, he is not a noble savage, but an ignoble one. For the general public, reports of looting are easy to incorporate into their images of the "criminal elements" who clean out the corner grocery during a racial disturbance, or the fiends and ghouls who roam disaster-stricken areas.

After the Galveston hurricane of 1900, published accounts told of people being summarily shot when they were caught with pocketsful of severed fingers with rings on them. In 1906, after the San Francisco earthquake and fire, the *Los Angeles Times* reported that "looting by fiends incarnate made a hell broth of the center of the ruined district. Sixteen looters were shot out of hand on April 19, while robbing the dead." In his reconstruction of events after the earthquake, reporter Q.A. Bronson noted "reports . . . of . . . looters wantonly shot in their tracks by Federal troops, miscreants hanged in public squares, and ghouls found cutting off the fingers and ears of corpses for rings and earrings attached."

Today, most radio and television accounts of disasters are less dramatic, but looting is still a major theme. After a tornado hit some suburbs of Chicago in April 1967, a county sheriff reportedly announced that "orders had gone out that beginning at 10 P.M. Friday, any looters . . . were to be shot on sight." After a power failure blacked out the Cincinnati area in May 1967, a wire-service story told of the smashing of store windows and looting in Cincinnati and in neighboring Newport and Covington, Ky.

Public officials, expecting certain kinds of community emergencies to activate human depravity, often request additional law enforcement. They mobilize National Guard units and take extra security measures. These steps are often taken upon the first reports of a civil disturbance or a natural disaster. Frequently, before the situation has even developed, television and radio will report what *is expected to happen*—the fear of looting and the steps being taken to prevent it.

That most people are concerned about looting in civil disorders and disasters is beyond dispute. Reliable evidence, however, points to a surprising fact: While looting clearly does occur in civil disturbances, in disaster situations it is very rare.

Many studies of disasters mention *reports* of looting, but very few cite authenticated cases. One study that did inquire into actual cases of looting was the National Opinion Research Center (N.O.R.C.) study of White County, Ark., after it was ravaged by a tornado in 1952. In the community that suffered the greatest damage, about 1000 of the 1200 residents were left homeless. A random sample of people from this town and adjacent areas were asked whether they had lost any property by looting. Only 9 percent reported that they, or members of their immediate household, had lost property that they even *felt* had been taken by looters. And fully one-third of these people were uncertain whether the loss was really due to looters, or whether the missing items had been blown away or buried in the debris. Finally, most of the articles were of little value.

In contrast, 58 percent of the people questioned said they had heard of *others'* property being stolen. In fact, 9 percent claimed that they had even seen looting in progress or had seen looters being arrested. The N.O.R.C. study team on the scene, however, could verify the theft of only two major items—a cash register and a piano.

Other disaster research confirms the rarity of looting. A study made after the 1953 floods in the Netherlands found that, although there were many reports of looting, law-enforcement agencies could discover not a single verified case. The Dutch researchers attributed many of the reports of looting to memory lapses in the immediate post-flood period, and pointed out that a number of people who reported thefts later found the missing items. Charles Fritz and J.H. Mathewson, in a review of disaster studies published up to 1956, concluded that "the number of verified cases of actual looting in peacetime disasters, in the United States and in foreign countries, is small."

More recent studies point in the same direction. The Disaster Research Center at Ohio State University, in field studies of more than 40 disasters both in the United States and abroad, has found extremely few verified cases of looting. Actual police records support these findings. For example, in September 1965, the month Hurricane Betsy struck New Orleans, major crimes in the city fell

26.6 percent below the rate for the same month in the previous year. Burglaries reported to the police fell from 617 to 425. Thefts of over $50 dropped from 303 to 264, and those under $50 fell from 516 to 366.

Misinterpreted Motives

Since all evidence is that looting is rare or nonexistent in natural disasters, why do reports of looting in disaster situations occur over and over again? And why are these reports persistently believed, even when there is no clear evidence to back them up?

To answer these questions, we need to look at four conditions that usually prevail in the immediate post-impact period: misinterpretations of observed behavior; misunderstandings over property ownership; inflated reports of looting; and sensational coverage of disaster situations by the news media.

Reports of looting are often based on misinterpretation of people's motives. After a disaster, masses of people—often numbering in the thousands—converge on the impact area. Local officials, particularly those with little experience in large-scale emergencies, frequently regard these convergers as sightseers—and, by extension, as potential looters. However, Fritz and Mathewson have shown that there are at least five different types of convergers: the returnees—the disaster survivors who want to go back to the impact area; the anxious—those concerned with the safety of kin and friends; the helpers—those who want to donate their services; the curious—those attempting to make some sense out of the unusual events that have occurred; and the exploiters—those seeking private gain from public misfortune. The number in this last category is small and includes, in addition to potential looters, souvenir hunters, relief stealers, and profiteers.

The important point is that those who converge on a disaster area have a variety of motives. Community officials often do not seem to recognize this. For example, a property owner whose house has been destroyed may return to the area to sift through the debris of his own home in the hope of recovering lost articles. To a casual observer, his behavior may look like looting. Out-of-town relatives may come into a disaster area with a truck to help their kin collect and store their remaining possessions. People engaged in informal search-and-rescue activities of this sort may also appear to be looters. The souvenir hunter is looking for something that has symbolic rather than material value. But in the disaster context, his behavior too becomes suspect.

Another source of false looting reports is the fact that, although little or no property is stolen in disaster situations, goods are frequently given away. Sometimes there is confusion about which items are free, and who is entitled to them.

In one disaster, the report began circulating that a grocery store had been looted. Investigation revealed that the owner had placed damaged goods outside on the sidewalk, announcing that anyone was welcome to take them. Since his store front had been demolished, however, the line between the free goods and the owner's undamaged stock was vague—and some people who came to get the free goods inadvertently took items from the undamaged stock instead. This misunderstanding was soon cleared up. But an early report of the incident, given to the military authorities in the area, quickly spread throughout the community as an authentic case of looting. And what's more, the looting report was later accepted as valid even by members of the military who had established that it was false.

Overblown estimates of disaster losses are the third source of unfounded looting reports. Officials in a disaster area frequently tend to overestimate the seriousness of the situation. Messages about either the quantity of aid needed or the extent of the damage tend to mushroom as they pass from one person to another. If one official asks another for 100 cots, the second official may relay a request to a third official for 150 cots, and so on. In much the same way, reports of looting get blown out of proportion.

The following incident occurred at a communications center in a major metropolitan area that had been hit by a hurricane: A patrolman in the field, talking over his radio, made a casual comment that, since some store fronts were open and could easily be entered, perhaps a policeman might be dispatched to that location. The patrolman who received this call was busy for a few minutes with other queries. Then he made a call to the state police requesting that a force be rushed to that location—since, he said, "a hell of a lot of looting is going on there."

Sensational news accounts round out the picture. Naturally, the mass media emphasize the dramatic. The atypical and the unique are what catch the newsman's attention. Photographs of disaster areas depict the buildings that are destroyed, not the ones that are still intact. And in press accounts, any stories about looting—including the stories that are inaccurate and inflated—are quickly seized upon and highlighted.

These accounts are often accepted as reasonable descriptions of what is occurring even by community officials themselves. In the absence of up-to-date and direct information, what happened or what is happening is not easy to determine. The phone system may be disrupted, preventing direct feedback of information from field points. Movement may be severely restricted. Direct observation is often impossible. And the pressure for immediate action may prevent anyone from keeping accurate records. Since few people in any community have much first-hand experience with large-scale disasters, journalistic accounts become a major means of defining reality. As one police chief said in reply to a question about his knowledge of looting, "Well, I'm not sure. All I know right now is the reports I've heard over the radio."

The upshot of all this is that many reported cases of post-disaster "looting," based on misinterpretation or misunderstanding and publicized by exaggerated or sensational accounts, are not really cases of looting at all. They involve no unlawful appropriations of property.

Still, the fact remains that certain "illegal" appropriations of property *do* occur in disaster situations. For example, people sometimes break into stores and warehouses without the owner's consent and take medical supplies, cots, generators, and flashlights. Now, is this looting? And if not, why not?

Here we come to the critical element of "property redefinition." Incidents of this sort are *not* looting. The notion of "property" involves a shared understanding about who can do what with the valued resources within a community. When a disaster strikes, property rights are temporarily redefined: There is general agreement among community members that the resources of individuals become *community property*. Individual property rights are suspended, so appropriation of private resources—which would normally be considered looting—is temporarily condoned. Before these resources can be given back to private use, the needs of the disoriented larger community have to be met.

When a natural crisis occurs, the usual plurality of individual goals gives way to the single, overriding goal of the community—the goal of saving as many lives as possible. Any way of achieving this becomes legitimate. People who are trapped have to be rescued; people who are in dangerous areas have to be evacuated; people who have been injured have to be given medical attention; people who are missing, and perhaps injured, must be found. If this means community appropriation of private search equipment, medical material, and even vehicles, it is implicitly viewed as necessary. In one case, a city attorney even made it official: He announced that people were to disregard any laws that would interfere with the search-and-rescue efforts going forward in the central part of the city. This meant formally sanctioning breaking into and entering private stores and offices in the city.

The redefinition of property that occurs during natural disasters, then, almost defines looting out of existence. Almost, but not quite. For implicit in the redefinition is the idea that access to the redefined property is limited to community members, and for community ends. If outsiders enter the disaster area and begin appropriating private property for their own use, it is still looting. And in fact, evidence indicates that the few verified instances of looting that do occur in natural disasters are almost always of this sort—that is, they are committed by outsiders.

Occasionally there are authenticated reports that seem to contradict our finding that looting in natural disasters is very rare. One example is the looting that occurred during the very heavy snowstorms that paralyzed Chicago in late January and early February 1967. A few of the incidents reported were probably routine burglaries, but others were clearly looting. They were not randomly distributed by location, and most of the cases occurred in the same neighborhoods—and sometimes on exactly the same streets—where looting had taken place in the civil disturbances during the summer months of 1966. Along Chicago's Roosevelt Road, for example, looting took place on some of the very same blocks.

This suggests that the looting that occurred in Chicago during the snowstorm, was actually a continuation, or perhaps a resurgence, of the earlier civil disturbance. For the general public, the habit of viewing civil disturbances as exclusively summer events probably obscured the true nature of the snowstorm looting. But some local policemen clearly interpreted the looting as a winter recurrence of the summer's civil disorders.

In contrast to what happens in a disaster situation, looting in civil disturbances is widespread, and the looters are usually members of the immediate community. During the past few summers, films and photographs have shown looting actually in progress. The McCone Commission reported that about 600 stores were looted or burned in Watts. In Newark, around 1300 people were arrested, mostly for taking goods. In the July 1967 holocaust in Detroit, unofficial estimates were that about 2700 stores were ransacked.

REDEFINITION OF PROPERTY

Disasters and civil disturbances are alike in that the normal order and organization of the community is disrupted. In addition, there is, in both situations, a temporary redefinition of property rights. But the two situations differ in other respects. In a disaster, there is general agreement among community members about community goals, especially about saving lives. As a result, by general agreement, all the resources are put at the disposal of the total community until emergency needs are met. A civil disturbance, on the other hand, represents conflict—not consensus—on community goals. The outbreak itself represents disagreement over property rights within the community. Access to existing resources is questionable, and often there is open challenge to prior ownership.

The critical role of attitudes toward property in determining the nature of looting is best seen by contrasting the looting that occurs in civil disturbances with that found in disasters. There are three significant differences. As already noted, widespread looting *does* occur in civil disturbances, while it is infrequent in disasters. Further, the looting in civil disturbances is selective, focusing on particular types of goods or possessions, often symbolic of other values. And, while out-and-out looting is strongly condemned in disaster situations, looters in civil disturbances receive, from certain segments of the local community, strong social support for their actions.

The occurrence of looting in civil disturbances needs no further documentation. And selectivity can be seen in the fact that, in racial outbreaks, looters have concentrated overwhelmingly on certain kinds of stores. In Watts, Newark, and Detroit, the main businesses affected were groceries, supermarkets, and furniture and liquor stores. In contrast, banks, utility stations, industrial plants, and private residences have been generally ignored. Apartments and homes have been damaged, but only because they were in or near burned business establishments. Public installations such as schools and Office of Economic Opportunity centers have also been spared. There has not been indiscriminate looting. Certain kinds of consumer goods have been almost the only targets.

Looters in civil disturbances are also likely to receive support from many people in their community. Spiraling support coincides with shifts in property redefinitions, and these shifts occur in three stages. Initial looting is often a symbolic act of defiance. The second phase, in which more conscious and deliberate plundering develops, is possibly spurred on by the presence of delinquent gangs that loot more from need or for profit than for ideological reasons. Finally, in the third stage, there is widespread seizure of goods. At this point, looting becomes the socially expected thing to do. For example, a sociological survey at U.C.L.A. found that nearly one-fourth of the population participated in the Watts outbreak (although all of these participants probably did not engage in the looting).

If looting means strictly the taking of goods, little of it occurs in the first phase of civil disturbances. Instead, destructive attacks are most frequently directed against symbols of authority in the community. Police cars and fire trucks are pillaged and burned. What is involved here is perhaps illustrated most clearly in other kinds of civil disturbances, such as some of those created by college students. One of the authors once watched a crowd of students determinedly attack, for over an hour, an overhead traffic light. It conveniently symbolized the city administration and police—the actual target of the demonstrators' wrath. In racial civil disturbances, the police and their equipment are also seen as obvious symbols of the larger community toward which the outbreak is directed. How intense this focus can be was shown in the Watts disturbance. About 168 police cars and 100 pieces of fire-fighting equipment were damaged or destroyed.

The full redefinition of certain property rights occurs next. The "carnival spirit" observed in the Newark and Detroit disturbances did not represent anarchy. It represented widespread social support for the new definition of property. In this phase, there is little competition for goods. In fact, in contrast to the stealthy looting that occasionally occurs in disaster situations, looting in civil disturbances is quite open and frequently collective. The looters often work together in pairs, as family units, or in small groups. Bystanders are frequently told about potential loot. And in some instances, as in the Watts outbreak, looters coming out of stores hand strangers goods as "gifts."

Looting in civil disturbances is by insiders—by local community members. These looters apparently come not only from the low socioeconomic levels and from delinquent gangs, but from all segments of the population. During disturbances in Toledo, 91 percent of the 126 adults arrested for taking goods had jobs. A random sample in Detroit found that participants in the outbreak came more or less equally from all income brackets.

In both disasters and civil disturbances, there is a redefinition of property rights within the community. The community authorities, however, respond very differently to the two situations. In disasters, responsible officials tolerate, accept, and encourage the transition from private to community property. In civil disturbances, community authorities see looting as essentially criminal behavior—as a legal problem to be handled forcefully by the police. And many segments of the larger community, especially middle-class people, with their almost sacred conception of private property, tend to hold the same view. This view of looting in civil disturbances fits in neatly with the ideas they already have about the criminal propensities of certain ethnic groups, notably Negroes.

Looting as a Mass Protest

At one level, there is no question that looting in civil disturbances is criminal behavior. But the laws that make it so are themselves based on dominant conceptions of property rights. Widespread looting, then, may perhaps be interpreted as a kind of mass protest against our dominant conceptions of property.

Mass protest is not new in history. According to George Rudé's analysis, in his book *The Crowd in History,* demonstrating mobs from 1730 to 1848 in England and France were typically composed of local, respectable, employed people rather than the pauperized, the unemployed, or the "rabble" of the slums. The privileged classes naturally regarded these popular agitations as criminal—as fundamentally and unconditionally illegitimate. Rudé notes, however, that such protest effectively communicated the desires of a segment of the urban population to the élite. E.J. Hobsbawm, in his analysis of the preindustrial "city mob," takes the same position: "The classical mob did not merely riot as a protest, but because it expected to achieve something by its riot. It assumed that the authorities would be sensitive to its movements, and probably also that they would make some immediate concession. . . . This mechanism was perfectly understood by both sides."

In current civil disturbances, a similar mechanism and a similar message may be evolving. An attack against property rights is not necessarily "irrational," "criminal," or "pointless" if it leads to a clearer system of demands and responses, in which the needs and obligations of the contending parties are reasonably clear to themselves and to one another. The scope and intensity of current attacks indicate the presence of large numbers of outsiders living within most American cities. If property is seen as a shared understanding about the allocation of resources, and if a greater consensus can be reached on the proper allocation of these resources, many of these outsiders will become insiders, with an established stake in the communities in which they live.

This, then, is the most fundamental way in which looting in civil disturbances differs from looting after natural disasters: The looting that has occurred in recent racial outbreaks is a bid for the redistribution of property. It is a message that certain deprived sectors of the population want what they consider their fair share—and that they will resort to violence to get it. The fact that looting in riots is more widespread than in disasters, that it concentrates on the prestige items that symbolize the good life, and that it receives the support and approval of many within the deprived sectors who do not participate themselves, merely indicates the true nature and intention of looting under conditions of mass protest.

The basic question now is whether American community leaders can or will recognize that such looting is more than "pointless" or "criminal" behavior. If they do, it may mark the beginning of a new political dialogue, in which the outsiders in our urban communities can express their desires nonviolently to the insiders—insiders who will have finally learned to listen. If not, then in the summers to come, and perhaps in the winters as well, many men and women from the growing urban population may continue to demand a redefinition of property rights through disorder and violence.

Reflective Questions

1. What is the origin of the term looting?

2. How does looting after disasters differ from looting following a civil disturbance?

3. What do the authors mean by a "redefinition of property" occurring during a disaster and civil disturbance?

4. How might an attack against property rights be viewed as a "rational" action?

25 □ Sniping—A New Pattern of Violence?

Terry Ann Knopf

The main question posed by this article is whether a new pattern of violence has emerged in the current course of racial conflict in America, a phase of deliberate planning and conspiracy—that is, sniping attacks on police in the United States. Terry Knopf of the Lemberg Center for the Study of Violence at Brandeis University has performed a valuable service by systematically examining newspaper coverage of "alleged" conspiracies and interviews with police. The author found that (1) the press distorted incidents; (2) there was more evidence of precipitating events causing violence than evidence of conspiracy, a conclusion similar to that of other investigations; (3) police casualties were exaggerated and failed to distinguish between sniper fire and other forms of gun play; and (4) press reports exaggerated the amount of sniping and shots fired.

It is not accurate, therefore, to assume that a new pattern of racial violence in the form of sniping has emerged. Indeed, it is quite possible that the American political character, as developed by Hofstadter, is highly conducive to conspiratorial theories of one kind or another. In some instances, it is quite possible that sniping may emerge out of the conflicting situation, but a more important question might be that of what official purpose is served by the claim of sniper attack. In a number of recent incidents where black and white students have been killed, the justification for the killings has been the unproven assertion of sniper fire. The assumption of such fire might well be a most convenient device for the exercise of social control and political repression. □

© Copyright July/August 1969, by TRANS-action, Inc., New Brunswick, New Jersey. Reprinted by permission.

ON JULY 23, 1968, AT 2:15 P.M., CLEVELAND'S MAYOR, CARL B. STOKES, WHO was in Washington, D.C., that day, made what he expected to be a routine telephone call to his office back home. He was told of information from military, F.B.I., and local police intelligence sources indicating that an armed uprising by black militants was scheduled to take place at 8 A.M. the next day. According to the reports, Ahmed Evans, a militant leader who headed a group called the Black Nationalists of New Libya, planned to drive to Detroit that night to secure automatic weapons. There were further reports that Evans' followers had already purchased bandoliers, ammunition pouches, and first-aid kits that same day. Simultaneous uprisings were reportedly being planned for Detroit, Pittsburgh, and Chicago.

At 6 P.M., in response to these reports, several unmarked police cars were assigned to the area of Evans' house. At about 8:20 P.M. a group of armed men, some of whom were wearing bandoliers of ammunition, emerged from the house. Almost at once, an intense gun battle broke out between the police and the armed men, lasting for roughly an hour. A second gun battle between the police and snipers broke out shortly after midnight about 40 blocks away. In the wake of these shoot-outs, sporadic looting and firebombing erupted and continued for several days. By the time the disorder was over, 16,400 National Guardsmen had been mobilized, at least nine persons had been killed (including three policemen), while the property damage was estimated at $1.5 million. Police listed most of their casualties as "shot by sniper."

Immediately, the Cleveland tragedy was described as a deliberate plot against the police and said to signal a new phase in the current course of racial conflict. *The Cleveland Press* (July 24, 1968) compared the violence in Cleveland to guerrilla activity in Saigon and noted: ". . . It didn't seem to be a Watts, or a Detroit, or a Newark. Or even a Hough of two years ago. No, this tragic night seemed to be part of a plan." Thomas A. Johnson writing in *The New York Times* (July 28, 1968) stated: ". . . It marks perhaps the first documented case in recent history of black, armed, and organized violence against the police."

As the notion that police were being "ambushed" took hold in the public's mind, many observers reporting on the events in Cleveland and similar confrontations in other cities, such as Gary, Peoria, Seattle, and York, Pennsylvania, emphasized that the outbreaks had several prominent features in common.

The first was the element of planning. Racial outbursts have traditionally been spontaneous affairs, without organization and without leadership. While no two disorders are similar in every respect, studies conducted in the past have indicated that a riot is a dynamic process that goes through stages of development. John P. Spiegel of Brandeis' Lemberg Center for the Study of Violence, has discerned four stages in the usual sort of rioting: the precipitating event, street confrontation, "Roman holiday," and seige. A sequence of stages is outlined in somewhat similar terms in the section of the Kerner Report on "the riot process." It is significant, however, that neither the Lemberg Center nor the Kerner Commission found any evidence of an organized plan or "conspiracy" in civil disorders prior to 1968. According to the Kerner Report: ". . . The Commission has found no evidence that all or any of the disorders or the incidents that led to them were planned or directed by any organization or group—international, national, or local."

Since the Cleveland shoot-out, however, many observers have suggested that civil disorders are beginning to take a new form, characterized by some degree of planning, organization, and leadership.

The second new feature discerned in many of 1968's summer outbreaks was the attacks on the police. In the past, much of the racial violence that occurred was directed at property rather than persons. Cars were stoned, stores were looted, business establishments were firebombed, and residences, in some instances, were damaged or destroyed. However, since the Cleveland gun battle, there have been suggestions that policemen have become the primary targets of violence. A rising curve of ambushes of the police was noted in the October 7, 1968 issue of the *U.S. News & World Report* which maintained that at least 8 policemen were killed and 47 wounded in such attacks last summer.

Finally, attacks on the police are now said to be *regularly* characterized by hit-and-run sniping. Using either home-made weapons or commercial and military weapons, such as automatics, bands of snipers are pictured initiating guerrilla warfare in our cities.

This view of the changing nature of racial violence can be found across a broad spectrum of the press, ranging from the moderately liberal *New York Times* to the militantly rightist *American Opinion*. On August 3, 1968, *The New York Times* suggested in an editorial:

. . . The pattern in 1967 has not proved to be the pattern of 1968.
Instead of violence almost haphazardly exploding, it has sometimes
been deliberately planned. And while the 1967 disorders
served to rip away false facades of racial progress and expose
rusting junkyards of broken promises, the 1968 disorders also
reveal a festering militancy that prompts some to resort to open
warfare.

Shortly afterward (August 14, 1968), *Crime Control Digest,* a biweekly periodical read by many law-enforcement officials across the country, declared:

The pattern of civil disorders in 1968 has changed from the pattern
that prevailed in 1967, and the elaborate U.S. Army, National
Guard and police riot control program prepared to meet this year's

"long hot summer" will have to be changed if this year's type of
civil disturbance is to be prevented or controlled.

This year's riot tactics have featured sniping and hit-and-run attacks on the police, principally by Black Power extremists, but by teen-agers in an increasing number of instances. The type of crimes being committed by the teen-agers and the vast increase in their participation has already brought demands that they be tried and punished as adults.

On September 13, 1968, *Time* took note of an "ominous trend" in the country:

Violence as a form of Negro protest appears to be changing from
the spontaneous combustion of a mob to the premeditated shoot-outs
of a far-out few. Many battles have started with well-planned
sniping at police.

Predictably, the November 1968 issue of *American Opinion* went beyond the other accounts by linking reported attacks on the police to a Communist plot:

The opening shots of the Communists' long-planned terror offensive
against our local police were fired in Cleveland on the night of July
23, 1968, when the city's Glenville area rattled with the scream
of automatic weapons. . . . What happened in Cleveland, alas,
was only a beginning.

To further emphasize the point, a large headline crying "terrorism" was included on the cover of the November issue.

Despite its relative lack of objectivity, *American Opinion* is the only publication that has attempted to list sniping incidents. Twenty-five specific instances of attacks on police were cited in the November issue. Virtually every other publication claiming a change in the nature of racial violence pointing to the "scores of American cities" affected and the "many battles" between blacks and the police has confined itself to a few perfunctory examples as evidence. Even when a few examples have been offered, the reporters usually have not attempted to investigate and confirm them.

Without attempting an exhaustive survey, we at the Lemberg Center were able to collect local and national press clippings, as well as wire-service stories, that described 25 separate incidents of racial violence in July and August of last summer. In all these stories, sniping was alleged to have taken place at some point or other in the fracas, and in most of them, the police were alleged to have been the primary targets of the sharpshooters. Often, too, the reports held that evidence had been found of planning on the part of "urban guerrillas," and at times it was claimed that the police had been deliberately ambushed. Needless to say, the specter of the Black Panthers haunts a number of the accounts. Throughout, one finds such phrases as these: "snipers hidden behind bushes . . . ," "isolated sniper fire . . . ," "scattered sniping directed at the police . . . ," "exchange of gunfire between snipers and police . . . ," "snipers atop buildings in the area. . . ." It is small wonder that the rewrite men at *Time* and other national magazines discerned a new and sinister pattern in the events of that summer. Small wonder that many concerned observers are convinced that the country's racial agony has entered a new phase of deliberate covert violence.

Conspirational Planning of Incidents

But how valid is this sometimes conspiratorial, sometimes apocalyptic view? What is the evidence for it, apart from these newspaper accounts?

Our assessment is based on an analysis of newspaper clippings, including a comparison of initial and subsequent reports, local and national press coverage, and on telephone interviews with high-ranking police officials. The selection of police officials was deliberate on our part. In the absence of city or state investigations of most of the incidents, police departments were found to be the best (and in many cases the only) source of information. Moreover, as the reported targets of sniping, police officials understandably had a direct interest in the subject.

Of course, the selection of this group did involve an element of risk. A tendency of some police officials to exaggerate and inflate sniping reports was thought to be unavoidable. We felt, though, that every group involved would have a certain bias and that in the absence of interviewing every important group in the cities, the views of police officials were potentially the most illuminating and therefore the most useful. Our interviews with them aimed at the following points: (1) evidence of planning; (2) the number of snipers; (3) the number of shots fired; (4) affiliation of the sniper or snipers with an organization; (5) statistical breakdowns of police and civilian casualties by sniping; and (6) press coverage of the incident.

As the press reports showed, a central feature in the scheme of those alleging a new pattern involves the notion of planning. Hypothesizing a local (if not national) conspiracy, observers have pictured black militants luring the police to predetermined spots where the policemen become the defenseless victims of an armed attack. No precipitating incident is involved in these cases except perhaps for a false citizen's call.

Despite this view, the information we gathered indicates that at least 17 out of the 25 disorders surveyed (about 70 percent) *did* begin with an identifiable precipitating event (such as an arrest seen by the black community as insulting or unjust) similar to those uncovered for "traditional" disorders. The figure of 70 percent is entirely consistent with the percentage of known precipitating incidents isolated by researchers at the Lemberg Center for past disorders (also about 70 percent).

In Gary, Indiana, the alleged sniping began shortly after two young members of a gang were arrested on charges of rape. In York, Pennsylvania, the violence began after a white man fired a shotgun from his apartment at some blacks on the street. Blacks were reportedly angered upon learning that the police had failed to arrest the gunman. In Peoria, Illinois, police arrested a couple for creating a disturbance in a predominantly black housing-project area. A group of young people then appeared on the scene and began throwing missiles at the police. In Seattle, Washington, a disturbance erupted shortly after a rally was held to protest the arrest of two men at the local Black Panther headquarters. Yet the disorders that followed these incidents are among the most prominently mentioned as examples of planned violence.

Many of the precipitating events were tied to the actions of the police and in some instances they were what the Kerner Commission has referred to as "tension-heightening incidents," meaning that the incident (or the disorder itself) merely crystallized tensions already existing in the community. Shortly before an outbreak in Harvey-Dixmoor, Illinois, on August 6–7, for example, a coroner's jury had ruled that the fatal shooting by police of a young, suspected car thief one month earlier was justifiable homicide. It was the second time in four months that a local policeman had shot a black youth. In Miami, the rally held by blacks shortly before the violence erupted coincided with the Republican National Convention being held about 10 miles away. The crowd was reportedly disappointed when the Reverend Ralph Abernathy and basketball star Wilt Chamberlain failed to appear as announced. In addition, tensions had risen in recent months following increased police canine patrols in the area. Although no immediate precipitating incident was uncovered for the outbreak at Jackson, Michigan on August 5, it is noteworthy that the disorder occurred in front of a Catholic-sponsored center aimed at promoting better race relations, and several weeks earlier, some 30 blacks had attempted to take over the center in the name of "a black group run by black people."

Let us turn briefly to the eight disorders in which triggering events do not appear to have occurred. Despite the absence of such an incident in the Chicago Heights-East Chicago Heights disorder, Chief of Police Robert A. Stone (East Chicago Heights) and Captain Jack Ziegler (Chicago Heights) indicated that they had no evidence of planning and that the disorder was in all probability spontaneous. In particular, Chief Stone indicated that the participants were individuals rather than members of an organization. The same holds true for the "ambuscade" in Brooklyn, New York, which the district attorney said at the time was the work of the Black Panthers. Although no precipitating event was uncovered, R. Harcourt Dodds, Deputy Commissioner for Legal Matters in the New York City Police Department, indicated there was no evidence of planning by anyone or any group. In Jackson, Michigan, as previously noted, tensions in the community had increased in recent weeks prior to the August disorder over a controversial center which some members of the community thought they should control. Thus the absence of precipitating events in at least three cases does not appear to be significant, least of all as evidence of a deliberate conspiracy to kill.

An assessment of the other five cases is considerably more difficult. In Inkster, Michigan, where four nights of isolated sniper fire were reported in August, Chief of Police James L. Fyke did not identify any precipitating event with the disorder and indicated that the state planned to make a case for conspiracy at a forthcoming trial. On the grounds that the two disorders in his city were under police investigation, Lieutenant Norman H. Judd of the Los Angeles Police Department declined comment on possible triggering events. In San Francisco, Chief of Police Thomas J. Cahill said there was evidence of planning. He said that "a firebomb was ignited and the shots were fired as the police vehicle arrived at the scene."

This brings us to Cleveland and Ahmed Evans, the fifth case in this instance. Because of the dramatic nature of the events and the tremendous amount of attention they received in the national press, any findings concerning Cleveland are of utmost importance. It is significant, therefore, that more recent reports have revealed that the July bloodletting was something less than a planned uprising and that the situation at the time was considerably more complicated than indicated initially.

A series of articles appearing in *The New York Times* is instructive. At the time of the disorder, in an account by Thomas A. Johnson, entitled "This Was Real Revolution," *The New York Times* gave strong hints of a plot against the police: "Early indications here were that a small, angry band of Negro men decided to shoot it out with the police. . . ." The article dwelt upon past statements of Ahmed Evans predicting armed uprisings across the nation on May 9, 1967 (they never materialized), rumors of arms caches across the country, and the revolutionary talk of black militants. No mention was made of any precipitating event, nor was there any reference to "tension-heightening incidents" in the community at the time.

One month later, in early September, *The New York Times* published the results of its investigation of the disorder. The report was prepared by three newsmen, all of whom had covered the disorder earlier. Their findings shed new light on the case by suggesting that a series of tension-heightening factors were indeed present in the community at the time of the disorder. For one thing, Mayor Stokes attended a meeting with police officials several hours before the first outbreak and felt that the information about a planned uprising was "probably not correct." Ahmed Evans himself was seen, retrospectively, less as the mastermind of a plot than as just another militant. Anthony Ripley of *The New York Times* wrote of him: "Evans, a tall, former Army Ranger who had been dishonorably discharged after striking an officer, was not regarded as a leading black nationalist. He was an amateur astrologer, 40 years old, given more to angry speeches than to action." Numerous grievances in the community—particularly against the police—which had been overlooked at the time of the disorder, were cited later. For example, it was noted that there were only 165 blacks on a police force of more than 2,000 officers, and there was a deep resentment felt by blacks toward their treatment by the police. The reporters also turned up the fact that in 1966 an investigation committee had given a low professional rating to the police department.

Ahmed Evans himself had some more specific grievances, according to Thomas A. Johnson's follow-up article. He noted that Evans had arranged to rent a vacant tavern for the purpose of teaching the manufacture of African-style clothes and carvings to black youths but that the white landlady had changed her mind. He said that Evans had been further angered upon receiving an eviction order from his home. The Ripley article noted that, two hours before the shooting began, Evans said he had been asleep until his associates informed him that police surveillance cars had been stationed in the area. (Evans was accustomed to posting lookouts on top of buildings.) According to Evans, it was then that the group made the decision to arm.

Did the presence of the police in the area serve to trigger the gun battle that followed? What was the role of the civilian tow-truck driver wearing a police-like uniform? Did his hitching up an old pink Cadillac heighten tensions to the breaking point? Were intelligence reports of a plot in error? Why were arms so readily available to the group? What was the group's intention upon emerging from the house? These questions cannot be answered with any degree of absolute certainty. Nevertheless, it is significant that the earliest interpretations appearing in *The New York Times* were greatly modified by the subsequent articles revealing the complexities of the disorder and suggesting it may have been more spontaneous than planned. As Ripley wrote in his September 2 article:

The Cleveland explosion has been called both an ambush of police and an armed uprising by Negroes. However, the weight of evidence indicates that it was closer to spontaneous combustion.

More recent developments on the controversial Cleveland case deserve mention also. On May 12, 1969, an all-white jury found Ahmed Evans guilty of seven counts of first-degree murder arising out of four slayings during the disorder last July. Evans was sentenced to die in the electric chair on September 22, 1969.

Then, on May 29, 1969, the National Commission on the Causes and Prevention of Violence authorized the release of a report entitled *Shoot-Out in Cleveland; Black Militants and the Police: July 23, 1968* by Louis H. Masotti and Jerome R. Corsi. The report was partially underwritten by the Lemberg Center. Its findings confirmed many of the results of *The Times* investigation and provided additional insights into the case.

Doubt was cast on prior intelligence reports that the Evans group had been assembling an arsenal of handguns and carbines, that Evans planned a trip to Detroit to secure weapons, and that simultaneous outbreaks in other northern cities were planned. ("The truth of these reports was questionable.") Further, it was revealed that these reports came from a single individual and that "other intelligence sources did not corroborate his story." In addition, the Commission report underscored certain provocative actions by the police:

It was glaringly evident that the police had established a stationary surveillance rather than a moving one. In fact, another surveillance car was facing Ahmed's apartment building from the opposite direction. . . . Both cars contained only white officers; both were in plain view of Ahmed's home. . . . Rightly or wrongly, Ahmed regarded the obvious presence of the surveillance cars over several hours' time as threatening.

The report stressed that "against theories of an ambush or well-planned conspiracy stands the evidence that on Tuesday evening [July 23, 1968] Ahmed was annoyed and apprehensive about the police surveillance."

The Times experience, together with the report of the National Commission on the Causes and Prevention of Violence, strongly suggest that the assumption that the Cleveland disorder was planned is as yet unproved.

It may be significant that 14 out of the 19 police officials who expressed a view on the matter could find no evidence of planning in the disorders in their respective cities. In another instance, the police official said the disorder was planned, but he could offer no evidence in support of his statement. If this and the Cleveland case are added, the number of outbreaks that do not appear to have been planned comes to at least 16 out of 19.

In their assertions that police are now the principal targets of snipers, some observers give the impression that there have been large numbers of police casualties. In most cases, the reports have not been explicit in stating figures. However, as mentioned earlier, *U.S. News & World Report* cited 8 police deaths and 47 police woundings this past summer. In order to assess these reports, we obtained from police officials a breakdown of police casualties as a result of gunfire.

What we learned was that a total of four policemen were killed and that each death was by gunfire. But three of these occurred in one city, Cleveland; the other was in Inkster, Michigan. In other words, in 23 out of 25 cases where sniping was originally reported, no policemen were killed.

POLICE CASUALTIES

Our total agreed with figures initially taken from local press reports. However, our count of four dead was only half the figure reported in *U.S. News & World Report.* We learned why when we found that the story appearing in that magazine originally came from an Associated Press "roundup," which said that eight policemen had been killed by gunfire since July 1, 1968. But four of these eight cases were in the nature of individual acts of purely criminal—and not racial—violence. On July 2, a Washington, D.C., policeman was killed when he tried to arrest a man on a robbery complaint. A Philadelphia policeman was killed July 15 while investigating a $59 streetcar robbery. On August 5, in San Antonio, a policeman was killed by a 14-year-old boy he had arrested. The youth was a Mexican-American who had been arrested on a drinking charge. And, in Detroit, a policeman was shot to death on August 5 following a domestic quarrel. The circumstances concerning these four cases in no way display the features of a "new pattern" of violence.

The question of how many police *injuries* came from sniper fire is more complicated. A total of 92 policemen were injured, accounting for 14 out of 25 cases. Almost half the injuries—44—came from gunfire. In some instances, our findings showed a downward revision of our earlier information. In Gary, for example, somebody reportedly took a shot at Police Chief James F. Hilton as he cruised the troubled area shortly after the disturbance began. However, when interviewed, Chief Hilton vigorously denied the earlier report. In Peoria, 11 police officers were reportedly injured by shotgun blasts. However, Bernard J. Kennedy, Director of Public Safety, indicated that initial reports "were highly exaggerated" and that only seven officers were actually wounded. In East Point, Georgia, a white policeman had reportedly been injured during the disorder. Yet Acting Police Chief Hugh D. Brown indicated that there were no injuries to the police. In Little Rock, a policeman swore that he had been shot by a sniper. However, Chief of Police R. E. Brians told us that there was no injury and no broken skin. The Chief added that the policeman had been new and was not of the highest caliber. In fact, he is no longer with the department.

In addition, a closer look at the data reveals that the highest figures for numbers of policemen wounded by gunfire are misleading and need to be placed in perspective. Let us examine the three cases with the highest number of injuries: Cleveland with 10 policemen wounded by gunfire; Peoria, with seven; and Harvey-Dixmoor, Illinois, also with seven.

In Peoria, all seven policemen were wounded by the pellets from *a single shotgun blast*. In an interview, Safety Director Kennedy stressed that "none of the injuries incurred were serious." The Harvey-Dixmoor incident was similar. There, five out of the seven injured were also hit by a single shotgun blast. Chief of Police Leroy H. Knapp Jr. informed us that only two or three shots were fired during the entire disorder. (A similar scattering of pellets occurred in St. Paul, where three out of four policemen hit by gunfire received their injuries from one shotgun blast.)

Sniping vs. Accidental Shooting

In Cleveland, almost every injury to a policeman came as a result of gunfire. However, it is not at all clear whether snipers inflicted the damage. In the chaos that accompanies many disorders, shots have sometimes been fired accidentally—by both rioters and policemen. Ripley's September 2 article in *The New York Times* stated the problem very well: "Only by setting the exact position of each man when he was shot, tracing the bullet paths, and locating all other policemen at the scene can a reasonable answer be found." Thus far, no information concerning the circumstances of each casualty in the Cleveland disorder has been disclosed, and this goes for deaths as well as injuries.

Moreover, what applies to Cleveland applies to the other disorders as well. The Little Rock case illustrates the point. Chief of Police Brians verified the shooting of a National Guardsman. However, he also clarified the circumstances of the shooting. He said that during the disorder a group of people gathered on a patio above a courtyard near the area where the National Guard was stationed. One individual, under the influence of alcohol, fired indiscriminately into the crowd, hitting a guardsman in the foot. Chief Brians added: "He might just as easily have hit a [civil-rights] protestor as a guardsman." What is clear is that the circumstances concerning all casualties need to be clarified so as to avoid faulty inferences and incorrect judgments as much as possible.

Concerning the amount of sniping, there were numerous discrepancies between early and later reports, suggesting that many initial reports were exaggerated.

According to the police officials themselves, other than in the case of Cleveland where 25 to 30 snipers were allegedly involved, there were relatively few snipers. In 15 out of 17 cases where such information was available, police officials said there were three snipers or less. And in 7 out of 17 cases, the officials directly contradicted press reports at the time and said that no snipers were involved!

As for the number of gunshots fired by snipers, the reality, as reported by police, was again a lot less exciting than the newspapers indicated. In 15 out of 18 cases where information was available, "snipers" fired fewer than 10 shots. In 12 out of 18 cases, snipers fired fewer than five. Generally, then, in more than one-quarter of the cases in which sniping was originally reported, later indications were that no sniping had actually occurred.

In Evansville, initial reports indicated that a minimum of eight shots were fired. Yet Assistant Chief of Police Charles M. Gash told us that only one shot was fired.

A more dramatic illustration is found in the case of East Point, Georgia. Although 50 shots were reportedly fired at the time, Acting Chief of Police Hugh Brown informed us that no shots were fired.

In York, 11 persons were wounded in a "gun battle" on the first night. However, it turns out that 10 out of 11 persons were civilians and were injured by shotgun pellets. Only two snipers were involved, and only two to four shots were fired throughout the entire disturbance.

In Waterloo, Iowa, Chief of Police Robert S. Wright acknowledged that shots were fired, but he added: "We wouldn't consider it sniper fire." He told us that there was "no ambush, no concealment of participants, or anything like that." Moreover, he stated that not more than three persons out of a crowd of 50 youths carried weapons and "not a great number of shots were fired." The weapons used were small handguns.

In St. Paul, where 10 shots were reportedly fired at police and four officers were wounded by gunshots, Chief of Police Lester McAuliffe also acknowledged that though there was gunfire, there "wasn't any sniper fire as such."

A similar situation was found in Peoria. Safety Director Kennedy said that the three shots believed fired did not constitute actual sniping.

In Little Rock, Chief Brians discounted reports of widespread sniping and indicated that many "shots" were really firecrackers.

In Gary, early reports were that Chief of Police James Hilton had been fired upon and six persons had been wounded by snipers. Assistant Chief of Police Charles Boone told us that while a few shots might have been "fired in the air," no actual sniping occurred. No one was shot during the disturbance, and no one was injured. Chief Hilton indicated that the fireman who was supposed to have been hit during the outbreak was actually shot by a drunk *prior* to the disorder.

In a few instances, discrepancies between first reports and sober reappraisal can be traced to exaggerations of the policemen themselves. However, most of the discrepancies already cited throughout this report can be attributed to the press—at both the local and national level. In some instances, the early press reports (those appearing at the time of the incident) were so inexplicit as to give the *impression* of a great deal of sniping. In other instances, the early figures given were simply exaggerated. In still other instances, the early reports failed to distinguish between sniper fire and other forms of gunplay.

The Role of the Press

Moreover, the press generally gave far too little attention to the immediate cause or causes of the disturbance. Even in the aftermath of the violence, few attempts were made to verify previous statements or to survey the tensions and grievances rooted in the community. Instead, newspapers in many instances placed an unusually heavy (and at times distorted) emphasis on the most dramatic aspects of the violence, particularly where sniping was concerned.

A look at some of the newspaper headlines during the disorders is most revealing, especially where the "pellet cases" are involved. As mentioned earlier, large numbers of casualties were sustained from the pellets of a single shotgun blast—in Peoria, seven policemen; in Harvey-Dixmoor, five policemen, and in York, 10 civilians were injured in this way; the most commonly cited examples of a "new pattern" of violence. Unfortunately, inaccurate and sensational headlines created an impression of widespread sniping, with the police singled out as the principal targets. A few individual acts of violence were so enlarged as to convey to the reader a series of "bloodbaths." In some cases, an explanation of the circumstances surrounding the injuries was buried in the news story. In other cases, no explanation was given. In still other cases, the number of casualties was exaggerated.

Distorted headlines were found in the local press:

RACE VIOLENCE ERUPTS: DOZEN SHOT IN PEORIA
Chicago (Ill.) *Tribune,*
July 31, 1968

6 COPS ARE SHOT IN HARVEY STRIFE
Chicago *Sun-Times,*
August 7, 1968

20 HURT AS NEW VIOLENCE RAKES WEST END AREA
11 FELLED BY GUN FIRE, FOUR FIREMAN INJURED FIGHTING FIVE BLAZES
York (Pa.) *Dispatch,*
August 5, 1968

These distortions were transmitted on the wire services as well. For example, in Ann Arbor, Michigan, readers were given the following accounts of Peoria and Harvey-Dixmoor in their local newspapers. The first account was based upon a United Press International news dispatch; the second is from an Associated Press dispatch.

10 POLICEMEN SHOT IN PEORIA VIOLENCE
By *United Press International*
Ann Arbor (Mich.) *News,*
July 30, 1968

Ten policemen were wounded by shotgun blasts today during a four-hour flareup of violence in Peoria, Ill. . . .

EIGHT WOUNDED IN CHICAGO AREA
Ann Arbor *News,*
August 7, 1968

Harvey, Ill. (AP)—Sporadic gunfire wounded seven policemen and a woman during a disturbance caused by Negro youths, and scores of law enforcement officers moved in early today to secure the troubled area. . . .

Finally, they were repeated in headlines and stories appearing in the national press:

GUNFIRE HITS 11 POLICEMEN IN ILL. VIOLENCE
Washington Post,
July 31, 1968

SHOTGUN ASSAULTS IN PEORIA GHETTO WOUND 9 POLICEMEN
The Law Officer,
Fall, 1968

Chicago—On August 6, in the suburbs of Harvey and Dixmoor, seven policemen and a woman were shot in Negro disturbances which a Cook County undersheriff said bore signs of having been planned.

U.S. News & World Report,
August 19, 1968

In all probability, few newspapers or reporters could withstand this type of criticism. Nevertheless, it does seem that the national press bears a special responsibility. Few of the nationally known newspapers and magazines attempted to verify sniping reports coming out of the cities; few were willing to undertake independent investigations of their own; and far too many were overly zealous in their reports of a "trend" based on limited and unconfirmed evidence. Stated very simply: The national press overreacted.

For some time now, many observers (including members of the academic community) have been predicting a change from spontaneous to premeditated outbreaks resembling guerrilla warfare. Their predictions have largely been based upon limited evidence such as unconfirmed reports of arms caches and the defiant, sometimes revolutionary rhetoric of militants.

And then came Cleveland. At the time, the July disorder in that city appeared to fulfill all the predictions—intelligence reports of planning prior to the disorder, intensive sniping directed at the police, the absence of a precipitating incident, and so on. Few people at the time quarreled with the appraisal in *The New York Times* that Cleveland was "perhaps the first documented case" of a planned uprising against the police. Following the events in Cleveland, disorders in which shots may have been fired were immediately suspected to be part of a "wave."

Unwittingly or not, the press has been constructing a scenario on armed uprisings. The story line of this scenario is not totally removed from reality. There *have* been a few shoot-outs with the police, and a handful may have been planned. But no wave of uprisings and no set pattern of murderous conflict have developed—at least not yet. Has the press provided the script for future conspiracies? Why hasn't the scenario been acted out until now? The answers to these questions are by no means certain. What is clear is that the press has critical responsibilities in this area, for any act of violence easily attracts the attention of the vicarious viewer as well as the participant.

Moreover, in an era when most Americans are informed by radio and television, the press should place far greater emphasis on interpreting, rather than merely reporting, the news. Background pieces on the precipitating events and tension-heightening incidents, more detailed information on the sniper himself, and investigations concerning police and cvilian casualties represent fertile areas for the news analyst. To close, here is one concrete example: While four policemen were killed in the violence reviewed in this article, at least 16 civilians were also killed. A report on the circumstances of these deaths might provide some important insights into the disorders.

Reflective Questions

1. What factors are related to the view that sniping may be a new pattern of violence?

2. What existing social conditions contribute to the willingness of Americans to accept conspiratorial theories concerning violence?

3. How might you account for the divergent views of media reports and police accounts regarding instances of sniping?

4. What should be the role of the media in reporting acts of violence?

PART FIVE □ REACTIONS TO A SOCIETY IN TURMOIL

The present war has made it clear that we can no longer regard Western Europe and North America as the world for which civilization exists; nor can we look upon European culture as the norm for all peoples. Henceforth the majority of the inhabitants of earth, who happen for the most part to be colored, must be regarded as having the right and capacity to share in human progress and to become co-partners in that democracy which alone can ensure peace among men, by the abolition of poverty, the education of the masses, protection from disease, and the scientific treatment of crime.

W. E. B. DU BOIS

FLETCHER DRAKE / PIX

For many Americans our nation's history has been viewed as tranquil until the advent of the current generation. Such, of course, has not been the case. Our nation has, instead, fluctuated between crisis and mild unrest during most of its existence. If it is true that American society is currently experiencing a state of turmoil, this condition has been developing for several years. Although unrest is certainly not new to American society, we appear to have attained a heightened polarization of our population. This present chasm seems to focus around establishing national priorities and defining the means to achieve these goals.

Several significant issues urgently demand attention. These may be categorized as either technical or social. Americans have long possessed great confidence in their ability to find solutions to technical problems, usually without altering the nature of the social and economic systems. Plans are now in motion to relieve the problems created by water and air pollution, urban development, transportation inadequacies, and population growth. The above technical problems might be called the nonissue issues. The approach to social issues is much more widely debated. Some of the most critical of these issues confronting Americans in the 1970's are centered around (1) civil liberties, (2) an equitable distribution of goods and services, (3) racial, ethnic, and sexual equality, (4) war and peace, (5) unemployment and underemployment, (6) normative inconsistencies, and (7) dissent and repression.

The above issues have served to divide our nation and have contributed to the development of hard-core extremism on both the left and the right. Similar tactics are frequently used by both groups. Demagogues are developing throughout America, on both local and national levels. The demagogue often substitutes rhetoric for logic, passion for rationality, and destruction for constructive behavior. From the far right, we commonly hear the pleas, so reminiscent of Nazi Germany, for order, unquestioned obedience, and support of the fatherland; from the extreme left are the sounds of violence, revolution, and anarchy.

Somewhere between the extremists are numerous Americans, many of whom have internalized our cultural values regarding brotherhood, social justice, and the right to control one's life. Some of these Americans are now demanding that a bridge be built to span the gap between the real and ideal culture values. On the other hand, many advance the gradualist's argument that more patience is needed and that desired changes require time. Time, however, is a relative concept; what is a short time or a long time? Time may be used to delay the promotion of positive social humanism in our national life. Time as an ethic to frustrate programs designed to insure individual freedom, social justice, equality, peace, and the overall liberation and survival of mankind can only lead to turmoil, moral sterility, social casualties, apathy, and the demise of a viable civilization.

The review of any society's reaction to a state of turmoil is, in a very real sense, the study of social movements. The American Revolution, the labor movement, the feminist movement, the civil rights movement, and the peace movement have all left an indelible print on the social structure and value system of our nation. We have all recognized that there are certain countries and certain historic periods that seem more susceptible to the flourishing of social movements than are others. What unique social environments contributes to the development of social movements? Why does the United States appear particularly susceptible to the formation and impact of social movements?

Cameron contributes to a better understanding of the above questions by citing three special conditions that lead to social movements:[1]

1. Men must consciously recognize their dissatisfactions and share these with others.
2. Men must believe in their own ability to reshape the course of their lives.
3. Men must live under conditions in which banding together to change something is both possible and plausibly effective.

A consideration of the three conditions offered by Cameron suggests that the social environment most conducive to the spawning of social movements is a democracy with a highly developed technology that is experiencing a state of turmoil. From the above discussion, it becomes clear that the study of social movements is inseparable from the understanding of the dynamics of social change. As we embark on the decade of the 1970's, our society would be wise to heed the admonishment of the late John F. Kennedy: "If we make peaceful revolution impossible, we make violent revolution inevitable."

[1] Wm. Bruce Cameron. *Modern Social Movements* (New York: Random House, 1966) pp. 10.

26 □ SOCIAL CHANGE, DISSENT, AND VIOLENCE

James H. Laue

Laue provides us with an analytical and theoretical paper on the nature of contemporary urban violence, dissent, and change. One of the main points in the article is that the day of the urban crisis is "in," that physical and social structures of every metropolitan area are becoming inadequate in meeting social needs. The author states three ways of viewing the urban crisis, (1) as a crisis in disparities, (2) as a crisis in systems, and (3) as a crisis in accountability. In addition, he states that one of the greatest paradoxes of our time is white America's fixation on sporadic black violence in a nation formed in violent revolution, expanded by the aid of aggressive violence, and maintained by a "defense" complex of about $100 billion per year.

A significant feature of the article is the creation of a comparative typology of violence based on two dimensions: (1) the *function* of violence (goal or anticipated outcome of violent activity) and (2) degree of *rationality* (degree of planning). Along the first dimension, three types of functions are specified— revolt, control, and expansion—while along the second dimension, two types of rationality are listed—expressive and political.

The prediction is that urban violence and dissent in the future will depend on flexibility of the power structure in moving toward the democratization of institutions. □

THE AIM OF THIS PAPER IS TO PLACE IN SOCIOLOGICAL PERSPECTIVE contemporary urban violence and dissent in the United States. The immediacy

From *Violence and Dissent in Urban America*, edited by Fred R. Crawford. (Atlanta: Southern Newspaper Publishers Association Foundation, 1969) pp. 25–39. Reprinted with permission.

and intensity of white/black confrontations in American cities today have been stamped into our minds by the media. So has been a common sense set of categories for interpreting violence and dissent, but it does not well serve the needs of detached sociological analysis. As a sociologist who came from the civil rights movement and has spent the last four years in the federal government, I seek to achieve a perspective on what is happening by viewing violence and dissent in America: (1) historically; (2) comparatively, in the context of a typology of group violence; and (3) processually, as related to social change.

I

"Urban problems" are very "in" now, and they have reached crisis proportions in the public's perception. It is important to establish early, I believe, that "urban problems" are not really new to us, nor should it be surprising that they are upon us. For they are manifestations of basic spiritual problems (or value positions, if you wish) that have been with America for some time. Those problems include our national romance with "progress" and individualism, with the profit motive, with our enduring self-righteousness about our nation's cause and destiny, and with our doctrine of man—what people are, how they should relate, how and when they may be "used" and for what ends.

All of these things have caught up with us now. They have been catching up with us for some time. The physical and social structures of virtually every metropolitan area in the United States have become increasingly unable to meet the needs of rapidly growing populations for jobs, housing, education, and other services. Now that the inadequacy of institutions has spilled over into overt racial conflict, the "urban crisis" is "in."

This is not to downgrade the intensity of the crisis. The human, social, and technical problems from which dissent and violence have arisen are real. The usual level on which we approach such problems is that of a statistical description of the conditions of various physical and social segments of the city —ghettos and barrios, unemployment and job discrimination rates, education, housing, health and welfare services, transportation facilities, etc. There is no need to catalog the problems at this level for our purposes; anyone who can read and use a telephone can easily determine the grim realities of his own city in as specific detail as he can stomach.

But there are at least three other—and, I think, more illuminating—ways of looking at the "urban crisis": as a crisis in disparities, in systems, and in accountability.

Disparities

The absolute statistics are bad enough, but it is the comparison of groups and the discovery of the disparities between their living conditions that underscore how really tragic urban life is for millions of American citizens. Starting with the ecological distribution of the population, it is clear that something unusual is operating. Of the total population growth of urban areas in the last twenty years, nearly 80 percent of the non-white increase has been in central cities, and approximately the same percentage of the white increase has been outside central cities. You do not have to know anything about sociology or ecology to know that a whole structure of assumptions and institutions operates to cause people to distribute themselves over the land in that particular way. The structure includes zoning commissions, the profit motive, land developers, realtors, and myths about property values and race.

Here and now, on the crest of seeming progress in race relations, consider some other indices of disparities between whites and non-whites in America:

1. The gap between death rates for non-white and white infants has become wider, increasing from 66 percent in 1950 to 90 percent in 1964.[1]

2. Black and Mexican-American living areas contain 3.5 times the proportion of substandard housing found in white areas.

3. Non-white unemployment rates consistently run two to four times that of white rates, with rates among young males as high as 40 percent in some cities.[2]

4. As recently as 1964, a non-white American with four years of college education could expect to earn less in his lifetime ($185,000) than a white who had completed eighth grade ($191,000).[3]

5. Black median income as a percentage of white median income has dropped to 53 percent from a previous figure of 57 percent.[4]

Thurgood Marshall and Bill Cosby notwithstanding, we're not making much headway.

Systems

The absolute figures and disparity indices gain greater coherence by viewing them in the context of systems theory. The urban area may be seen as a total system, with a series of interlocking and interdependent subsystems, each with inputs and outputs, boundaries, functions, and reciprocal relationships with other subsystems.

[1] "White/Negro Disparity Statistics," paper prepared for the Community Relations Service, U.S. Department of Justice, by Mary M. Chapnick, September 13, 1966.
[2] *Ibid.* and "Riot Prevention," advertisement in *The Washington Post*, July 10, 1967, by the National Association for the Advancement of Colored People.
[3] "Employment and Earning," Bureau of Labor Statistics (Washington D.C.: U.S. Government Printing Office, 1964).
[4] Cf. footnote 2, "Riot Prevention."

Examples are (1) the taxes/municipal services system; (2) migration (both into and within the area); and (3) planning/development systems.

"Urban crisis" then means that more and more of these essential subsystems are breaking down in more and more urban areas: (1) shifting and woefully inadequate tax bases; (2) too rapid in-migration of rural peoples whose lifestyle, education, and job-skills do not well fit them for an urban environment; and (3) inability to coordinate community planning and to achieve consensus for public-spirited action in the face of narrow, vested interests.

ACCOUNTABILITY

The crisis in accountability weighs most heavily on me. Daniel Moynihan and others are saying that it is impossible to assess responsibility for the deteriorating situation in cities today—the variables are too many and the interrelationships too complex. But unless we can trace the steps leading us to the present crisis, how are we to avoid similar mistakes in the future? Decisions were made, perhaps by default, leading to existing patterns of land-use and zoning, to placement of municipal facilities, to allocation of fiscal resources. The dispersal of black and white population growth to the central city and suburbs respectively did not happen by chance. That more than 60 percent of all new industrial building since 1962 has occurred in the suburbs is not a chance happening. That Hemisfair in San Antonio displaced poor blacks and browns, and not middle-class white, did not happen by chance. That the Atlanta Stadium could be constructed in record time in the middle of a still-unrenewed, black ghetto (many of the residents call it "Our Magnificent Neighbor") did not happen by chance. Until we can trace the interplay of private and public vested interests which resulted in the public policy decisions represented in these examples, we cannot hope to move far forward in attack on the problems at the base of urban dissent and violence.

II

The causal relationship between dissent, violence, and social change is not clear,[5] but we do know that in virtually every case of significant social change,[6] the other two phenomena are present in various forms at some point(s) during the process. I will offer brief definitions of the three phenomena which do not claim to be comprehensive or exhaustive; rather they are meant to serve as a

---

[5]For a recent, comprehensive treatment of the problems in assessing causation, see Henry Bienen, *Violence and Social Change* (Chicago: University of Chicago Press, 1968).

[6]By "significant social change" I mean shifts of power and influence that are relatively rapid, and require new behaviors in many areas of life for large proportions of the population in the system.

point of focus for beginning our considerations of urban violence in contemporary America. The phenomena are defined in descending order from most to least generic: social change is the most general, continuous, inclusive social process; dissent is part of the conflict process involved in much social change; violence is an intensified type of conflict which may or may not involve formal dissent.

Social Change

Societies are always in flux. Social change is an ever-present phenomenon in all human communities. It may be defined as the continuous process of redistribution of power. Power is the control over decisions—the decisions that affect peoples' lives. The more persons affected in significant ways by a particular decision, the greater the power of the decisionmaker. Since power never gives itself up willingly, most social change is accompanied by conflict between vested interests—i.e., those having the prerogatives to make or participate in important decisions. When the stakes are high, the conflict is great.[7] Such is the case in American's urban areas where various institutional systems are not adequately serving the population's needs, and more and more people are asking to be included in the decisions that govern those institutions and the allocation of their outputs.

There are many typologies of social change; for our purposes a distinction between reformist and revolutionary types of change will be helpful.

TYPES OF SOCIAL CHANGE

Reform
(modify institutional functioning)

Revolution
(change values, replace institutions)

All social change can be assessed in terms of its impact on institutions: does it simply modify them in an attempt to improve their functioning and thus bring them more closely in line with stated but unrealized values (reform), or does it replace them with institutions whose proper functioning would express another set of values (revolution)? Adjusting economic institutions so that every able-bodied person holds a wage-earning job would be an example of reform in the American system; abolishing the job-wage system and replacing it with some other form of economic resources distribution would be revolutionary.

Dissent, protest, and movements for change similarly may be assessed in

---

[7] For an elaboration of this way of viewing social change, see James H. Laue, "Power, Conflict and Social Change" in Louis H. Masotti and Don R. Bowen (ed.), *Riots and Rebellion: Civil Violence in the Urban Community*, (Beverly Hills, Calif.: Sage Publications, 1968), pp. 85–96.

terms of this continuum: is their aim to modify existing institutions (reform) or replace them (revolution)? Despite the loose talk in the popular media about "revolution,"[8] the civil rights movement of the 1960s has been by-and-large reformist, with such "getting-in" goals as eating at lunch counters, voting, having decent housing, holding a job, owning income-producing property. As military and foreign policy issues have become more frequent targets of protest and dissent in the last five years, a good deal of revolutionary ideology has emerged, but with little strategic planning and support for actual institutional overthrow and replacement. Slow progress in race relations is moving many blacks and browns in this direction, too. It is fair to say that the goals of movements among blacks, browns, students, and anti-war groups are indeed closer to the revolutionary end of the continuum at the end of 1960s than they were at the beginning. Serious questioning of the value-assumptions underlying America's foreign and domestic policies is intensifying. The nation's response may largely determine whether revolutionary sentiment gains support. Current repressive tendencies make me believe it will.[9]

Dissent

Social order and stability in a society depend on maintenance of at least the tacit consent of the great majority of the members of that society. Dissent—opposition to established institutions and/or values—is continuously present in every social system. In the America of the 1960s the most substantial dissent has been directed toward issues of poverty, militarism, and racism. As in every system, it is directed against those persons and social groupings who control the decisions regarding salient issues. It has been said that since the beginning, all the important decisions in the United States have been made by rich, adult, white males. Sociologically, it is no accident that in the vanguard of overt dissent in America have been the poor, the young, the non-white, and the women.

Dissent may take the form of covert disagreement which is never overtly

---

[8] Notably *Newsweek's* special issues on "The Negro Revolution" in 1963 which were expanded into a book on the same subject by William Brink and Louis Harris, *The Negro Revolution in America* (New York: Simon and Schuster, 1964).

[9] For example, the responses to the Pentagon demonstration in October, 1967, and the Chicago convention demonstrations in 1968, and responses to racial disorders in many cities by local police departments which led to upwards of 85 percent of the dead and 60 percent of the injured coming from the minority community. Virtually every city and state in the country now have prepared riot contingency plans which rely heavily on repressive military force. For a discussion of trends toward repressive action, see Martin Oppenheimer, *The Urban Guerrilla* (Chicago: Quadrangle, 1969). See also the *Report of the National Advisory Commission on Civil Disorders* (Washington: U.S. G.P.O., 1968) and *Rights in Conflict*, a report submitted by Daniel Walker, Director of the Chicago Study Team, to the National Commission on the Causes and Prevention of Violence (New York: New American Library, Signet Books, 1968).

expressed. It may be verbal, or it may be actively expressed through political organization, protest, or violence. Dissent, then, takes many forms, is of varying degrees of intensity and organization, and is a threat of greater or lesser concern to the established order. To counteract the popular tendency to lump all dissenters together,[10] and prepare us for further analysis of urban dissent and violence, I call attention to a simple continuum which is a way of looking at the degree of activeness of dissent (see Table 1).

TABLE 1 □ DEGREE OF ACTIVENESS OF DISSENT

Passive	Active	Violent
Covert opinions	Political or community organizing	Expressive violence against property or persons
Private verbal disagreement	Direct action demonstrations	
Public verbal disagreement		Political violence against property or persons

The examples arrayed along the continuum are not comprehensive. They simply suggest that dissent comes in all sizes, shapes, and varieties, and that we do ourselves a disservice unless we approach analysis of current urban problems with such distinctions (e.g., in addition, variations in goals, tactics, degree of organization, etc.) in mind.

Violence

The conflict accompanying social change and dissent varies in intensity. Violence is an escalated form of social conflict involving the violating of boundaries by one or more parties against another or others, often through use of physical force. It may or may not be reciprocal. The boundaries violated may be personal or social, psychic, physical, territorial, or economic. There may be violence against a man's psyche or his livelihood without use of direct physical force against him by the violating party.

---

[10]The public's growing inability to distinguish between "riots" and peaceful protest demonstrations is the most general expression of this tendency. The media contribute to this analytical confusion in this and other ways. As the manuscript of this paper is finalized in Boston in April, 1969, the print and broadcast media in the city are repeatedly and indiscriminately labeling the student protestors at Harvard and elsewhere "radicals" and "radical students" in much the same stereotyping (and, in some instances, plain inaccurate) manner as with ethnic minorities and "Reds" in recent years.

So violence may be: direct or indirect, directed against persons or property, individual or group in character, and involve physical force or not.

The violence which is of popular concern in the United States today (i.e., by blacks, in cities) is a particular kind of direct, largely property-oriented group violence involving physical force. It is popularly and often incorrectly called a "riot."[11] It must be understood that this phenomenon of blacks striking out against the two major symbols of white power—property and, to some extent, police—is only part of the total picture of violence in the cities. This point is elaborated in the last section of this paper.

III

One of the greatest paradoxes of our time is white America's fixation on sporadic black violence (largely against property) in a nation formed in violent revolution, expanded with the aid of aggressive violence, and maintained by a "defense" complex costing upwards of $100 billion per year.

This is not to "justify violence," which is the cry raised almost automatically in response to analysis of this issue.[12] It is simply to describe the violence occurring today in its appropriate historical context in an attempt to overcome the ahistoricity kindled in us by our intense concern and fear about the immediate racial violence in cities.

Allen Grimshaw's work provides a powerful summary of the role of social violence[13] in American history:

> The history of social violence in the United States is varied and colorful. Race, creed, color, and place of national origin have all, at one time or another, served as bases for social categorization and social violence. Orientals, Africans, and American Indians have all been the victims of massive group assault. Catholics, Mormons, and Jews, as well as a variety of Protestant sects, have at some time been the focus of systematic campaigns of discrimination and, occasionally, of social violence. Loyalists in the American Revolution and Copperheads in the Civil War were frequently deprived of civil liberties including safety of life and limb. Economic strife has erupted into violence countless times during the brief history of the United States, particularly in the

---

[11] A "riot" involves direct physical clashes between two groups, as occurred in race riots in Philadelphia, Los Angeles, and Detroit in the 1940s, and in other cities earlier.

[12] The group to whom this paper was originally presented was no exception.

[13] I.e., violence, often group in nature, directed at persons or their property "solely or primarily because of their membership in social categories." Allen Grimshaw, "Changing Patterns of Racial Violence in the United States," *Notre Dame Lawyer*, XL, 5 (Symposium, 1965), p. 1. Page references are to the author's mimeographed reprint.

last 100 years. No major industry accepted unionization without a struggle, but in some, such as the railroads and the mines, the struggle assumed the character of class warfare.

America has been, then, a land of lawlessness and violence. Spontaneous brawls between servicemen of different branches are remembered by people who lived through World War II. Violence between schoolboys from different schools or young gang members fighting over "turf" are a part of the American scene today. The gangster warfare of the thirties is celebrated in movies and in television series; famous blood feuds are remembered in folk and popular songs. Our tradition of lawlessness includes, on one hand, a generalized contempt of parking regulations, and an apparent admiration of gangster heroes, and, on the other, an excessive zeal in the administration of "Vigilante justice," "lynch law" and "six-shooter law" on the frontier.

Racial disturbances and teenage gang "wars" are colorful and dramatic manifestations of conflict. But violent disturbances of a racial character or among delinquents, which have a high visibility, have claimed and continue to claim fewer lives than many other varieties of violence, individual or social. There are more criminal homicides in some American metropolises every year than there have been deaths from all the urban race riots of the twentieth century combined. A few famous feuds, and some major labor disputes, have rolled up casualty lists which compare in length with the most spectacular interracial disorders. Juvenile violence, although an important problem, probably receives disproportionate attention because of the random and sporadic pattern it takes and because victims have increasingly been people from the middle class.[14]

Looking at the history of only one type of violence in the United States (black-white), Grimshaw delineates at least seven major periods:[15]

1. 1740-1861—Slave insurrections and resistance against the system of forced chattel slavery.
2. 1861-1877—Civil War and Reconstruction, which produced the "bloodiest case of interracial violence in American history, the so-called 'Draft Riots' of 1863 in which several thousand persons apparently died in New York." Night-riding began in the postwar period as the forerunner of lynching (which was to take a minimum of 4,500 black lives reported to the present) and other violent forms of social control against Negroes.

[14]*Ibid.*, p. 2.
[15]The following material is adapted from *ibid.*, pp. 2-5.

3. 1878–1914—Second Reconstruction and the beginning of the Great Migration, including labor violence in the North, Jim Crow legislation, night-riding, and lynching bees in the South, as well as riots in Atlanta; Wilmington, North Carolina; and Springfield, Illinois.

4. 1915–1929—World War I and postwar boom and racial adjustment, characterized by increasing outbreaks of interracial violence in Northern urban areas and continued Southern violence. Common examples were lynching, mutiny and insurrection, individual interracial assaults, and homicides (especially on returning Negro servicemen), racially-based arson and bombings, Northern and Southern-style race riots.

5. 1930–1941—Interwar and depression period, in which reported racial violence declined in frequency of incidents if not in barbarity. The 1935 New York disturbance was the major "riot" of the period, and extremist political movements grew.

6. 1942–1947—World War II and immediate postwar years, marked by an increase in interracial violence, including the Detroit riot of 1943 and others in Los Angeles, New York and elsewhere, intimidation and assaults on returning Negro veterans. Increased militance of Negroes in challenging the segregated system no doubt contributed to more repressive measures of social control by the dominant group.

7. Post-1948—Grimshaw believes that "the pattern of events has changed so rapidly in the years since 1948 that it seems specious to attempt to isolate and label specific periods." Major developments in black-white conflict have included (a) increasing resort to (and effectiveness of) the courts and legislation for conflict-resolution and redress; (b) increasing support of minority rights by local, state and federal governments[16] ("however flagrant the activities of some local law enforcement officers may be, however slowly the majesty of federal power may move"); (c) the widespread application and success of non-violent direct action techniques such as the sit-ins and Freedom Rides; (d) the growth of black nationalism and its subsequent rejection of the goal of "becoming white" (i.e., being integrated); and (e) the urban racial disorders since summer 1964, notably in Los Angeles, Newark, and Detroit.

Note that this interpretation deals with only certain kinds of violence in American history—those having to do with black-white relationships. Equally significant for our understanding of what is happening today in the cities are such other instances of group violence in our nation's past and present history as:

1. The winning of the Revolutionary War against a disciplined British

---

[16]With a major exception being, until very recently, Southern cities, counties and states, which formally resisted and tacitly sanctioned violent resistance to school desegregation and other legal mandates against discrimination.

army by a volunteer band of pick-ups, the first great guerrilla warriors in early modern warfare;

2. The Indian wars, which nearly led to extinction of this land's original inhabitants by the invading Euro-Americans, with incarceration of most of the remaining descendents on reservations;

3. The severe intergroup conflict and violence that accompanied the arrival and attempts at assimilation of each ethnic group;

4. The Japanese "relocation" in World War II, in which tens of thousands of American citizens of Japanese origin were stripped of liberty and property and summarily shipped to concentration camps without due process; and

5. The institutionalized militarism and violence of the present day (called "defense"), which maintains nearly 3½ million persons in the armed forces and 432 major military bases in at least sixty-eight foreign countries, and will be operated in fiscal 1970 at a price of more than $80 billion,[17] not counting additional billions in hidden benefits and subsidiary advantages to corporations and universities. And enter the ABM.

Yet, incredulously our national leaders say repeatedly that "violence never solved anything" when talking to blacks and students about their grievances, and urge calm, reason, and persuasion.[18] Blacks, students, and others displeased with things as they are have learned confrontational and violent styles of conflict-resolution from the nation's history and present activities in areas of foreign policy (e.g., the network of military bases and a 30-billion-dollar non-war) as well as domestic affairs (repression of ghetto uprisings by superior police violence and the national fixation of "law 'n' order").

The point is that most middle-class, white Americans are continuously blinded to an objective analysis of current black violence because different oxen are now being gored—namely theirs. Somehow current black violence seems "different" to us than the more barbarous and pervasive history partially described above. It is a question of legitimacy—whether the violence is defined as appropriate or not. The legitimacy of violent behavior is determined by (1) who is defining it, and (2) what he is trying to protect or achieve. Analytically, the Great Britain of the 1760s and 70s is the white middle-class America of the 1960s and 70s—both defending their institutionalized positions of power against revolutionary challengers defined as so "radical," "violent," and "irresponsible" as to be unfit to manage the resources and affairs of western civilization.

The legitimacy of violence is in the eyes of the legitimator. And if he is

---

[17]Edward P. Morgan, "Elementary Lesson on the Armed Forces," *The Washington Post* (February 15, 1969).

[18]The latest and best example: the implications of President Nixon's statement on student unrest, issued March 22, 1969.

of the dominant or controlling group in society, the moral righteousness of his use of violence is assured. Machiavelli saw the principle clearly: national greatness legitimates violence.[19] Until we can see that our moral positions on the "necessity," "justifiability," and even "righteousness" of violence flow from our power positions, objective analysis of contemporary American urban violence is impossible.

IV

By now it should be clear that conflict and violence are ongoing and in a real sense, natural parts of all human communities. They are not abnormal or pathological except in extreme forms, just as intrapsychic conflict is not abnormal until it reaches an extreme intensity that impairs the normal functioning of the organism and may be defined as psychotic.

The "urban violence" which is of popular concern today therefore may be seen in two contexts: (1) the historical, as we have described its roots in the American traditions of slavery, segregation, militarism, frontier justice, and media glorification of violence; and (2) the comparative, as a particular type of group violence among many types. This section turns to the second perspective and develops a typology of group violence.

We start by asking, "What are the most important dimensions to examine if we are to understand group violence?" I have chosen two: the function of violence (aim, goal, or anticipated outcome of violent activity) and the rationality of violence (degree of rational planning for goal-achievement through violent means).

FUNCTION

Any instance of violent activity may be placed on a continuum ranging from revolt to control to expansion.[20] Violence for revolt is employed by subordinate groups against the controlling interests of the system. Violence for control is one of many techniques available to the power structure for keeping the behavior of the system's members, and especially dissident groups, within acceptable limits. Group violence for expansion is the most aggressive type, and is usually employed to enlarge limits of territorial or political dominance. It is commonly associated with whole societies and their leadership, but may be used by subgroups trying to take new turf for themselves within the host society.

[19] Bienen, *Violence and Social Change*, p. 74.
[20] The categories of revolt and control were suggested to me by Thomas Rose's paper, "Violence as Political Control and Revolt" (draft copy of material to be published in *Readings in Public Policy and Politics* edited by Edgar Litt, Holt, Rinehart and Winston).

Rationality

Similarly, a continuum may be constructed signifying degree of rationality or planning of group violence, with expressive and political categories representing the two extremes. Expressive violence refers to that which has no planning, but rather grows spontaneously and "naturally" from the conditions of everyday life. Political violence is the fully pre-planned type, specifically employed as a means to a particular goal. Every instance of violence fits somewhere between those two extremes in its degree of spontaneity or pre-planning.

Combining the two continua produces a chart on which representative examples of the various types of group violence may be placed.

TABLE 2 □ TYPES OF GROUP VIOLENCE

Degree of Rationality	Function		
	Revolt	Control	Expansion
Expressive (spontaneous, no planning)	Disorder "riot" 1	Lynching 3	(Primitive raiding parties? youth gang wars?) 5
Political (planned, directed toward preconceived goals)	Guerrilla warfare 2	Law enforcement (police and military) 4	War, military aggression 6

The examples included here (Table 2) are intended to represent the most extreme or "pure" form of each of the six types produced by crossing the function and rationality axes. Several important dimensions of group violence are not covered by this typology, notably targets and legitimacy. Within each cell could be specified the target of that type of violence. In cell 1, for example, property has been the most frequent target of citizens in the urban racial disorders of the last five years, while persons have been the most frequent target of law enforcement officials. Persons or property are common targets in cell 2, depending on the specific ends sought by the violent groups. In both "control" cells, 3 and 4, persons are the immediate target of the violent activities of the informal (3) or official (4) agents of social control of the power structure. The long-range goals of expansion (5 and 6) usually include territorial acquisitions, but both persons and property are involved as immediate targets.[21]

Which types of violence are legitimate? Again, it depends on the position and loyalties of the definer of legitimacy. Cell 4 (the planned and ordered use of violence for law enforcement) clearly is the most commonly accepted type of group violence in any society, with cell 6 (war) running a close second. The American public has been particularly upset by (i.e., strongly convinced of the illegitimacy of) recent cell 1 violence—the disorders and "riots" in urban areas. While those activities represent only a small portion of the total violence occurring in the United States and in relation to its foreign involvements, they have high saliency because they represent revolt against establishment targets who naturally define such revolt as illegitimate.

V

Having considered contemporary urban dissent and violence in historical and comparative terms, we return to an examination of these phenomena in relation to the process of social change.

My research on race relations in the United States has viewed change as the generic process, and conflict as one part of that process. Through studies of the sit-ins and freedom rides,[22] and of the pressures for racial change in our major urban areas, I have developed a phase-structure of the change process which provides a model for studying today's urban violence in a perspective beyond the violence itself. Space does not permit elaboration, but the sequency leading to major change in racial and other patterns observed in virtually every American community may be briefly summarized:

1. A continuous condition of power (the control of decisions) never giving itself up willingly.

2. A period of rational, persuasive, non-threatening overtures for change from subordinate groups to dominant groups.

3. Eventually, a last-resort series of open, dramatic challenges to the *status quo* on given issues.

---

[21]There may be no pure type of expansion/expressive group violence; the examples in cell 5 on the chart seem closest to the type.

[22]See James Laue, "Direct Action and Desegregation: Toward a Theory of the Rationalization of Protest," doctoral dissertation submitted to Harvard University, 1965; and Laue and Martin Oppenheimer, *Black Protest: Toward a Theory of Movements*, in preparation for Blaisdell and Company.

4. A period of overt community conflict emerging as latent competition is forced to the surface by an accumulation of challenges which can no longer be adequately dealt with by the normal methods of social control.

5. A cresting of the conflict cycle in a crisis, drawing hitherto-uninvolved elements of community power into honest negotiation for change. Crisis is phenomenological: it is achieved when the persons with power to make some of the changes demanded define the situation as a serious enough threat to their self-interest to change priorities for action.

6. The working out of some change through communication and compromise—with the whole process cycling again and again in communities on each new issue.

While there are examples from every American city of how change has emerged through this process, I now question whether the theory will have long-range applicability as the focus of conflict moves North and becomes progressively urban, because of two conditions which must be met if a social system is to achieve change through conflict. First, the superordinate power in the system must permit conflict as a way of doing change. The model would not have applied in Nazi Germany; rather a kind of short-circuiting from initial challenge to repressive change would have taken place. Second, I am coming to be convinced that the superordinate power must not only permit conflict, but must, in fact approve of the goals of the protestors.

What operated in the South in the early 1960s, then, was a concessions model in which Negroes challenged politically-expendable cities, counties and states, while the federal government permitted the conflict process to run its course through to change, and tacitly (and often openly) supported the goals of the protestors as being consistent with basic American values. The permissive superordinate power was the federal government, supported by the mass media and the white, liberal-labor coalition.

But now it is the superordinate power itself which is under attack. The targets are now the federal government, the large Northern cities (with their nonexpendable Democratic machines), "white liberals," the mass media, judges who do not enforce housing codes, the real estate industry—in short, the whole middle-class establishment. It was easy for the superordinate power in its various forms to support conflict in Alabama and Mississippi: the moral issues were seemingly clear, the devils were readily available in brutal sheriffs and unattractive politicians, and it was far away. But many of the same persons, newspapers, private organizations and government officials who endorsed the movement's use of conflict for change in the South, now confuse demonstrations with riots and label Southern protest techniques turned northward as "irresponsible."

In light of these recent shifts in targets and allies—and of the urban racial violence of past summers—we need to ask, "Under what conditions will the crisis-definition become repressive?" The crisis-definition I have been using is essentially oriented to positive change. It assumes, within the context of a sympathetic superordinate power, that crisis always moves the targets of the challenge in the direction of democratic change. The intensity of urban violence and dissent in the foreseeable future will depend largely on whether the power structure can respond to the challenges with flexibility—and with rapid movement toward further democratization of institutions.

Reflective Questions

1. What similarities exist between the present urban violence and violence in the early cities of America and the world?

2. Is it true that for every case of significant social change, violence and dissent are present?

3. If a superordinate power, such as the Federal government, is under constant attack, is it more likely to be repressive than sympathetic to urban problems and needs?

4. Given the growing proportion of blacks in American cities and their increased political participation, what prospects do you see for a more conducive and supportive atmosphere for urban rehabilitation and change?

27 □ THE BLACK REVOLUTION: A PRIMER FOR WHITE LIBERALS

Charles V. Hamilton

Charles V. Hamilton, who with Stokely Carmichael wrote *Black Power: The Politics of Liberation,* offers a penetrating analysis of the relation of the Black Revolution to white liberals. In the following article, Hamilton asserts that among persons most confused and disgusted by the Black Revolution are white liberals. The latter believe in rationality, color blindness, compromise, integration, consensus and "law." Blacks, however, are pursuing a principle of legitimacy, according to Hamilton, outside the traditional liberal framework, a principle of group development that is not predicated on consensus but on self-awareness and identity. The call of white liberals for blacks to forget race and think of themselves as Americans is meaningful only to those who have power and cultural identity. Although there are differences between white liberals and black-power advocates, the article assures us that the latter group has more in common with white liberals than with white conservatives. □

AMONG THE AMERICANS WHO HAVE BEEN MOST CONFUSED, DISTRESSED, AND even disgusted by recent manifestations of the Black Revolution are many of those whites who have traditionally been known as liberals, and who have long been committed to the betterment of race relations and the attainment of civil rights in such fields as employment, education, and housing.

By word and deed, Black Power advocates—and I am one—have brought

From *The Progressive,* January, 1969, pp. 29-31. Copyright © 1968 by The Progressive, Inc. Reprinted with permission.

tension, uncertainty, and pain to the ranks of liberals. A few liberals have become active, outspoken opponents of the Black Revolution. Many are washing their hands entirely of "the race issue." Still others, while maintaining their commitment to civil rights, are plainly perplexed by the new issues raised by black militants.

It is an uncomfortable state of affairs, and one that is often depicted as dangerous to society. Yet I believe that the processes now at work can lead to constructive results—provided we are willing to examine those processes, understand them, and adapt ourselves to the changes that may be necessary.

In attempting to assess, briefly, some aspects of the Black Revolution that have proven so troublesome to white liberals, I will try not to repeat the points made by James Farmer in his article, "Are White Liberals Obsolete in the Black Struggle?" in *The Progressive* for January, 1968. I am in full agreement with those points. My comments will attempt to extend Mr. Farmer's discussion.

White liberals should recognize that their discomfort is well-founded: the Black Revolution challenges—and, indeed, rejects—many of the values they hold dear. To an extent that even most liberals fail to recognize, these values have been broadly accepted by much (though not all) of American society. They are the values of individual freedom and equality, founded on John Locke's doctrine that man is basically rational, capable of knowing his self-interest and capable of reaching an accommodation based on that self-interest.

In the realm of race relations, these principles are articulated in terms of color-blindness. ("We don't hire on the basis of color; we hire on the basis of merit.") Racial integration is regarded as a highly desirable goal and one that is consciously sought.

Politics, in the liberal tradition, is seen as a protracted process. Men bargain, negotiate, and ultimately reach a compromise. Consensus is presumed, and political conflict is confined to certain predetermined rules of the game. Change is expected to be gradual, and the goal of objectivity is sought. Passion and subjectivity are eschewed. Considerable reliance is placed on discussion, debate— dialogue. There is an assumption that social problems can be resolved, especially if all parties are sincere and work "within the system."

There is an assumption, too, that "law" must be obeyed, and that "law" (meaning, of course, particular legal statutes) is made by legitimate processes. The authority of law-making bodies is not to be questioned; their particular decrees and statutes, perhaps, but not their fundamental authority to issue such decrees and statutes.

If one wishes to change the particular outputs, one does so "legally"— that is, by resort to the courts and the ballot box, primarily, and by pressure group lobbying in the legislature, although this last approach is suspect; it smacks of undue favors and "dirty politics." Liberal concern about "dirty politics" has led to a spate of reforms aimed at democratizing the political process: referendum, initiative, recall; party primaries; blue-ribbon reform candidates; anti-patronage measures. (It has been pointed out too infrequently that many of these liberal reforms have operated against the interests of masses of black people.)

All this is part of the liberal approach to politics in America. And black Americans have for years subscribed to this egalitarian, libertarian orientation. Their goal has been to enter the mainstream of the American polity by pursuing the liberal principle of legitimacy. But after years of fashioning alliances with liberals along these lines, the black masses find themselves confronted with the fact that they have not only failed to improve their condition, but that they have steadily lost ground in relation to the progress of whites.

The various educational systems, in the more liberal North as well as in the South, have failed to come to terms with the cultural (as well as the educational) needs of black children. Northern liberals showed no concern about the deficiencies in textbooks until black parents and students began to call this to their attention. The liberals had assumed the superior efficacy of *their* approach to education, and were convinced it would behoove black children to take advantage of it—even if they had to be bussed across town to do so. It never occurred to those white liberals that their standardized tests might be culturally biased. And even if they were, were not the little black children "culturally disadvantaged," "slow learners," "high risks"?

The liberals never gave much thought to the ultimate effect on black people of years of urban renewal; many were on the faculties of universities using urban renewal to relieve their "land-locked" condition. Some liberal professors raised their voices against the destruction of black neighborhoods. But most of the social scientists, more interested in their methodology and their correlations than in the social product (some call it value-free social science), took no interest in black community participation in urban renewal decision-making.

Today, some of these faculties are trying to rush to relevancy by adding courses dealing with black Americans to their curricula. They are groping to understand the demands of black student groups on the campuses, but many of the white liberal professors now find they are simply not relevant to a vast segment, an important segment, of this society—precisely because *their* (not just the students') education has been blindly incomplete.

Black people have been complaining about police brutality for years, but many white liberals did not get "up tight" about this issue until they began protesting against the war in Vietnam and experiencing the brutality themselves. Anti-war demonstrators have often described police tactics as "unbelievable," but they have long been quite believable to black people. I would suggest that if those same white liberals were to start protesting this country's policies and practices toward South Africa, they would run up against the same firm billy clubs. (It is most instructive, incidentally, that white liberal America is not overly concerned about the economic support of South Africa's apartheid system offered by interests in this country. But this may become the next liberal fad when the Vietnam war is over.)

The point I want to make is that the white liberals' approach to problems of race in this country has not been as viable as many would like to think. Their agenda simply has not been as enlightened as a first glance would indicate. And this has been the case largely because they have been operating under a principle of legitimacy not particularly applicable to the development of black people. The liberal approach has specific relevance for a relatively secure, relatively "arrived" group, and it is capable of manipulating the system to permit a few to enter—as a few blacks have.

White liberals have never come to terms with the phenomenon of *institutional* racism in this country. It was Stokely Carmichael who broached this subject in the present-day context, and he was *followed* by the President's Commission on Civil Disorders (Kerner Commission). It is small wonder that few black people could get excited about the Commission's report. It merely articulated what many of us had been saying for years, and if many white liberals did not know it, then it is apparent they were operating on a different set of principles and premises.

I am suggesting that black people are pursuing a principle of legitimacy outside the traditional liberal framework—one that is concerned with *group* development, and that does not presume the existence of a consensus, especially on matters regarding race. This principle is very color-conscious. ("We want black principals to head schools in the black communities.") Racial integration is not regarded as a matter of immediate, high priority, because it is recognized that before any group can enter the open society it must first close ranks. Prolonged debate, discussion—dialogue—are luxuries which frequently cannot be afforded.

This principle is most usually associated with a society on the make, with a people coming out from under colonial rule into political independence and economic development. In the present-day American context, it is manifested in demands for black community control of schools and law enforcement agencies; in such moves as black ownership of businesses in the black community.

Pursuing this principle, black people cannot assume the Lockeian notion of the rationality of man; in fact, in regards to race, they must assume that Western, Anglo-Saxon man might well be irreconcilably irrational. Politics as a protracted process becomes only a frustrating exercise, especially when one realizes the extent to which black people have been *systematically* excluded from decision-making.

The goal of the Black Revolution is development, and those institutions of society which put as much stock in procedure as in performance must be looked upon as obstacles to that goal. When people are excluded from participating, they see political delay in solving their problems as deliberate procrastination and unwillingness to act, not as inevitable, pluralist constraints on institutions.

Black people understand that the best way to pursue the fulfillment of their potentiality is to start from a firm base of self-awareness and identity. When liberals tell them to forget race and think of themselves only as Americans, they know that this is an invitation which only those in power can entertain—an invitation to cultural absorption. And such absorption will occur while other groups in the society protect and maintain their own cultural identity.

It is important to point out that in examining the contrast between liberal values and those of the Black Revolution, I am discussing two principles of *legitimacy:* one is not legitimate and the other illegitimate. Rather, one is more valid than the other for a previously colonized people set on rapid social change and development. The concerns and motivations of such people often simply do not coincide with those of people proceeding under an egalitarian, libertarian principle. Herein, I suggest, lies the major tension between white liberals and advocates of Black Power. Black Power groups must be viewed as new, relevant intermediary groups for a people who no longer trust the established, traditional, frequently liberal-oriented associations.

Should one conclude that black people have more in common with white conservatives than with liberals? Conservatives oppose bussing and are resistant to open housing; they see Black Power as a modern-day extension of Booker T. Washington—a misreading of both Mr. Washington and Black Power. At the same time, Black Power advocates push for community control of the schools (not for integration), and they call for consolidated, unified community groups (not dispersal).

A close examination will reveal, however, that ultimately the advocates of Black Power still have more in common with liberals than with conservatives. The former recognize, for example, the importance of the Federal government's role in the development of black communities—a role as crucial, in its way, as the in-put of external economic resources and technical assistance for the development of previously colonized countries. Conservatives, with their basically anti-centrist and anti-government views (i.e., anti-government for all but themselves), offer no useful partnership to the Black Revolution. They see Black Power as decentralist, when, in fact, it is an effort to build a more meaningful central relationship.

There is nothing irreconcilable about black people pursuing their own principle of legitimacy and subsequently taking their place as full-fledged members of the American pluralist society. This process, in itself, would lead to a vast transformation of the system. I see this process as comparable to new nations of

Africa and Asia gaining their political independence, then adopting a particular principle of development and ultimately assuming their places as developed members of the society of nations.

The more dynamic the process of social change and the more we are personally involved in it, the more difficult it is to see such change in its overall, long-term developmental stages—and the easier it is to "lose our cool." But such is the challenge to those who would understand system transformation in a modern, industrial, heterogeneous society and who would create—during that delicate period of transformation—necessary and vital forms of communication and cooperation.

Reflective Questions

1. Given the status differences between the races in America, can one achieve equality between them without some kind of preferential treatment or reparations for blacks?

2. What is black power? Is it a permanent goal of the Black Revolution, or is it best understood as a strategy for integration and equality?

3. What is the relationship between black awareness, black pride, and black power? Are the three separate concepts? Can black people have one without the others?

4. What is the most appropriate role for white liberals in terms of the Black Revolution? Should they work primarily in their own white communities to bring about changes?

28 □ THE KLAN REVIVAL[1]

James W. Vander Zanden

Using 153 klansmen as direct-resource persons, and a wealth of secondary information, Vander Zanden presents a view of the Klan and its members as a resistance movement. The author describes the Klan member as a highly marginal man—marginal with reference to economics, social status, and self-identity. The techniques employed by the Klan in attempting to achieve their ends are classic textbook methods used by various social movements. The author points out that the Klan member, "having internalized both the common success goals and the socially sanctioned norms for their achievement, . . . does not turn to attack the social system" but rather, personalizes his "enemy," for example, Earl Warren, former President Johnson, Justice Douglas, and "evil" groups like the Black Panthers, the national political parties, and foreigners. □

Since 1955 there has been a Ku Klux Klan revival in the South, but as a resistance organization, its course of development and ecological distribution is atypical. The occupational positions of 153 klansmen are examined, and the atypical course and distribution are interpreted on the basis of the position klansmen occupy in the social structure.

SINCE 1955 THE NATION'S PRESS HAS CARRIED PERIODIC REPORTS OF REVIVED Ku Klux Klan activity in the South. Fiery crosses, motorcades, torchlight rallies, floggings, bomb terror, and the castration of a Negro have followed in its

From *The American Journal of Sociology*, Volume LXV, No. 5, March 1960, pp. 456–462. Copyright © 1960 by the University of Chicago Press. Reprinted by permission of the University of Chicago Press and the author.

[1] The data for this paper was secured by field research in Georgia and South Carolina late in 1955 and in 1956 and from the extensive materials in the Library of the Southern Educational Reporting Service in Nashville, Tenn.

wake.[2] The hooded order, a reconstruction-era organization, had previously been revived in 1915, and again following World War II. The post-World War II revival, however, was short lived, and by 1952 the Klan had been suppressed through state and federal action.

Then came May 17, 1954, and the Supreme Court school desegregation ruling. Racial tensions slowly mounted during the year that followed. Nevertheless, even in the states of the Deep South, the belief was widespread that some desegregation would be inescapable. Delay was the major tactic of state officials. When, on May 31, 1955, the Supreme Court handed down its implementing decree, the NAACP quickly followed with at least forty-two petitions for immediate school desegregation in as many communities of Virginia and the Deep South. The result was an immediate and marked upsurge in counteractivity by the whites. Deep South states no longer were thinking in terms of buying time; compromise was being ruled out; die-hard, adamant opposition was the order of the day. In the rural Black Belt areas of the Deep South the citizens councils, until this time relatively small, isolated groups, gained momentum. Drastic, stringent punishment was meted out to Negro signers of integration petitions. In Deep South states politicians increasingly made segregation their chief campaign issue. In Mississippi fourteen-year-old Emmett Till was mutilated, murdered, and his body dumped into the Tallahatchie River. In Alabama a mob and the developments that followed in its wake successfully blocked the admittance of Autherine Lucy to the state university, where the Negro woman had enrolled under court order. Increasingly, whites believed they could defeat integration.[3]

In this atmosphere of mounting tension and resistance the Klan made its reappearance. But, as contrasted with the citizens councils, its strength did not reside in the rural Black Belt areas of the South;[4] on the contrary, it has been an urban phenomenon, with the preponderance of its strength located in the

[2] At least three floggings have been linked with the Klan, one of which, near Travelers Rest, S.C., resulted in the conviction of four Greenville, S.C., klansmen. Klansmen have been implicated in the Montgomery and Atlanta church bombings and in the attempted bombing of a Negro elementary school near Charlotte, N.C. Acquittals resulted in the former cases, but convictions were secured in the Charlotte case. Four klansmen were subsequently convicted of mayhem and sentenced to twenty years imprisonment for the Labor Day, 1957, castration of a Negro handyman near Birmingham, Ala. The act had been perpetrated, according to the courtroom testimony of the klansmen, as a test for one of their number to prove his worthiness "of becoming assistant exalted cyclops."

[3] For a detailed account and analysis of the Southern resistance movement following in the wake of the Supreme Court school rulings, see James W. Vander Zanden, "The Southern White Resistance Movement to Integration" (unpublished doctoral dissertation, University of North Carolina, Chapel Hill, 1958).

[4] *Ibid.*, pp. 313–15, and James W. Vander Zanden, "The Citizens' Councils," *Alpha Kappa Deltan*, XXIX (Spring, 1959), 3–10.

Piedmont of the Southeast.[5] In the last half of 1955 and the first half of 1956 came the zenith of citizens council activity throughout the Deep South. After this period organized council activity subsided: economic sanctions and pressures against Negroes became infrequent; attendance at mass meetings dropped sharply; chapters in wide areas became inactive; only a scattering of new chapters were formed; and renewals of membership and financial contributions dropped sharply. With the crushing of the integrationist movement in the Deep South, the citizens councils became, for the most part, inactive. The situation was summarized by Charles N. Plowden, banker, large landowner, and a prominent figure in the Summerton, South Carolina, council, the community from which had come one of the original cases before the Supreme Court. Speaking of the Summerton citizens council, Plowden remarked: "There's no need to meet. Everything's going along quiet."[6] But the Klan exhibited a different course. It gathered slow momentum in 1955 and 1956 but did not reach its peak until late 1956, 1957, and early 1958, after which it, too, experienced a sharp tapering-off.

The growth and activity of the citizens council has been closely associated with the whites' perception of the imminence of desegregation. Robert Patterson, leader of the Mississippi councils, has repeatedly asserted in organizing speeches: "Organized aggression must be met with organized resistance." In short, movement begets countermovement. The corollary has also tended to hold true,

[5] Klan strength has resided in the following areas of the South. Alabama: Birmingham and vicinity (Jefferson, Shelby, Tuscaloosa, and St. Clair Counties), the Montgomery-Prattville vicinity and Mobile; Florida: Jacksonville and vicinity (Duval and Nassau Counties), Tampa, and Tallahassee, with a scattering of members in the north-central area of the state between these three urban centers; Georgia: Atlanta and vicinity (DeKalb, Fulton, and Cobb Counties), Macon, Savannah, and Columbus, with a scattering of members in Americus, Warner-Robbins, Cochran, Vienna, Moultrie, Albany, Waycross, and Nashville; North Carolina: membership and activity centered in a triangular area with Reidsville on the north, Charlotte on the west, and Hamlet on the southeast; South Carolina: Greenville and vicinity (York, Cherokee, Spartanburg, and Greenville Counties), Columbia and vicinity, and Florence, with a scattering of members in Darlington, Dillon, and Horry Counties; and Tennessee: the Chattanooga-Rossville, Ga., vicinity, Maryville-Alcoa-Knoxville vicinity, and Nashville. Small chapters have also been reported in Baton Rouge, La., Waco, Tex., Little Rock, Ark., and southern Delaware.

Since fiery crosses, torchlight rallies, floggings, and bombings are the sort of activity that commands newspaper headlines, it is easy to exaggerate the size of Klan membership. Some estimates have placed it as high as 100,000. But such estimates appear to be stimulated by the Klan's sensationalism and boasting. Although Klan membership figures are secret, the figure surely did not exceed 10,000 at the organization's zenith in late 1956 and 1957.

[6] John Bartlow Martin, "The Deep South Says Never," *The Saturday Evening Post*, Part II, CCXXIX (June 22, 1957), 101.

namely, if movement subsides, so, too, does countermovement.[7] The Klan development, on the other hand, has not followed a similar course. Nor, as has been noted, has its strength resided (with the exception of Tallahassee and Montgomery where the Negroes' movement for integration on buses was under way) in areas where the threat of integration was thought of by the general populace as immediate or especially threatening. This paper suggests that in part these incongruities can be explained and the appeal of the Klan understood by examining the position which klansmen occupy within the social structure.

The "mission" of the Klan is set forth in the handbook of the U.S. Klans, Knights of the Ku Klux Klan:

We invite all men who can qualify to become citizens of the Invisible Empire, to approach the portal of our beneficent domain, join us in our noble work of extending its boundaries, and in disseminating the gospel of Klankraft, thereby encouraging, conserving, protecting and making vital the fraternal relationship in the practice of an honorable clannishness; to share with us the sacred duty of protecting womanhood; to maintain forever the God-given supremacy of the White Race; to commemorate the holy and chivalric achievement of our fathers; to safeguard the sacred rights, privileges and institutions of our civil government; to bless mankind and to keep eternally ablaze the sacred fire of a fervent devotion to a pure Americanism.

Since the Klan is a secret society, membership lists are not available. However, from a number of sources the names and occupational positions of 153 klansmen were identified.[8] They fall into four occupational groups: (1) skilled workers (e.g., garage mechanics, machinists, carpenters, and stonemasons); (2) marginal, small businessmen (e.g., small building-trade contractors and proprietors of food markets, grills, and gasoline stations); (3) marginal white-collar workers (e.g., grocery-store clerks, service-station attendants, policemen, and salesmen); and (4) transportation workers (primarily truck drivers) and unskilled and semiskilled workers in the textile, construction, automotive, aircraft, coal, and steel industries. This sample is of unknown representativeness and it is undoubtedly biased, yet it probably reflects the occupational breadth of the Klan's membership. Accordingly, caution should be taken into account in evaluating the following interpretations.

[7] See James W. Vander Zanden, "Resistance and Social Movements," *Social Forces,* XXXVII (May, 1959), 312–16, and "The Theory of Social Movements," *Sociology and Social Research,* XLIV (September–October, 1959), 3–8.

[8] The names were obtained from those listed on charter applications for Klan incorporation in the several states, from police arrests for Klan activity, from a police-seized membership list in Charlotte, N.C., and from Klan spokesmen named in the press.

Of the 153 klansmen, 98 were in the first three occupational categories: skilled workers, 51; marginal businessmen, 11; and marginal white-collar workers, 36. These are commonly ranked in the upper rungs of the working class and the lower rungs of the middle class, that is, in an intermediate position between clear-cut "blue-collar" manual jobs and white-collar jobs, their status is insecure and they are anxious. At the same time, they generally lack the resources, skills, or education necessary to improve their life-chances.

The situation for the workers in the fourth category is different in that middle-class status is not teasingly and just immediately ahead of them. But the frustration may nevertheless be as acute, where the common success goals are internalized, yet they lack means of access to the approved goals.[9] And their plight is made worse by the insecurity that has traditionally characterized employment in these industries (construction, automotive, textile, aircraft, steel, and coal). Furthermore, the automotive and aircraft industries are relatively recent arrivals on the Southern scene—part of a rapidly growing Southern industrial complex—which have drawn large numbers of workers from small towns and rural communities of the region. Often the workers have been uprooted from what are almost folk communities[10] and propelled into an urban industrial world, with the consequent destruction of old rural values and lifeways, disruption of social ties, and isolation from durable personal ties and roots. Ambiguities regarding one's position, role, and status are the result. In a word, status disorientation occurs.

The picture has not been too different in the expanding Birmingham steel-coal complex. In the textile industry recent studies have pointed to the sharp undermining of the folk relationships that had characterized the mill villages. Increasingly, the mill hands are being engulfed in currents of social change. Traditional castelike barriers between the textile workers and "townspeople" are breaking down, and the mill villagers are becoming more heterogeneous in socioeconomic characteristics. Status, once predominantly ascribed, is becoming

---

[9] In this connection see Wendell Bell, "Anomie, Social Isolation, and the Class Structure," *Sociometry*, XX (June, 1957), 105–16; Dorothy L. Meier and Wendell Bell, "Anomia and Differential Access to the Achievement of Life Goals," *American Sociological Review*, XXIV (April, 1959), 189–202; Richard M. Stephenson, Mobility Orientation and Stratification: A Study of One Thousand Ninth Graders (unpublished doctoral dissertation, Columbia University, 1956); Robert H. Guest, "Work Careers and Aspirations of Automobile Workers," *American Sociological Review*, XIX (April, 1954), 155–63; Ely Chinoy, *Automobile Workers and the American Dream* (Garden City, N.Y.: Doubleday & Co., Inc., 1955); Genevieve Kupfer, "Portrait of the Underdog," *in* Reinhard Bendix and Seymour Martin Lipset (eds.), *Class, Status and Power: A Reader in Social Stratification* (Glencoe, Ill.: Free Press, 1953), pp. 255–63; and Herbert Hyman, "The Value Systems of Different Classes: A Social Psychological Contribution to the Analysis of Stratification," *in* Bendix and Lipset, *op. cit.,* pp. 426–41.

[10] See Howard W. Odum, *The Way of the South* (New York: Macmillan Co., 1947), esp. p. 61.

increasingly achieved.[11] With the shift there has developed a growing disparity between the commonly extolled success goals of our society and the socially sanctioned means whereby they may be attained.

The klansman appears to have internalized *both* the success goals of American society and the institutionalized means for their realization. Thwarted in progressing toward the goals, he does not reject them, nor does he have recourse to socially prescribed means. Rather, he seizes upon the symbols of 100 per cent Americanism and his membership in the superordinately defined white race—and elevates and magnifies these out of proportion. He overconforms to the institutionalized caste pattern of the South and to patriotic identification with America.[12] Judged by white-group standards, his adherence to the dominant white-racial values and Americanism is excessive.[13] And this leads to conflict with other values, most particularly the sanctity of the individual and private property.

Tormented by his ambiguous status, the klansman, by emphasizing the difference between himself as a white and the Negro, may achieve, at least negatively, a sense of group identification. By conforming to the dominant white group, he gets some sense of identification and security. Nevertheless, insecurity and uncertainty lead to his compensating for his lacks through an exaggerated overconformity with the white-caste value system and exaggerated

---

[11] Glen Gilman, *Human Relations in the Industrial Southeast* (Chapel Hill, N.C.: University of North Carolina Press, 1956); Harriet H. Herring, *Passing of the Mill Village* (Chapel Hill, N.C.: University of North Carolina Press, 1952); and James W. Vander Zanden, "The Ways of Big Daddy," *American Mercury,* LXXXVIII (April, 1959), 120–25. See also, Liston Pope, *Millhands and Preachers* (New Haven: Yale University Press, 1942), esp. chaps. iv–vi; Lois MacDonald, *Southern Mill Hands* (New York: Alex L. Hillman, 1928), pp. 98–99 and 149; Harriet L. Herring, *Welfare Work in Mill Villages* (Chapel Hill, N.C.: University of North Carolina Press, 1929), pp. 104, 333 ff.; Gilman, *op. cit.,* pp. 226 ff.; and James W. Vander Zanden, "Some Religious Trends in the Past Thirty Years in Southern Cotton Mill Villages" (unpublished paper, 1957).

[12] On overconformity see Percy Black and Ruth Davidson Atkins, "Conformity versus prejudice as Exemplified in White-Negro Relations in the South: Some Methodological Considerations," *Journal of Psychology,* XXX (July, 1950), 109–21; Richard T. LaPiere, *A Theory of Social Control* (New York: McGraw-Hill, 1954), pp. 121 ff.; and Talcott Parsons, *The Social System* (Glencoe, Ill.: Free Press, 1951), pp. 323–24.

[13] At times such excessiveness may be condoned if not actually welcomed by the population at large, which sees it as a temporary expedient arising from a definition of the situation as unusual and frequently threatening. Means normally prescribed are seen as effective for accomplishing the task at hand, and their employment is justified by the atypical situation and its temporary character. At the same time, those more inhibited through a greater internalization of the prevailing societal norms are "saved" from violating the norms and from consequent anxiety. Thus the reaction among some Southern whites to Klan bombings and floggings has been: "I don't approve of violence. But they (Negroes) were asking for it. They had it coming to them." This situation is reminiscent of the reaction of many to Senator Joseph R. McCarthy.

100 per cent Americanism. For his props are not *any* props: they are props esteemed by society.

Secrecy plays a role similar to exaggerated conformity: the strongly emphasized exclusion of all outsiders makes for a feeling of possession.[14] Klan secrets give the klansman a highly tangible and explicit group identification because they set him apart from the amorphorous mass of humanity.

There are still other consequences. One's own weakness, inferiority, and ambivalence are not infrequently concealed from others and even from one's self, and the substitute often is compensatory self-aggrandizement,[15] seen in the superpatriot and militant white supremacist and frequently expressed in Klan addresses:

Our kind of whites were elected to rule the world and everything in it.[16]

The Ku Klux Klan is the only white Christian Protestant 100 per cent American organization in America today. . . . Klansmen are the cleanest and most perfect people on earth.[17]

The exaggerated emphasis given by the Klan to symbols of status suggests a similar effort. The elaborate Klan regalia conspicuously establishes the individual's membership in the "Invisible Empire" and sets him apart from the mass of humanity. The concern with status and individual aggrandizement is reflected in the organization's preoccupation with insignia, with the assignment of status-denoting colors for the robes of officials, and with the use of an exaggerated status-exalting nomenclature (e.g., Imperial Wizard, Grand Dragon, Grand Titan, Grand Giant, and Exalted Cyclops). Likewise, the respective authority and power of Klan officials have been major issues since the recent Klan revival and have also been crucial contributing factors in Klan factionalism and splintering.[18] In Birmingham a heated argument during a Klan meeting over "one-man rule" resulted in gun play and the wounding of two klansmen. In Tampa the self-styled Grand Dragon of the Associated Florida Ku Klux Klans, W. J. Griffin, named six other Klans operating in the Tampa area and lamented to the press: "We have too many chiefs and not enough

---

[14] George Simmel, *The Sociology of George Simmel*, translated by Kurt H. Wolff (Glencoe, Ill.: Fress Press, 1950), p. 332.
[15] Nathan W. Ackerman and Marie Jahoda, *Anti-Semitism and Emotional Disorder* (New York: Harper & Bros., 1950), p. 31.
[16] Klan speaker at a rally at Lakeland, Fla.; Memphis *Commercial Appeal*, July 22, 1956.
[17] Klan speaker at a rally at Pontiac, S.C.; Charlotte *Observer*, October 2, 1955.
[18] The largest of the Klans is the U.S. Klans, Knights of the Ku Klux Klan chartered in Georgia. There have been at least fifteen splinter groups, six in addition to the U.S. Klans in South Carolina, four in Alabama, one each in North Carolina, Texas, and Louisiana, and at least two in Florida.

Indians to stage a war dance." Griffin asserted that "the old countersign and password won't work because all klansmen are strangers to each other." His answer: The Klan should adopt old Indian customs "and force grand dragons to wear tusks in their noses. . . . Members should be forced to be stamped with the branding iron or clip their ears with leather punches like farmers mark their livestock."

The excessive vehemence with which some klansmen extol their white status and disassociate themselves from Negro status suggests that basically they may feel themselves as weak, deprived, and helpless as they imagine the Negro to be. This appears reflected in statements such as these: "The Communists would have you believe that the nigger's blackness is only skin deep. All I gotta say to that is they ought to go skin one and find out for themselves. We are gonna stay white, we are gonna keep the nigger black, with the help of our Lord and Savior, Jesus Christ;"[19] and "I've been a white man all my life and I always will be."[20] Such individuals may tend to equate their own lower status with the subordinate Negro-caste position, and their vehement dissociation from the Negro and their avowal of membership in the dominant group may be efforts to convince both themselves and others that they do not occupy an inferior position.

The Klan offers its members a chance to acquire importance, hope, and a sense of worthiness. It gives him a "cause," a sacred mission with meaningfulness and purposiveness. A strong sense of "mission" is a recurring theme in Klan speeches, e.g., "America was saved by the Knights of the Ku Klux Klan [at the time of the reconstruction] and if it is saved again, the Ku Klux Klan will do it."[21] A hooded klansman observed to the writer at a Klan rally outside of Orangeburg, South Carolina: "Believe me, mister—we ain't no hoodlum outfit. The reds and fools say we are, but we ain't. We're goin' to save this here country. You just watch and see!"

Finding his group identity ambiguous and/or his aspirations thwarted, the klansman can identify himself with something beyond and greater than himself—"The Invisible Empire." Since the organization lays claim to his whole person (not merely to a segment, as do most American voluntary associations),[22] his social being tends to become submerged within a greater whole. The success which was not forthcoming through normal channels promises to

[19] Klan speaker at a Montgomery, Ala., rally; Montgomery *Advertiser,* November 25, 1956.
[20] Klan speaker at a Lakeland, Fla., rally; Memphis *Commercial Appeal,* July 22, 1956.
[21] A speaker at a Klan rally at Montgomery, Ala., September 9, 1956.
[22] As Simmel observes: ". . . [the secret society] quite characteristically claims to a greater extent the whole individual, connects its members in more of their totality, and mutually obligates them more closely, than does an open society of identical content. Through the symbolism of the ritual, which excites a whole range of vaguely delimited feelings beyond all particular, rational interests, the secret society synthesizes those interests into a total claim upon the individual" (Simmel, *op. cit.,* p. 360).

come through the organization and cause to which he has dedicated himself. At the same time, the Klan demands unconditional obedience to its rules and norms and enforces them. It is quite possible that individuals lacking stable or explicit group identification in the society-at-large find assurance, stability, and identification in such dogmatic and totalitarian commitments. By the same token, social change, as represented by integrationist and liberal movements, confronts him with indefiniteness, unconventionality, and loss of familiar anchorage.

But such inclusive commitment, by tying him with incomparable closeness to the group, makes him dependent. Severance from the group threatens him with a loss of substance and a part of his social being—with rootlessness and the loss of a stable life-feeling. The cohesion of the secret society is obtained in part by partially secluding the individual from other meaningful social relationships. This is reinforced through the definition of the klansman as a deviant by society-at-large, social sanctions not infrequently awaiting the "known" member. The result is that the individual tends to evaluate his behavior according to the norms of the Klan rather than of society-at-large.

Within this context the individual can legitimatize the use of violence, proscribed by society-at-large. Despite frequent disavowing of the use of violence, hardly veiled threats of violence are a repeated theme in Klan speeches. Examples include: "The way I feel about them niggers who want to integrate education is this—they don't want an education, they want a funeral."[23] "I'd shed every drop of my blood to keep kids from going to school with niggers."[24] "A Negro who tries to get into a white swimming pool [referring to a Negro who sought to enter a white pool at Durham, N.C.] is not looking for a bath, he's looking to get killed."[25]

Likewise, impulses toward aggressive behavior and violence deriving from thwarted aspirations can be justified by the standards of his group—or so he thinks. The Klan regalia hiding the individual's identity operates toward a similar end. Not alone does it protect the individual from recognition and possible social sanctions, but it obliterates the individual as a member of society-at-large while accentuating his Klan identification. And as an object of what the klansman frequently perceives to be unfair treatment from society-at-large, he can feel himself morally freed from the obligations that society would impose upon him. The use of symbols incrusted with emotional meaning, the performance of hallowed rituals, the singing of hymns—all these help in the breaking down of resistances that inhibit the responsiveness desired in the members of the fold.

Thwarted in realizing goals which society holds to be worthwhile and

[23] Klan speaker at a Montgomery, Ala., rally; Montgomery *Advertiser,* November 25, 1956.
[24] Klan speaker at a Lakeland, Fla., rally; St. Petersburg *Times,* July 22, 1956.
[25] A Klan speaker at a rally outside of Monroe, N.C.; Charlotte *Observer,* August 9, 1957.

frequently occupying a precarious position within the social structure, the individual easily comes to see himself as the victim of inscrutable conspiracies and enemies. Time and again failing in his encounters with life, he develops a generalized feeling of inadequacy, but his "faults" appear to him as wholly outside of himself. It is he who is blameless, virtuous, more sinned against than sinning—and so his self-esteem is restored. All is reflected in the endless recurrence in Klan speeches of such words as *plot, conspiracy, hoax, corruption* and the like.

But the Klan, as contrasted with reformist or revolutionary movements, does not offer a program of basic social change. The source of discontent is not seen as the social system, social conditions, or the government. The difficulty is personified as an "enemy"—as "evil" persons, e.g., Eleanor Roosevelt, Richard Nixon, the justices of the Supreme Court, and Harry S Truman; and "evil" groups, e.g., Jews, Communists, Catholics, foreigners, the "big-city" press, and "scalawags." Having internalized both the common success goals and the socially sanctioned norms for their achievement, he does not turn to attack the social system. On the other hand, members of reformist and revolutionary groups reject both the cultural goals and the institutionalized means, seeking to substitute others for them. But overidentifying himself with the existing order, the klansman seeks to realize success within the existing social structure: the obstacles barring success are, to him, merely the work of "evil" agents.

At times the obsession with "enemies" and "plots" reaches paranoid proportions; it appears as if everywhere there is a conspiracy afoot. This is reflected in the speech of a Klan leader at a Nashville rally who, in the course of his address, depicts as enemies Negroes, Communists, the press, the FBI, Russia, the Nashville school board, the Red Cross, the United Fund (the latter two for allegedly "using their money to transport Negroes around the country to break-down segregation"), food dyes, the use of Salk Polio vaccine (referred to as a "Communist plot"), and the fluoridation of water (referred to as "rat poison").[26] Because of their own insecure and weak position within the social structure and their negligible insight into their situation, the world about them seems hostile and evil.

[26] Nashville *Tennessean,* June 9, 1957.

Reflective Questions

1. Why would the Klan appear to be gaining support in suburban areas?

2. What techniques are employed by the Klan to gain "respectability"?

3. Why might Klan membership appeal to the marginal man?

4. What purpose is served by the exaggerated emphasis given by the Klan to grandiose titles?

5. What is the possible impact of the Klan on American society during the decade of the 1970's?

29 □ AN INTERVIEW WITH ABBIE HOFFMAN AND JERRY RUBIN

Paul Kurtz

Paul Kurtz, editor of *The Humanist,* presents an interview with the self-proclaimed leaders of the Yippie movement in an attempt to determine the thinking of these particular young radicals. Kurtz analytically probes and searches in an effort to find meaning and clarification amidst the wealth of ideas expressed by Hoffman and Rubin. The following dialogue provides considerable insight into the intellectual rationale that serves as justification for the recent actions taken by supporters of the Yippie ideology. In the ensuing discussion, Hoffman and Rubin reflect on the goals of the Yippie movement, the hypocritical values in American life, revolutions, capitalism, toleration, youth and the "old left." □

PAUL KURTZ: You're both key figures in the Yippie movement. What would you say is the purpose of the Youth International party?

JERRY RUBIN: To overthrow the Government.

ABBIE HOFFMAN: It's not the Youth International party; that's a slogan used by *The New York Times*—which needs it. It's Yippie, and there is an exclamation point after it! Yippies are just people struggling to make a new society, one based on human values rather than property values. It's people doing that—all kinds of different people.

RUBIN: Yippies are more a style than a concrete thing. It's not a card you have and say, well, I'm a member of the Yippies. It's just where your head's at and what you're doing. It involves drugs and working out your own life-style, and primarily it's saying that American society as it exists right now is immoral and has no

This article first appeared in *The Humanist,* May/June, 1969, and is reprinted by permission.

place for its youth. Youth had to create something new and different, and Yippies are just part of that creation.

KURTZ: Now, you gave two different answers. For Jerry Rubin the purpose of the Yippies is a revolution to overthrow society, and for Abbie Hoffman to build a new society.

HOFFMAN: One can't be done without the other. When we talk about a system rather than a society, because a system is the machinery that holds that society together, we're talking about decision-making—how decisions are made in the country—and that's the system. And the way in which decisions are made, the kind of people, and how you get to a position where you can make a decision where you have power over another person's life—that's what we're talking about changing.

KURTZ: The first thing then is to destroy the Establishment, and then, second, to build a new society, as you've indicated.

HOFFMAN: Well, what do we have to do then? We *are* the new society.

RUBIN: The Establishment is dead. Its myths don't have any power anymore; the people who work for the Establishment don't have their hearts in it, don't have their lives involved; it's lost the will of the majority of the world. It's on a suicide trip. Our fathers and the people who have power are on a suicide trip. And the young kids are on their own; they have to create their own thing.

KURTZ: In other words, the Yippies are both negative and positive at the same time. A lot of people, of course, think that the Yippie movement is primarily negative: destroy the Establishment, period. But do you really have a positive aim as well?

HOFFMAN: Well, when we went to Chicago during the Democratic Convention, we went to have a festival of life. That's a very positive thing. We're saying that nobody looks at the Democrats and says, "That's decay, that's destruction; they aren't doing anything positive." That's ridiculous. What we were doing was very positive. We are saying: "We are the new society. How are we going to survive together?"

RUBIN: Let me put it in one sentence: To destroy a society that is primarily involved in destruction is a positive act.

KURTZ: All right, one destroys the Establishment. What is the next stage? Do you have some notion of what a Utopia might be?

RUBIN: It's not a program, like the program they had in the '30's, or like what came out of Marxism: a 10-point program. It's a new value system that is in people's bodies. Let's just take the question of money. An old value is that a man's property is his own, and he can pass it on to his children through inheritance, and those who are poor have their own problems. And I think among the youth of America there is an entirely different attitude toward money. That it is just a means, and that it confuses and fucks* up things more than anything else—we've got to get beyond it and share everything.

HOFFMAN: When the factory becomes a community and all the people participate in the decisions that go on in that factory, you have a new society because they are a part of it. And then the revolution becomes a whole community effort of working things out together. There is a vision.

RUBIN: Let me just say one thing about the Yippie thing that is important. It says to us and to a young kid that "you have all the answers." America says, listen to the expert; the person who knows about poverty is a rich person who studied it; a person who knows how to eliminate racism is a white person who's studied it. In our heads, the people who can eliminate poverty are the poor people, the people who can eliminate racism are the people who are the victims of racism, and the only people who can build the future are the young kids. Society is constantly telling young kids: "Keep your place; listen to your teachers; listen to your parents; be good; fulfill your role."

HOFFMAN: Yippies try to switch it around and say, "Trust your impulses." The revolution will come out of you. It'll come out of your impulses; it will come out of your guts; and the way that it will come is when you struggle. Mao Tse-tung said that the way to learn is to do. You do, then you learn, then you do, then you learn again. I just sat down with an intellectual, and he said, "Well, we've got to think, we've got to talk, and we've got to think." Well, we did that for an hour, and I said, "Well, here we are. I haven't learned anything about you because we aren't brothers; we aren't struggling for the same things. We aren't sharing our blood together; we aren't sharing our food together. We aren't sharing our dope, we aren't living in the same area."

KURTZ: I'd like to focus first on the values in American life that you particularly find to be hypocritical or contradictory; and then let's focus on the values that you would substitute for them.

HOFFMAN: That's a long list.

---

* Editorial Note: Those who have had any dialogue with radical students know that this word has become as common as "damn" and "hell." Therefore, we have retained its use.

RUBIN: We'll have to be very general: America separates people. Separates blacks and whites, separates wetbacks; separates them through competition; separates them through geography. People in private homes, students, are separated from one another, students compete for exams, and when one student fucks up, another student's happy: I'm getting ahead of him. In every institution the idea is to get the people in one position to fight each other, so what's the result? The result is that there's no community, and people really have no basis for feeling an identity with each other. Also, all the energy that would go toward fighting against the Establishment for people's common goals is diverted to fighting against one another.

KURTZ: It's separation, competition, and the lack of community, then, that you particularly indict?

HOFFMAN: That's right.

RUBIN: So black power, and youth power, and Yippie power, and Viet Cong power—all that is an attempt to get the people to recognize themselves as brothers, no matter what their small differences are, and to fight against those powers and those institutions that are dividing them.

HOFFMAN: And there's also one thing that Jerry left out: the fight between men and women, how they are separated. All this is done so that you can maintain a capitalist consumer economy. Once you get the people divided up like that, playing certain kinds of roles, being certain kinds of cogs in the whole machinery, then you can program them easier, and you can sell things to them quicker, and they can buy things. To be a woman, you have to buy Virginia Slims, you see? And it's easier to do that. And now you feel inadequate because you don't buy Virginia Slims and smoke them.

RUBIN: That's what America says to the blacks: "Well, there's room in our society for *some* blacks." And the goal is to get some blacks into the middle class, so that the majority of the blacks have as their ambition to follow those few blacks in the middle class. The black-power movement says, "We're going to advance as a total, loving community, and the benefit of the lowest guy is going to be the final judgment of all." No one guy benefits while another guy suffers.

KURTZ: You find the separation of the sexes and class distinctions to be wicked, but do you also find the consumer economy of capitalism to be a basic source of difficulty?

HOFFMAN: Of course it's basic, because it leads to the perpetuation of competition. It says that man is basically a competitive animal, which I believe to be incorrect fundamentally. I think man is a cooperative animal. And then there are all those studies about animals: I don't go in for all that intellectual shit, because it's there—the stuff to prove it either way. But a revolutionary attitude is one that says the people are basically good, they're basically creative, and they're basically cooperative.

KURTZ: Are you saying that you find in our society that the competition and the striving tend to destroy creativity and cooperation?

HOFFMAN: Well, of course. Capitalism is an economic jungle.

KURTZ: Then you also attack the system because it thwarts the ability to enjoy pleasure?

RUBIN: It's a religious war; it causes ulcers.

KURTZ: This is an interesting point. Why do you view it as a religious war?

RUBIN: There is no single reform that could satisfy the worldwide revolutionary movement. It's a war of ideas, and, let's say, it's against Christianity. Our Christian inheritance tells us that this life is a steppingstone to the next life; therefore, no matter what suffering we experience in this life, it is in a sense good because we're going to go to the bank when we're dead. That's a way to keep poor people down, because they're thinking about the next life. The body is bad, pleasure is bad, and out of all this comes the 8-hour day, the bank accounts, the insurance policy. The question implied that the revolution is a decision you make, which it really isn't.

KURTZ: When you say it's a religious war, does that mean that you're opposed to the Judeo-Christian system of values that we've inherited?

HOFFMAN: Yes, maybe like the Protestant ethic, as Max Weber has defined it: postponement of pleasure. Keep your nose clean, keep your mouth shut, upward mobility, move upward in the system, become successful, get life insurance.

KURTZ: Are you saying that you wish to enhance the present enjoyment of pleasure and not lose it, by deferring it for some future pleasure—as the Puritan does? Is this your point?

HOFFMAN: Sure. But let's define pleasure.

RUBIN: Yes, let's not confuse it. The Viet Cong are having more fun than the American soldiers.

HOFFMAN: Pleasure is struggling for what you believe in.

KURTZ: You're not opposed to actual struggle or activity?

HOFFMAN: No, oh, no.

KURTZ: Then you're not advocating simply the contemplative withdrawal from the world of events. This is not what you mean, release from action?

HOFFMAN: Oh, no. We're rarely accused of that. We're talking about a change in the value system, like Christianity's struggle against the Roman Empire. You see, that also was an economic struggle, because the Christians were slaves. America is an empire, and it's dissolving. There are people all around the world who say we aren't going to put up with this anymore. And there are young people here who say we aren't going to buy that, we aren't going to participate. And there are blacks who are saying we don't want that; we don't want that honky style of life.

KURTZ: Some who have observed the Yippies are struck by the fact that the movement performs many functions of religion. It's interesting that earlier you described the revolt as a religious protest. Obviously the kids in the Yippie movement reject traditional religion. But many of the forms and functions of a new kind of religion have seemed to develop. How would you define this? Is it a kind of religion?

RUBIN: It's like the churches are antireligious, because you go to church and justify that another man goes to hell. And the churches primarily divide people, and, in a sense, the churches justify the evil of the state. So the churches have failed, the schools have failed, the economy has failed, and the politicians have failed. All the experts have failed.

KURTZ: Would you call the youth movement a new religious reawakening—not in the theistic sense, but in the humanistic sense?

HOFFMAN: Well, there's a religious experience involved, because there are visions, and there is magic involved, and there's belief, and there's faith in what we're doing. That's a religious experience. And we can't explain it in a nice rational way, because if we did that, we'd be like ministers in a church. We don't have the building. We're in the catacombs—in the catacomb state of religion.

RUBIN: People's entire lives are involved. The revolution is people living their lives. I say the Viet Cong is a religious movement. The blacks are involved in a religious movement. The blacks are trying to redeem the culture that was destroyed, and redeeming the culture means redefining what life means, and out of that comes a search for power to implement that, because when you're working on a new way of life, you've also got to defend yourselves. As I see it, America is trying to wipe out its youth. It has no need for youth, and we feel useless, and we're on our own.

KURTZ: Would you consider your movement in some sense humanistic?

HOFFMAN: How could it not be? Even to call it a religion gets us a little nervous, because that's a Western concept. There's religion here, there's play here, there's work here, and all those things. We just don't relate to it that way. We relate to it as a life experience. We go to the Pentagon and we meditate, and we play, and we struggle, and we are political.

KURTZ: But in what sense is it humanistic? In that human experience, the human body, and human cooperation are fundamental, and that your ideals are primarily humanistic?

RUBIN: It's humanistic in that there are no borders. A suffering thousands of miles away is my suffering. The entire life, the entire universe, is just one big planet.

HOFFMAN: It's also humanistic on a very specific level. We had a celebration on the first day of spring last year in Grand Central Station, at midnight. Eight thousand people came to be there and to experience community. And some kids happened to take the hands off a clock in the middle. And what happened, right after that, with no warning 200 or 300 police charged in and started beating people all over the place. I was knocked unconscious. A friend of mine came to defend me. The cops picked him up, threw him through a glass window, and broke both his hands. Now, everybody forgot this kid's hands. The only questions we'd get from people who wanted to defend the system was why did those kids take the hands off the clock? And there we are: two sets of hands. We're concerned about that guy's hands. How can you be that fucked up? Ten dollars for a lousy set of hands on a clock!

KURTZ: You emphasize the humanistic values in your movement, but Herbert Marcuse has said that humanism is "bourgeois."

RUBIN: Humanism is only a word. Marcuse is relating to it in a different way. I don't know what you mean by humanism.

KURTZ: Briefly, it is antisupernatural, emphasizes the positive sphere of human experience, and expresses a genuine concern for all humans.

HOFFMAN: What are you saying, let's all get together and love? That's a bunch of bull.

RUBIN: Brotherhood week? Is that what you mean by humanism? Then it is not a humanistic movement. That's like keep the blacks in their place, but be nice to them one day a week. That's not the kind of humanism we're talking about.

HOFFMAN: When the lion gobbles up the lamb, he is at peace.

KURTZ: By humanism I mean that you're committed to a humanitarian goal of mankind, and you're interested in releasing human potentialities.

HOFFMAN: There's nobody struggling in the world to make a revolution that isn't.

KURTZ: How would this relate to Marxism? The early Marx was a humanist, and there is a rediscovery of Marxist humanism in Eastern Europe today. In what sense would the student movement relate to Marxism?

RUBIN: I think of Marx as myth. The myth of Marxism says people should get together and overthrow governments to improve new structures. That whole myth is part of our unconscious. It's not really relevant, because it's not like we went into a library and read a book and got a theory and then went out to implement the theory. A lot of the people who call themselves Marxists take a lot of the specific mechanisms that Marx pointed out and treat them as catechism and a religion and say that this is what we have to do. It eliminates the spontaneity and the excitement. See, you ask us a lot of questions that imply answers none of us have.

KURTZ: But the Marxist indictment of the Establishment, as viewed from the Old Left, finds in the economic structure the basic problem; and there is a very conscious effort to overthrow the structure.

RUBIN: If you understand what both of us say, there is an incredible emphasis on economics. The economic system divides people, destroys them spiritually, confines them to boring work. The whole economic structure has to be changed.

HOFFMAN: We are for a change in the economic system because the economic system is based upon property.

KURTZ: Is it primarily the capitalist economic system, then, that is for you the main problem?

HOFFMAN: If we want to start there, we can start there. You can start at a lot of places because there are values that come out of that system: There's religion, the political system, and the information system.

KURTZ: But what is crucial or basic?

RUBIN: I don't think that you can implement the values we're stating without a revolution in the economic structure.

KURTZ: But how do you differ from Marx?

HOFFMAN: I think where it differs from Marx is that we don't see the working class at General Motors ready to have the uprising. Maybe it's coming, but it isn't there right now. And what we see is a very strange phenomenon: Where people who have a relatively good materialistic deal in life, like young people—their parents had it, lived through the depression, you know, and work, and all that—they're rejecting that; they're saying, no, we don't want that kind of life. Therefore, it becomes more existential than deterministic Marxist. It's more unexplainable—you don't know why, you just know why because that thing isn't working.

KURTZ: Let's focus on what you consider to be your positive values. Obviously you're committed to the liberty of the individual. This is fundamental, as I see it. You want the individual to be free, in morality, in sex, in drugs, in enjoyment, and in appreciation of his body.

RUBIN: That's only part of it. Liberty is a bad word because it implies that it's okay if the individual is part of a bad society so long as he has freedom to go by himself and do what he wants to do. We're saying that American society and Western society are societies that do not allow the individual to develop his potentiality with the other people.

KURTZ: So then you haven't abandoned the collective ideal? Many people find, you see, a kind of contradiction: on the one hand, individual freedom, and on the other hand, the collective. But can you have both at the same time?

RUBIN: Now take the university. Students are working for grades and competing against one another. There are just so many places in the society they can get into. So they may have individual freedom in a certain sense, but they don't feel satisfied, because they don't feel part of a family. When you feel part of a family, then you can express your own individuality.

KURTZ: What if the family suppresses you? Or the collective suppresses you? Doesn't this occur? And if so, what happens to the freedom of the individual?

HOFFMAN: Then you get another collective.

KURTZ: Do you ever live outside the collective, in any sense? Is this a kind of Thoreau's *Walden* that you're emphasizing in positive terms?

HOFFMAN: Well, no. Say, like, dig the Beatles. They're like making a community kind of art form. But they're all individuals—we know them as individuals. They have different personalities; they maintain their individuality. There are families that work like that.

RUBIN: Take a baseball team—they're all a team, and when one guy gets a home run, the other guys are happy, because the team is getting the point, but they are all doing their best within.

KURTZ: I see, so it's a kind of cooperative ideal in which you hope individual freedom will develop, but it's not individual freedom separate from the cooperative?

HOFFMAN: Oh, no, I don't believe there is such a thing. I think that's an illusion pumped in by a capitalist economy, a mass economy that wants to keep it that way.

KURTZ: Would your indictment of modern society also apply to socialist or communist economies?

RUBIN: It would apply to Russia and Eastern Europe. It would not apply to Cuba. I was in Cuba in 1964, and I have to say that the idea that a family was possible in a society first entered my head when I was in Cuba. You'd go into a factory and every worker would say, "Hey, look at our factory!" That doesn't happen when you walk into an American factory. It's just a whole different attitude. Everyone's talking about everyone else. And if you try to explain what it's like in America, it's a foreign idea.

KURTZ: Don't you find bureaucracy there? And doesn't bureaucracy deaden both the collective and the individual? In Eastern Europe and the Soviet Union one often finds that to be the case.

HOFFMAN: I think every struggle has a basic respect for individuals. Even the National Liberation Front. When they go on a mission, they sit down as a group outside the town that they're going to raid and they talk about it. And the privates and the captains all talk. And they made a kind of collective thing, and they go into action. And they have their individuality. In the American Revolution it was the same way. They were standing at Lexington, and one guy in the Lexington militia said they ought to have uniforms. And they all laughed that down. And then the captain came over and said, well, the British are coming, and they said, well, nine hours, and they haven't got here. I'm going back and tend my farm. I'll stay, another guy says. It was anarchistic; it was also a very unpopular war.

KURTZ: But do the Yippies find the Eastern European countries and the Soviet Union, too, in a sense, also to be consumer economics with all their defects and problems? At the Humanist-Marxist Dialogue held last September [1968], we found that the same kind of indictment of Western capitalism also applies to Communist countries, where the individual is sacrificed to vast organizational complexes.

HOFFMAN: They have state capitalism.

RUBIN: We have brothers in Russia: the young kids, fighting against the state. It is the same in Eastern Europe. Those are our brothers, you know? What's happening across the world is a rebellion of the youth against the old state governments, no matter what they are. We'd be doing the same thing if we were in Russia.

KURTZ: What about China? Aren't there similar problems? Can one really destroy all bureaucratic organizations? Or is this an illusion?

HOFFMAN: I tend to respect what's going on in China, but I think it's impossible for me to find out what's going on in China.

RUBIN: I have a positive attitude without knowing that much.

KURTZ: If we may turn to another issue, there are many people who are disturbed at what they think is the anti-intellectualism in the Yippie movement.

HOFFMAN: Hey, man, do you realize how *intellectual* this discussion has been? It's almost boring its so goddamn intellectual!
RUBIN: The university is anti-intellectual. The books that we were made to read as kids and as teenagers were anti-intellectual, because they didn't describe reality as it existed, and they got our head all fucked up with concepts and theories that made it all a mental game that never touched our bodies and never became real. What we're trying to do is work out a theory that comes right out of the body, that comes right out of blood, comes right out of guts.
KURTZ: But what about the intellect? Are you offering a new theory or a new set of concepts?
RUBIN: It's an action.
HOFFMAN: It's wasted motion to come to a university and tell people that they ought to think. They've been told for 16 years that they ought to think, they ought to analyze, they ought to consider both sides.
KURTZ: Are you opposed to logical analysis?
RUBIN: I'm opposed to a certain kind of thinking. For example, while white cops are wiping out black people in the ghetto, I'm opposed to intellectuals sitting around and writing books and thinking about it, because that's masturbation on thinking.
KURTZ: But you're not opposed to thinking, are you? You want a different kind of thinking related to the body or related to reality as you find it. But you're not attacking all thinking, or analyses, or concepts?
HOFFMAN: The thought should be in tune with the actions of the person. You see it's not that way with the intellectual who sits in the university and makes 20 or 25,000 dollars a year and writes a book about the evils of the society. Like Galbraith: We live in an affluent society—so?
KURTZ: Is there a literature that you refer to, are there any classics, any writers that you find to be fundamental in any sense to your position?
HOFFMAN: Well, Marvel comics are great, and movies are good.
RUBIN: When I was young I dug *Catcher in the Rye* by Salinger.
HOFFMAN: When I was young I had a course from Marcuse on Soviet Marxism.
KURTZ: Do you find Marcuse important, then?
RUBIN: I can't understand him.
HOFFMAN: I can't understand his latest book. It's six dollars for 70

pages and I can't understand that at all. Men like Marcuse, McLuhan, Maslow—who's a great humanist; he had a lot to say about Freud and where he went off the track a little—I respect them, but I don't love them. They have good minds, and they see certain things.

KURTZ: Do you respect good minds?

HOFFMAN: I respect them because they have a way of looking at society that might be correct and there may be something to learn from that. But dammit, I don't love them; they're not participating in the struggle, and they're not going to build a new society.

RUBIN: And I don't see how you can have a good analysis if you haven't felt it, and tasted it, and experienced it. I don't know whether anybody can really write something about someone else really well. Take Eldridge Cleaver's book *Soul on Ice*. It's beautiful, it's analytical, it's poetic, it's everything. And it's coming out of his gut. It's better than all the books that have ever been written by white people about what it's like to be black. You can't study something abstractly; you can't study life in a test tube. And the university is a plastic environment that has a Chinese wall around it. And it tells people to read books, think, and out of this will come some answers. And I find that the people in the university don't know what's happening. They don't have any experience.

KURTZ: Many liberals and members of the Old Left may sympathize with part of your critical indictment and also with some of your positive values. One of the basic values of humanism is democracy. And this involves a commitment to tolerance and a belief in reasoned dialogue. But I take it that you are critical of the notion of toleration or of reasoned dialogue.

RUBIN: What do you mean by toleration?

KURTZ: Tolerating different points of view. Not being tolerant of hypocrisy, in the sense that you won't criticize it, but toleration in John Stuart Mill's sense; that is, that you have an open dialogue and respect different points of view.

RUBIN: The Yippie movement is like the youth movement—there's so many differences within it. You can hardly describe it. But it's all within the family.

KURTZ: Do you tolerate those who disagree with you?

HOFFMAN: Sure.

KURTZ: In an open society, a democratic society, there are a variety of points of view, and one who believes in democracy is willing to tolerate people expressing different points of view. Do you welcome this?

RUBIN: Do you mean tolerate in a sense that black people should tolerate white cops?

KURTZ: I was talking about toleration in the sense of freedom of speech and discussion. Are you committed to that?

RUBIN: Oh. Yeah. I think that George Wallace should have a free hour every night on TV because he indicts himself.

KURTZ: Yet many people in the New Left seem to deny that we should be committed to open dialogue and free speech. Marcuse even says that one should not tolerate the intolerable.

RUBIN: Yes, but he's talking about something else. He's talking about the fact that this university allows the military to come in and use it for militaristic purposes. There comes a point where you don't allow a public structure to be used for the incineration of brown people thousands of miles away. I don't tolerate that. I will not tolerate concentration camps. But anyone can say what he wants. That's fine. We're talking about tolerating people who have the power to kill, and who do kill.

HOFFMAN: I was at a symposium at Dartmouth just two days ago, and there was a liberal guy who had run for Senator and had gotten beaten, and he was answering all these questions. He was good on Biafra—they're always good on Biafra, and they're good on Mississippi. But some student asked him a question: What do you think about what's going on on the campuses, and are the students right? And he paused for about 30 seconds, because there were votes there, and he came out 50–50. And the last part of his statement said, "I don't believe in violence as a means to social change." Well, that's a nice thing to say, but if he [the student] had said, are you a pacifist—oh, no, he's not a pacifist. He should give that speech to the military, he should give that speech to proponents of institutional violence, landlords. Landlords are violent people. Why doesn't he talk to them? Why doesn't he talk to the American Legion that way? You don't talk to students that way. You don't try to stem the flow of energy that's coming up to change things. You say, well, if you believe in that as a technique, okay. We're not saying you've got to use violence. You weigh 110 pounds, and you should go up and beat up that cop? You fight in your own way.

KURTZ: Are you willing to use violence if need be?

HOFFMAN: You use whatever you've got, and whatever you're good at.

RUBIN: What should the Jews have done in Nazi Germany? Should they have written letters to the editor? Should they have picketed? Should they have had legal demonstrations? What should blacks do when whites come in carrying clubs, guns, and the official uniform of the state with license to do whatever they want to do in the streets, and then the courts give their approval?

KURTZ: In other words, you think that peaceful methods of persuasion within the established system are not adequate, and that you have to use civil disobedience, confrontation politics, and possibly violence?

HOFFMAN: If we just go around living our life, doing what we think is right, and working towards a humanist society, there's confrontation.

RUBIN: Look, it's happening. The Establishment has no means that are legitimate for change. No means at all. The moment that someone challenges the Establishment effectively, the means close, and the person becomes a problem to be dealt with, through force.

HOFFMAN: Even if they are reformers they are killed.

KURTZ: But do you think that these methods will in the long run succeed? Will the youth movement, as it is now developing, be successful? Will more youth be radicalized and the system overthrown?

RUBIN: It can't lose.

HOFFMAN: See, what we're talking about is the future. There are a lot of roads into the future. The future is all out there—there's a lot of space.

KURTZ: Perhaps there is one thing that you have overlooked: the possibility that the adults may become reactionized. Many people who consider themselves to be liberal and even radical are turned off by the tactics of confrontation. There is a very startling phenomenon—a right-wing reaction—building up. In what sense will the methods you employ achieve what you want?

RUBIN: Our allies are the babies being born right now. The young kids are with us. You can see it in high schools, you can see it in the colleges. The young kids are fighting for their lives; the old people are fighting for their reputations or for something else. We can't lose. The structure is illegitimate and is on a suicide trip. Private property is not going to be the future in 25 or 50 years.

KURTZ: But the adults have the power. And the question is whether or not these methods will in some sense boomerang.

RUBIN: America has a lot of power, but the Viet Congs are kicking her ass.

KURTZ: Will you work cooperatively with those within the Establishment to achieve common aims?

HOFFMAN: No. Of course not.

RUBIN: There are no common aims.

KURTZ: Do you think that either of you have been already coopted by the system? You're both "news" for the media.

RUBIN: They're trying to put us both in jail.

KURTZ: But you, Abbie Hoffman, have a book published that has a large sale.

HOFFMAN: Yeah, but the profits from that book—I don't even have a bank account—the profits from that get spread into the projects, and get spread into what we're doing.

KURTZ: But won't the same thing that happened to liberals, who were radicals 20 or 30 years ago and now are successful, also happen to you?

RUBIN: No chance.

KURTZ: Remember the Marxists and radicals of the last generation are now professors in the universities.

HOFFMAN: If it happens to us—as two individuals—so what? The movement is growing. Ten years ago when I was in school, radicals went to Pete Seeger concerts; that was it. And then a struggle came that was outside the universities—somebody else's struggle in the South. About in 1964, with the free-speech movement, it came back in the universities again. People started to struggle. Now it's into the high schools. In 10 years it'll be in the grammar schools. And we know that. We know that it's happening. And we can see it: You go out to high schools and you see it. The same demands that went on in the free-speech movement in 1964 are going on in high schools today.

RUBIN: You see long hair and drugs become the major issues among the teenagers, both against the parents and against school.

KURTZ: But these issues—drugs, long hair, dress—are really minor in your view, are they not? Surely they are not essential to any revolutionary movement?

RUBIN: Oh, no, they're major issues, you see, because they're part of a counterculture.

HOFFMAN: They're major issues, but to focus your life in on one issue while not recognizing that there are other issues—

RUBIN: If there had not been a Vietnam war we would have had to invent it, because the Vietnam war was our excuse to fight for our own freedom. Long hair is an expression of that; dope is an expression of that; every issue blends into the same thing, which is to fight for our own bodies and our own freedom.

HOFFMAN: Given our political system and our economic system, there had to be a Vietnam war. In fact there's always been. You know, the Philippines, they were our colonies and all that; I don't know when this country has had a good war.

KURTZ: Do you find any redeeming virtues at all in America? In a sense what you're saying is really an elaboration of many liberal and progressive principles, for example, as defended by Dewey and others in this country earlier.

HOFFMAN AND RUBIN: Who's Dewey—Thomas E. Dewey?

KURTZ: John Dewey, the father of progressive education in this country. Much of what you say, but surely, not all—for he had faith in the democratic process—is very much like what he argued for: his demand for liberation of individuals on the one hand and for social responsibility on the other.

HOFFMAN: Well, if he did, then he was right.

RUBIN: We're using a lot of the ideas that we've heard against a society that doesn't implement them. We're for the underdog. The Viet Cong are the underdog; the blacks are the underdog. This society wants to wipe out the underdog. Everybody should be equal, right? But being equal within the private-property structure means that the poor can stay poor until they can solve their own individual problems. Well, we want everybody to be equal *right now*. The difference between Dewey and us is that we're part of a massive, human, social movement that is overwhelming, that can't be stopped. And so, there is no thinker we can point to and say "Here he is, here's the thinker." It's like a river, and people flowing in the streets. And we're applying it right now.

KURTZ: Apparently both of you have had difficulty with local, state, and Federal indictments. Where do you stand in regard to them?

RUBIN: The cops are trying very hard to put us in jail for our ideas. Not because we have them in our heads, but because we're trying to act on them. In the past eight months, I've been arrested for possession of marijuana—an alleged 3 ounces—which is intent to sell. Now, I don't know how many readers of *The Humanist* smoke marijuana, but marijuana is great, and nobody should go to jail for it. As a matter of fact, it ought to be a major thing in the schools. It's more important than textbooks. The cops had a phony search warrant and broke into my apartment; the rap is 2 to 15 years. And it's still pending. Then in Chicago, I got a state indictment—a felony for "solicitation to commit mob action," in which they charged that I incited a mob to attack cops.

KURTZ: Are you under indictment too, Abbie Hoffman?

HOFFMAN: By the time this magazine comes out, we're also both going to be indicted by the Federal Government for the crime of crossing state lines with intent to riot. I have a couple trials under appeal—30 days in Washington for wearing a flag shirt, and 15 days for resisting arrest in Chicago, and a trial pending for Columbia University, and a lot of trials. The age of innocence is flying away. I have over 30 arrests—I used to get away with it a lot. Now, it's tough. They follow you around.

RUBIN: It's unbelievable—the FBI harassment.

HOFFMAN: In the week after Chicago that I was home, I was visited no less than five times by some official Government agency.

KURTZ: The fear is that your confrontation tactics will provoke a dangerous counterreaction.

RUBIN: If the right wing cracks down, that means all the brothers have got to get together in a united mass against the right wing. You can't go hide under a blanket if they're going to crack down.

KURTZ: But the liberals have been polarized. I mean the Left movement has been split between the Old and New Left, liberals and radicals. Dialogue is difficult, and there is a serious hostility gap.

RUBIN: People have got to make a choice.

KURTZ: In the present context, if you don't have any allies among the liberals, then this may provide a real opportunity for the emergence of a New Right.

HOFFMAN: We have each other and we have the future.

RUBIN: The liberals have got to make their choice. They either close their eyes and let fascism come down, or they put their bodies in between us and the cops.

HOFFMAN: They've shown for a number of years that they're going to allow the society to commit genocide on blacks, and gobble up the blacks, and they've shown for a number of years that they'll let the country gobble up other nations. Now the question is, are they going to let the country gobble up their kids? You see, we're bringing it right home. Here it is, America. We are your children. No matter what age we are, we all fly youth fare. You've got long hair, you fly youth fare, and you are young. You're a freak; you are young forever.

KURTZ: The liberals and the Old Left may be your last line of defense in this country. In vilifying them, who will be left to defend your civil liberties if and when they are attacked?

RUBIN: The liberals, unfortunately, are impotent. Our only protection is ourselves. People can help us, but they really can do something only by joining us and being with us. People were very upset about Chicago, but now I stand a good chance of being put behind bars for Chicago. So I hope that people will translate the tears that they shed that week into active support.

Reflective Questions

1. How do Hoffman and Rubin reconcile their apparently contradictory statements regarding the purpose of the Yippie movement?

2. What do Hoffman and Rubin regard as the primary sources of the current polarization that they claim is taking place in American society?

3. In what manner do Hoffman and Rubin correlate the Yippie movement with a religious experience?

4. What is the basis behind the optimistic view held by Hoffman and Rubin regarding the eventual success of the Yippie Movement?

5. Do you see any impact of the Yippie Movement on policy making among governmental officials? If so, describe it.

6. Do you envision the Yippie Movement as gaining or losing support among the young during the coming decade? Support your position by rationally examining the Yippie Movement as a social movement that is attempting to initiate social change.

30 □ CONTENT ANALYSIS OF A SUPER PATRIOT PROTEST*

James McEvoy □ Mark Chesler □ Richard Schmuck

The authors examine, through the method of content analysis, a specific right-wing protest to an article appearing in a national publication. The article that served as the source of protest is described by its author and publisher as pro-American; however, more than 2000 letter writers considered the article as subversive and/or Communistic. The social and demographic characteristics of the letter writers reveal considerable insight into the background of the super-patriot protester. This study would appear to lend support to many of Hofstadter's propositions and to Adorno's statement that ethnocentrism in one area of life tends to be accompanied by ethnocentrism in other areas. □

That story in your last issue was the most brazen and infuriating piece of propaganda against God and Country that I have ever read.

THIS QUOTATION IS AN EXAMPLE OF ONE OF THE MOST SIGNIFICANT phenomena of mid-twentieth century America—super patriotism. Variously called extreme conservatism, right-wing extremism, and radical rightism, super patriotism is a manifestation of the ideologies and energies of persons who reject aspects of contemporary American social and political life. Super patriotism is characterized by political conservatism and fervent nationalism, by active

From *Social Problems,* Volume 14, No. 4 (Spring, 1967), pp. 455–463. Reprinted by permission.
* This research was sponsored by the Office of Research Administration of the University of Michigan, Ann Arbor, Michigan, and administered by the Center for Research on Utilization of Scientific Knowledge, Institute for Social Research.

participation in conservative social and political organizations, and by the perception of a major and dangerous internal Communist conspiracy operating to influence many areas of American life.[1] Some of the areas of change figuring most prominently as targets of right-wing protest involve international relations, civil rights activity and domestic welfare policies, modernist religious and educational institutions, and community mental health services. In many cases, super patriots view the mass media as channels through which "Communists" brainwash Americans into accepting these changes in American society and therefore through which Americans will eventually be entrapped by Communism.

A short story in a recent issue of a national magazine seemed to some super patriots to be an example of just such usage of the mass media. It depicted the rapid and dramatic takeover of a group of children's minds through the use of rather crude techniques of brainwashing. In a few minutes, a "new teacher" was able to convert her students' beliefs in the authority of their parents, their allegiance to their country, and their faith in God, into faith in and adulation of "Our Leader," a figure with a strong likeness to the "Big Brother" of Orwell's *1984*. Included in the story were incidents depicting the destruction of the American flag, the teaching of atheism, and the encouragement of disrespect for parents.

In the *Bulletin* of the John Birch Society, a publication which presents a monthly program of action for local chapters, this story was presented by Robert Welch, founder and leader of the John Birch Society, as being strikingly anti-religious, un-American, and Communistic; and as a result, several thousand protest letters were received by the author and editors of the magazine. It is not possible to identify all of the letters as the result of the instructions in the *Bulletin*, or as in any sense being written only by members of the John Birch Society; however, the issue to which they were directed and their observed content strongly suggest that much of this sample of writers is exceptionally sensitive to patriotic and nationalistic content in the media to which it is exposed.

The editors of the magazine and the author of the story defended its theme and content as pro-American, claiming that it tried to exemplify the subtlety with which a Communist takeover of the country might be performed. Despite what the authors of this paper, the editors of the magazine, and the author of the story all believed to be the unmistakable anti-Communism of the story, it was, nevertheless, seen by more than two thousand letter writers as subversive or Communistic. It is the nature of these writers' responses to the story and their demographic, sociological, and psychological characteristics that are the subjects of this paper.

---

[1] R. Schmuck and M. Chesler, "Super Patriotism: A Definition and Analysis," *Journal of Social Issues*, 19 (1963), pp. 31–50.

Methods

The total population of letters numbered 2,254. A random number was selected as a starting point and every tenth letter was then drawn for inclusion in the sample. This sample was then coded and a second sample was drawn in the same way and compared with the first. No significant differences were found between these two samples; they were therefore considered to be representative of the population and combined. The entire sample of letters upon which this study is based was 453, or 20 per cent of the population. Content analysis of the letters sampled, was employed as the method of study. The following groups of categories were designed for use in the analysis.[2]

Several *demographic* categories were designed to describe data as the census region of the letter's origin and the population of the city of its origin.

Estimates of a very general nature were made about the *social status* of the writers on the basis of coding each letter for the type of writing implement used by its author, the author's occupation, and the quality (imprinted, unimprinted, tablet) of the stationery used by the writer.

The level of *literacy* of each letter was measured by a count of the grammatical, spelling, and syntactical errors occurring in the letter.

Group *salience*, or the nature and frequency of references made to groups or associates, was recorded by several different categories. These included indications of group salience by mentions of families in general or the writer's family, references to secondary groups or voluntary associations such as clubs or lodges, and indications that the writer had discussed or would discuss the story with a group with which he was in some way affiliated. Also recorded were statements about the responses (actual or expected) that these groups had or were expected to have to the story.

The *identity* of the writer was assessed by two categories. One simply recorded whether or not the writer said he was a member of the John Birch Society; the second was the self-expressed identity of the writer, such as "I am a long time reader . . ." or "I am a mother. . . ."

Another category was employed to discriminate between the writers' reactions in terms of *personal* or *general values*. In other words, did the writer see the story as a personal affront, or, rather, did he couch his objections in terms of the story being an attack on such broad general values as patriotism, God, religion, and the like.

Several code categories were devised to measure roughly the *hostility* and affect of each letter. One of these, threats, provided a count of those writers who cancelled or threatened to cancel their subscriptions and those who said

---

[2] For a more complete description of the categories and coding methods, see the monograph *Letters from the Right*, J. McEvoy with R. Schmuck and M. Chesler, Ann Arbor: Center for Research on Utilization of Scientific Knowledge, University of Michigan, 1966.

they would stop reading or in other ways employ negative sanctions against the magazine.

Another set of categories measured the *mimetic frequency* of each letter. The particular editor to whom the letter was addressed and the number of arguments in the letter which paralleled those in the *Bulletin* were coded. The instructions in the *Bulletin* were broken down into twenty-five separate phrases and the frequency of occurrence of these phrases was recorded for each letter.

Finally, two categories were used to code the letter on the dimensions of *patriotism* and *religiosity* using the frequency of references of these themes as the basis for a scale of relative intensity.

THE SOCIOLOGICAL AND DEMOGRAPHIC CHARACTERISTICS OF WRITERS OF PROTEST LETTERS

For the most part, letter writing campaigns have been studied by researchers interested in political mail as a reflection of public opinion.[3] But recent studies[4] have focused more on the characteristics of the letter writers themselves. Wartenburg and Thielens's study is especially pertinent here because it analyzed another set of protest letters solicited by Welch in the John Birch Society *Bulletin*. Although that campaign and the one studied here focus on different issues, some demographic comparisons can be made of the characteristics of the writers studied by Wartenburg and Thielens and those studied by McEvoy, Chesler, and Schmuck.

The writers in this study were nearly identical with Wartenburg and Thielens's population in the proportion coming from suburbs of major cities larger than 100,000. However, the letters in this sample indicated a greater proportion of writers from cities ranging in size from 5,000 to 50,000 than we would expect on the basis of the distribution of the national population. The data indicated that relatively few residents of rural areas were among the writers and that at least 80 per cent of this sample is located in urban and suburban centers or small towns as compared with 60 per cent of the national population residing in these areas. Table 1 summarizes these data.

An early study of letter writing[5] demonstrated that some regions and states, particularly California, had a high rate of political letter writing. For the sample studied here, and that studied by Wartenburg and Thielens, California

---

[3] E. Kefauver and J. Levin, "Letters That Really Count," in Katz *et al., Public Opinion and Propaganda,* New York: Holt, Rinehart & Winston, 1954. See especially L. Sussmann, *Dear FDR: A Study of Political Letter Writing,* Totowa, N.J.: Bedminster Press, 1963.
[4] H. Wartenberg and W. Thielens, *Against the United Nations: A Letter Writing Campaign by the Birch Movement,* New York: Columbia University, 1964, mimeo.
[5] R. Wyant, "Voting via the Senate Mailbag," *Public Opinion Quarterly,* 5 (1941), pp. 359–382.

TABLE 1 □ POPULATION OF WRITER'S HOME COMMUNITY BY PER CENT OF PROTEST WRITERS AND NATIONAL POPULATION[a]

Size of Community	Letters (%)	National Population (%)[a]
Below 5,000	19.2	40.2
5–10,000	7.1	5.5
10–25,000	13.5	9.8
25–50,000	13.2	8.3
50–100,000	11.0	7.7
100–500,000	22.5	12.5
Above 500,000	11.0	16.0
Not available	2.4	—
	100.0%	100.0%

[a] Based on current urban definition, 1960 census, *Statistical Abstract of the United States,* 1966, p. 15, including both rural and urban population.

outranked all other states in this regard. Indeed, in both studies it supplied four times as many letter writers than would be expected on the basis of its population. Moreover, of those letters in our sample from California, over four-fifths were from Southern California, mostly from Orange and Los Angeles counties. Thirty-three per cent of those letters analyzed by Wartenburg and Thielens were from the same state.

Table 2 demonstrates the distribution patterns of our study and Wartenburg and Thielens's study as compared with the national population.

TABLE 2 □ PERCENTAGE, BY REGION, OF LETTER WRITERS AND NATIONAL POPULATION

Region	National[a] Population (%)	Wartenburg and Thielens (%)	Letters (%)
California	8.8	33	30
Other Far West	6.8	9	11
South	30.7	29	29
North Central	28.8	18	19
North East	24.9	11	10
Unknown	—	—	2
	100.0%	100%	100%

[a] *Statistical Abstract of the United States,* 1966.

Some other studies of political mail, however, suggest a heavy concentration of writers in the Eastern states, with only 12 per cent coming from the West.[6] An interesting parallel to these sources of super patriots' protest letters is found in the "Western" conservative hegemony which eventually placed Barry Goldwater as the Republican presidential nominee in 1964. That letter writing played an important part in his nomination has been suggested by Converse, Clausen, and Miller.[7] These authors draw on survey interview data to propose that the "reality" basis of the Goldwater campaign was in part created by a massive letter writing campaign which encouraged the Goldwater camp in its belief that it could win the election. "It is to the world of letter opinion or one like it that the Goldwater campaign, in its original design, was addressed."[8] These same authors discovered that 15 per cent of the adult population had written politically relevant letters, but that the majority of all political letters were written by only 3 per cent of the population. Of those who wrote in 1964, well over 50 per cent favored the candidacy of Goldwater. The kind of letter writing campaign that we have been analyzing here may have been a training ground for those writers who inflated the expectations of the Goldwater camp in the Spring of 1964.

In this analysis an attempt was made to gather data on the socioeconomic status and the occupations of the writers. In comparison with the letter writers studied by Wartenburg and Thielens, these writers were slightly lower in socio-economic status. While only 8 per cent of the letters gave any indication of occupation, there seemed to be an extraordinary number of doctors of medicine and doctors of osteopathy who wrote in protest. After the sampling was completed and the overrepresentation of doctors discovered, all the letters in the population were examined once again in order to extract all doctors from the population. The result was a total of 48 letters or 2.13 per cent of our total population being so identified. This represents twenty-one times the number of M.D.'s and D.O.'s in the resident civilian population for the year in which the letters were written.[9]

Stylistic Dimensions of Protest

In this section we review the relevance of variables such as literacy, education, dogmatism, and flexibility of protest for these letter writers. Literacy, and per-

---

[6] Sussmann, *op. cit.*

[7] P. Converse, A. Clausen, and W. Miller, "Electoral Myth and Reality: The 1964 Election," *American Political Science Review*, 59 (1965), pp. 321–336.

[8] *Ibid.*, p. 335. Letter opinion was obtained by analyzing the interviews of persons who indicated that they had written a letter with political relevance to any editor, public official, or the like, determining the frequency of writing, and then comparing these responses with expressed vote preference.

[9] A forthcoming report will discuss this group in detail: J. McEvoy, *Medicine and Super Patriotism: An Analysis of Physicians' Protest Letters*, in preparation.

haps by inference education, has been related to relative flexibility and openness to differences in conservative populations.[10] In this sample the more literate writers significantly more often asked for an explanation for the appearance of story than did less literate writers ($X^2 = 7.92$, p. $< .01$). Asking for an explanation suggests a more open-minded posture toward the story and the media, indicative of greater cognitive flexibility. Literacy was also found to be closely connected with another set of categories which were devised to measure the overall group salience or the generalized indications of group support and consciousness found among our writers. Within these categories, we coded each letter for indications that its writer saw himself as part of a larger group or that he was attempting to elicit real or mythical group support for his feelings toward the magazine. An example of this sort of letter is:

Dear Editor,
    After reading_____ I asked several friends to do likewise. We all agreed it is a very pro-Communist story.
    We are surprised and shocked that the _____ with its standing should stoop so low.
    You have just lost five faithful readers.
                             Sincerely,

A high level of literacy more often produced letters which *lacked* indications of group salience. That is, the more literate writers did not as frequently try to justify their position with attempts to magnify the effect of their protest by introducing groups who, they claimed, also supported their position. These findings are illustrated in Table 3.

Organized political letter writing campaigns are, according to Kefauver and Levin, destined to the same fate as huge petitions to Congress: "No one reads them. They gather dust in Capitol files until finally carried away. They seldom influence legislation."[11] Therefore, some of the more sophisticated mail campaigns and more sophisticated people might consciously attempt to avoid sponsoring group references in protests such as this one. The pattern of avoiding reference to the sponsoring group is evident in these letters where the John Birch Society, the *Bulletin,* or Robert Welch were mentioned only four times. One of these references was made by a public health physician—one of the few writers who saw the story as anti-Communist—who violently criticized the magazine for its "Birch-like" stories, and went on to denounce it as right-wing. One other reference to Welch in which the story was interpreted as anti-Communist

---

[10] See H. McCloskey, "Conservatism and Personality," *American Political Science Review,* 52 (1958), pp. 27–45; and T. Adorno, E. Frenkel-Brunswick, D. Levinson, and N. Sanford, *The Authoritarian Personality,* New York: Harper, 1950.
[11] Kefauver and Levin, *op. cit.,* pp. 221–226.

TABLE 3 □ LITERACY OF LETTER RELATED TO TWO MEASURES OF GROUP SALIENCE

	Group Salience[a]				
	(A) Would Make Contact with Others		(B) Cite Reactions of Others		
Literacy	High	Low	High	Low	N
High literacy	25 (11%)	203 (89%)	38 (17%)	190 (83%)	228
Low literacy	45 (20%)	180 (80%)	61 (27%)	164 (73%)	225
N	70	383	99	354	453

[a] $X^2 A = 7.11, p. < .01; X^2 B = 7.30, p. < .01.$

was made by a self-identified member of the John Birch Society who had read both the instructions in the *Bulletin* and the story and had then decided that Welch was wrong. He wrote complimenting the magazine for its anti-Communism. The other two references to Society membership were in protest letters, one of which was a threatening note signed "Birch Chapter XYZ." Two additional letters contained references to membership in a "conservative club."

On the other hand, 38 per cent of the writers used one or more of the assertions contained in the *Bulletin's* commentary and instructions, and 30 per cent used one or more of the phrases taken directly from the *Bulletin*. Occasionally a letter would be simply a word for word copy of the *Bulletin's* statement. More often, however, one or two phrases—particularly those describing the writer's supposed interpretation of and emotional reaction to the story—were integrated into an otherwise original text. Wartenburg and Thielens also found that 29 per cent of their population used verbatim quotations and that "closely parallel" arguments appeared in more than 50 per cent of their letters. Noting the obvious consequences of this sort of copying, they conclude: ". . . some writers were transparently unsuccessful in their efforts to present the appearance of independent thought."[12]

Even though these letters were easily detected as a "campaign," the editors answered every letter personally, trying to explain their interpretation of the story. They also made a brief analysis of the letters, published an editorial report to their readers about the campaign, and allowed these letters to be used for research. The magazine lost, if the writers are to be believed, about 485 readers or subscribers as a direct result of publishing this story. Moreover, 27 per

[12] Wartenburg and Thielens, *op. cit.*, p. 22.

cent of those cancelling stated that they would attempt to get other people to do likewise. These statistics say nothing about the thousands of people who must have seen the *Bulletin* and who may have retaliated in other ways but did not write to the magazine. Nevertheless, economic sanctions were not the major threats of the protest. For every person who wrote to cancel, there are four who simply protested; this, of course, may be in part due to the fact that many writers were not subscribers.

ADDITIONAL CHARACTERISTICS: THE TRUE BELIEVERS AND RELIGIOSITY

Some of the methods used by elites to control mass behavior are to supply a population susceptible to mobilization with an identity, proffer a set of abstract, de-personalized symbols, and control as much as possible the information which reaches this population. Eric Hoffer's description of the True Believer, whose "rejected self ceases to assert its claim to distinctiveness, and there is nothing to resist the propensity to copy," seems quite relevant here.[13] On a small scale, those writers who relied on the leadership of the John Birch Society for literal formulation of their opinions exemplify these processes. Those persons would be expected to have a high score on *mimetic frequency* in our coding procedure. Indeed, the fact that 30 per cent of this sample was marked by the use of phrasing copied directly from the *Bulletin* indicated to us that a significant number of our writers lacked sufficient autonomy to formulate their own responses and suggested that they might differ in other ways from the remainder of the population. Some examples of their letters follow:

> It must be pseudo-leaders like you who have created the turmoil of today, causing tens of thousands of citizens and taxpayers to begin a tide of protest against our federal lack of resistance to infiltration of the red butchers. . . . This (story) was the most brazen and infuriating piece of propaganda against God and Country that I have ever read.
>
> A writer

> If the _____ story in your last issue was intended to bring all red-blooded Americans up fighting, then you've succeeded.
> . . . This (story) was the most brazen and infuriating piece of propaganda against God and Country that I have ever read.
> Taken at face value this story makes Communism appear right and beautiful and taken at face value, you deserve the anger and contempt of all who love God and Country.
>
> A writer

[13] E. Hoffer, *The True Believer,* New York: Mentor, 1963, p. 95.

On almost all measures, the writers who quoted from the John Birch Society *Bulletin* tended to be slightly lower in their socio-economic status than were those who did not so quote. They were also slightly less literate than writers who did not include quotations from the *Bulletin's* text. But perhaps more important, the writers who copied from the *Bulletin* more often came from rural areas or small towns than did those who did not quote from it. Of the 137 people who quoted from the *Bulletin,* 34 per cent came from cities of less than 10,000 people. Only 23 per cent of the writers who did not use direct quotations resided in cities of that size. These figures compare with 34 per cent of the national population which live in cities of 10,000 or smaller. Perhaps an absence of cross-pressures in the small town environments of these writers may in turn result in more rigid adherence to the ideas of their leaders than would be the case for persons of similar ideology living in larger cities. In these latter areas social and occupational interaction is likely to be more frequently experienced by a given individual.

The rigidity or conformity indicated by the writers' use of quotations from the *Bulletin* was further reflected in their interpretation of, and response to, the story. Each letter was coded on the dimension of personal or general value reaction: whether or not the writer saw the story as threatening to his personal values—e.g., "I do not believe that this story is in good taste and I don't want it in my house"—or to general values he believed to be characteristic of American society—e.g., "Your publishing of this story is wicked. Men have died for liberty and Our Flag. This story is a disgrace to those men." Twenty-eight per cent of those persons responding with personal values conformed to the *Bulletin* text, while 39 per cent of those responding with only general values so conformed ($p. < .05$).

The propensity to respond at a general value level can be seen as another indication of the loss of self-relevant values of the True Believer. In this particular regard, however, it must be recognized that the statement in the *Bulletin* was written primarily in abstract or "general value" form, and, as a result, these findings are in some ways confounded due to the nature of the symbols taken over by the writers who quoted from the *Bulletin*. These same limitations apply to the analysis of the ambiguity perceived in the story, that is, whether the story was seen as a clear cut example of the Communist line or not. Nevertheless, it is readily apparent that those writers quoting from the *Bulletin* were far more often willing to accept Welch's conclusions than were those who did not use the *Bulletin* text. This is a further indication of the high degree of conformity characteristic of those writers who quoted from the *Bulletin;* they not only used symbols of their leaders to initiate or reinforce a reaction of their own, but they also apparently internalized the meaning of these symbols as well. This behavior is also a close approximation of the profile of the True

Believer's response to the directions of his significant elites, and gives additional support to the application of Hoffer's thesis to this group of writers.

Additionally, those writers who quoted from the *Bulletin* were slightly more likely to threaten the magazine than were those who did not; another element of this picture is the slightly more threatening posture on the dimension of group contact taken by those quoting. They more often said that they could attempt to get others to act against the magazine than did those writers who wrote original letters. They also more often wrote group letters, apparently trying to invoke greater sanctions by making their letters the product of more than one writer.

In conclusion, those writers who quoted from the *Bulletin* are, in some ways, strikingly different from the remainder of our population. The variables apparently most significant are the population of the cities in which they reside, and those which attempted to measure the nature of their response to the story in terms of ambiguity and personal-general value interpretation. As measured by their threat of cancellation and their frequency of group signatures, their protests toward the magazine appear to be more hostile than those writers who did not quote. As we have noted, however, these differences often do not reach an acceptable level of significance and appear only to suggest the possible existence of a relationship.

Religious fundamentalism and super patriotism have been demonstrated to occur together,[14] and rigid adherence to religious doctrine and practice is often a manifestation of the True Believer's impulse toward identification with a cause. In our sample, however, we found that only 7 per cent of the letters received by the magazine were predominantly religious in content. Some examples follow:

Dear Sir:

I have just read . . . and I am shocked. How could you print such a story, telling the children to believe there is no God? It smacks of Communism.

I am deeply hurt, and raise my voice in protest against such literature being printed in _____. I am a firm believer in God and have been a teacher in our local Sunday School for over fifty years, teaching little children to believe THERE IS A GOD.

Most Sincerely,

---

[14] See R. Schmuck and M. Chesler (eds.), *Super Patriots and Radical Rightists: Social Psychological Studies,* in preparation; S. Lipset, *Political Man,* New York: Doubleday, 1960; and D. Danzig, "Radical Right and the Rise of the Fundamentalist Minority," *Commentary,* April, 1962, pp. 291–298.

Dear Sir:

... I couldn't believe that you would put such an article (story) before the public's eyes. To me it was brazen, and the most anti-Christ article I have ever read. Do you know, actually know, that God gave us this country? That God only is the One, who not only made a place in our Wonderful Country for a good magazine and He only has brought you forth to success? Why did you do it? Why brainwash people with Communist slants? When on Judgment Day you will be asked "Why sell my people into slavery by printing as you did?" No one can help you then. I know I can't allow such stories in my home and therefore, I can't buy the _____ anymore. I wanted you to know why (*sic*).

Former Subscriber

The thirty-two highly religious letters were extracted from the sample and, like those letters which employed phrases from the *Bulletin,* analyzed and compared with the remaining portion of the sample. As might be expected, this group of writers was different in several respects from the sample as a whole. Indications of group salience in these writers' letters centered mainly on the family. In 38 per cent of the letters some mention of the family occurred, as compared with 18 per cent of the non-religiously oriented group which indicated family group salience. Most often this concern with families was general rather than specific to the writer's own primary group. Very frequently a writer would state that this story was, for example, "sure to help break up more American homes. ..." Furthermore, he saw the story's result as primarily disintegrative of present social institutions. Thus, a primary group anxiety is characteristic of this group; and it may be the case that their strong religious beliefs are an attempt to increase the solidarity of the family unit of which they are a part.

This concern with certain social institutions is evident in the fact that 56 per cent of these highly religious writers expressed their protests wholly on the grounds that publication of the story was in conflict with most important general and common values of the nation. Finally, the highly religious writers tended to be less punitive than the remainder of the population as expressed in their threats of cancellation of their subscription and the like. Unfortunately, there were too few highly religious letters to permit meaningful statistical analysis along these several dimensions.

These empirical referents of character and attitudes constitute one way of identifying the letter writers. Observations or interviews with these protestors would, of course, shed more light both on their characteristics and the concepts employed here. The limitations of these data also prohibit more diverse theorizing into the social psychological qualities and attributes of the writers. However, the data that are available and have been analyzed here provide an instructive description of one expression of super patriot protest.

Reflective Questions

1. What do the authors mean by the label super patriot?

2. What is the method of content analysis?

3. Why are political letter-writing campaigns seldom effective agents of influence?

4. Why are "true believers" particularly susceptible to social movements?

31 □ THE REVOLT AGAINST DEMOCRACY

Edgar Z. Friedenberg

Professor Friedenberg provides a lucid and analytic examination of the factors underlying the current revolutionary dissent that is being expressed by expanding numbers of young American citizens. Friedenberg argues that many young people consider authority to be illegitimate, as well as oppressive. The crux of today's conflict, according to Friedenberg, is that American society lacks a device by which social class differences may be legitimated. The solution to our conflict, he suggests, lies not in replacing our present democratic system, but rather in developing a mass mentality that will demand that the system respond to the needs of the people whose lives it affects. □

THERE IS A WIDESPREAD CONVICTION AMONG DISSENTING YOUTH TODAY THAT they are oppressed by a fundamentally illegitimate authority. For the younger members of a gerontocracy like ours to regard the authority of the older generation as oppressive is a rational act; that such authority should be logically regarded as oppressive is implicit in the fact that it occasions revolt. But for authority to be regarded likewise as illegitimate is something new. It makes conflict far more disruptive. It is, in fact, the characteristic that most clearly distinguishes today's intergenerational conflict from that which commonly occurs between successive generations.

Legitimacy is the chief lubricant of the social mechanism; it prevents friction by inducing collaboration among its several parts even in situations in which conflict of interest is apparent. The extreme example is the quiet dignity with which the condemned so often cooperate with their executioners. In the ultimately terrifying situation, the victim takes what comfort he can from

From *Change*, May/June, 1969, pp. 11–17. Reprinted by permission of *Change* and the author.

identifying himself as a member of the society which has officially certified him as so worthless that he must be publicly destroyed. By so doing, he is not alone in his moment of mortal terror.

In a social system that has exhausted its legitimate authority, however, executions are regarded as publicly planned assassinations that invite resistance, escalation and, ultimately, role-confusion, as Danton and Robespierre discovered. Declining legitimacy leads to a rise in coercive violence, which is usually attributed to the disorderly provocation of those who have no respect for "authority" or "law and order." Analysis of the actual events more often discloses that the contrary is true: violence is launched and maintained by terrified officials who feel their authority threatened. As their legitimacy ebbs, they fall back on the resources for coercion which their official position affords, and modern technology has made these resources enormous. Whether this results in the re-establishment of legitimacy depends on whether a stable regime can be built on the wastelands of terror. In the past it has usually been possible, but it does take time—more than a generation.

Terror thus is not a very useful device for restoring the faith of the younger generation in the legitimacy of the authority of their elders. Indeed, the authorities in this country have so structured their recent confrontations with the young as to reveal their own cognizance of the illegitimacy of their authority. This is the era of *plainclothes* police cracking the skulls of students, of *undercover* narcotics agents busting students for smoking pot. A uniform is an asset to the officer of a society whose legitimacy is accepted; the uniform, as with the soldier, legitimates even lethal hostility, if there is any legitimacy left. But out of uniform the adversary is a spy, and he himself becomes the legitimate object of condemnation. The widespread use of covert surveillance and coercion in a society indicates that the forces that bind it together have become even less legitimate than those that link hostile belligerents in the traditional context of war.

Authority, however, is no less dangerous because it lacks legitimacy; rather, because of its own anxieties, it is more dangerous. The more sensitive and intelligent young people I know today consider themselves to be living in some degree the lives of outlaws. They attempt to resign themselves to the prospects of being busted for smoking pot or dropping acid, imprisoned for draft evasion either directly or under a loose charge of conspiracy, or locked away in a concentration camp if resistance to the Vietnam war or revolt in the urban slums results in the declaration of a State of National Emergency or invocation of the Internal Security Act of 1950. All these are valid fears. There *is* real danger of becoming a political prisoner in the United States today through the normal operation of due process. Our military adventures and our treatment of poor and black people are political questions, and therefore offenses related to opposition to such policies are political offenses. It is less clear that classifying marijuana as a "dangerous drug"—in the absence of substantial evidence to that effect—and making its use a felony, and its distribution under some circumstances punishable by life imprisonment, are legal definitions designed to curb political offenses. But they are, and the very fact that the political character of such laws seems paradoxical makes the political function of the pot issue worth scrutinizing.

Smoking marijuana is essentially a ritual action by which young people assert a moral position. Careful research has shown that both the dangers and joys associated with its use have been grossly exaggerated. The satisfactions it affords are derived far less from its mildly stimulating effect on the central nervous system—which may be agreeable or disagreeable, depending on the circumstances—than from the sense of affirming a particular view of the world and of one's place in it. Potblowing is ideological; examination of the ideology it expresses reveals several characteristic components. The most important of these are:

1. People who are enjoying themselves without harming others have an inalienable right to privacy.
2. A drug whose effect is to turn its users inward upon their own experience, enriching their fantasy life at the expense of their sense of the need to achieve or relate to others, is as moral as alcohol, which encourages a false gregariousness and increasingly pugnacious or competitive behavior.
3. Much of the solicitude of the older generation for the welfare of the young merely expresses a desire to dominate and control them for the sake of adult interests and the preservation of adult status and authority.

Pot is clearly less dangerous than pot-busts. It is also less dangerous to youth than the Selective Service System; parents who become hysterical and punitive about the dangers of drug abuse while being equally insistent that their sons go quietly to Vietnam when summoned are more concerned with the embarrassment of having children who are in trouble with the law than with their children's welfare. So we are back again to the issue of legitimacy, which is what the potblower's ideology basically questions. On their own terms, there can be no doubt that their position is valid: there are no demonstrable dangers to either the individual or society sufficient to justify or even explain the treatment accorded marijuana users. The effects of the drug are less obnoxious than those of alcohol; the solicitude of adults masks intense hostility and anxiety.

Institutionalized hostility toward marijuana users is intelligible, however, when the potblower's ideology is considered in relation to the class structure of American society. For that ideology expresses essentially an upper-middle to upper-class attitude toward life; indeed, for this century, it expresses one that is remarkably aristocratic. To value privacy and a rich inner life at the expense of achievement and the development of social skills in manipulating and competing with others—to value these is to reject the fundamental and official attitudes of American society, to fly in the face (and perhaps up the nose) of the school system, the Little League and the core virtues of the Land of Opportunity. The fact that marijuana is too mild a drug to do much for the fantasy-life does not affect the controversy. People get out of psychedelic drugs about what they expect and the use of marijuana has evolved in such a way that custom provides what the drug cannot—as it does for alcohol. Pot-parties have therefore become almost a photographic negative of cocktail parties: communal experiences at which the joint is passed from mouth to mouth like a peace pipe or communion cup; the scene is tranquil rather than gregarious, with no one-upping permitted; there is not even much moving around.

Pot, then, both evokes and symbolizes a whole set of attitudes and behavior that are anathema to the lower-middle classes: laziness and fantastic ease, grooving with one's neighbor instead of competing with him, drifting into bed with the partner of your choice rather than conning her into it as proof of your none-too-evident manhood. Pot-busts have become primarily a form of interclass hostility, in which the working class attacks the sloth, depravity and decadence of gilded, long-haired youth.

Interclass hostility of this kind is ancient, of course. What is novel, and very dangerous, in the form of pot-bust is that the customary class roles have been fundamentally reversed. For here it is the lower of the adversary classes which, armed with legitimacy, attacks the upper in the name of law and order. And the upper defends itself, when it does so at all, by appealing to such values as civil liberty, the right to privacy, and freedom from arbitrary search and seizure which, although recognized in general terms in the Constitution or reflected in certain court decisions, have never been accepted by the American masses which see them as essentially a form of privilege.

And so they are; and this is the heart of the conflict. For what American society most apparently lacks today is a device by which social class differences may be legitimated. This, in fact, is what our institutions have evolved, since Jackson's time, to prevent. Privilege in America is illegitimate *per se*. Or in de Tocqueville's words, written in Jackson's day:

> The Americans hold, that, in every state, the supreme power ought to emanate from the people; but when once that power is constituted, they can conceive, as it were, no limits to it, and they are ready to admit that it has the right to do whatever it pleases. They have not the slightest notion of peculiar privileges granted to cities, families or persons: their minds appear never to have foreseen that it might be possible not to apply the same laws to every part of the state and to all its inhabitants.

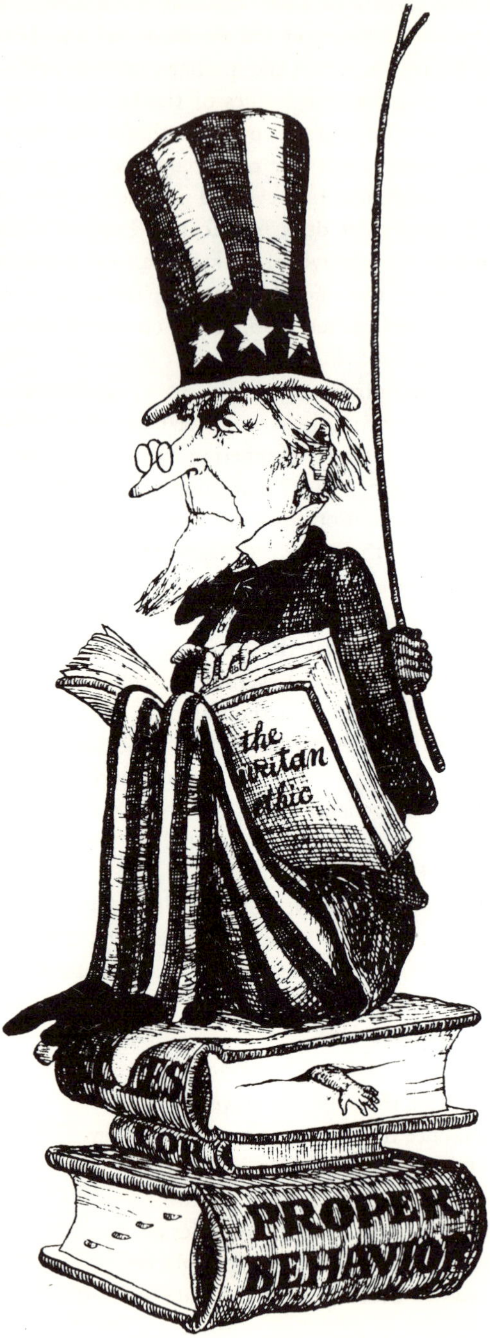
the
PROPER
BEHAVIOR

This is not quite accurate. The Bill of Rights *does* conceive of limits to the supreme power of the people, and attempts to establish them—which is why the working class so often perceives the Supreme Court as opposed to law and order. The people certainly *do* have a notion of peculiar privileges granted to cities, families or persons—it is what they are most determined to prevent. They *do* foresee that it might be possible *not* to apply the same laws to every part of the state, and to all its inhabitants—which is why they enjoy lurid fantasies of the university as a privileged sanctuary for draft-dodgers, addicts and perverts. What they *don't* grant, even as a possibility, is that such privileges, and such a sanctuary, might have social value.

And for most of them, perhaps it would not. This is not an issue that need be debated, for American society is as receptive to the claim of vested interest as it is hostile to that of privilege. There are social classes in America as elsewhere, and a society that recognizes and defers to the special interests and needs of oil-producers, speculative builders and labor unions can hardly justify rejection of the special interests of middle-class youth, which sorely needs a place to call its own. American society as a whole would surely be far better off if its most sensitive and articulate youth did not feel themselves to be outlaws. No more need be demanded on behalf of hippies or turned-on youth than is accorded Standard Oil or the friendly Chase Manhattan Bank: that their needs be recognized and reflected in the law of the land, and that they be allowed to go about their business unmolested without having to prove that what is good for them is good for the entire world.

But even this cannot be vouchsafed under our system. The answer adults give the beleaguered and fugitive young when finally forced to admit that the marijuana laws are Draconian and irrational, and the Selective Service Act capricious and inequitable, is to assert that for the sake of a stable and orderly society even unjust and unwise laws must be respected, and that procedures exist by which laws may be changed to make them wiser and more just. Unfortunately the idea that unwise and unjust laws—which reflect the hostilities and assuage the inferiority feelings and envy of the masses—can be effectively changed by due process and lawful means in a mass democracy is probably false. American law and public policy are almost always unresponsive to moral issues or minority needs, unless these find expression in terms of raw power. The fall of the Johnson administration, and subsequently of the Democratic party, under the impact of war protest may seem to belie this statement; so may the actual social progress the nation has made in the past fifty years. It is the blindness of the New Left to this record of past achievement, in fact, which most offends the surviving members of the Old Left. But neither case is a convincing indication that the American social or legal structure might be capable of a generous response to the demands of dissenting middle-class youth today. It seems very obvious that the Johnson administration would have been unaffected had the Vietnam war been prosecuted more successfully. Failure is punished by the electorate; but the war protest did not occasion the failure. Lyndon Johnson's defeat was not brought about by Benjamin Spock, Tom Hayden or Eugene McCarthy, but by the Vietnamese themselves. And they did not do it by winning their case before the bar of American public opinion or through the channels of American legal process.

The accomplishments of the Old Left are more solid, and unquestionably theirs. It is quite true that virtually all the social legislation they fought for in the thirties—against opposition fully as repressive as anything the New Left faces today—has not only been enacted but is now taken wholly for granted. What is sad, as Norman Thomas observed a few years before his death, is that nobody seems to have much pleasure out of it. But the goals of the New Left have a different political, and a different moral, significance than those of the Old; their tasks are not really comparable and they cannot really be allies.

Broadly speaking, the reforms of the thirties were economic and addressed to the improvement of social justice and the abatement of the grossest economic insecurity. What was achieved was solid, and new to a country which still provides much less in the way of social services, especially to the ill and aged, than an Englishman or Scandinavian would expect as a matter of right. In any case, the radicals of the thirties emphasized economic need and the improvement of the political power of the working class far more than civil rights, civil liberty or personal freedom. This was not because they were oblivious of these issues, but because they saw economic threat and vulnerability to poverty and economic pressure as the most serious threats to freedom. Job security and a decent wage, and essential social services, were to serve as shields against coercion by bosses and the slings and arrows of outrageous fortune. The Wagner Act and the Federal Minimum Wage Law were thought of not only as guaranteeing certain important economic and political rights but also as part of the foundation on which human liberty would rest.

As such, they have not been particularly effective. They serve as necessary instruments of social justice in guaranteeing certain important economic rights to the organized working class, which is quite sufficient to justify them as legislation. But the working class has not proved to be devoted to liberty; it is more inclined to be devoted to George Wallace or Mayor Daley. It supports the war more zealously than the financial and industrial leadership of the country—a paradox in terms of the stereotypes of the thirties, which envisioned rough, honest, warmhearted labor as the undauntable defender of peace and international brotherhood against the rapacity of capitalist warmongers. The capitalist warmongers have proved rapacious enough. Nevertheless, I do not think the American economy as a whole is as committed to a policy of perpetual military and political malevolence as the mass of the American people; it is too easy to conceive of other and more pleasant ways of profiting by our not-altogether-free associations with our neighbors. Where generals and corporate executives support the Vietnam war out of economic and status interests, both labor leaders and the working-class people one meets from day to day actively hate the draft-dodgers, peaceniks and troublemakers who harass their country while their boy is risking his life to defend it against the savage and treacherous gook. *If he hadn't —if he had ever started to talk like those long-haired punks, they'd have had his ass themselves.* However the various factors add, support for the war is now strongest in the working class, at least among parents; their sons, chased by the draft, may be less enthusiastic. But resistance to the war remains primarily a middle-class value.

The reforms of the Old Left have thus added to the difficulties of the New by greatly strengthening the political power of what has proved to be the most repressive segment of the population—the real control-addicts, in William Burroughs' phrase: the supporters of law and order, so long as the law does not shackle their local police or protect fresh kids and hippies. The reforms of the Old Left have created also one final problem of legitimacy that the New Left is, I think, reluctant to face. For the Old Left reforms proved ultimately popular; they benefitted the masses at the expense of the classes, which not only gave the old radicals great satisfaction, it made their programs legitimate *per se*. They were on the side of democracy and they knew it; with the final triumph of FDR they could prove it. It is true that the forces of law were often arrayed against them, sometimes with a brutality equal—discounting the greater technological efficiency of the sixties—to anything the war-resisters encounter now. But when this happened in the thirties, just as when it happened later to civil-rights workers in the South, it was the law itself which had become illegitimate. This thought affords little protection to the body in confronting a group of murderous sheriff's deputies, but it does enhance the victim's self-esteem.

What seems to be the hardest today for young radicals to face, in their conviction that authority has become illegitimate, is the implication that the source of the illegitimacy is the American democratic process itself. It is one thing to assert that "the system" is corrupt, that the mass media conceal essential data and misrepresent what they do report, that political parties do not respond to the will of the electorate. It is another, and more difficult for a radical American, to grant that what is wrong with America may be characteristic of mass democracy itself.

Yet this seems to be the more valid conclusion. The mass media, for example, do not, I think, mislead people so much as they confirm them in the fantasies they wish to hold. When, as in the Chicago Convention coverage, they do not, all hell breaks loose as the public, in paroxysms of rage and self-pity, demands that its prejudices be confirmed. The public does not accept discordant interpretations of reality any more than a neurotic patient accepts an unwelcome interpretation; it was Walter Cronkite, not the public, who learned from the experience. And the American political process *does* respond to the will of the people; it is the mass of the people that does not respond to the moral imperatives of Vietnam and the plight of the poor and the black—or, rather, it responds with greater hostility as its own destructiveness mounts.

As the twentieth century, along perhaps with everything else, approaches its conclusion, it becomes apparent that democracy and fascism are not contrasting and opposing political systems, but different stages of evolution in the responsiveness of society to the fears, envies and resentments that pervade the lives of lower status groups. Democratic political structures are devised to legitimate the demands to which these feelings naturally give rise, and to increase the political power of the masses, and hence their capacity to command a better life. But in a society as open, invidious and competitive as ours, the kinds of people who succeed are usually incapable of responding to human demands;

and the political power of the masses is used merely to express the hatreds and the envy, and to destroy anything that looks like genuine human satisfaction, especially among the more vulnerable members of the higher social classes. Higher status youth—whose style of life infuriates the working class and whose status by no means compensates for their political helplessness as a disfranchised group with few established civil rights in law—have become the chief target of the working-class sense of outrage and defeat. It is difficult for white, middle-class parents to imagine—and most don't want to—the degree of harassment to which their adolescent children are subjected by hostile and vigilant school authorities, and by police who feel, and are, perfectly free to disperse groups of youngsters whose behavior is not at all threatening and who could not, if adults, be held to have given probable cause for suspicion of any offense.

Tyranny has taken many forms in history, but the graceless vulgarity and egregious, clumsy brutality of fascism are its most hideous form; and these grow best out of the democratic process itself. The masses came onto the stage of history too late to be credited with having invented tyranny—even the Russians have made no such claim—but they have made something new and more terrible of it by depriving it of style.

Those who complain of the failures of democracy are expected to provide a better political plan and, even more confidently, expected to recoil in fear or perplexity from the demand that they do so. Winston Churchill's much-quoted comment that democracy is the worst system of government in the world—except for all the others—is supposed to have settled the matter.

But, in fact, there is no reason to feel embarrassed by this demand. Our political system, like the rest of our society, has not become the way it is in response to free and conscious choice, and—unless we commit national suicide—it cannot be transformed by an act of will. It reflects, rather, the effects of years of use and abuse, insight and misunderstanding, discipline and indulgence—both often equally ill-considered—of its inherited structures. There is no question of choosing elitism or oligarchy or fascism or anything else instead of democracy. There is only the question of how our present democratic system can respond to the demands placed on it by the needs of the people whose lives it affects, including those subject to its military and economic caprice who do not live within our borders. It is not possible to change or exchange political systems at will—even revolution does nothing like this; the new one grows back, often monstrously deformed, on the roots of the old.

The comprehensive public school, in its commendable attempt to give children of all social classes some experience of one another's lives, has become an institution in which lower- and upper-class children alike find themselves held hostage—if they do not escape—to the values and behavior patterns prized by the lower-middle class and imposed by it as a universal norm of conduct and moral judgment. Release with a satisfactory credential depends on the student's good conduct, and that of his parents, in not rejecting those norms or the values of the school system itself.

The pattern of anxieties thus established in the name of socialization has done much to cement our society together—as well as to make it more rigid when facing the need to devise alternative norms. But that need is now pressing, and the society is coming apart anyway. A major force in its disruption is the irritation that the upper and lower classes feel with each other; our society is splitting right down the middle-middle. And in a society that denies the legitimacy, if not the very existence, of class interests, and whose political leaders prattle of "law and order" as a remedy for "violence in the streets"—as if they had not seen a dozen times by now that the violence in the streets is often committed by the forces of law and order—nothing realistic can be done to recognize the serious nature of the conflict between those interests, or to resolve it.

It is almost certain that any effective measures to keep the American social system from bitter dissolution must indeed transcend present structural limits and political arrangements. The crucial question is whether this is possible. The present political structure of America is precisely what is wrong, and there is no *a priori* reason to assume that it bears within itself the seeds of its own reform. But I am sure that if any radical improvement in the quality of our national life can be made—and our survival depends on this—the devices by which it can be done will seem outrageous, and will, indeed, cause widespread outrage. But as perhaps most surviving American Indians and Vietnamese might agree, there is no great risk in devising a system more outrageous than that which America already has, and has had for nearly two centuries.

Reflective Questions

1. How might today's youthful protester argue that authority is illegitimate?

2. What does Friedenberg mean when he describes legitimacy as the ". . . chief lubricant of the social mechanism?"

3. How might you explain the relationship between declining legitimacy and coercive violence?

4. How can the intergenerational conflict discussed by Friedenberg be considered a type of interclass hostility?

5. What are the basic points of differences between the Old Left and the New Left?

6. Why does Friedenberg argue that any effective measures to keep the American social system from dissolution must transcend present structural limits and political arrangements?

32 □ NOTES ON THE LIBERATION OF WOMEN

Carol Andreas

Women no longer describe themselves as suffragettes or abolitionists. These terms are too limited in the options they denote. Liberation means equality, power, and a continual widening of choices and options. Women are refusing to be defined solely in terms of housewife and mother roles or as persons whose sole significance and worth emanates from their attachment to men. Carol Andreas, a sociologist and activist in the women's liberation movement, describes what has happened as women have viewed themselves as productive members of society instead of accepting an ideology in support of a dependent status. The author sees extensive possibilities for the movement if it develops an ideology with broadly defined aims that are responsive to new left organizations and goals. □

'Tis not a year or two shows us a man. They are all but stomachs, and we all but food; they eat us hungrily, and when they are full, they belch us.
EMILIA, in *Othello*

ALIENATION AND THE SEXUAL CASTE SYSTEM

TO BE LIBERATED AS AN INDIVIDUAL IS, MORE THAN ANYTHING ELSE, TO BE taken seriously in all of one's human relationships—and to be thereby in a position to take oneself seriously.

To be a liberated individual is very much akin to becoming "a man" as

From Carol Andreas, "Notes on the Liberation of Women," a previously unpublished paper.

Paul Goodman describes that unlikely occurrence in his critique of American society, *Growing Up Absurd*. And it has very little to do with becoming "a woman" as that process is understood by most people within and without the discipline of sociology.

It is time for radical scholars to make serious analyses of the relationships between men and women, to postulate connections between the alienation experienced by modern men and the structure of the organization of society by sex, to describe the peculiar forms of women's alienation, and to determine how these are related to the material and social conditions of society in an advanced stage of corporate capitalism.

If most men in such a society are hindered from taking themselves seriously because they have no control over the allocation of basic resources and over the productive processes that determine standards and styles of living in their material worlds, how much more are women hindered from assuming such control? They are not even expected to know anything about basic resources or productive processes. They are taken seriously only as consumers of nonessential goods and services, as oppressors of alienated men, and as purveyors of patriarchal culture.

If most men are denied the opportunity to communicate honestly and intensively with their peers because they are essentially in competition with each other for power and prestige, how much less are women able to carry on adult conversation at all, let alone to join regularly with others in purposeful activity? And how much more demeaning is the competition among women who seek their own social rewards precariously through the achievements of men and children?

If most men are unable to move out of roles ascribed to them by a cultural expectation that separates them from enjoyment of sentiment, and which demands that they not indulge in admission of failure or ignorance, that they choose vocations that promise extrinsic rather than intrinsic reward, and that they pretend not to notice the nefarious ends to which their work is devoted, how many women can claim to have given any thought to the ends of their existence or to the extent to which they are able to test the limits of their own capabilities?

If most men cannot clearly define for themselves beliefs that might give them some criterion of self-worth, but can only strive continually for ephemeral successes, how many women even know the joy of striving beyond the next catcall, the next stack of neatly folded diapers, or the next increase in their husbands' incomes? The sexual caste system seriously limits the aspirations of individuals, especially women, and it does not provide clear measures of success other than those that are transitory within one's life-span.

These are conditions of life that make it impossible for people to be taken seriously except as their activities serve the interests of others who are not concerned about mutuality. And in activities of the latter kind, people must finally despise themselves by their performance. They cannot take themselves seriously because in doing so they deny their own human potential and they deny themselves the right to participate fully in the creation of human culture.

Women, especially, are without a legitimate rationale for intervening in history except as they are permitted to do so during periods of historical crisis. And it is during such periods that they begin to discover themselves as alienated human beings, and to work towards achieving self-understanding and self-determination—de-alienation.

The preconditions for the alienation of modern women can, according to one line of thought, be found in the loss of communal productivity at a time when accumulation of the products of cooperative labor made exploitation possible. When women, working together, initiated the cultivation of land and the domestication of animals, the hunting activities of men became peripheral endeavors, and men began to engage themselves in assuring their own maximum advantage from the new forms of production, insisting on private appropriation of surplus goods, on usurpation of communal productive life, and on the restriction of sexual activity by women so that accumulated wealth could be transmitted to their progeny.[1]

Whether or not this is an accurate historical account of the way exploitative relationships among people first became legitimated, it cannot be denied that the growth of familism supported such relationships. And it cannot be denied that those few societies still in existence in which productive activities are shared among men and women are also characterized by laxity of regulations with regard to the sexual conduct of males and females and by an absence of competitive, proprietary behavior.[2]

But all of this is not too helpful to us unless we are able to define the kind of sexual oppression that exists in present societies in terms that will make clear the conditions for liberation.

Capitalism and the Sexual Caste System

In the United States, as in all societies where the acquisition of private wealth is permitted, there is a category of persons who are economically independent in the sense that whatever labor they perform is not necessary for their sustenance. Those who labor at increasing their private wealth through investing in the labor of others and who thereby profit personally from the "surplus value" they can glean from such exploitation are capitalists, and those who serve not only

---

[1] Evelyn Reed, *Problems of Women's Liberation: a Marxist Approach,* Merit Publishers, New York, 1969.
[2] Karen Sacks, "Social Bases for Sexual Equality," *Women in Revolt,* Random House, New York, 1970.

themselves but also each other as a class of people who engage in economic exploitation by acting as directors of corporations and of the subsidiary institutions that support those corporations are, in a classical sense, ruling elites.

The economically dependent persons in such a society, or those who must sell their labor in order to sustain themselves, are encouraged to succumb to their condition by various means that include perpetuation by ruling elites of a myth that equal opportunities exist in the society and that ruling bodies represent the interests of all the people because public elections are held to determine who shall be chief executive and who shall be legislators. People are prevented from struggling to achieve control of their lives by union bureaucrats who bargain for increased benefits for those who sell their labor, benefits that do not threaten the ability of corporate elites to increase their own profits at the expense of consumers or of more vulnerable groups of workers such as women, racial minorities, and the like. And they are prevented from engaging in struggle by the creation of their own dependent category of persons whose services can be acquired for whatever price the market can bear—wives.

Although wifely work has no exchange value in an advanced capitalist economy—that is, it is thought to exist outside the economic system—it not only allows those who invest in the labor of others to buy the labor of two for the price of one; it also allows those who sell their labor for money within the system to work under the illusion that they are independent rather than dependent beings. The control they are able to exert over the lives of their own dependents, women and children, disguises for them the fact of their dependency on ruling elites.

When a wife decides to work for money within the economic system, the mask of her dependency on her husband is partially removed, and a man who endured his own dependence only because it gave him a measure of control over others in turn feels threatened and shamed by his new condition of open servitude. Whether the wife was previously engaged in productive but unpaid work within the household, or whether she was primarily engaged in enhancing the status of her husband by glorifying her dependent state and advertising it through conspicuous consumption or through frivolous pursuits, as a wife and mother she justified the existence of her husband—however intolerable or reprehensible his work might otherwise have been.

The control that women are given over household matters is a small price to pay for *their* acquiescence to the state of affairs described above, and if their modest feelings of importance are threatened when their children are no longer in need of their services or attentions, and when their sphere of control is thereby narrowed, corporate elites can use such new misery profitably. If a middle-aged woman bears a heavy load of dependency-consciousness, she can still gain a measure of satisfaction and an illusion of competence by hunting for bargains. If she is less attached to her dependent status, she can try to find a job that, however little it may pay or however intrinsically unrewarding it may be, can decrease her misery enough to keep her quiescent, at least in her relationship to the society at large. Whatever her status within that society (a status that is acquired largely by the occupational "success" or "failure" of her husband), she can be enticed to cope with the misery of middle age by buying more and more products to rescue her fading beauty and youth, both of which once gave her a certain kind of control in her associations with others and a feeling of self-worth. Or she can be urged to devote herself more tirelessly to the task of assisting in her husband's occupational and social achievement—a choice that may or may not be welcomed by him.

Whatever merit or demerit each of these alternatives may have for particular individuals, they all have in common the attribute of being useful to ruling elites, both in preserving the caste system itself and in providing more markets and services that profit those who control societal institutions.

Even the breakup of families at those junctures of life when immiserization is most severe can be used to increase the wealth of corporate elites. Proliferating family units can consume a tremendous amount of waste, that is, products needed because of competition for status within the society and because of the necessity of duplication of products that are not used cooperatively by larger numbers of people. There may be some tendency for the acquisition of material goods to diminish in importance as a mode of attaining status in a society to the extent that the rearrangement of familial commitments, such as occurs through divorce, becomes an extremely frequent or acceptable mode of existence. But so long as such behavior is defined as deviant, the institution of the family is externalized by its collection of properties and its standard of living, both of which can mitigate the connotation of deviance that makes people so uncomfortable. Men who are driven to provide the accoutrements of respectability for several families are good servants of corporate elites, as are women who must maintain a family that has no male head or benefactor. And within a family system that defines commitment to other persons over time as a matter not only of economic and emotional responsibility toward each other, within a well-defined structure, but mainly and primarily as a matter of exclusiveness toward each other in these realms, the competition among persons and between families who must seek in privatism the security that can never, finally, be found there, is highly profitable for the ruling class.

Familial privatism and the caste system itself (both that of male and female and that of race, ethnicity, or whatever other divisions can be maintained by the ruling elites) effectively prevent exploited categories of people from becoming politically self-conscious classes within the society, classes that can expose and overcome the true nature of exploitative relationships within the system. Each of the exploited groups can be led to blame the others for their common misery, and each does in fact threaten the other within a structure that produces artificial scarcity—of jobs, living accommodations, services, friends, and opportunities for self-development and creative expression.

People are given an opportunity within the family system to gain a measure of purposefulness in their work through the goal of establishing family wealth, wealth that can be passed on from generation to generation. And they are forced to purposefully accumulate private wealth in a society where basic needs are not defined as human rights to be provided in common for all members of the society. The fear of loss of private wealth in the face of a physical disaster or a social crisis is partially mitigated by insurance and social-welfare programs, but it is never entirely overcome as long as artificial scarcities are maintained. While this remains the case, the risk of uniting to change the power configurations within the society is very great for all social groupings, with the possible exception of students and of those intellectuals who are willing and able to live off the system rather than in it.

It is primarily within the social institution where the sexual caste system is most clearly exemplified, that is, within the family, that patterns of authority are learned by new generations of people. Not only are the habits of deference toward men and toward age established (if at all) within the family; habits of deference toward illegitimate authority, or authority acquired largely through birth or through bureaucratic machinery within the church or state, are largely taught by socializing agents within the family. It is the *function* of motherhood and fatherhood to assert the credibility of such authorities, and to produce "good citizens," which typically means obedient functionaries. The fact that mothers and fathers are not succeeding very well in doing so today does not alter the character of the institution itself—it only means that the institution is not surviving the pressures that now exist in the society. In some respects, the extended family was more suited to the task of acculturation than is the highly mobile nuclear family that evolved from it, so that expectations placed on parents today are not only of questionable merit but also impossible of fulfillment. If the nation-state needs "good citizens" for its own survival, and if these are not readily forthcoming, that is, if the control that ruling elites are able to exert in the socialization process is not sufficient to produce compliant individuals, then a heavier investment in police apparatus is made, and increased pressure is brought to bear on all social institutions to maintain "law and order."

Social institutions, and especially the family, have been under pressure at many times in history to produce people who will readily accept totalitarianism. This kind of pressure is not peculiar to capitalistic societies, and it may even be the difficulty of maintaining it in such a society that will appear as the Achilles' heel of the present economic order in the United States. The family as an agent of socialization into a rigid hierarchical social system is difficult to maintain at the same time that individual competitiveness is being stressed as an ideal, and individual competitiveness was openly stressed in the United States during its earlier periods of laissez-faire economic development. The survival of individualism as a cultural goal makes it difficult to develop those social institutions that can effectively maintain the rule of corporate elites.

Nevertheless, ruling elites can be expected to continue striving to meet such contradictions in one way or another. While the support they give to religious and state authority, to maintaining educational institutions in the service of their own purposes, and to creating and maintaining divisions among the populace whose real interests would be served only by unity, is far from peculiar to the particular kind of economic and political control that corporate capitalists are able to exert in a modern society such as the United States, the perpetuation of sexism through the creation of a blatant consumption-orientation and through an emphasis on privatism are aspects of control that can be located precisely in history as accompanying the development of corporate capitalism, as can the growth of the myth of personal choice in an open society, the admission of caste being destructive of stability in a society where competition is glamorized in order to veil its own dehumanizing qualities.

Capitalism is served well by continued development of propertylike relationships among people, by the basic notion of a division of labor by sex along the lines of maintenance (female) versus production (male) with the granting of social status through the male members of the society, by the continuation of the double standard that makes of men the hunters and wooers and of women the hunted or seducers, and by the standardization of cultural ideals of feminine and masculine attractiveness; but the origins of these social conditions cannot be attributed so much to any of the stages of capitalist development as to the older and more fundamental concepts of private property and of the authoritarian nation-state.

Creating the New Society

Many men and women have begun to recognize that the social institutions that define the boundaries of their lives thrive on sexism, and that much of the pain and frustration that they have silently or not so silently endured for years can be explained as a product of the sexual caste system. Those who have come to these understandings during the present period know that to struggle for a redefinition of the boundaries of their existence in relation to each other is to call for revolutionary change in society. What kind of revolution is needed to free human beings from the oppression of sexism? Is such a revolution possible? If it has in fact already begun, what are its theoretical premises, and how is it being carried out?

Perhaps these questions can be answered at least in part by looking carefully at the issues that are being raised by the various constituencies of the contemporary women's liberation movement in the United States.

Since the winter of 1970, the movement for the liberation of women has spread rapidly to the point where it can claim active participation of persons in every subcultural, socioeconomic, and geographic position within the society. Youth, education, urbanity, and previous involvement in radical politics are no longer primary distinguishing characteristics of membership. However, women's liberation movement publications and leadership still reflect a system of thought that derives from the civil rights movement and the antiwar movement. Male chauvinism is linked with the chauvinistic political and economic institutions of the society as a whole, and with the condoning of those power-dependence relationships among people that serve to perpetuate personal profiteering and expansion of national business advantages all over the world. There is a great deal of discussion within the movement about the relative merit of subsuming the liberation of women under the overall struggle for a socialist revolution or subsuming the struggle for new forms of political and economic existence under the overall struggle to revolutionize relationships between the men and women who compose that existence.

Regardless of their positions in this matter, activists engage themselves in campaigns to repeal abortion legislation, to equalize work opportunity, to change the image of women in the media, and to establish group child-care facilities. But it is not these issues that bind together the women who meet for long hours of discussion concerning their oppression. Nor are women in the contemporary movement particularly concerned about demonstrating their competence relative to that of men. They are primarily concerned about defining the new society that is bound to emerge from their struggle over these issues. As the movement has gained adherents, it has tended more and more to define itself in revolutionary terms, that is, to assume that its progress will in fact change all of the institutions of the society in fundamental ways. Significantly, the movement has intensified rather than backed away from its critique of the legally constituted nuclear family.

Among those who have been working out the meaning of their own personal liberation, forms of communal life are emerging—not only among those who are just entering adulthood, but also among young professionals in the middle stages of their careers, and among older professionals whose child-rearing years are over. The emphasis is not so much on "destroying the family" as on extending and transforming it. Male liberation groups, gay liberation groups, and male-female groups are joining with all-female groups in helping to define a new society and to deal with the personal conflicts and complex relationships produced by that effort.

Collective modes of existence can be expected to make people less vulnerable to manipulation by those who reap benefits from the kind of insecurity that is fostered by privatism and consumerism. At the same time, these forms will in all likelihood enable individuals to experience less constraint in pursuing occupational interests that may not always coincide with "jobs available" in the marketplace, interests that may well include subversive political activity. Women who are willing and able to find meaningful work for pay may do so without having at the same time to assume ultimate responsibility for children, since a collectivity can assume this responsibility. Men who want to explore their own potentials for creative activity outside the paid labor market may do so without abandoning their families and friends, or being abandoned by them. This is not to say that men readily recognize the liberating consequences for themselves of the demands that movement women place on them. What often happens as a result of women's-movement activity is a defensive response on the part of men who counter the claims of women by describing their own oppression as males. A dialogue then ensues that inevitably involves sensitive men in a process of painful but ultimately liberating change.

An interesting aspect of this development of a transexual movement, more affected by the contemporary cultural revolution than by the political activity of the past decade, is the potential it has for taking the steam out of media-inspired programs directed against man-eating lesbians who are characterized as movement leaders. The Establishment must finally grapple with the women's liberation movement, not because of the danger of usurpation of male power alone, but because of its challenge to those institutions—private property and the legally constituted nuclear family—that support the present economy and its necessary adjunct, the authoritarian nation-state.

The origin of the movement for the liberation of women seems to have come, as in earlier eras, from the discovery by certain women of their potential and of their oppression when their services were needed outside the home. During World War II and again during the era of heightened political activity, domestically and internationally, in the 1960's, women experienced collective oppression upon assuming new prerogatives. In the first case the resultant assertion of independence was effectively, if temporarily, squelched by the wholesale cultivation of a "feminine mystique." In the second case the advent of simple and effective contraceptives that gave women the possibility of real control over their procreative functions, combined with the moral power of a larger humanist movement, made the movement for the liberation of women both broader in its demands and less easily controlled. Its capacity now to give both direction and force to other movement demands, and to ultimately devise new means of control of resources for maximum human use rather than for destruction and despoilation, is limited only by the extent to which the contradictions of the present society have already rendered its people powerless to effect change.

Bibliography

Simone de Beauvoir, *The Second Sex,* Alfred A. Knopf, Bantam Books, New York, 1961 (first published in France, 1949).

Margaret Benston, "The Political Economy of Women's Liberation," *Monthly Review,* September, 1969 (reprinted by Radical Education Project, Box 561-A, Detroit, Michigan 48232).

Myron Brenton, *The American Male,* Fawcett Publications, Inc., Greenwich, Conn., 1966.

Frederick Engels, *The Origin of the Family, Private Property and the State,* International Publishers, New York, 1969 (first published in 1898).

Paul Goodman, *Growing Up Absurd,* Random House, New York, 1956.

Herbert Marcuse, *Eros and Civilization: A Philosophical Inquiry into Freud,* Vintage Books, Random House, New York, 1962 (first published in 1955).

Juliet Mitchell, "Women: the Longest Revolution," *New Left Review,* November-December, 1966 (reprinted by Radical Education Project, Box 561-A, Detroit, Mich. 48223).

Reflective Questions

1. How unified is the women's liberation movement?

2. Should the women's liberation movement form coalitions with other liberation groups and causes?

3. Does the fight for equality mean different things to different socio-economic and racial segments of the female population? How might these differences among women be incorporated into a common women's liberation movement?

4. In what ways are women discriminated against in American culture? Cite examples.

33 □ "So That Man Might Live Better"

Athelstan Spilhaus

Spilhaus analyzes one of the most pressing ecological problems currently confronting mankind—the quest for living space. Specifically, he examines the "urban dilemma," which is simultaneously an American and world problem. He presents a state-of-the-population message and contributes a suggested plan for alleviating the distinct possibility of an approaching intolerable living situation. After citing the lack of long-range planning as directly related to our present situation, he offers a careful plan, consisting of a system of dispersed cities as a possible solution. Although some students of ecology may consider Spilhaus' plan utopian, the fact is that few long-range alternatives are currently being projected to meet this formidable crisis confronting mankind. □

THERE ARE TOO MANY PEOPLE ON EARTH, THE UNITED STATES NOT EXCEPTED. Significant as that may be, however, more critical is the fact that the numbers of people are increasing faster than we can provide the human services which people need to remain human.

The mandate is clear. We must restrict the increase of population worldwide, and we must provide a better way of living for the present and future populations. Presently we are doing neither. We merely whittle timidly at the edges of an expanding entanglement that grows more serious each year.

Restricting population growth is not the theme of this discussion. I submit, nevertheless, that the words of biologist Garrett Hardin merit consideration: "To couple the concept of freedom to breed, with the belief that everyone born has

Reprinted by permission from *Bell Telephone Magazine* (September/October, 1969), pp. 20–25.

an equal right to the commons, is to lock the world into a tragic course of action."

Former Secretary of the Interior Stewart Udall phrased it this way: "We have learned neither how to grow, nor at what pace, and *that* is our failing and our future trouble."

While sociologists, biologists, and theologians discuss the control of population growth, the search for a better way of living continues. The crux of this problem is the city.

The urban dilemma is an American problem and a worldwide problem. At its root is the fact that too many people drift into too few cities or their immediate environs. Consequently, 70 percent of all Americans now live on one percent of the land.

Urban renewal too frequently encourages such movement. Two- or three-story slum buildings are torn down, and sterile, high-rise, so-called low-cost housing brings more people into the center of the metropolis. Such a quandary can be rationally explained: Our system seldom rewards long-range planning and experimentation in government; the reward to a public servant is continuation in office; incumbency is usually based upon ability to find a quick fix that shows instant benefits.

Countries vary in their material resources and in the degree of development of these resources. But every country has human resources in excess of its ability to use them fully. Therefore we should concentrate on "people services" in a new culture, recognizing that we are all in the service of others, without servility.

I dream of a city where the dwelling units are simple and adequate but the services in education, sanitation, health, recreation, and all forms of culture are outstanding. To achieve this in realistic dimensions, I am convinced that we need, as a corrective, the development of a system of dispersed cities of controlled size, differing in many respects from conventional cities, and surrounded by ample areas of open land. Present "model city," "satellite city," and "new town" projects do not fulfill all of these criteria.

The cities I have in mind would be "planned"—carefully planned before construction to reasonably assure that the people services effectively intermesh with adequate physical facilities and essential governmental procedure in an atmosphere of flexibility. This would be feasible because the critical factor of population size would be known rather than unknown.

Needless to say, the first planned cities would have to be dedicated to experiment before a "grand system" of dispersed cities could be fully conceived. The proposed Minnesota Experimental City (MXC) would be a prototype.

MXC is a cooperative venture of the business and industrial community, the Federal government, and the State of Minnesota and its university. The subject of serious discussion and planning since 1967, it will be a complete city of some 250,000 people outside the commuting range of existing cities. It will also be a huge urban laboratory effecting actions which are necessary to alter the social, economic, and physical environment to achieve otherwise unattainable ends over a relatively brief period—about 10 years. Construction is expected to begin in 1973.

The potential gains of a grand system of dispersed cities are great enough to justify huge calculated experimental risks. It is mystifying that we reserve great risks and toleration of great mistakes for wars.

People like to live in cities. Dispersal, as I see it, does not mean that the whole United States would become a single sprawling suburb on the order of a Los Angeles. Dispersal refers to cities big enough to offer the advantages of city living yet small enough not to be subject to unplanned overgrowth.

The city is a system. It requires synergism. Each of the interlocking services affects each of the others. It is unwise to study the status of education without the center of one city to the center of its neighbor in the same acceptable commuting time of 15 minutes. Thus, mobility, not only within a city but between cities, is a vital part of the concept since it would multiply the choices offered to any individual in any of the different cities.

The high-speed network between dispersed cities would also provide access to long distance airports serving several of the cities from an open land area. Vertical takeoff and landing craft, for short distance flights, would use terminals inside the city.

The ultimate solution to the population problem for a closed-system earth is to use, reuse and recycle wastes. One step is to control waste at the source to avoid mixing and dispersing. Another is the redesign of many systems so that less waste is produced. For example, a sterile pneumatic system for delivering food might reduce the vast quantities of wrapping paper and containers now required.

Utility tunnels, hydraulic conveyors, or unitized trains might carry many solid wastes as well as liquid and gaseous wastes to processing plants. Reduction of bulk and suitable packaging of wastes would allow deadheading trains and trucks to take them away from the city to open areas where they could be processed and stored or reused, perhaps to build ski slopes, arenas, or other recreation facilities. Wastes not immediately reused could be sorted and stored in "mountains" to be mined when reuse becomes economically desirable.

In water-rich areas, water can be used first for drinking and then reused at least twice, for cooling and then for recreation. But, if experimental cities are to show the way for cities in arid areas, complete recycling of part of the water must be attempted.

Large industries dedicated to pollution control are springing up, and while complete recycling might not be possible to achieve for most wastes immediately, that objective should remain in all planning.

Between now and the year 2000, we shall need to build a family unit for two and one-half people every 27 seconds. This will simply accommodate the increase in population and does not take into account the razing of substandard units. It means mass production of buildings on an assembly line basis, perhaps in the vein of Moshe Safdie's mass producible, privacy-respecting, and aesthetically pleasing Habitat at Canada's Expo 67.

Simple construction is an essential in mass-produced housing. In an experimental city, materials could be brought up from the city substructure inside the growing building itself so that growth could take place without clogging the surroundings. Easy dismantling is also important. As needs change, buildings would be taken apart and the materials moved back into the substructure to be stored and reused later.

The city's infrastructure might contain all the services: power, communication, water, gas, pneumatic tubes for parcel delivery, express tunnels for police and other emergency vehicles, fume sewers, conveyer mchanisms. For most of these services new technologies already exist, but they haven't been tried as a system.

For information transfer in densely populated communities the "wired city" approach may be preferable to a radiation system. Perhaps radiation should be reserved for needs—such as communication to and from moving vehicles—that wires cannot fulfill.

In a city with a suitably wired or piped substructure, a large spectrum of sight and sound terminal devices would be applicable. Telephones or typewriter consoles can already tie into computer services of schools, hospitals, libraries, stores, and banks. Advances being made today in cable circuits and in considering the ramifications of housing, transportation, communication, labor, welfare, etc. For example, institutions such as schools and churches could probably share facilities with much greater efficiency of operation than either can now muster separately. If noise and filth are eliminated from factories, zoning becomes unnecessary, and transportation needs change because people aren't as apt to move to another part of town. Better communications change patterns of travel, medical care, and education. Clearly, we cannot continue to experiment in bits because each new technology affects other technologies.

It is obvious that the planning, construction, populating and managing of a dispersed city system that is highly suitable for industry, commerce, and human occupation will require leadership, imagination, and enthusiasm of scientists, industrialists, and educators alike. We must be prepared to discard convention and to experiment with new and radical ideas.

It is also obvious that the project cannot be accomplished through any attempt to rebuild a present city, regardless of its size or location; for, without exception, our cities are bound by tradition, outmoded building codes, restrictive legislation, and the consequences of unplanned, unhealthy growth.

The urgency of such an ambitious and large-scale experiment is readily evident. Even if a newly conceived city accommodating a quarter of a million people were built in every one of the 50 states within the next three years, these cities would barely absorb the predicted increase of population in the United States during that time and would do nothing to alleviate the problems of overgrowth in existing cities.

An experimental planned city such as the Minnesota project will constitute an immense study not only in new technologies but in new social concepts and even morality. For instance, it should help to measure the degree to which we would be willing to give up security of ownership in favor of part or shared ownership that would lead to something better. How much beyond the compromised ownership of condominiums or time-bought automobiles are people willing to go?

Government? There is increasing evidence that the ballooning maze of physical and social complexities in our cities is undermining the theory that advocates the spreading of authority. Federal standards and controls are established to resolve the conflict. In new experimentation, an attempt at management of the city-hotel-corporation type is worthy of consideration. Many public services might be contracted to private businesses on a performance basis. Population balance can be achieved through careful selection of the type of industries participating and the commercial operations established.

Consider also the possibilities for significant innovations in transportation, waste management, housing and construction, and communications.

Now in the process of design are systems that can move people motorless, driverless, and noiseless in semiprivate pods, computer-controlled so that passengers travel from where they are to where they want to go without stopping. The various systems have a common denominator: they are driven by a propulsion system built into a track. Eliminating the automobile in cities by means of a modern transport system of this kind would do away with the need for freeways and traffic control. It would lessen smog, save lives, and free valuable space.

In a city of controlled size, two miles square, one could reach the edge of the city walking on the trafficless ground level in 15 minutes or less. More importantly, using 400-miles-per-hour underground tube transit systems presently in design, one could go from waveguide, satellite and laser transmission could also be put to good use.

The communications system in a planned city would provide access from any point to large high-speed computers for purposes of city management on the basis of real information, crime prevention through video monitors, and advanced social experimentation through up-to-the-minute data banks. Such an advanced system would furnish an ideal laboratory for determining how to insure privacy of computer use while realizing maximum computer benefits to society.

And what about the cost for an experimental city of 250,000 inhabitants? If we take 2.5 people as an average family unit and $20,000 as the average cost per unit, we arrive at $2 billion. But the city would be planned from scratch with large substructures housing equipment for city services, and it would involve extensive experimentation. Thus we double the first figure and arrive at a guess of $4 billion.

However, not all these costs constitute an additional burden on the national economy. New housing and businesses will be built in any case, somewhere.

Certainly the plan must prove attractive to industries if they are to participate and bear part of the cost. Some construction cost could legitimately be funded by FHA mortgage. Part of the experimentation and research would be met by the private sector. Imaginative American industry needs a place, a city laboratory, in which to try out new technologies of waste management, communication, transportation, and construction. This laboratory would also serve those in business who are showing greater concern for urban social problems.

If these ideas are subject to charges of impracticality, consider the possible consequences of failure to innovate on a scale broader than any we've known.

Look ahead, for instance, and suppose that the world population, if we do little about population control, reaches 15 billion by A.D. 2069. And let us assume that our technology permits us to build cities on any solid land, from Antarctica to the tropics, from desert to rain forest. The area of all the continents is about 2.3 billion acres. Thus, if we built cities of controlled size, dispersed throughout the world, there would be 60,000 cities of a quarter of a million people each, and each city would be surrounded by 40,000 acres, or 64 square miles, of open land. The alternative of allowing the present big cities to grow unplanned or to accelerate their growth through so-called urban renewal would mean that vast tracts of the earth's surface would be uninhabited and the urban complexes would be intolerable.

There is no magic in the number 250,000 as a desirable population level for a planned city. Perhaps a half million would better provide the choices people want, or cities of different sizes may be needed. But size must be controlled and cities must be kept within a small area, with clearly defined bounds, so that they would remain surrounded by open land.

These ideas are not totally new, but they have been treated with little sense of urgency. There are new insights, new technologies, new inventions, and there are resources. What has been lacking so far, in the words of Economist Barbara Ward, "is the unifying vision of the whole urban order as a proper field of coordinated inquiry and action."

We have witnessed how commitment and imagination of the best in government and the best in industry can work as a team to achieve, within a few years, almost incredible accomplishments in outer space. To provide a better environment for people on earth can we not explore space on this planet with similar commitment and imagination and with the involvement of people in a grand national experiment?

Reflective Questions

1. What is the mandate, according to the author, facing humanity?

2. What does Spilhaus see as the root of the urban dilemma?

3. Why do urban renewal and similar projects appear so fruitless as long-range plans to provide for a higher quality of life?

4. What are the restrictions facing the implementation of a plan similar to the one offered by Spilhaus?

5. What alternatives or plans could you offer to resolve the problem discussed in this article?